Hebrews' Cosmogonic Presuppositions

Hebrews' Cosmogonic Presuppositions

Its First-Century Philosophical Context

BENJAMIN ROJAS YAURI

Foreword by Jeremy Punt

WIPF & STOCK · Eugene, Oregon

HEBREWS' COSMOGONIC PRESUPPOSITIONS
Its First-Century Philosophical Context

Copyright © 2022 Benjamin Rojas Yauri. All rights reserved. Except for brief quotations in critical publications or reviews, no part of this book may be reproduced in any manner without prior written permission from the publisher. Write: Permissions, Wipf and Stock Publishers, 199 W. 8th Ave., Suite 3, Eugene, OR 97401.

Wipf & Stock
An Imprint of Wipf and Stock Publishers
199 W. 8th Ave., Suite 3
Eugene, OR 97401

www.wipfandstock.com

PAPERBACK ISBN: 978-1-6667-1929-1
HARDCOVER ISBN: 978-1-6667-1930-7
EBOOK ISBN: 978-1-6667-1931-4

10/21/22

This work is dedicated to my dear wife, Elena B. Zubieta, with whom
I became one flesh and since she shares her life with me,
I will share the authorship of this book with her.

As regards this world, God's work of creation is completed. For "the works were finished from the foundation of the world." Hebrews 4:3. But His energy is still exerted in upholding the objects of His creation. It is not because the mechanism that has once been set in motion continues to act by its own inherent energy that the pulse beats and breath follows breath; but every breath, every pulsation of the heart, is an evidence of the all-pervading care of Him in whom "we live, and move, and have our being." Acts 17:28. It is not because of inherent power that year by year the earth produces her bounties and continues her motion around the sun. The hand of God guides the planets and keeps them in position in their orderly march through the heavens.

—Ellen G. White

Contents

List of Illustrations | ix
List of Tables | xi
Foreword by Jeremy Punt | xiii
Preface | xvii
Acknowledgments | xix
Abbreviations | xxi

1. Introduction | 1
    Research Motivation: Importance of Presuppositions | 2
    Research Background: Hebrew's Presuppositions | 4
    Research Problem | 6
    Research Purpose | 8
    Preliminary Studies Already Undertaken | 8
    Research Scope and Delimitations | 10
    Research Methodology and Procedure | 11
    Research Significance | 14

2. Introductory Issues and Hebrews' Cosmogony | 17
    Chapter Introduction | 17
    Genre of Hebrews | 18
    Authorship: Implications for Its Cosmogony | 20
    Audience: Implications for Its Cosmogony | 23
    Background of Thought: Implications for Its Cosmogony | 27
    Other Introductory Issues: Implications in Its Cosmogony | 31
    Chapter Conclusion | 34

3. First-Century Cosmogony | 35
    Chapter Introduction | 35
    Forerunner Thoughts for First-Century Cosmogonies | 36
    Cosmogonic Thoughts in the First Century | 48
    Chapter Conclusion | 66

4. Text-Linguistic Analysis in Hebrews' Cosmogony | 73
   Chapter Introduction | 73
   Literary Component of Hebrews' Cosmogony | 74
   Structural Analysis in Hebrews' Cosmogony | 94
   Genre and Figures of Speech in Hebrews' Cosmogony | 102
   Textual Dependence of Hebrews' Cosmogony | 103
   Linguistic Analysis of Hebrews' Cosmogony | 107
   Chapter Conclusion | 113

5. Grammatical Analysis of Cosmogonic Hebrews' Text | 115
   Chapter Introduction | 115
   Methodology and Procedure | 116
   Grammatical Analysis | 118
   Chapter Conclusion | 181

6. Cosmogonic Presuppositions in Hebrews | 183
   Chapter Introduction | 183
   Development of Ancient Cosmogonic Presuppositions | 185
   The Creator in Hebrews' Cosmogony | 189
   Procedure in Hebrews' Cosmogony | 298
   The Creation in Hebrews' Cosmogony | 213
   Chapter Conclusion | 231

7. Hebrews' Cosmogony and First-Century Cosmogonies | 234
   The Literary Component | 236
   The Creator | 244
   The Procedure | 249
   The Creation | 256

8. General Conclusion | 261
   Brief Research Summary | 261
   Main Research Findings | 264
   Future Research Questions | 266

Bibliography | 269

Ancient Document Index | 285

List of Illustrations

Figure 2.1	Soterio-cosmology in Apocalyptic Judaism and Christian tradition	29
Figure 3.1	Stoics' cosmogony: its contradictions	51
Figure 4.1	Keywords of first-century cosmogony present in Hebrews	78
Figure 4.2	Classification of Hebrews' verses with presence of first-century cosmogony keywords	80
Figure 4.3	Hebrews' texts with cosmogony perspectives	81
Figure 4.4	Key-verses within syntactic structure of Hebrews' cosmogony	83
Figure 4.5	Key-sentences with literary component of Hebrews' cosmogony	84
Figure 4.6	Simplification of Hebrews 1:1–4	90
Figure 4.7	Different structure proposals for Hebrews	96
Figure 5.1	Line diagram of key-section 1: Hebrews 1:1–4	120
Figure 5.2	Use of αἰών in Hebrews' cosmogonic literary context	124
Figure 5.3	Line diagram of key-section 2: Hebrews 1:10–12	128
Figure 5.4	Line diagram of key-section 3: Hebrews 2:10	138
Figure 5.5	Line diagram of key-section 4: Hebrews 3:3–4	140
Figure 5.6	Line diagram of key-section 5: Hebrews 4:3–5	144
Figure 5.7	Line diagram of key-section 6: Hebrews 4:10	150
Figure 5.8	Line diagram of key-section 7: Hebrews 8:1–2	153
Figure 5.9	Line diagram of key-section 8: Hebrews 9:11–12	158

Figure 5.10	Line diagram of key-section 9: Hebrews 9:24–26	164
Figure 5.11	Line diagram of key-section 10: Hebrews 11:3	167
Figure 5.12	Line diagram of key-section 11: Hebrews 11:9–10	174
Figure 5.13	Line diagram of key-section 12: Hebrews 12:25–27	179
Figure 6.1	Prepositions that complete the idea of Hebrews 11:3	207
Figure 6.2	Chiastic structure of Hebrews 1:10–12	219

List of Tables

Table 3.1	Main cosmogonic presuppositions present in cosmogonic exclusion	67
Table 3.2	Main cosmogonic presuppositions present in cosmogonic speculation	68
Table 3.3	Main cosmogonic presuppositions present in cosmogonic contemplation	69
Table 3.4	Main cosmogonic presuppositions present in Greek-Roman philosophy	70
Table 3.5	Main cosmogonic presuppositions present in Jewish cosmogony	71
Table 3.6	Main cosmogonic vocabulary present in first-century philosophy	72
Table 4.1	Correlation between Hebrews' text and first-century cosmogony	77
Table 4.2	Key-sentence or literary component of Hebrews' cosmogony	93
Table 4.3	Morphological organization of the literary component of Hebrews' cosmogony	95
Table 4.4	Textual issues in the literary component of Hebrews' cosmogony	111
Table 6.1	Old and contemporaneous cosmogonic presuppositions	189
Table 7.1	Comparison of cosmogonic verbs in first-century literature	238
Table 7.2	Comparison of cosmogonic nouns in first-century literature	241
Table 7.3	Comparison of cosmogonic adjectives in first-century literature	243

Foreword

WE LIVE IN A day and age where all but the totally withdrawn are only too aware of climate change and its, often devastating, role and impact on the planet on which we live. Writing here in the middle of 2021, countries throughout the world are suffering various natural disasters, ranging from extreme heat and resulting runaway fires to heavy rain downpours with devastating flash floods. Most people do not have the scientific understanding needed to fully comprehend the changes to which we all contribute wittingly or otherwise through our lifestyles and choices. However, the subtle but unmistakable connections between personal convictions and responsible behavior, also eco-ethical behavior, are becoming increasingly clear. In large parts of the world, such human convictions as well as behaviors are influenced by religious persuasion if not affiliation.[1]

Benjamin Rojas Yauri's work is not aimed at the modern-day climate crisis, or even how people's religious persuasions impact their behavior also when it comes to ecological concerns. Benjamin rather goes in search of the cosmogonic presuppositions of the book of Hebrews in the New Testament or Christian Bible. With his focus on Hebrews' assertions about the origin of everything, his work wants to contribute to the study of ancient cosmogony and to that of Hebrews in particular. He situates his quest in the first-century philosophical context, using a multi-methodological research approach that has a threefold focus that employs a historic-grammatical, socio-rhetorical, and content analysis of the Hebrews texts. In addition, as part of his research, he develops a methodology that allows for the discovery of a document's position

---

1. See recently, Yoo and Watts, *Cosmologies of Pure Realms*. They argue, based on notions of purity and pollution in religion, that a culture's beliefs about cosmological realms shapes its pollution ideas and its purification practices.

on topics other than its main topic. He describes his novel and intricate methodology as *text-linguistic exclusion*, which consists of four steps, namely identification, exclusion, simplification, and organization, and uses it to provide a very detailed analysis of the vocabulary and syntax of key passages in Hebrews. Through the rigorous application of his model to the text of Hebrews, Benjamin can then offer synthetic discussions of cosmogonic presuppositions but also of possible interconnections with ancient philosophical cosmogonic passages.

The book starts out by tackling relevant introductory issues as far they pertain to Hebrews, before he turns to an analysis of important cosmogonic presuppositions found in first-century philosophies. Benjamin proceeds to analyze the Hebrews text and provides a close-reading analysis of its Greek text upon which its cosmogonic presuppositions were established, by turning his attention to the mechanics of the Greek text, as well as its grammatical, textual, and literary issues. Applying the four steps of his text-linguistic exclusion approach to Hebrews, he identifies twelve key-sentences in the text, which he argues are the core sentences around which the cosmogony of Hebrews is developed. His analysis, which includes attention to words' part of speech, morphology, lexicology, and, even more broadly, their syntax, subsequently measures and assesses the correspondences with cosmogonic vocabulary in other writings and, in this way, indicates what is unique to Hebrews. His presentation of the cosmogonic presuppositions in Hebrews, and comparison of these with the cosmogonic presuppositions readily present in first-century philosophy, in the end focuses on four key aspects: the literary component; the creator; the procedure of creating; and, the creation itself.

The central finding of this research is that Hebrews embraces a new cosmogonic perspective for its time, built on coherent presuppositions developed mostly in its reading of Jewish literature, among which the Old Testament and in particular Genesis 1–3, which takes a predominant place in Hebrews. Benjamin's comparison of Hebrews' cosmogeny with those of other Greek and Roman first-century philosophies and their presuppositions, shows how Hebrews' cosmogony are different even where vocabulary may be shared. He shows how Hebrews offers a new cosmogonic perspective that stands apart from first-century cosmogonic presuppositions which were a plethoric mixture of thoughts. Interestingly, and importantly, he insists on difference but avoids claims to exceptionalism by emphasizing that the relationship between Hebrews and first-century philosophies was anything but antagonistic—Hebrews' overall interest does not seem to be in the confrontation of other, contemporary cosmogonies but rather to present its particular point of view coherently. In short, Benjamin's work advances the knowledge of cosmogeny on Hebrews, and at the same time provides a base and opens the door for further investigations. His research makes a new contribution to scholarship on Hebrews because this topic has not been discussed in a systematic way before in a dissertation of monograph.

In the end, Benjamin is modest when he, on his own terms, points out that his work on Hebrews entails two messages of exhortation for the global theological community: to rethink its interpretative approach to the Scriptures; and, to be tolerant, through humility regarding one's own positions while offering them with clarity and with respect for others and their positions. Benjamin Rojas Yauri's work on the Hebrews text and first-century contexts in fact also highlights ancient interest in the understanding of how the cosmos came into being what it is, and provides valuable resources for its ongoing theological understanding and appropriation. This careful, painstaking investigation of an ancient text's cosmogonic perspectives in their ancient contexts can feed into also our contemporary cosmological concerns, particularly in theological discussions and also within communities of faith, with the potential to enrich contemporary debates about ecological concerns.

Jeremy Punt, Stellenbosch
July 2021

Preface

THE BOOK THAT YOU are holding is a revised version of my doctoral dissertation under the supervision of Prof. Jeremy Punt at Stellenbosch University, entitled "Cosmogonic Presuppositions in Hebrews and Its First-Century Philosophical Context." The dissertation as well the book aims to consider the relationship between Hebrews' cosmogonic presuppositions and its first-century philosophical context. It is a multi-methodological research focusing on the historic-grammatical, socio-rhetorical, and content analysis methodologies applied to biblical studies. In addition, this research develops a methodology that allows the discovery of a document's position on topics other than its main topic, i.e., a methodology that could be termed a "Text-linguistic exclusion" and which consists of four steps: 1) Identification, 2) Exclusion, 3) Simplification, and 4) Organization. By using these four steps, twelve key-sentences have been identified in Hebrews which must be considered as the core sentences around which the cosmogony of Hebrews is developed.

This dissertation comprises eight chapters: chapters 1–3 tackle the problem of some of the introductory issues pertaining to Hebrews and analyze the cosmogonic presuppositions found in first-century philosophy. Chapters 4 and 5 analyze Hebrews' text and provide the foundational analysis of the Greek text upon which the cosmogonic presuppositions in Hebrews were established, i.e., it displays the mechanics of the Greek text, as well as its grammatical, textual, and literary issues. Chapter 6 presents the cosmogonic presuppositions in Hebrews, and chapter 7 compares these with the cosmogonic presuppositions present in first-century philosophy by focusing on four main aspects: 1) the literary component; 2) the Creator; 3) the procedure of creating; and 4) the creation itself. Chapter 8 follows as both a comprehensive summary and conclusion of this research.

Even though it cannot be asserted that this research is complete, in the sense that there is nothing more to say about cosmogony in Hebrews, it can be asserted with absolute certainty that Hebrew's cosmogony holds a positive view about the creation, in that everything has its origin in God. In addition, the present creation will be transformed—i.e., recreated—in order that God's holy people will inherit a perfect world. Among this and other findings, the main finding of this dissertation answers the primary question of this research, which reads as follows: "What are the relationships between Hebrews' cosmogonic presuppositions and its first-century philosophical context?" This research allows one to answer the question by asserting that there is no relationship of dependence in presuppositions but only in the usage of some general vocabulary. Further, Hebrews embraces a new cosmogonic perspective for its time, built on coherent presuppositions developed mostly in its reading of Jewish literature, among which the Old Testament, and particularly Genesis 1–3, takes a predominant place. This new perspective stands apart from first-century cosmogonic presuppositions which were a plethoric mixture of thoughts. But on the other hand, it is clear that the relationship between Hebrews and its first-century philosophy is not antagonistic or confrontational, since Hebrews seems not to try to correct these other cosmogonies but only presents its particular and coherent point of view.

Finally, it is possible to assert that the book that you have in your hands, in addition to the insights and conclusions that it can share with us about Hebrew's cosmogony and its relationship with the current cosmogony—and without minimizing it—it has two great words of exhortation for the global theological community: Firstly, rethink your way in which you interpret the Scriptures, that is to say, rethink your hermeneutics and therefore your interpretation. Secondly, be tolerant, don't argue with each other—i.e., don't try to correct others as you could also be wrong—try only to support your position with clarity and with respect to others.

Acknowledgments

I WOULD LIKE TO express my gratitude to Professor Jeremy Punt, for his friendly, careful, critical, and excellent supervision, as well as for his encouragement to be academically rigorous and for his patience with my English and other countless deficiencies of mine. But also, I would like to gratefully acknowledge people, institutions, and God above all, since they have been journeying with me these past years as I have worked on this dissertation now a book.

Among the people: first I owe enormous gratitude to my dear wife, Elena, and to my children Ashelén, Solange, and Yajdiel, who, while at my side and even while away from me, have given support and attention during the whole process of developing this document. Thank you. Secondly, I would like to thank Felipe Rojas and Valeriana Yauri, my dearest parents, and with them, Demesio Rosales and Teodomira Melgarejo—their prayers are a source of strength and wisdom in my life. Thirdly, special thanks to Dr. Máximina Contreras who believed in me from the beginning and gave me all her support. Fourthly, to you who are reading this document, if I know you personally, I would put your name here, because I owe you more than you think; and if I do not know you personally, thank you for sharing the interest in this topic with me. Finally, I owe enormous gratitude to all the scholars who through their writings have been the main support, as well as motivation, during the realization of my dissertation.

Among institutions: firstly, I am hugely indebted to the Universidad Peruana Unión (UPeU) for their financial support—of not only me, but also my family—throughout my academic years at the University. More specifically, I would like to express my gratitude to the past and present administrators of UPeU, and particularly to its Faculty of Theology: my dear friends, Barito Lazo, Jesús Hanco, Felipe Esteban, Gluder Quispe,

Edgard Horna, Víctor Choroco, Juan Choque, S. Teófilo Correa, Nilton Acuña and Walter Murillo. Secondly, I would like to thank Stellenbosch University, and particularly its Faculty of Theology for taking me in as part of its doctoral students. Thirdly, I must give thanks to the Seventh-day Adventist Church and the global Christian community which encourage me every day to prepare myself more in order to serve God, the church, and our society better.

I also like to thank the team of editors at Wipf and Stock Publishers, for considering my proposal as a publication. It is an honor to be included among so many important scholarly works. Thank you to the external reader who provided helpful feedback on the manuscript. Lastly, and most of all, I would like to thank ὁ θεός who, in Jesus, identified himself to me to help and to save me, and to make me a useful person in his creation. He is the only One Who can save completely, because he lives to intercede for me (cf. Heb 7:25), and he will appear a second time, apart from sin, for my salvation (cf. Heb 9:28).

Abbreviations

General

AD	*anno Domini* (in the year of our Lord)
BC	before Christ
BCE	before the Common Era
ca.	circa
CE	Common Era
cf.	[Lat.] *confer*, compare
diss.	dissertation
ed(s).	editor(s), edited by, edition
fl.	flourished (or the Latin equivalent, *floruit*)
ms(s).	manuscript(s)
NT	New Testament
OT	Old Testament
viz.	*videlicet*, namely

Modern Documents

Journals

AmJT	*American Journal of Theology*
ARJ	*Answers Research Journal*
AThR	*Anglican Theological Review*
AUSS	*Andrews University Seminary Studies*
BASOR	*Bulletin of the American Schools of Oriental Research*
BSac	*Bibliotheca Sacra*
CBQ	*Catholic Biblical Quarterly*
Chm	*Churchman*
CurBR	*Currents in Biblical Research* (formerly *Currents in Research: Biblical Studies*)
DavarLogos	*DavarLogos: Revista bíblico-teológica*

EFN	Estudios de Filología Neotestamentaria	Mnemosyne	Mnemosyne: A Journal of Classical Studies
Eur. J. Phys.	European Journal of Physics	MSJ	The Master's Seminary Journal
EvQ	Evangelical Quarterly	Neot	Neotestamentica
GOTR	Greek Orthodox Theological Review	NTS	New Testament Studies
GR	Greece and Rome	PEW	Philosophy East and West
HSCP	Harvard Studies in Classical Philology	Phil. Q.	Philosophical Quarterly
Hum. Rel.	Human Relations	PLB	Physics Letters B
IBS	Irish Biblical Studies	PSBS	Procedia—Social and Behavioral Sciences
IDS	In die Skriflig		
JATS	Journal of the Adventist Theological Society	QHR	Qualitative Health Research
JBL	Journal of Biblical Literature	QMMR	Qualitative and Multi-Method Research
JGRChJ	Journal of Greco-Roman Christianity and Judaism	Semeia	Semeia
		Them	Themelios
JMT	Journal of Ministry and Theology	VR	Vox Reformata
		WTJ	Westminster Theological Journal
JRThe	Journal of Reformed Theology	ZNW	Zeitschrift für die neutestamentliche Wissenschaft und die Kunde der älteren
JSNT	Journal for the Study of the New Testament		
JTS	Journal of Theological Studies		

ZNW	*Zeitschrift für die neutestamentliche Wissenschaft und die Kunde der älteren Kirche*	SVF	Arnim, H. von, ed. *Stoicorum veterum fragmenta*. 3 vols. Leipzing: Teubner, 1903.

Reference Books

ABD	Freedman, D. N. ed. *Anchor Bible Dictionary*. 6 vols. New York: Doubleday, 1992.
COEDLE	Stevenson, Angus and Maurice Waite, eds. *Concise Oxford English Dictionary: Luxury Edition*. 12th ed. New York: Oxford University Press, 2011.
EBD	Myers, Allen C., ed. *The Eerdmans Bible Dictionary*. Grand Rapids, MI: Eerdmans, 1987.
ODE	*Oxford Dictionary of English*. Copyright © 2010, 2016 by Oxford University Press.
OED	*The Oxford English Dictionary*. 20 vols., 3rd ed. Oxford: Oxford University Press, 1989.

Greek Texts

Byz.	Byzantine
LXX	Septuagint, Alfred Rahlfs
NA^{28}	Novum Testamentum Graece, Nestle-Aland, 28th ed.
TR	Textus Receptus
UBS^5	The Greek New Testament, United Bible Societies, 5th ed.

Modern Versions

BTX	Biblia Textual
CJB	Complete Jewish Bible
CSB	Christian Standard Bible, 2017
ESV	English Standard Version
HCSB	Holman Christian Standard Bible
ISV	International Standard Version

LBLA	La Biblia de las Américas	\multicolumn{2}{l}{**Augustine**}

LBLA	La Biblia de las Américas		
		Conf.	Confessions
LEB	The Lexham English Bible	De civ.D.	De civitate Dei
NASB95	New American Standard Bible, 1995	**Josephus**	
NIrV	New International Reader's Version	Ant.	Jewish Antiquities
		J.W.	Jewish War
NIV	New International Version		
NKJV	The New King James Version	**Lactantius**	
		De Ira D.	De Ira Dei
NLT	New Living Translation	Epit.	Epitome Divinarum Institutionum
NTV	Nueva Traducción Viviente	Inst.	Divinae institutions
RV60	Reina Valera, 1960		
		Plato	
		Crat.	Cratylus
Ancient Documents		Soph.	Sophista
Aristotle		Theaet.	Theaetetus
[Plant.]	De plantis		
[Xen.]	De Xenophane	**Philo**	
Cael.	De caelo		
De an.	De anima	Abr	De Abrahamo
Frag.	Fragmenta varia	Aet.	De aeternitate mundi
Met.	Metaphysica	Conf.	De confusione linguarum
Mete.	Meteorologica		
Ph.	Physica	Contempl.	De vita contemplative

Det.	Quod deterius potiori insidari soleat	\multicolumn{2}{l}{Plutarch (Pseudo = Ps)}
		De Defect.	De defectu oraculorum
Flacc.	In Flaccum	Plac.	Placita Philosophorum
Fug.	De fuga et invention		
Gig.	De gigantibus	Plat.	Platonicae quaestiones
Her.	Quis rerum divinarum heres sit	Stoi. Repug.	De Stoicorum repugnantiis
Ios.	De Iosepho		
Leg. 1, 2, 3	Legum allegoriae I, II, III		
Legat.	Legatio ad Gaium	\multicolumn{2}{l}{Various Authors}
Migr.	De migratione Abrahami	Acad.	Academicae quaestiones (Cicero)
Mos. 1, 2	De vita Mosis I, II	Auth. Teach.	Authoritative Teaching (The Nag Hammadi Library)
Mut.	De mutatione nominum		
Opif.	De opificio mundi	De pud.	De pudicitia (Tertullian)
Plant.	De plantatione		
Post.	De posteritate Caini	His. eccl.	Historia ecclesiastica (Eusebius)
Praem.	De praemiis et poenis		
		Magn.	Ignatius to the Magnesians (Ignatius)
Prov. 1, 2	De providentia I, II		
QE 1, 2	Quaestiones et Solutiones in Exodum I, II.	Plant.	De plantis (Nicolaus Damascenus)
Sacr.	De sacrificiis Abelis et Caini	Ref.	The Refutation of All Heresies (Hippolytus)
Sobr.	De sobrietate		
Somn. 1, 2	De somniis I, II.	STh.	Summa Theologica (Aquinas)
Spec. 1, 2, 3, 4	De specialibus legibus I, II, III, IV		

Vit. Phil.	Vitae Philosophorum (Diogenes Laertius)	𝔓⁴⁶	Chester Beatty Papyrus II
		sa	Sahidic
		sy	Syriac versions
Witnesses of the Greek New Testament Text		vg	Vulgate
		Ψ	Codex Athous Laurae
A	Codex Alexandrinus	ℵ	Codex Sinaiticus
Ath	Athanasius of Alexandria		
b	Codex Verona (Veronensis)	**Grammatical Abbreviations**	
B	Codex Vaticanus	Syntax	
bo	Bohairic	AJ	Adjunct (s)
C	Codex Ephraemi Rescriptus	EC	Embedded clauses
		PC	Primary clause
D	Codex Bezae or Claromontanus	SC	Secondary clause
H	Codex Coislinianus	SP	Supplements
K	Codex Cyprius		
L	Codex Regius	Morphology	
l	Lectionary	B	Adverb
lat	The Vulgate and a part of Old Latin witnesses	C	Conjunction
		DAPM	Article accusative plural masculine
𝔪	Majority text: the text of the majority of Greek manuscripts	DASF	Article accusative singular feminine
		DASM	Article accusative singular masculine
P	Codex Guelferbytanus A or Porphyrianus	DASN	Article accusative singular neuter

DDSF	Article dative singular feminine	NASF	Noun accusative singular feminine
DGPF	Article genitive plural feminine	NASM	Noun accusative singular masculine
DGPN	Article genitive plural neuter	NASN	Noun accusative singular neuter
DGSF	Article genitive singular feminine	NC-SA	Noun common singular absolute
DNPM	Article nominative plural masculine	NDPM	Noun dative plural masculine
DNPN	Article nominative plural neuter	NDSF	Noun dative singular feminine
DNSM	Article nominative singular masculine	NDSM	Noun dative singular masculine
JAPN	Adjective accusative plural neuter	NDSN	Noun dative singular neuter
		NGPF	Noun genitive plural feminine
JDSF	Adjective dative singular feminine	NGPN	Noun genitive plural neuter
JGPN	Adjective genitive plural neuter	NGSF	Noun genitive singular feminine
JGSF	Adjective genitive singular feminine	NGSM	Noun genitive singular masculine
JNPM	Adjective nominative plural masculine	NNPM	Noun nominative plural masculine
JNPN	Adjective nominative plural neuter	NNPN	Noun nominative plural neuter
NAPF	Noun accusative plural feminine	NNSM	Noun nominative singular masculine
NAPM	Noun accusative plural masculine	NNSN	Noun nominative singular neuter
		NVSM	Noun vocative singular masculine

P	Preposition	RP3NPM	Pronoun personal third-person nominative plural masculine
RD-GSF	Pronoun demonstrative genitive singular feminine		
		RR-ASM	Pronoun relative accusative singular masculine
RD-NSN	Pronoun demonstrative nominative singular neuter		
		RR-GSF	Pronoun relative genitive singular feminine
RF3ASM	Pronoun reflexive third-person accusative singular masculine		
		RR-GSM	Pronoun relative genitive singular masculine
RP1DP	Pronoun personal first-person dative plural	VAAI2S	Verb aorist active indicative second-person singular
RP2GS	Pronoun personal second-person genitive singular	VAAI3S	Verb aorist active indicative third-person singular
RP2NS	Pronoun personal second-person nominative singular	VAAN	Verb aorist active infinitive
		VAAP-SNM	Verb aorist active participle singular nominative masculine
RP3APM	Pronoun personal third-person accusative plural masculine		
		VAAS3S	Verb aorist active subjunctive third-person singular
RP3ASM	Pronoun personal third-person accusative singular masculine		
		VAPP-PGN	Verb aorist passive participle plural genitive neuter
RP3DSM	Pronoun personal third-person dative singular masculine		
		VFAI2S	Verb future active indicative second-person singular
RP3GSM	Pronoun personal third-person genitive singular masculine		
		VFMI3P	Verb future middle indicative third-person plural

VFPI3P	Verb future passive indicative third-person plural	VPPI3S	Verb present passive indicative third-person singular
VIAI3S	Verb imperfect active indicative third-person singular	VPPP-PGN	Verb present passive participle plural genitive neuter
VIUI3S	Verb imperfect either middle or passive indicative third-person singular	VPPP-PNN	Verb present passive participle plural nominative neuter
VPAI1P	Verb present active indicative first-person plural	VPPP-SAN	Verb present passive participle singular accusative neuter
VPAI3P	Verb present active indicative third-person plural	VPUP-PGN	Verb present either middle or passive participle plural genitive neuter
VPAI3S	Verb present active indicative third-person singular	VRAN	Verb perfect active infinitive
VPAP-SNM	Verb present active participle singular nominative masculine	VRPN	Verb perfect passive infinitive
VPAS3S	Verb present active subjunctive third-person singular	VRPP-PGN	Verb perfect passive participle plural genitive neuter

1

Introduction

THE EPISTLE TO THE Hebrews, recognized as the document under study, "is the most elegant and sophisticated, and perhaps the most enigmatic, text of first-century Christianity."[1] But, as Allen states, from the earliest days of Christian history, this epistle has also "been shrouded in obscurity."[2] Researchers have encountered many problematic topics through their studies of Hebrews,[3] however, the scope of this research is not excessively ambitious nor does it aim to solve every problem in Hebrews. Consequently, this document only aims to uncover the nature of Hebrews' cosmogonic presuppositions[4] and its relationship with first-century philosophy.

1. Attridge, *Epistle to the Hebrews*, 1.

2. Allen, *Hebrews*, 23.

3. As Dyer clearly shows, during the last decade the study of Hebrews has increased extensively and with it issues regarding its hermeneutics, theology, and generalities have resurged. See Dyer, "Epistle to the Hebrews in Recent Research." However, the plethora of problematic issues in Hebrews was also observed by others and this resulted in a resurgence of interest among the scholars, as also expressed before by Guthrie, "Hebrews' Use of the Old Testament," 272; McCullough, "Some Recent Developments (Part I)," 153; McCullough, "Some Recent Developments (Part II)," 42.

4. "Cosmogony" or "cosmology": this research will use the term "cosmogony." Robert A. Oden Jr. stated scholars occasionally maintained that it is important to make a firm distinction between these two terms, since some understand "cosmogony" as a mythical account of the original events that produced an ordered universe, and "cosmology" as speculation about meaning and value in the universe in the most general sense. Oden also recognizes that such a terminological division may be useful in discussing nonbiblical issues. See *ABD*, s.v. "cosmogony." But also important

Research Motivation: Importance of Presuppositions

All research begins with some motivation, and to understand the Bible and what it communicates could be considered the main motivation for this research—but to understand implies the need to interpret. However, interpreting the Bible—with the New Testament being the focus here—depends mainly on presuppositions, because as Heidegger hints, it is impossible to start the interpretation process without a certain horizon of pre-understanding.[5] The pre-understanding horizon referred to by Heidegger is the set of assumptions in the hermeneut's mind. Therefore, an important question also arises in the interpreter's mind: "How can I get to an understanding that is not based on the arbitrariness of my own statements, but that lets me hear the text message and not something coming from my own self?"[6] But answering this question is not easy, because postmodern philosophical hermeneutic argues that it is not legitimately possible to talk about the meaning of the text as the meaning is not in the text but in the readers. Consequently, the different interpretations are legitimate, and since therefore no particular interpretation is correct, all interpretations are wrong or all are equally correct.[7] Therefore, these new hermeneutics considers all interpretations to be valid, except the one that claims to be correct and maintains that all others are incorrect.

The above gives rise to a debate that could start with the question: Does it mean that interpretation basically depends on the presuppositions of the interpreter? If this is so, then the work of biblical scholarship must seek to discover the presuppositions that allow for proper

---

in this respect is the fact that the actual definition of this word entails "the branch of science that deals with the origin of the universe, especially the solar system," see *ODE*, s.v. "cosmogony." And since this research deals mainly with the origin and not the development or actual condition of the cosmos, it is appropriate to use the word "cosmogony" instead of "cosmology."

5. Heidegger, *Being and Time*, 136, 274. It is important to recognize that Gadamer developed Heidegger's idea of "explication," and "interpretation originates in understanding and is always derived from it." Following Heidegger's significant stance, "Gadamer insists that all forms of interpretation in real life and in human sciences are grounded in understanding and are nothing but the explication of what has already been understood." Mueller-Vollmer, *Hermeneutics Reader*, 34–35. More about it can be found in, Gadamer, *Truth and Method*, 179–387; Costache, *Gadamer and the Question of Understanding*, 51–90.

6. Ratzinger, "La Interpretación Bíblica en Conflicto," 29–30.

7. See Donald A. Carson's "Acercandonos a la Biblia" in Martínez and Zorzoli, *Nuevo Comentario Bíblico*, 23.

and correct understanding of the message that the biblical text wishes to convey. Therefore, presuppositions are crucial to the interpretation of the Bible.[8] However, inasmuch as no one comes to the text with a blank mind, that is, without presuppositions, it is necessary that the interpreter of the Bible takes the arguments of the New Zealand theologian Graham Stanton into account:

> The interpreter must allow his [sic] own presuppositions and his own pre-understanding to be modified or even completely reshaped by the text itself. Unless this is allowed to happen, the interpreter will be unable to avoid projecting his own ideas on to the text. Exegesis guided rigidly by pre-understanding will be able to establish only what the interpreter already knows.[9]

Therefore, the hermeneutical presuppositions—defined as early assumption, prior conjecture, and previous presumption—with which the biblical hermeneut approaches the Bible, in certain cases, should be replaced or reformulated, because only then can the Bible be interpreted in an appropriate way. So, as can be seen, the main motivation of this research is to attempt to discover biblical presuppositions, and in order to reach this goal one book—Hebrews—and one topic—cosmogony—were chosen, both of which will be developed in the coming section.

---

8. The experience of persons such as David Friedrich Strauss, Ferdinand Christian Baur, Rudolph Bultmann, and others can demonstrate that which is being claimed here. For instance, Strauss viewed the New Testament as mythology due to his presupposition about the limited sphere regarding the action of God. For this reason, he does not accept miracles. Bruce, *New Testament History*, 40. Baur considered most New Testament books as the work of second-century pseudonymous writers, for he considered a deep rift between Paul's ministry and the church at Jerusalem. Karleen, *Handbook to Bible Study*, 90, 91. Stanton indicates that Rudolph Bultmann's approach to the New Testament involved existentialist presuppositions that determined much of what he felt the text to be saying. Interestingly enough, he set forth in writing his views on the need to attempt to be aware of one's presuppositions, although he concluded that no interpreter could ever really operate without them. Stanton, "Presuppositions in New Testament Criticism," 67. Other examples are the commentators who do not believe that God can reveal the future; for some cases, see Archer, *Encyclopedia of Bible Difficulties*.

9. Stanton, "Presuppositions in New Testament Criticism," 68. Bultmann also asserted, "The question whether exegesis without presuppositions is possible must be answered affirmatively if 'without presuppositions' means 'without presupposing the results of the exegesis.' In this sense, exegesis without presuppositions is not only possible but demanded." Bultmann, "Is Exegesis without Presuppositions Possible?," 289.

Research Background: Hebrew's Presuppositions

Hebrews seems to present a reading of the Old Testament not shared by any other document of the New Testament and which represents a new interpretation based on presuppositions different from those of the other New Testament writers. For this reason, Hebrews has for centuries drawn attention from scholars,[10] since it seemingly shows a new view of the Old Testament.[11] For instance, George Holley Gilbert, who argues that while the Gospels put the climax of Christ's redeeming activity on earth, Hebrews puts it in heaven.[12] To Gilbert, the presuppositions on which Hebrews built its theology shows a Hellenistic character—he asserts that Hebrews has similar ideas to those found in Philo and Plato and interprets the Old Testament with Greek presuppositions. He states,

> These then, as it seems to me, are the Greek elements in the Epistle to the Hebrews. Its conception of Christ is wholly interpenetrated with the widely current views of the Logos, its conception of a heavenly tabernacle of which the Mosaic was only a copy and shadow is based on the Platonic doctrine of Ideas, and its conception of Scripture is Greek in the underlying view of inspiration, Greek in that Christ is sometimes represented as speaking in the Old Testament—for this view probably sprang out of the Logos influence—and Greek in its profoundly allegorical character.[13]

---

10. Today Dyer also asserts that it "no longer seems appropriate to consider Hebrews as among the neglected in the New Testament canon." Dyer, "Epistle to the Hebrews in Recent Research," 104. To Guthrie, problems such as no readily identifiable author nor recipients, the imprecise date, unrecognizable patterns of thought, and its clearly superior style put Hebrews out of place in the New Testament, and for this reason this book, called "the Cinderella," has been studied by many scholars in past years. Guthrie, "Hebrews in Its First-Century Context," 414–15. Meanwhile Punt reminds us that though some have seen Hebrews as "a riddle," irrelevant and incomprehensible, its relevance and value for the task of scholars, ministers and Christians, is more significant than they think, as it shows the method of delivering the biblical message to the contemporary mind. Punt, "Hebrews, Thought-Patterns and Context," 119, 122–54.

11. The Old Testament is understood here as the thirty-nine books accepted as part of the biblical canon in most Protestant Christian circles. The titles "Old Testament," "Scriptures of Israel," and "Hebrew Bible" are used in this document interchangeably. Regarding the apparently new view of the Old Testament in Hebrews, see Guthrie, "Hebrews in Its First-Century Context," 430–33.

12. Gilbert, "Greek Element," 521.

13. Gilbert, "Greek Element," 532.

On the other hand, Estrada Zesati, recognizes that although some words and sentences of Plato and Philo appear in Hebrews, he affirms in his extensive and significant work about Hebrews 5:7–8[14] that there is no dependency between the Gospels and Hebrews,[15] and it is improbable that the writer of Hebrews had been influenced by Greek philosophy.[16] Nevertheless, and even though Hebrews shows evidence of Jewish influence, Mackie more recently stated that the motifs of the Old Testament used in Hebrews are opposed to the message they convey in the Old Testament. One example, he maintains, is the role of the throne of God, which instills fear and prevents the people from approaching God—the Old Testament message according to Mackie—while in Hebrews it is referred to as τῷ θρόνῳ τῆς χάριτος (the throne of grace) which all are invited to approach. Moreover, according to Mackie, a close examination of the motifs, such as the temple veil, and the glory of God and the angels, reveals that they present similar features.[17]

These authors—as others, both older and more recent—have argued directly or indirectly that Hebrews shows a Greek mindset,[18] just as Philo of Alexandria does.[19] Therefore, Greek presuppositions—or at least the current presuppositions of its time, i.e., first-century philosophy—could

14. In all quotations from Hebrews the name of the biblical book will be omitted. In addition, wherever the biblical version is not specified, it is a personal translation, otherwise the version will follow the text, and—if it is pertinent—the abbreviation of the ancient version.

15. Zesati states that the terminology used is evidence of the independence between the Gospels and Hebrews. For example, in the suffering of Christ in Gethsemane, Matthew uses the terms λυπεῖσθαι καὶ ἀδημονεῖν (sorrowful and distressed), Mark uses ἐκθαμβεῖσθαι καὶ ἀδημονεῖν (troubled and distressed), Luke uses ἀγονία (agony), and John uses τετάρακται (troubled), while Hebrews uses the term κραυγή and δάκρυα (cries and tears). Zesati Estrada, *Hebreos 5:7–8*, 28.

16. Zesati Estrada, *Hebreos 5:7–8*, 58, 299.

17. Mackie, "Ancient Jewish Mystical Motifs," 103.

18. Svendsen in his PhD dissertation argues that Hebrews was deeply steeped in Hellenistic philosophy, and also states, "The hermeneutics of Hebrews should rather be seen as a variation of Philo's allegorical method." Svendsen, *Allegory Transformed*, 57. Also, Barclay accepts that the writer to the Hebrews had a dual background, namely, a Greek and Hebrew background. Barclay, *Letter to the Hebrews*, 2–3.

19. Gilbert not only states that Philo and the writer of Hebrews share ideas, he asserts that the writer of Hebrews built his reasoning on Philo's ideas: "It remains to notice the magnitude of the contribution . . . made to the thought of Hebrews when Philo's conception of the Logos as a high priest was adopted by the Christian writer. It may not be too much to say that he regarded this thought as the special burden of his message." Gilbert, "Greek Element," 526.

be found in Hebrews. Two influential works which differ on the background of Hebrews are the work of Spicq, which argues a Greek mindset, and the work of Williamson, which maintains that Spicq was wrong.[20] On the other hand, Hurst in his analysis of possible backgrounds of Hebrews asserts, "The numerous backgrounds proposed this century for Hebrews cannot all be correct." Nevertheless, he also concludes that in most cases it will be "determined by the subjective judgments of individual scholars."[21] And although it must be accepted that understanding the mindset of the writer of Hebrews is almost impossible, this study, based on Hebrews' text, will focus only on the background of one point of its content, i.e., its cosmogony.

Research Problem

To consider the cosmogony of Hebrews is to consider its religion and its beliefs, i.e., its presuppositions about the origin of the world, the universe and reality, since, to paraphrase Durkheim, it can be stated that every cosmogony is a kind of religion.[22] Hebrews, as Johnson asserted, can be considered one of the most "powerfully argued, and theologically profound writings in the New Testament,"[23] therefore it is certainly an important source of knowledge concerning biblical cosmogony. "It holds second place among New Testament documents in references to Genesis 1–[3] and creation in general."[24]

Moreover, it contains the most well-known affirmation on the topic: "By faith we understand that the worlds were framed by the word of God, so that the things which are seen were not made of things which are visible" (11:3, NKJV). On the other hand, it must be recognized that cosmogonic ideas are usually expressed indirectly, as part of the worldview

---

20. See Ceslas Spicq, *L'épître aux Hébreux*; Williamson, *Philo and the Epistle to the Hebrews*.

21. Hurst's analysis of Christian and non-Christian backgrounds concludes by asserting that to tie Hebrews with the outlook of Philo, Qumran, Gnosticism, the Samaritans or *Merkabah* mysticism, Jewish Apocalyptic, Paul, Acts 7, or 1 Peter presents difficulties since all of them always leave some sort of inconformity, even though some of them could be more appropriate. See Hurst, *Epistle to the Hebrews*, 131–33.

22. Durkheim, *Elementary Forms of the Religious Life*, 141.

23. Johnson, *Hebrews: A Commentary*, 1.

24. Cortez, "Creation in Hebrews," 279, cf. Mueller, "Creation in the New Testament," 48.

Introduction

of the biblical writer. Moreover, as Lucas asserts, cosmogony is "often expressed using imagery and ideas which were shared with other cultures with which the biblical writers were in contact."[25] Therefore, knowledge of current cosmogonies in the first century can illuminate the understanding of Hebrews' cosmogony. Hence this research will tackle the cosmogonic presuppositions in Hebrews and its first-century philosophical context, by considering a statement that will be split into one primary question and six secondary questions in order to facilitate its consideration.

Primary Research Question

What has been mentioned up to now could raise numerous questions in the mind of the reader in respect of presuppositions, Hebrews, first-century philosophy and cosmogony, which would be impossible to answer fully and completely. However, this research aims to address a problem related only to the cosmogonic presuppositions in Hebrews and its relation to the cosmogonies present in first-century philosophy.

In brief, the specific problem that will be discussed in this research is: What are the relationships between Hebrews' cosmogonic presuppositions and its first-century philosophical context?

Secondary Research Questions

In order to answer the primary question of this research, six secondary questions will be addressed which will be tackled in different chapters:

1. Does the comprehension of introductory questions about Hebrews influence the understanding of its cosmogony?
2. What are the cosmogonic presuppositions and literary content present in first-century philosophy?
3. What is the cosmogonic literary component of Hebrews?
4. What are the grammatical features that can help to extract the cosmogonic presuppositions in Hebrews?
5. What are the cosmogonic presuppositions in Hebrews?
6. What are the similarities and differences between the cosmogonic presuppositions in Hebrews and in first-century philosophy?

25. Lucas, "Cosmogony," 1:132.

Research Purpose

Consequently, in relation to the research problem, the purpose of this research is first to judge the relationship between Hebrews' cosmogonic presuppositions and its first-century philosophical context, and in order to fulfill this main purpose, it is necessary to establish six minor purposes:

1. To evaluate if the comprehension of introductory questions about Hebrews influences the understanding of its cosmogony.

2. To display the cosmogonic presuppositions and literary content present in first-century philosophy.

3. To determine the cosmogonic literary component in Hebrews.

4. To evaluate the grammatical features that can help to extract the cosmogonic presuppositions in Hebrews.

5. To establish the cosmogonic presuppositions in Hebrews.

6. To determine the similarities and differences between the cosmogonic presuppositions in Hebrews and its first-century philosophical context.

Preliminary Studies Already Undertaken

Some preliminary studies related to the topic of this research include the following: *Cosmology and Eschatology in Hebrews: The Settings of the Sacrifice*, written by Schenck. Although the writer approaches the cosmology in Hebrews—a topic closely related with cosmogony—his emphasis is on the eschatology. He approaches the relationship between Hebrews and the writings of Philo and Plato, and he observes that in some topics there is influence, but in others there is no such influence. Concerning the specific focus of this research, Schenck's book has little to say; however, he portrays the λόγος as the medium of creation, but declares nothing about the origin of matter. In other words, Schenck briefly shows a cosmology of Hebrews, but does not approach its cosmogony, which is the main topic of this research.[26] Another significant book is *The Theology of the Letter to the Hebrews*. In this book, Lindars writes on presuppositions that arise in Hebrews, and groups them into four categories:

---

26. Schenck, *Cosmology and Eschatology in Hebrews*.

Introduction

1. The plan of salvation;
2. The use of Scripture;
3. The atonement ritual; and
4. The *rigorism* of Hebrews.

However, although he states, for example, that the writer of Hebrews "presupposes that God is in control of history in a way that is difficult to square with our global perspective,"[27] he does not assert anything about cosmogonic presuppositions in Hebrews.

Some articles also touch on the topic of this research; for example, O'Neill affirms that the doctrine of *creatio ex nihilo* has full support in the New Testament. He asserts that no one doubts this doctrine, but he also states that a difference exists between the creation of matter—the very beginning—and the creation of the world—the fashioning of matter—as we see it today.[28] Likewise, more recently, some books and articles[29] have appeared that relate significantly to the topic under study; however, most of them focus on general cosmogony, i.e., they do not focus on Hebrews as the document of evaluation. Nonetheless, among the articles that hold a close relation to the topic of study in this research, two hold a special position. The first, written by Stewart, is an older document; short, but very significant, since it deals almost directly with the topic under study. In it Stewart asserts that "Hebrews is not directly concerned with the manner of creation or the nature of matter, but there are scattered allusions which presuppose underlying conceptions of cosmology, ontology and epistemology."[30] The problem with Stewart's article is its brevity—nine pages are not sufficient to address a topic as complicated as cosmogony. The second article was written by Felix Cortez and was published during the time this research was being done. It deals directly with the creation

---

27. Lindars, *Hebrews*, 129.
28. O'Neill, "How Early Is the Doctrine," 449–65.
29. Among these documents are the following outstanding works: Copan and Craig, *Creation Out of Nothing*; Gregory, *Ancient Greek Cosmogony*; Pennington and McDonough, *Cosmology and New Testament Theology*; Samuelson, *Judaism and the Doctrine of Creation*; Burrell et al., *Creation and the God of Abraham*; Hubler, "Creatio Ex Nihilo"; Filtvedt, "Creation and Salvation in Hebrews," 280–303.
30. Stewart in his important article tackles five issues: 1) Form and archetype, copy and *ectype*. 2) The world: single, dual or multiple? 3) Types and worlds in the epistle to the Hebrews. 4) The creative word: fiat or hypostatic intermediary? And 5) The creation and duration of the world. See Stewart, "Creation and Matter," 284–93.

in Hebrews, and as Cortez explicitly states, the purpose of his article is to answer four questions:

> 1) What does the Letter to the Hebrews say about the creation of our world? 2) What role does the creation of our world play in the broader argument of the Letter to the Hebrews? 3) How did Hebrews' views on creation relate to the debate on the origin of the world in antiquity (especially to Plato whose views held a prominent position in the intellectual landscape of the ancient Greco-Roman world)? And 4) What are the implications of Hebrews' views on creation for the current debate between creationism and evolution?[31]

However, it must be pointed out that none of the documents mentioned above, including the last two, try to extract the cosmogonic presuppositions veiled in Hebrews in order to compare them with the cosmogonic presuppositions present in first-century philosophy. In summary, the authors of these studies can be divided into two groups: authors who think the writers of the New Testament, including the writer of Hebrews, presupposed a creation from nothing, *creatio ex nihilo*; and authors who argue that the New Testament, Hebrews included, hold the conviction that creation was made from preexisting and eternal matter.

Research Scope and Delimitations

This research has one specific goal: to identify the main cosmogonic presuppositions as they emerge in Hebrews. This research therefore wants to ascertain whether the writer of Hebrews believed that matter is eternal and pre-existing or that it had an origin. Likewise, it wants to ascertain the relationship between the creator and matter, as well as the process by which the world became the habitat of human beings from the text and perspective of Hebrews. On the other hand, it must be asserted that this research is based on the Greek text of Hebrews, and the results obtained in exegetical work will be compared with the main cosmogonic vocabulary and thoughts present in first-century philosophy. This will be done in order to determine if the cosmogonic presuppositions in Hebrews were influenced to some degree by the thoughts of its philosophical context. Finally, regarding the scope of the investigation, it should be noted that the study of the Greek terms relevant to the investigation will

---

31. Cortez, "Creation in Hebrews," 279–320.

be based primarily on Hebrews and secondarily on the contemporary philosophical writers.

This research is not meant to be a commentary on Hebrews, nor does it aim to give the final word on its interpretation. It does not propose a new hermeneutical methodology, nor does it expect to identify the author of Hebrews or resolve any other introductory issue. This research also does not aim to discover all the presuppositions present in Hebrews, nor intends to give the final word on the relationship between Philo and the writer of Hebrews, nor between Hebrews and any other specific personality of its context. Furthermore, this research does not aim primarily to undertake a study of some single Greek word in Hebrews such as λόγος, nor of any other Greek word. Finally, it must be asserted that this research is not going to seek a relationship between Hebrews' cosmogony and modern cosmogonic philosophical theories—sometimes called scientific theories—and it does not purport to discuss current positions on cosmogony or creation among different Christian traditions.[32]

Research Methodology and Procedure

Since this study comprises theological research, the methodology for it will mainly be the one generally used in theoretical and documentary research. The literary analysis will be based on academic literature that

---

32. Firstly, the following modern cosmogonic philosophical theories can be mentioned: 1) The primeval-atom theory, which basically posits that an all-inclusive primeval atom suddenly radioactively burst over thirteen billion years ago—the "big bang"—when time and space came into being concurrently and the natural laws came into force. 2) The steady-state theory, which basically posits that there is no beginning nor end for everything. 3) The superdense state theory, which posits that all matter plus energy can be charted back in time to a more concentrated conglomerate mass some six billion years ago, when the extremely high temperature of this mass produced an explosion—the "big bang"—that propelled matter and radiation outward, which in time formed the planets, stars, and galaxies. Secondly, according to Mare, there are at least eight theories about the origin of the universe among professed Christians: 1) The Progressive Creative Catastrophism or "Gap" theory; 2) The Day-Age Catastrophism theory; 3) The Alternate Day-Age theory; 4) The Eden-Only theory, namely Genesis only describes garden of Eden creation in six literal days; 5) The Concurrent or Overlapping Ages theory; 6) The Revelation Day theory; 7) The Split Week or Double Symmetry theory which is developed on the assumption that God is timeless; and 8) The Progressive Creationism theory which holds that there is no need to posit a "gap" between verse 1 and 2 in the first chapter of Genesis. More about cosmogonic theories can be found in Hetherington, *Encyclopedia of Cosmology*; Mare, "Cosmogony, Cosmology," 1:1044; Zinke, "Faith-Science Issues," 63–90.

deals with cosmogony, cosmology, creation, biblical hermeneutics, biblical languages and Hebrews. However, it will be focused on a deep grammatical, syntactic, and semantic analysis of Hebrews' text, and throughout this process, the NA^{28} edition and the textual witness that is present in its apparatus will be taken into account.[33]

Much has been written about the importance of method and methodology in research. There are several forms of investigation that are grouped by methodology, purpose, time, variables, the level of measurement, and data analysis, etc.[34] The theological research can be considered qualitative research or research in humanities, which has as its primary purpose the interpretation of documents and acts, which contribute to the advancement of human knowledge. Therefore, this research must be considered in these categories and more specifically as documentary constructive research.[35]

On the other hand, current research methodology into biblical studies is constituted by a broad spectrum of proposals, besides which, the author of this study believes that there is no single perfect method or methodology for biblical interpretation. Namely, methods of interpretation exist which, when used, can lead to a better understanding of the biblical text.[36] Therefore, this research will use a variety of methodologies, giving preference to the historic-grammatical methodology. Further, because this research will be multi-methodological, it will make significant use of some procedures posited by methodologies such as

---

33. Nevertheless, it must be clarified that, when necessary, other versions of the New Testament Greek as well as other Greek documents, such as writings of Plato, Philo, Josephus, and Laertius, amongst others, will be taken into account.

34. More about methods and methodology in biblical or religious studies can be found in LeMon and Richards, *Method Matters*; McGowan and Richards, *Method and Meaning*; Stausberg and Engler, *Routledge Handbook of Research Methods*.

35. Bohnsack et al., *Qualitative Analysis and Documentary Method*, 60–68; Jupp, *Sage Dictionary of Social Research Methods*, 207, 63.

36. Correa affirms that there are as many methods for doing theology, as there are theologians, but he also recognizes that there are methods that have a more respectful approach to the text, that value its authority and originality based on the same Bible. Correa, "Intertextualidad y Exégesis Intra-Bíblica," 2, 11.

content analysis,[37] and socio-rhetorical interpretation.[38] Socio-rhetorical interpretation is well-known, but with regard to content analysis, it is necessary to clarify it as being defined as a method that "emphasizes an integrated view of speech/texts and their specific contexts," that "goes beyond merely counting words or extracting objective content from texts to examine meanings, themes, and patterns that may be manifest or latent in a particular text."[39] Thus, this method allows for empirical study and not a subjective approach to the text.

The methodology will specifically include the following stages, and in doing so, will emphasize the internal analysis of Hebrews and the external analysis of the philosophical writings in the first century. Such analysis will include:

1. Display of the internal and external Hebrews' cosmogony context, which will be dealing with two aspects: firstly, with the introductory issues of Hebrews and their influence in its cosmogony; and secondly, with the selection of relevant cosmogonic texts and thoughts present in first-century philosophy. The criteria for this selection are topics pertaining to this research—cosmogony—and usage of special cosmogonic Greek words.

2. Selection of relevant texts and words for cosmogony in Hebrews, which include the analysis of textual witnesses—if some selected text requires it—as well as the text-linguistic and grammatical analysis. More specifically, it will analyze elements such as: structure, rhetorical figures, aspects of style, genres, linguistic issues,

---

37. Content analysis is a methodology of research inspired by hermeneutic analysis and comparison of the texts and is mostly used in research in humanities sciences. Content analysis must not be confused with "content criticism" (*Sachkritik*), which is characteristic of the new hermeneutic, although its beginnings precede content analysis. The term *Sachkritik*, although first applied in 1922 and 1926 to the task of Barth by Bultmann, can be considered as the basis of the task of demythologizing of the New Testament. See Henry, *God, Revelation, and Authority*, 4:301; Ramm, "New Hermeneutic," 139–43. In order to better understand the content analysis method, see also Neuendorf, *Content Analysis Guidebook*; Patton, *Qualitative Research & Evaluation Methods*; Hsieh and Shannon, "Three Approaches to Qualitative Content Analysis," 1277–88; Herrera and Braumoeller, "Symposium," 15–39.

38. Robbins, *Exploring the Texture of Texts*. An extensive bibliography and aid for the employment of this method is presented on the website dedicated to this type of research, http://www.religion.emory.edu/faculty/robbins/SRI/index.cfm. See also Gowler, "Socio-Rhetorical Interpretation," 191–206.

39. Zhang and Wildemuth, "Qualitative Analysis of Content," 308–19.

semantic and syntax, among other particular features that are pertinent to this study.

3. Disclosure of Hebrews' cosmogonic presuppositions, and in order to achieve this, a conceptual analysis will be done on the basis of the grammar, syntactic, and semantic features of the selected texts which will be included in the content analysis. Further, it will be identifying and systematizing the units of analysis and context.

4. Statement of Hebrews' cosmogonic presuppositions and its relationship with its first-century philosophical context, in order to assess the independence or dependence between Hebrews and its philosophical context on the cosmogonic issue.

It is also important to make clear that this research is not inductive research, but on the contrary, is deductive research; namely, this research will not commence in social reality, but will rather commence in the text, in order to be pertinent in social reality. Finally, it needs to be stated that the author of this research believes in and will employ the simple and old method of meditation,[40] namely, prayer, faith, and trust in the providence of a real God Who directs the minds of those who study his word.

Research Significance

There are always significant contributions from any research, this research is important to global theology, for the following reasons:

1. To ascertain whether Hebrews was influenced to some degree by first-century philosophy, regardless of whether their ideas are similar or different. This is something that has profound implications for the current hermeneutical debate, because presuppositions influence both the methods and results.

2. To contribute to a better understanding of biblical cosmogony, namely, the locating of time, actions, events, and happenings referred to in the Mosaic רֵאשִׁית (the beginning) and ἀρχῇ (the beginning) Johannine.

3. Perhaps the most important contribution of this research is the advance toward an understanding of the presupposition regarding the origin of all things, which also has profound implications for

---

40. Roothaan, *Method of Meditation*, 16–76.

the work of current biblical hermeneutics. Nevertheless, it is more pertinent to the individual, since as Lucas and Waltke appropriately assert about cosmogony,

> It [cosmogony] shapes one's answers—consciously or subconsciously—to the "big" questions such as "Who am I?" and "Why am I here?" For most people, their worldview is something that they have never fully articulated and made coherent.[41]

> It is important because the question of cosmogony is closely related to one's entire world view. Someone has said that our world view is like the umpire at a ball game. He seems unimportant and the players are hardly aware of him, but in reality he decides the ball game. So likewise one's world view lies behind every decision a person makes. It makes a difference whether we come from a mass of matter or from the hand of God. How we think the world started will greatly influence our understanding of our identity, our relationship to others, our values, and our behavior. Because the question of cosmogony is important for understanding some of the basic issues of life, intelligent men throughout recorded history have sought the answer to this question. Just as the knowledge of the future is crucial for making basic choices in life, so also the knowledge of beginnings is decisive in establishing a man's or a culture's *Weltanschauung* ("world view"). No wonder the Bible reveals both.[42]

Therefore, a major consequence of this research could be considered to be its assistance in answering the existential question, which, in turn, could be considered to be the primary question and perhaps even the basis on which other existential questions are elaborated and answered.

4. Finally, since the change of beliefs and practices into Christendom is deeply related to biblical interpretation,[43] which in turn is greatly influenced by the change of its cosmogonic presuppositions,[44] it

---

41. Lucas, "Cosmogony," 1:131.

42. Waltke, "Creation Account in Genesis 1:1–3," 28.

43. All interpretation rests on presuppositions and hermeneutical methods, but methods also rest on presuppositions, therefore if the presuppositions are false the method could be wrong and truth will be distorted, so some methods for determining truth are not applicable to the study of the Bible. For more about it see Story, *Christianity on the Offense*, 51–52.

44. Perhaps this is the reason for the emergence of such plurality of denominations

can be stated that the conclusions of this research could help future studies by biblical scholars and Christendom in general.

---

into Christendom, especially during the nineteenth and twentieth centuries, since these years were witnesses of a veritable explosion of growth of many denominations into the Christendom. More specific information on it can be found in "Center for the Study of Global Christianity," and also in the document "Status of Global Christianity, 1970–2020: Society, Religion, and Mission," which can be found at http://www.gordonconwell.edu/ockenga/research/documents/2ChristianityinitsGlobalContext.pdf, and in "World Christian Database." See http://www.worldchristian database.org/wcd/.

2

Introductory Issues and Hebrews' Cosmogony

IT HAS BEEN CLAIMED that in order to have a better understanding of any writing a knowledge of its introductory issues are compulsory since it serves as a catalyst to its interpretation or understanding.[1] However, Hebrews could be considered to be a New Testament document with significant problems in its introductory issues, since an attempt to define items such as its authorship, audience, and background, amongst others, is a goal almost impossible of being achieved. Consequently, the purpose here is to position the backdrop to this research, not to solve the longstanding scholarly difficulties in Hebrews. Therefore, the focus of this chapter is on the cosmogonic implications of Hebrews' introductory issues.

Chapter Introduction

Hebrews, due to it being a handwritten document, has some features in common with other writings of the time, some of which are relevant to this research. This chapter tackles some of these difficult issues in Hebrews, since as Mosser asserts,

> The positions one takes on specific introductory questions regarding the epistle's destination, recipients, purpose, date and

---

1. For instance, Schreiner asserts that "the value of studying introductory issues is that it assists the student in interpreting a letter in its historical context." Schreiner, *Interpreting the Pauline Epistles*, 63.

genre—or whether one thinks there is enough evidence to take positions on these issues—have particular bearing on how one understands Hebrews as a whole. Unfortunately, Hebrews is notorious for refusing to reveal the correct answers to such questions and scholarship has had little success uncovering them.[2]

Therefore, assumptions regarding the introductory issues can influence the comprehension of Hebrews' cosmogony, and so, along with the genre, authorship and audience of Hebrews, this chapter also deals with the background of thought, date, and other features that are significant for our purpose.

Genre of Hebrews

Hughes affirmed that the introductory issues in Hebrews are "the battleground of discordant opinion and conjecture,"[3] and this is most evident when the genre of the book is tackled. There are various possibilities regarding the genre, which depend on what the reader wants emphasized: its epistolary nature or its sermonic character. However, it is also possible to label Hebrews as an essay, treatise, oration, or biblical exposition.[4] And, as already asserted, each of these possibilities will give a different understanding of its content, or at least of the document's focus. In order to determine the genre of some New Testament documents it is widely recognized that there are at least three things to consider:

1. There is literature that can be considered as sui-generis in the New Testament;
2. It is rooted in the Semitic world and Greek literary practices;[5] and
3. A single document can contain different literary genres.

---

2. Mosser, "No Lasting City," 6.
3. Hughes, *Commentary on the Epistle to the Hebrews*, 1.
4. An acceptable treatment of the genre of Hebrews, showing an extensive bibliography and explanations of diverse theories, can be found in Lane, *Hebrews 9–13*, lxix–lxxxiv. On the sermonic nature of Hebrews or as "paraclesis" and also for its classification as epideictic oration, see Attridge, "Paraenesis in a Homily," 210–26. More discussion and bibliography on this respect can be found in Allen, *Hebrews*, 24.
5. Ellingworth, *Epistle to the Hebrews*, 59–61.

Introductory Issues and Hebrews' Cosmogony

In the case of Hebrews, most writers and commentators label it as a kind of sermon,[6] while others label it as a midrash in rhetorical prose and epistle.[7] For instance, Cockerill states that "Hebrews is a Christian synagogue homily,"[8] while Hagner asserts that "the literary genre of Hebrews is an exhortatory sermon."[9] Nevertheless, regardless of the positions taken on the genre of Hebrews, commentators often leave an opening for new potential interpretations. So for instance, Koester—who labels Hebrews as a rhetorical sermon, even though he recognizes that there are those who consider Hebrews to be an epideictic speech—sustains that, "moreover, assessment of the genre depends in part upon the individual hearer."[10]

On the other hand, Hebrews' own assertion that the document is a τοῦ λόγου τῆς παρακλήσεως (a word of exhortation, cf. 13:22), has also been understood as being the genre of the document.[11] But since this section of the document has been labeled as not being part of the original document, it can hardly serve to determine the genre of Hebrews. However, it must be kept in mind that the purpose of this research is not to determine Hebrews' genre, and therefore it is enough to make some observations that can help to further research on this issue.

1. The document's vocabulary is not part of the common argot of common first-century Christendom, i.e., a sermon preached in an ordinary synagogue or in an ordinary Christian meeting could have been incomprehensible to most of its listeners. Therefore, if it is a sermon it must be addressed to specific people.

2. The document has an introduction and conclusion that appear to have no parallels in other first-century documents.

---

6. Allen for instance asserts, "It is now generally recognised that Hebrews is a written sermon." Allen, *Hebrews*, 25. Attridge asserts that it is a synagogue sermon, Attridge, *Hebrews*, 14, and Guthrie that it is a sermon, Guthrie, *Hebrews*, 24. Johnson asserts that "Hebrews presents itself as a work of deliberative rhetoric, careful in language and rich in metaphor." Johnson, *Hebrews*, 15.

7. For midrash in rhetorical prose see Bruce, *Epistle to the Hebrews*. And for epistle see Kistemaker, *Exposición de la Epístola*.

8. Cockerill, *Epistle to the Hebrews*, 15.

9. Hagner, *Hebrews*, 12.

10. Koester, *Hebrews*, 82.

11. Guthrie overvalued his argument when he stated that "this word of exhortation (τοῦ λόγου τῆς παρακλήσεως)" (13:22 NASB) is "a designation used elsewhere to refer to a sermon." Guthrie, *Hebrews*, 24.

3. The document seems to cover one topic—Christ's occupation in heaven after his resurrection—even though, in the process, it tackles other minor themes.

So it is possible that the original document of Hebrews was a treatise to which its author added a conclusion relating to its content and which gives the tone of a letter to the document. As already asserted, whatever position is taken about the genre of Hebrews will influence the comprehension of its cosmogony, the topic under study. So for instance, if Hebrews is a sermon, most of its cosmogonic information will be considered to be a kind of illustration in order to support its final appeal. But, if Hebrews is a treatise, the content on cosmogony is not an illustration, but the foundational issue on which its interpretation of the Old Testament and the formulation of its theology is built.

Authorship: Implications for Its Cosmogony

The authorship of Hebrews is perhaps the most important element to establish in order to comprehend the mind-set that contributed to the formation of the text and, with it, the presuppositions about its cosmogony. But the authorship of Hebrews has been in dispute since early times.[12] In fact, it can be affirmed along with Hacking that "this is one

---

12. The writing of Tertullian (ca. 150–200 CE) is perhaps the oldest register of Hebrews' authorship, and he believed that "Barnabas—a Levite associated with Paul—wrote it." See Tertullian, *De pud.* 20.2. In addition to it, Eusebius asserted that Pantaenus (ca. 190 CE) believed that Paul wrote it, while Clement of Alexandria (ca. 155–220 CE) believed that he—Paul—wrote it in Hebrew and Luke translated it to Greek. See Eusebius, *Hist. eccl.* 3.38.2; 6.13.1–2; 14.1–4. More recently, Utley affirms about the earliest problems concerning the authorship of Hebrews, that "the Eastern Church—Alexandria, Egypt—accepted Paul's authorship of Hebrews' book as it can be seen in the early papyrus manuscript called the Chester Beatty Papyri ($\mathfrak{P}^{46}$) which was copied at the end of the second century, since it places Hebrews after Romans. On the other hand, this book is omitted from the list of Paul's letters adopted by the Western Church called the Muratorian Fragment" (ca. 180–200 CE). Utley also states that Origen maintained "either Luke or Clement of Rome wrote it" following Paul's teaching, while Calvin asserted that "Clement of Rome—the first writer to quote Hebrews in 96 CE—or Luke was the author." Meanwhile, "Martin Luther stated that Apollos—an Alexandrian trained intellectual associated with Paul (cf. Acts 18:24)"—was the author. "Adolph von Harnack, however, posited that Aquila and Priscilla—since they taught Apollos the full gospel and were associated with Paul and Timothy (cf. Acts 18:26)—wrote it. Sir William Ramsey maintained Philip the evangelist wrote it for Paul while Paul was in prison at Caesarea. Others, moreover, have asserted Philip or Silas" as the author of Hebrews. Utley, *Superiority of the New Covenant*, 2–3.

of the great remaining mysteries of the New Testament."[13] Currently, it is possible to identify at least fifteen theories regarding the authorship of Hebrews, besides the one that posits it as unknown or anonymous, and the one that considers it a pseudepigraphic document.[14] However, the main question about this topic is not whether Hebrews was written by Clement of Rome, Maria, Priscilla, Barnabas, Luke, Apollos, Paul, or some other person, but rather whether "the author's own thought-world was predominantly Jewish or Greek."[15]

Nonetheless, even though the authorship of Hebrews is in dispute, the fact is that since the early first century it was considered part of the collection of authoritative Christian writings,[16] written by someone with extensive knowledge, someone well-known to the audience (cf. 6:9–10; 10:34; 13:7, 9), and someone of deep feeling with a benevolent heart for first-century Christendom. Moreover, it was apparently someone that did not listen to Jesus directly (cf. 2:3), someone who used some Greek translation of the Old Testament—perhaps the Septuagint—as his Bible, and someone very well-educated in the ancient tabernacle's procedures.[17] What is clear from the text is that it was someone capable of using Greek efficiently, well-educated in Hellenistic skills of drafting and rhetoric as the text's excellent Greek evidences.[18]

Hebrews has no subscription title and consequently, it is necessary to either speculate who the author was, or to deduce it from external or

---

13. Hacking, *Opening up Hebrews*, 8.

14. The names that have been suggested as possible authors of Hebrews are: 1) Barnabas, 2) Paul, 3) Clement of Rome, 4) Luke, 5) Apollos, 6) Silas, 7) Peter, 8) Philip, 9) Priscilla & Aquila, 10) Aristion, 11) Stephen, 12) Jude, 13) Epaphras, 14) Timothy, and 15) Mary, the Mother of Jesus. See Bateman, *Charts on the Book of Hebrews*, 17–26. Ellingworth deals with thirteen of these names, see Ellingworth, *Epistle to the Hebrews*, 3–21. For Hebrews as a pseudepigraphic document see Rothschild, *Hebrews as Pseudepigraphon*, 119–62.

15. Ellingworth, *Epistle to the Hebrews*, 22.

16. Helmbold and Utley stated that "several early gnostic works such as *Gospel of Truth*, *Gospel of Philip*, and *The Apocrypha of John* quote the book of Hebrews several times, which shows it was considered part of the authoritative Christian writings by the second century." Utley, *Superiority of the New Covenant*, 2; Helmbold, *Nag Hammadi Gnostic Texts*, 91.

17. Utley, *Superiority of the New Covenant*, 2.

18. Johnson claims that "by far the best Koine to be found among New Testament writings" is that which is present in the book of Hebrews. Johnson, *Hebrews*, 8. The book of Hebrews contains complex sentences and an elevated rhetorical. Attridge, *Hebrews*, 5.

internal evidence. And even though there is some speculation of Apollos as being the author—with apparent biblical support—it is better to determine its potential author from both its external and internal evidence. From before the time of Stuart (1780–1852) up until today, the questions regarding the authorship of Hebrews have been answered with much conjecture and perhaps less evidence, and very little advance has been made by more recent scholars in this respect—the same questions and the same answers for every theory have been constantly repeated during the centuries. Stuart answered many of the past concrete arguments against Pauline authorship of Hebrews through his extensive defense in 1827,[19] without fully satisfactorily answering every question in particular, but with enough support to continue to affirm with Origen,

> Therefore, if any church [ἐκκλησία] holds that this epistle is by Paul, let it be commended for this. For not without reason [εἰκῇ] have the ancients handed it down as Paul's. But who wrote [γράψας, i.e., penned it down] the epistle, in truth, God knows.[20]

But whether agreeing or disagreeing with Origen about the Pauline authorship of Hebrews, most scholars agree with him in the respect "that the thoughts are those of the apostle, but the diction and phraseology are those of someone who remembered the apostolic teachings, and wrote down at his leisure what had been said by his teacher."[21] Even those who disagree intensely are obliged to uphold:

> Traceable to no apostle, it teaches, exhorts, and warns with apostolic authority and power. Though not of Paul's pen, it has, somehow, the impress of his genius and influence, and is altogether worthy to occupy a place in the canon, *after his Epistles, or between* them and the Catholic Epistles. *Pauline in spirit*, it is catholic or encyclical in its aim.[22]

Therefore, in order to reach a better understanding of the cosmogony of Hebrews it is important to understand the cosmogony of Paul, or at least not deviate too far from it. Perhaps that is why Stuart maintained that the secondary clause "through whom also he made the universe (δι' οὗ καὶ ἐποίησεν τοὺς αἰῶνας)" (1:2, NIV)—must be interpreted as "*He* [i.e.,

19. Stuart, *Commentary on the Epistle to the Hebrews*, 77–235.
20. Eusebius, *Hist. eccl.* 6.25.13–14.
21. Eusebius, *Hist. eccl.* 6.25.13.
22. Schaff and Schaff, *History of the Christian Church*, 1:810. Second emphasis added.

θεός] *made the worlds*, or *the universe*." Moreover, he posits his interpretation of the noun plural αἰών in a clear sense of spatial realm and bases it on Pauline texts (cf. 1 Cor 8:6; Eph 3:9; Col 1:15–19; 1 Tim 1:17).[23]

On this same topic, O'Brien, who posits an unknown, but remarkable Christian mind besides Paul as the writer of Hebrews, states that the term, αἰῶνας, which means "ages," is used here for both temporal and spatial realms, and he also provides support for his position on the basis of Pauline and non-Pauline biblical texts.[24] The same treatment was given by Johnson who postulated Apollos as the writer of Hebrews.[25] But Westcott, who posits an anonymous writer to Hebrews—someone not closely linked with Paul—proposes that the meaning of αἰῶνας only has a temporal sense,[26] and in order to support his arguments he uses pseudepigraphal literature and also Philo.

Audience: Implications for Its Cosmogony

Speculation about the most probable audience of Hebrews will play a significant role in establishing the cosmogony—or any topic—embedded in the text of Hebrews, because, if the writer addresses his/her writing to a specific group of people, s/he must also compose the document according to the philosophical context of his/her readers.

But even though the quest for a profile of this potential audience must be built on the basis of the text itself, this has not been an easy task. Generally, most of the canonical New Testament documents identify their audience from their very title, but to identify Hebrews only by its title—To the Hebrews—might be wrong,[27] because as Allen states, it is generally recognized as not being part of the original composition, but as an addition of the second century.[28] Nevertheless, the title "To the He-

23. Stuart, *Commentary on the Epistle to the Hebrews*, 47–48.

24. O'Brien, *Letter to the Hebrews*, 9, 52.

25. Johnson, *Hebrews*, 68.

26. Westcott asserted that αἰῶνας must be understood in 1:2 as "The sum of the 'periods of time' including all that is manifested in and through them." See Westcott, *Epistle to the Hebrews*, 8–9.

27. Koester states that "the title is of little value for historical reconstruction," see Koester, *Hebrews*, 46.

28. Allen affirms, "Most think the title was deduced from the letter's content. In and of itself, the title is virtually no help in identifying the recipients of the epistle." Allen, *Hebrews*, 24. To see more about the discussion on the title in relationship to the epistle's canonicity see, Childs, *New Testament as Canon*, 413–15.

brews" can provide some insight about the intended audience to whom Hebrews was addressed,[29] a fact that is evidenced by the ancient witness, Clement of Alexandria,[30] and also by the inscriptions Πρὸς Ἑβραίους—to the Hebrews—as a title on the earliest manuscripts such as ℵ A B C.[31]

However, despite all the issues regarding the expected audience of Hebrews, as O'Brien asserts, most commentators "agree that the book was written for Christians,"[32] who are being encouraged to "hold fast the confession" (cf. 3:6, 14; 4:14; 10:23) of first-century Christendom. Also from its title—Πρὸς Ἑβραίους—it can be assumed that during the first centuries it was widely accepted that its audience consisted of Jewish Christians, and this was the traditional view.[33] In the nineteenth century, along with the traditional view, a second view developed which argued that the recipients were gentile Christians,[34] although this view has not garnered much support as the internal evidence of the epistle argues so strongly against it. More recently, a third view arose advocating a mixed audience composed of Christians of both Jewish and gentile origin.[35] The

---

29. Ellingworth states, "The title Πρὸς Ἑβραίους is attested in all Greek manuscripts and in the ancient versions. There is no evidence that the writing was ever known by any other name." He affirms, "The suggestion that Πρὸς Ἑβραίους means 'against the Hebrews' is a priori unlikely, since the title corresponds to those of the Pauline epistles, which were certainly not written 'against' the Romans etc. It also goes against the content of Hebrews, which is consistently unpolemical in its discussion of Jewish matters. In any case πρός + acc. in a hostile sense would mean rather 'In response to . . . ,' and there is no suggestion in Hebrews that its author is responding to Jewish arguments." Ellingworth, *Epistle to the Hebrews*, 21–22.

30. Eusebius, *Hist. eccl.* 6.14.1–4.

31. Westcott, *Epistle to the Hebrews*, xxvii. The full name of the earliest manuscripts can be found in the section of Abbreviations.

32. O'Brien, *Letter to the Hebrews*, 9.

33. Allen, *Hebrews*, 62. Koester affirms "Those who think that Hebrews was addressed to Jewish Christians usually understand the occasion to have been the threat of some Christians reverting to Judaism." See Koester, *Hebrews*, 46–47.

34. Ellingworth states, "Until modern times, the general assumption, perhaps too much influenced by the title, was that their background was Jewish. E. M. Roeth in 1836 was the first to propose the thesis of gentile addressees. He has had many successors, but the traditional view, that the readers were of Jewish origin, is still widespread." See Ellingworth, *Epistle to the Hebrews*, 22. Then also, Moffatt offered one of the best presentations of this theory in the twentieth century, see Moffatt, *Hebrews*, xxiv–xxvi. See also deSilva, *Perseverance in Gratitude*, 2–7.

35. G. Guthrie asserts, "Although some scholars have taken these insights to indicate a thoroughly Jewish audience for Hebrews, one must remember that many Gentiles affiliated themselves with first-century synagogues, either as proselytes or

main question is whether the original readers'—or maybe listeners'—own thought-world was predominantly Jewish or Greek, no matter whether they were from Italy (cf. 13:24b) or from some other place.³⁶

Some features of Hebrews, such as its consistent avoidance of gnostic language and of terms relating to the distinction between Jews and gentiles, as well as the use of "the fathers" (cf. 1:1) rather than "our fathers"—besides the presupposition that its author shared an Alexandrine mind-set—have made scholars believe that the expected audience of Hebrews ought to be identified as Christians of gentile origin. But, as Ellingworth asserts, Hebrews contains overwhelming evidence that points to a Jewish Christian setting.³⁷

So in order to more accurately pinpoint the mind-set of the audience, it is necessary to establish the very identity of its audience. In 1923 Brown suggested that the readers were a group of the former Jewish priests who had become Christians according to Acts 6:7.³⁸ Also, he affirms that they did not constitute an entire church, but, in effect, they were a special class, particularly distinguished from their "leaders" (cf. 13:7, 17, 24), and from the "saints" (cf. 13:24).³⁹ Allen sustains that this theory was broadly followed and in some cases developed by well-known scholars such as Bornhäuser in 1932, Clarkson in 1947, Ketter in 1950, Spicq in 1952, Sandegren in 1955, Yadin in 1966, Rissi in 1987, Pixner in 1992, and P. Grelot in 2003.⁴⁰ Allen, in 2010, can also be added to this

---

God-fearers. Consequently, some Gentiles came to Christ with a rich background in Jewish worship and extensive knowledge of the Jewish Scriptures. Therefore, the exact mix of Jews and Gentiles in this church group must remain a mystery." See Guthrie, *Hebrews*, 20.

36. As James P. Sweeney asserts, "Some went even further, maintaining that Hebrews was addressed to a group sympathetic with the views of the Qumran community and the broader Essene movement." See Sweeney, "Hebrews, Letter to The." Ellingworth also affirms, "Kosmala's suggestion that the readers were unconverted Essenes has not won acceptance; among those who emphasise the links of Hebrews with Qumran, Yadin 1958 saw the readers rather as former Essenes, or at least Jews influenced by Qumran." See Ellingworth, *Epistle to the Hebrews*, 26.

37. Ellingworth, *Epistle to the Hebrews*, 23–24.

38. Brown, "Authorship and Circumstances of 'Hebrews,'" 505–38.

39. Brown, "Authorship and Circumstances of 'Hebrews,'" 537.

40. Allen explains that all of them have made some contribution to this topic, for instance, P. Grelot argued that the recipients were converted Jewish priests who were now refugees in a city where nationalist Jews brought increasing pressure and hostility on them. See Allen, *Hebrews*, 45–70; Bornhäuser, *Empfänger Und Verfasser*; Clarkson, "Antecedents of the High Priest Theme in Hebrews," 89–95; Ketter, *Hebräerbrief*,

group. Allen asserts that this theory about the possible audience has not been analyzed as it deserves,[41] but an exception to his assertion could be Spicq, who developed a list of twelve arguments in favor of this view.[42]

It is not the purpose of this document to define the intended audience of Hebrews, but to assert that any position taken in this respect could influence, albeit indirectly, the understanding of the cosmogony of Hebrews. For instance, William Lane argues in favor of an audience

---

Jakobusbrief, Petrusbrief, Judasbrief; Spicq, *Hébreux Introduction*, 1:226–31; Sandegren, "Addressees of the Epistle to the Hebrews," 221–24; Yadin, "Dead Sea Scrolls," 36–55; Rissi, *Die Theologie des Hebräerbriefs*, 52; Pixner, "Jerusalem Essenes, Barnabas," 167–78. Likewise, Grelot more recently argued that the recipients were converted Jewish priests who were now refugees in a city where nationalist Jews brought increasing pressure and hostility on them around 66 CE. These priests lived on the margin of the church, which he located as most likely in Antioch. See Grelot, *Une Lecture ae L'épître aux Hébreux*, 190–91.

41. Lindars, for instance, calls it a speculative reconstruction that "strains credulity," and his criticism is primarily based on his assumption that Spicq "assumes that they are exiled from Jerusalem, and long to return to their old life and to minister once more in the temple," and also he asserts that "Hebrews never once suggests that the readers might themselves have officiated in the temple," but he also agrees with a Christian Jewish identity of the readers. See Lindars, *Hebrews*, 2–15. D. Guthrie was more optimistic when he affirms that "this must remain a conjecture, although a conjecture that deserves careful consideration." See Guthrie, *New Testament Introduction*, 691.

42. According to Allen, Spicq asserts the next twelve statements about the intended audience of Hebrews: 1) They were converted by the earliest disciples of the Lord (2:3); 2) They could have known the Roman Jews living in Jerusalem at the time of Pentecost who were converted (Acts 2:10) and who, after returning to Rome, would have added their greetings to those of the author of Hebrews (13:24); 3) They were fortified in the faith by the Holy Spirit through the work of Stephen (2:4; cf. Acts 6:8); 4) They should have been teachers (5:12), because this is the role that the priests had for the people as revealed in the Old Testament (Hag 2:11; Zech 7:8; Mal 2:7) as well as the New Testament; 5) The present tense ἀνίσταται ("arises," NKJV; "appears," NIV) in 7:15 is reminiscent of Acts 20:17, 18, 28, and could have a hierarchical connotation; 6) The priests in Jerusalem had been used to the splendor of temple worship. Now, as Christians, they had lost their material and spiritual privileges as sons of Levi; 7) Jewish priests were permitted by Mosaic law to eat a portion of the sacrifice that had been offered; 8) The conclusion (10:18) of the doctrinal section (7:1—10:18), affirms in absolute wording the elimination of the need for any sacrificial ritual; 9) Because he was addressing priestly descendants of Levi, the author took "psychological precautions" and used doctrinal "circumlocutions" in order to denounce the foolishness of their attempted continuation of their priesthood; 10) The vivid description of (6:6) and (10:29) is understood better against the backdrop of readers who had taken part in the death of Jesus; 11) The recipients of Hebrews had been victims of some persecution, including the loss of possessions (10:34); and 12) The traditional title given to the book, "To the Hebrews," implies a body of men closely united, a homogeneous group. See Allen, *Hebrews*, 68–70.

constituted of a small group of Jewish Christians who meet in a house church in an urban Italian setting with a rich legacy of Hellenistic Judaism,[43] whose world—i.e., their Jewish identity—was falling apart. And in the phrase ἔξω τῆς παρεμβολῆς (outside the camp, cf. 13:13, LEB) he finds an exhortation to sever the emotional and social ties with the Jewish community.[44] Westcott, however, argues in favor of an audience constituted of Jewish Christians who meet in "Jerusalem, or in the neighborhood of Jerusalem,"[45] and sustains about the phrase ἔξω τῆς παρεμβολῆς, that the author is encouraging his audience to abandon "not only the 'city,' which men made as the permanent home for God, but also to move to something better than 'the camp,' in which Israel was organized."[46]

However, even though the text apparently has no cosmological or cosmogonic elements, Thompson, who argues for an unknown audience not closely linked to Christian Judaism,[47] also argues that "outside the camp" signifies neither "outside Judaism" nor "outside Jerusalem," but rather that it implies a call to leave earthly assurances and to pursue the heavenly world. That is to say, ἔξω τῆς παρεμβολῆς (outside the camp, cf. 13:13, LEB), according to Thompson, means outside the earthly sphere,[48] an interpretation that has a clear cosmogonic connotation. Finally, and even though it could be strongly debated, it can be stated that it is very likely that the mindset of Hebrews' readers was the mindset of former priests converted to Christianity after having taken part, indirectly, in the crucifixion of Jesus Christ.

Background of Thought: Implications for Its Cosmogony

Determining the conceptual background of Hebrews is essential in order to clarify the distinctive cosmogony of the document. There are a significant number of views in this regard—Lane names most of them: Philo, Alexandria, Platonism, Qumran, Apocalyptic Judaism, Merkabah Mysticism, the Samaritans, Pre-Christian Gnosticism, Mystery Religions,

43. Lane, *Hebrews 9–13*, li–lx.
44. Lane, *Hebrews 1–8*, 545.
45. Westcott, *Epistle to the Hebrews*, xl.
46. Westcott, *Epistle to the Hebrews*, 443–44.
47. Thompson, *Hebrews*, 6–10.
48. Thompson, "Outside the Camp," 61–62. Cf. Thompson, *Hebrews*, 283.

Primitive Christian Tradition, Paul, John, Peter, Mark, and Luke.[49] For instance, Polkinghorne asserts, "There is a platonic cast of thought in the Epistle to the Hebrews, with its emphasis on a heavenly realm of eternal reality, compared to which the phenomena of this world are but transient intimations of something lying beyond."[50] On the other hand, Brown tried to establish beyond any doubt the presence of Stephen's mind-set in Hebrews,[51] while Spicq later claimed that Philo's mind-set was present in Hebrews,[52] a proposal that Williamson showed to be erroneous.[53]

However, in one respect all scholars agree: Hebrews is written in exceptional Greek, by someone evidently well-educated and with the advantage of training in rhetorical skills. And it is almost certain most scholars will agree that "Hebrews ranks with Paul and the Fourth Evangelist as one of the three great theologians of the New Testament,"[54] and that it "constitutes one of the most majestic presentations of Christology in the entire New Testament."[55] Although most of the theories regarding Hebrews' background were widely supported—as well as extensively

---

49. Lane, *Hebrews 9–13*, civ–cxii.

50. Polkinghorne, "Scientist Looks at the Epistle to the Hebrews," 113.

51. Brown, "Authorship and Circumstances of 'Hebrews,'" 507–12.

52. Hurst sustains that Spicq represents the climax of approximately sixty years of research, "during which there was an extraordinarily unanimous approach to the background of Hebrews. During this time, writers of immense erudition were convinced of the soundness of the case, and to many it seemed almost irrefutable. Yet there is irony in recalling that even as Spicq was assembling the ultimate case for Philonic influence in Hebrews, a group of texts was coming to light which would call it into question. Younger students who might have been persuaded by Spicq were distracted by the Qumran scrolls. A new background for the epistle was hence introduced, and the enthusiasm with which Spicq's findings were greeted dissipated quickly. Spicq himself was sufficiently impressed by the new evidence to modify his position. He now felt that the author (Apollos), having come from Alexandria, was writing to a group of Jewish priests who had been in contact with Qumran and who had fled from Jerusalem to Antioch." Hurst, *Epistle to the Hebrews*, 8.

53. Ronald Williamson brought the most serious challenge against the alleged Platonism of the author of Hebrews, as well as the alleged influence of Philo. He showed that the Old Testament Levitical cultus and typological milieu furnish a better explanation for the background of the thought of the author than Alexandrian influence. He further cataloged a host of differences between Alexandrian thought and Hebrews. His research concludes saying, "it is possible that the Writer of Hebrews had never been a Philonist, had never read Philo's works, had never come under the influence of Philo directly or indirectly." See Williamson, *Philo and the Epistle to the Hebrews*, 579.

54. Lindars, *Hebrews*, 1.

55. Allen, *Hebrews*, 24.

challenged—there are nonetheless supporters for all theories to date. Among them, the positions that argue for Christian tradition and Apocalyptic Judaism seem to be more relevant to Hebrews.

Nevertheless, Hebrews' soterio-cosmology, particularly concerning the future, has a marked difference with Apocalyptic Judaism, whereas it seems to be more analogous with early Christian tradition as presented in Hebrews. In Apocalyptic Judaism, "the present age, from creation . . . to the coming of Messiah . . . , is to be succeeded by a future age of peace and righteousness under the reign of God." But early Christian tradition posits an "already" kingdom of God with the resurrection of Messiah, along with a "not yet" kingdom of God. The distinction rests on the notion that "the kingdom of God had become present in hidden form in the midst of the present evil age, although its public manifestation awaits" eagerly for him for "He will appear a second time, apart from sin, for salvation" (9:28, NKJV).[56]

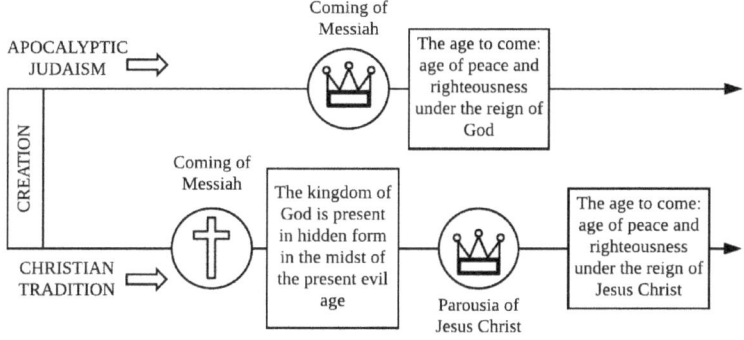

Figure 2.1 Soterio-cosmology in Apocalyptic Judaism and Christian tradition.[57]

Although there are some differences between early Christian writings and Hebrews, as was strongly argued by Ellingworth,[58] the history of its interpretation clearly shows that almost all scholars interested in Hebrews over the centuries recognized, to a larger or lesser degree, a

---

56. Ellis, "How the New Testament Uses the Old," 210.

57. Tables and Figures in this document are the author's original work, however, where the idea came from an external source it will be indicated as such in the footnote.

58. Ellingworth, *Epistle to the Hebrews*, 3–21.

connection between the other canonical documents of the New Testament and Hebrews. Therefore, even though it is plausible to agree with Allen when he affirms, "Certainly much of the book's content is unique. It does not fit readily into the scheme of the Pauline, Johannine, or Petrine writings,"[59] it is also imperative to establish that Hebrews fits perfectly with the general scheme of early New Testament writings.[60] Along with the above conclusions, Allen asserts that Hebrews exhibits a great affinity with Luke and Acts in the New Testament.[61]

Although it is well-known that the background of Hebrews—i.e., which first-century milieu(s) might best explain Hebrews' content—is a most crucial issue in which no decisive consensus exists, it is an issue that is impossible to avoid in order to understand its cosmogony.[62] For instance, Hebrews' use of σκιά (shadow, cf. 8:5) in connection with Moses and his vision—ὁράω—"of what is in heaven" (τῶν ἐπουρανίων, cf. 8:5, NIV) can be interpreted as a Platonic experience, clearly portrayed in Philo's treatment of Exodus texts (cf. Exod 25:40),[63] or as an objective experience, as Bruce does:

> This "pattern" (referred to also in Ex. 25:9; 26:30; 27:8) was something visible; it did not consist merely of the verbal directions of Ex. 25–30. It may have been a model for which the verbal directions served as a commentary; it may have been the heavenly dwelling-place of God which Moses was permitted to see. The

---

59. Allen, *Hebrews*, 24.

60. Although the writing dates of the New Testament books are widely arguable, of the twenty-seven books of the New Testament canon, twenty-two were likely written between 48 CE and 70 CE, and only the other five—the Johannine writings—are usually dated in the last decade of the first century.

61. Allen, *Hebrews*, 61.

62. Even though Schenck stated that it is judicious to avoid drawing conclusions on questions such as authorship or recipients and destination, he asserts, "On the other hand, we cannot avoid the matter of Hebrews' 'background of thought' in interpretation. Words do not have meaning independent of their use in some socio-conceptual framework. One cannot make a judgement on any text's meaning without either intentionally or accidentally investing its words with meanings from some cultural dictionary." Schenck, *Cosmology and Eschatology in Hebrews*, 3.

63. Philo affirms that Moses "saw with the soul's eye [τῇ ψυχῇ θεωρῶν] the immaterial patterns [ἀσωμάτους ἰδέας] of the material objects [σωμάτων] which were about to be made, and in accordance with these forms copies perceptible to the senses had to be reproduced, as from an archetypal drawing and patterns conceived in the mind." Philo, *Mos.* 2.74. Some commentators follow Philo's thought in this respect with some variations, see Lea, *Hebrews, James*, 153–54; Westcott, *Epistle to the Hebrews*, 219.

tabernacle was intended to serve as a dwelling-place for God in the midst of his people on earth, and it would be completely in keeping with current practice that such an earthly dwelling-place should be a replica of God's heavenly dwelling-place.[64]

And from these two different approaches to the Hebrews' text, two different cosmogonies can be developed from it: one with real things—e.g., the heavenly city—in the heavens, while the other one will interpret the heavenly city as merely a spiritual thing or as a motivational argument. Finally, even though it would be a mistake to make a conclusive assertion about Hebrews' background of thought, it is probable that it rests on a kind of apocalyptic Judaism, in which some Essene ideas were mixed with a new Christian interpretation of the Old Testament and a new view about the arrival, development, and future of the age to come.

Other Introductory Issues: Implications in Its Cosmogony

Although issues such as purpose, date, or location—of both audience and writer—could be considered less important in comprehending the cosmogony of Hebrews, it is wholly accepted that in historical studies, they play a significant role in the interpretation of biblical text.

For instance, if the purpose[65] of Hebrews is pastoral care, as Guthrie asserts,[66] it could possibly be stated that it has been influenced, in that respect, by the Epicureans and/or the Stoics. Since, as Klauck affirms, Epicureans and Stoics[67] were concerned with spiritual needs of the individual, they "sought to provide help so that the individual could attain a successful life and cope with the blows of fate. It is [Klauck maintains]

---

64. Bruce, *Epistle to the Hebrews*, 184.

65. Concerning the purpose of Hebrews and its influence on its interpretation, Allen, commenting on the first two verses of Hebrews, asserts, "The view that the author's purpose in writing was to dissuade his readers from apostatising to Judaism has coloured the way this passage and the entire book are interpreted." Allen, *Hebrews*, 108.

66. Guthrie asserts "When discouragement comes—the kind of discouragement that screams questions at the faith—we need encouragement and perspective; we need the community of faith; we need help to stay the course of commitment. Hebrews was written to offer such help." Guthrie, *Hebrews*, 18–19.

67. Nevertheless, even though it is probable that both schools have had a wide influence on Christendom of the first century—maybe it is for that reason that Luke concentrates on the Epicureans and Stoics in the Acts of the Apostles—it is necessary to look into the text—Hebrews' text—to find the most accurate purpose of the document.

not entirely wrong to call their activities pastoral care or spiritual direction, or even psychotherapy."[68] Thus, the Stoic cosmogony can also be imposed on Hebrews, but Hebrews itself affirms that its purpose is to be a "message of exhortation" (τοῦ λόγου τῆς παρακλήσεως, cf. 13:22, CSB).

Issues such as date or location will also influence the interpretation of Hebrews; for instance, if the interpreter thinks that it was written after 70 CE,[69] all the allusions to Jerusalem and its temple must be reinterpreted in this context. Likewise, the location of the recipients is very important in order to understand the content of Hebrews, and, similar to other introductory issues, it is a very controversial one. Consequently, there are different theories that locate them in either Jerusalem, Alexandria, Antioch of Syria, Caesarea, Rome, or even in Spain.[70] For instance, Voulgaris argued that Hebrews was sent to the church of Jerusalem,[71] and Allen declares, even though his schema is quite speculative, "some plausibility can be given to the suggestion that Hebrews was written to Jerusalem after the death of James."[72] On the other hand, Michaels believed that Paul or someone who lived in Rome—perhaps Timothy—was the author of Hebrews and that the location of recipients was Rome itself, although it is rather contradictory.[73] If Rome was the place where the audience of Hebrews resided, due to circumstances such as persecution, the purpose of the document, as Guthrie asserts, must be encouragement—i.e., pastoral in nature.[74] The same can be said

---

68. Klauck, *Religious Context of Early Christianity*, 334.

69. Among them are James Moffat, R. McLachlan Wilson, Simon J. Kistemaker, Alan C. Mitchell, among others. See Bateman, *Charts on the Book of Hebrews*, 43.

70. More information about this topic can be found in Bruce, *Epistle to the Hebrews*, 13–14; Ellingworth, *Epistle to the Hebrews*, 29; Lane, *Hebrews 1–8*, lviii–lx; Kistemaker, *Hebrews*, 13–16; Utley, *Superiority of the New Covenant*, 3.

71. Voulgaris, "Hebrews," 199–206.

72. Allen, *Hebrews*, 35.

73. It is interesting to note that even Michaels posits Timothy as the author of Hebrews, which he calls a modest proposal. Further, it is interesting to read some pages later that the phrase ἀσπάζονται ὑμᾶς οἱ ἀπὸ τῆς Ἰταλίας (those who are from Italy send you greetings, cf. 13:24, CSB) "could mean that the author was writing *from* Italy, where a number of Italian Christians join Paul in sending their greetings. Or it could mean that the writer was writing *to* Italy, and thus a group of Italian believers with him was sending back greetings to their Italian compatriots in Rome." Michaels, "Commentary on Hebrews," 305–11, 315–18.

74. Guthrie asserts, "Life, and thus the Christian life, is fraught with trials that suck the emotional winds from our sails. When discouragement comes—the kind of discouragement that screams questions at the faith—we need encouragement and

about Jerusalem, but if the area was Antioch of Syria, it is necessary to rethink the purpose of Hebrews, since Antioch of Syria became a more prominent Christian place, and it was a place where Jewish Christianity flourished, before and after the death of Paul.[75]

The view that posits Antioch of Syria as the destination of Hebrews was argued by Brown,[76] and more recently by Spicq and Allen.[77] Even though the Christians in Antioch had endured some hard times,[78] it was known as a very friendly and open city for Jews as well as for emergent Christianity.[79] This characteristic of Antioch as a multicultural city embracing religious freedom, allows one to infer that the new converts could easily practice their new faith, as well as develop a strong fraternity, which with time obtained its own name: χριστιανός (cf. Acts 11:26). In addition, a place like this could become the residence of people that "ought to be teachers" (5:12, CSB) but "become spiritually dull and indifferent" (νωθροὶ γένησθε, cf. 6:12, NLT), with "feeble knees" (παραλελυμένα γόνατα, cf. 12:12, NKJV). That is to say, people with the capacity to fulfil the Christian mission, but who have forgotten the real purpose of their lives, i.e., to go "outside the camp . . . for here we have no continuing city, but we seek the one to come" (13:13–14, NKJV).

It must also be recognized that Antioch of Syria as the destination is more suited to the phrase, "with the word of exhortation" (13:22), with which the document was defined by its own author. Moreover, the use of the preposition ἀπό in the phrase, "The believers from [ἀπό] Italy send you their greetings" (13:24, NIV), reinforces the likelihood of Antioch

---

perspective; we need the community of faith; we need help to stay the course of commitment. Hebrews was written to offer such help." Guthrie, *Hebrews*, 18–19.

75. McDonald, "Antioch (Syria)," 35; Tenney, *New Testament Times*, 209–37; Zetterholm, *Formation of Christianity in Antioch*, 53–110.

76. Brown, "Authorship and Circumstances of 'Hebrews,'" 530.

77. Allen, *Hebrews*, 63; Spicq, *Hébreux Introduction*, 220–52.

78. Josephus, *W.J.* 7.46–53.

79. Allen asserts, "One of the most likely and one of the safest places would be Antioch in Syria." Allen, *Hebrews*, 64. But also, Brown and Meier suggested that in the Christian community in Rome there may have been "elements of that Levitical heritage" referenced in Acts 6:7, but it cannot be proven that Jewish priests were relocated to Rome. Brown and Meier, *Antioch and Rome*, 153–55. On the other hand, Spicq argues that the converted priests who *remained* in Jerusalem were forced by persecution to relocate to some other place such as Caesarea, Antioch, or Ephesus. Spicq, *Hébreux Introduction*, 227. Josephus also gives some insight about the presence of priests in Antioch of Syria. Josephus, *J.W.* 7.43–45.

of Syria as the destination. According to Mosser—who after examining first-century manuscripts employing the preposition ἀπό—the preposition ἀπό is consistently used to indicate the place from which a document was written,[80] as is the case in 13:24. Thus the social conditions of Antioch could have been a facilitator for a change in the viewpoint of Hebrews' audience concerning the fate of this world, and with it, a change in their cosmogony, a reality that the author apparently glimpses and tries to adjust.

Chapter Conclusion

The analysis of Hebrews' introductory issues allows the assertion that in studying Hebrews, it is better to build every argument and conclusion from the text itself and not from matters such as genre, authorship, audience, background of thought, date, or any other issue. Nevertheless, it must also be emphasized that since assumptions about the introductory issues in Hebrews can determine the interpretation of its text, researchers must make any such assumptions clear. Finally, this chapter serves as a support for what will be presented in succeeding chapters, since, from chapter 4, in which cosmogony of the first century will be tackled, the research will deal mainly with Hebrews' text itself in order to establish its cosmogony.

---

80. Mosser, "No Lasting City," 157.

3

First-Century Cosmogony

To have a better understanding of Hebrews' cosmogony it is necessary to comprehend its context and, more specifically, its cosmogonic philosophical context—consequently this chapter deals with the main thoughts about cosmogony that were present during the first century, as well as with its main vocabulary.

Chapter Introduction

Hebrews, like all writings, emerged in a specific context, which it is crucial to establish. However, in order to achieve this, i.e., to reconstruct its philosophical context, is an almost unattainable objective particularly as far as ancient documents are concerned. And owing to the fact that the evidence to be gathered from the document itself is ambiguous and open to divergent interpretations, it will be addressed, as Lane asserts, "tentatively as a working proposal."[1] There are two main topics that will be addressed in this section: The forerunner thoughts of first-century cosmogony; and Cosmogonic thought into the first century; and both of these topics will be focused in Western schools of thought. However, even though the focus of this research is in the first century—mainly the Roman Period[2]—it contains some of the more significant thoughts which

---

1. Lane, *Hebrews 1–8*, liii.
2. We consider the Roman Period with respect to the Jews to be during the period from 63 BCE to 70 CE. Melvin, *History of Israel*. It is also necessary to state that others

were present during and before the period commonly called the Second Temple Period.³ The Greek world was rich in theories and philosophers, and to this day many of these ideas are the basis of accepted knowledge. Therefore, in order to understand the Greek cosmogony in the early Roman Period with respect to the Jews (63 BCE–70 CE),⁴ it is necessary to identify and consider the thoughts of the philosophers, which could be considered as precursors.⁵

Forerunner Thoughts for First-Century Cosmogonies

Hebrews has not been directly linked with the mainstream thought of that time—i.e., centuries prior to the first century CE—but has indirectly been linked with various former philosophers of its time, such as Plato, and also with some pre-Socratic and post-Socratic thinkers. Therefore,

---

view the hegemony of the Roman Empire to cover the period from 168 BCE to 476 CE. Davis wrote that "Pydna [The Battle of Pydna in which the Roman general Aemilius Paulus defeated King Perseus] marked the final destruction of Alexander's empire and introduced Roman authority over the Near East." Davis, *100 Decisive Battles*, 51.

3. The Second Temple Period corresponds with the Intertestamental Period, comprising the period between the building of the second Jewish temple in Jerusalem in 515/516 BCE and its destruction by the Romans in 70 CE. It may also be considered to commence as early as 538 BCE, the date of Cyrus' edict for Jews to return to Jerusalem (Ezra 1:2–4; 6:3–5; Isa 44:28). McCune, "Intertestamental Period."

4. Even though the historical accounts of these periods and dates are not unanimous, it is recognised that "the Jews in Judea came under Roman rule in 63 BCE and remained so until the Arab conquest in the seventh century." Grabbe, "Jewish History: Roman Period," 576. Consequently, in 63 BCE, when the civil war between the Pharisees and the Sadducees ended, when Pompey, a Roman general, arrived and helped the Pharisees defeat the Sadducees in Jerusalem, the Roman Period begins with respect to the Jews. On the other hand, it is important to consider the assertion of Evans when he asserts that "the middle Roman period covered AD 70–180." Evans, *NT307 Archaeology and the New Testament*; Negev, *Archaeological Encyclopedia of the Holy Land*. To Evans' assertion Bolen adds that "the Early Roman period is usually considered to extend from the 1st century BC until AD 70 and the Late Roman period concludes about AD 325." Bolen, "Where Did the Possessed-Pigs Drown?" Also, Adan-Bayewitz et al. also agreed that the early Roman period beginning in first-century BCE goes to 70 CE. See Adan-Bayewitz et al., "Preferential Distribution of Lamps." Consequently, 70 CE, when the prediction made by Jesus before his death in 33 CE that the Jewish temple would be completely destroyed (Luke 21:6) was fulfilled, and when the Roman armies destroyed the city of Jerusalem and its temple, killing hundreds of thousands of Jews and taking captive most of the survivors, ended the early Roman period with respect to the Jews.

5. Thompson, "What Has Middle Platonism to Do," 33.

this section will indicate the main theories concerning cosmogony present in centuries prior to CE, so that in the next chapters, it will be feasible to assess their possible influence on Hebrews. These forerunner thoughts of first-century cosmogonies will be divided in this research into three periods on the basis of the approach to cosmogony:

1. First period: Cosmogonic speculation;
2. Second period: Cosmogonic contemplation; and
3. Third period: Cosmogonic exclusion.

First Period: Cosmogonic Speculation

During this time—sixth and fifth century BCE—many significant changes took place in Greek thinking.[6] They transitioned from myth to philosophical thought—νοῦς or νόος—from barbarian to citizenship—πολίτης or πολιήτης—and democracy—δημοκρατία. This period comprises the pre-Socratic philosophy, in which five schools were predominant: the Ionian, the Pythagorean, the Eleatic, the Atomist, and the Sophist schools.[7]

---

6. Until this time every town had their own belief, but Homer sought to include all Greek divinities in one Pantheon of gods. However, this system collapsed when the Greeks began relationships with other towns, and they discovered that others had different beliefs. Due to this, the Greek thinking that existed prior to this period, had a variety of beliefs—each believed that they had the truth. This made the religious thinking collapse, and the need arose to explain everything based on reason. Dellutri and Dellutri, *La Aventura del Pensamiento*, 27–28.

7. The Sophist school is also part of this period, but for the purpose of this research, it will not be analysed, since as Plato points out, to accurately define the nature of the Sophist is very difficult. Plato, *Soph.* 218c. For instance, it seems that Protagoras taught that the universe is an atomistic series of events, namely nothing is and everything becomes, but even this becoming is relative. See Adamson, *Development of Greek Philosophy*, 65–66; Turner, *History of Philosophy*, 72, cf. Plato, *Crat.* 386. Also, Protagoras, the main personality among the Sophists, proposed the theory of the "homomensura," which states that the "man [ἄνθρωπος] is the measure [μέτρον] of all things [χρημάτων] of the things which are, that they are, and of the things which are not, that they are not [τῶν μὲν ὄντων ὡς ἔστιν, τῶν δὲ οὐκ ὄντων ὡς οὐκ ἔστιν]." Plato, *Theaet.* 152a 2–4, cf. Diogenes, *Vit. Phil.* 9.51. Likewise, according to Plato, Protagoras stated that "each thing appears (φαίνεται) to me, so it is for me, and as it appears to you, so it is for you—you and I each being a man." Plato, *Theaet.* 152a 6–8. Based on this theory Socrates thought that all things are as he thinks they are, and for others as they think they are, namely, each thing can be seen as a different thing, because each person can think differently. Secondly, he taught that everyone's perception of reality could take on a different form. See Mas Torres, *Historia de la Filosofía Antigua*, 62–63. Also, it is

The Ionian School[8] recognized the environment as κόσμος, and its first aim was to explain the beginning—ἀρχή—of all things.[9] Its cosmogony was based on physical elements, such as ὕδωρ (water), πῦρ (fire), ἀήρ (air), and γῆ (land)[10] and among its proponents, Heraclitus (525–475 BCE) developed a revolutionary idea for his time, when he spoke about constant movement, i.e., matter cannot be destroyed, it can only be changed—μεταβάλλω—from one form to another.[11] Thus he stated that the supreme reality is not *being*, but *becoming*. Further, he indicated that this constant change is not random, but is controlled by the λόγος—i.e.,

---

necessary to state that in the Sophist schools, the cosmology and cosmogony topics were not the main occupation, the preoccupation was humanistic and anthropologic, i.e., they were focused on the human being. In this time Gorgias (ca. 485–380 BCE) asserted that nothing exists, but if something existed, that would be incomprehensible and incommunicable. For Gorgias, even he himself does not exist. Weber, *History of Philosophy*, 32.

8. The Ionian School was probably the first representative school of thought during this new era, and even though there is very limited information available about this school of thought, it is now well accepted that persons like Thales (ca. 624–546 BCE), Anaximander (ca. 610–546 BCE), Anaximenes (ca. 585–525 BCE), Heraclitus of Ephesus (ca. 525–475 BCE), Empedocles (ca. 490–430 BCE) and Anaxagoras (ca. 510–428 BCE), were part of this school. We only have very limited information about the teachings of these men and this is thanks to references by subsequent writers. See Dellutri and Dellutri, *La Aventura del Pensamiento*, 28; Turner, *History of Philosophy*, 34, 53.

9. Henry states that philosophers like Thales, Anaximander and Anaximenes mainly worked on identifying the basic matter of the world. Henry, *God, Revelation, and Authority*, 5:43–44.

10. Thales thought that all things came from water, more precisely from a state of humidity, from eternity in the past. Aristotle, *Met.* 983b.3.20–24. On the other hand, Anaximenes proposed that the air, like mist, was the original substance. Ps. Plutarco, *Plac.* 1.3,4. Empedocles combined all of these ideas and stated that the original substances are the physical elements of water, fire, air and land. Anaximander held that the matter came from an eternal substance which he called ἄπειρον. Heraclitus stated that everything is in movement in constant change (see, Aristotle, *Met.* 1010a.10–14), while Parmenides stated that everything is constant. Although it is not clear whether the concept of eternal matter was held at this time, precursors to the thoughts of Socrates can be observed (ca. 470–399 BCE). This conclusion may be because they tried to explain the ἀρχή of the κόσμος rationally. Thiselton, *Concise Encyclopedia*, 279.

11. Aristotle, *Met.* 1010a.10–14; *De an.* 405.25–29; *Ph.* 185.2.15–24; *Cael.* 298.2.30–34. The best explanation for the Heraclitus theory has been given by Plato who affirms that in the opinion of Heraclitus all things flow and nothing stays, because the pushing principle [ὠθοῦν—the motive power] is the cause and ruling power of all things, therefore all things are in motion and nothing is at rest. Heraclitus compares existence to the flow of a river, and he stated that you cannot go down twice into the same river. See Plato, *Crat.* 401–2.

the universal and eternal law—but he did not consider the λόγος to be a person, but rather the cause of universal harmony.[12] Finally, Heraclitus believed that the final reduction of all things is their transformation into that which they were in their first moment, i.e., fire in the conflagration—ἐκπύρωσις.[13] Therefore, for Heraclitus, the beginning and end of all things is found in one element—fire—and the endless cycles—i.e., the law of constant movement—produce the series of transformations into the other elements.[14] Among the later Ionian philosophers, Anaxagoras (ca. 510–428 BCE) assumed that anything comes out of anything[15] to existence through the action of the eternal mind—νοῦς—which brought about everything from multitudes of tiny particles—ὁμοιομερεία—like seeds. He also stated that when they mix together they bring about the origin of every creature.[16] Maybe that is why Nicolaus of Damascus (64–5 BCE) states that Anaxagoras believed that the seeds of plants are borne down from the air, and why other philosophers following Nicolaus call the earth the mother, and the sun the father, of plants.[17]

With the Pythagorean School begins a "Philosophy" itself,[18] but unfortunately Pythagoras (ca. 570–495 BCE) does not reveal a clear cosmogony. He saw the cosmos as a structure built on numbers, and the Pythagorean School had a mixture of scientific and religious theories.[19]

12. Aristotle, *Ph.* 205.1.1–4. Henry states that Heraclitus (525–475 BCE) identified the single original element of the universe as fire, and affirmed that everything changes except the law of change. He also states that for him—Heraclitus—this law is the λόγος. Henry, *God, Revelation, and Authority*, 5: 44. Salvador Torres confirms that Heraclitus defines the λόγος as fire. Mas Torres, *Historia de la Filosofía Antigua*, 17.

13. Aristotle, *Mete.* 355.1.5–9; *Ph.* 205.1.1–4. But it is also necessary to assert that according to Aristotle, to Heraclitus "the first principle—the 'warm exhalation' of which, according to him, everything else is composed—is soul; further, that this exhalation is mostly incorporeal and in ceaseless flux." Aristotle, *De an.* 405.25–29.

14. For more explanations about the theory of Heraclitus, see Adamson, *The Development of Greek Philosophy*, 42–48.

15. Aristotle, *Ph.* 203.1.20–24.

16. Anaxagoras stated that this world exists because "All things were mixed together—πάντα χρήματα ἦν ὁμοῦ." Namely, everything came to existence by means of the development of chaos to order. Freeman, "Anaxagoras," 65.

17. Nicolaus, *Plant.* 1.2. Cf. Aristotle, *Plant.* 817a.1.25–29.

18. Long affirms that Pythagoras is the only one among other Pre-Socratic thinkers that can be called "Philosopher." The reason for this was that none of the other thinkers, until the time of Pythagoras, called their teachings "philosophy." See Long, "Scope of Early Greek Philosophy," 3.

19. Aristotle, *Met.* 987b.10–14; 1090a.20–24, 30–39; *Frag.* 28. But it is also necessary to note that Aristotle asserted that Pythagoras stated "that every man has been

Cornford observes that Pythagorean cosmogony states that everything came from an eternal fiery seed,[20] but, also as Adamson stated, for them the formed universe was regarded as being divided into the following three regions:

1. The region of the elemental fire, which is pure, perfect and does not admit change or movement;
2. The region of the heavenly bodies, where movement is present; and
3. The earthly region, which includes the moon and its immediate surroundings.[21]

But it is clear that in Pythagorean cosmogony a divine being is almost not present: i.e., the origin of all things—except of human beings apparently—is proposed as having no supernatural connection.[22]

On the other hand, the Eleatic School contrasts the "being" with the "becoming." Therefore, Xenophanes of Colophon (580–484 BCE), Parmenides (540–470 BCE), and Zeno of Elea (490–430 BCE), affirmed the existence of a single entity whose character is unchanging, and to them, this "Being" is unlimited, infinite, immobile, eternal and immutable, and they called this "Being" *God*.[23] They also considered that apart of this "Being" nothing exists,[24] because this Being is everything.[25] The idea here is pantheistic because they believed that everything is part of this *God*.

---

created by God in order to know and to observe." Aristotle, *Frag.* 61. More about Pythagoras can be found in Huffman, "Pythagoras."

20. Cornford explicitly states, "Pythagorean cosmogony, in which the living world expanded from a fiery seed, by taking in the surrounding darkness, and when formed, continued to breathe the vacant air from without. The sphere has always existed in its perfection and self-sufficiency, and outside it there is neither body nor void. It everlastingly fills the whole of space." Macdonald Cornford, *Plato's Cosmology*, 57.

21. Adamson, *Development of Greek Philosophy*, 24.

22. Stenudd states, "Then the mathematical cosmogony of Pythagoras would rightly be categorised as an atheist one." Stenudd, *Cosmos of the Ancients*, 61–63. It must be remembered that Laertius states that there are four personalities that share the name of Pythagoras, living at about the same time and at no great distance from each other, but he also states that there was another Pythagoras, a doctor, who wrote on Hernia and also made a compilation of the teachings of Homer. Laertius, *Vit. Phil.* 8.46. cf. Laertius, *Pythagoras*.

23. Aristotle, [*Xen.*] 977.1.10–14.
24. Henry, *God, Revelation, and Authority*, 5:44.
25. Plato, *Soph.* 242d.

This meant that the world was not created because it is part of this eternal *God*, and therefore they teach in their cosmogony that everything existed since eternity, but apparently not so with the human being.[26]

The Atomistic School represents the last phase of the period that here has been called cosmogonic speculation. This school, funded by Leucippus (ca. fifth century BCE), had as its best-known expounder Democritus of Abdera (ca. 460–370 BCE).[27] Democritus conceived reality as cyclic and his teachings were very similar to those of Anaxagoras, i.e., he taught that all things are composed of pure, invisible, indestructible[28] and indivisible tiny particles of matter, which he calls ἄτομος.[29] Thus the cosmogony of the Atomistic School stated that everything was built from the eternal tiny particle called atom,[30] but according to them the atoms are brought together by their equal weight[31] and not by any incorporeal agency or by chance. Thus in the cosmogony of Atomists there is no place for intelligent purpose, and as Adams sustains,

> [For Atomists] a κόσμος is formed when atoms collide, recoil and become entangled. Since there is no limit to the number of atoms and since space itself is boundless, the number of κόσμοι is infinite. There are innumerable κόσμοι both similar and dissimilar to our κόσμος. Some are at their peak; some are in process of disintegration. A κόσμος is destroyed when it comes into collision with another κόσμος.[32]

The seventh chapter of this document will examine the main differences and similarities—if any—between the cosmogony of Hebrews and the cosmogony of these four pre-Socratic schools.

---

26. Even though it may seem contradictory, it is necessary to state that according to Hippolytus of Rome (170–235 CE), Xenophanes asserted that "We all are sprung from water and from earth." Hippolytus, *Ref.* 10.3. Maybe he had a different position in respect of human being creation or maybe he understood that all people also are eternal in their essence.

27. Turner, *History of Philosophy*, 65–70.

28. However, Philo notes that Democritus believed in "the dissolution and breaking up of the combined particles." Philo, *Aet.* 8.

29. As Adams affirms, according to the Atomic hypothesis, these indivisible particles, "atoms," form the basis of all that exists. Adams, *Constructing the World*, 46.

30. Aristotle, *De an.* 403.2.30–404.1.29

31. Aristotle, *Ph.* 203.1.20–24; Lactantius, *Inst.* 7.3,7.

32. Adams, *Constructing the World*, 46.

Second Period: Cosmogonic Contemplation

In this period, Greek philosophy reaches its highest point of development.³³ The period is comparatively short and comprises the life spans of its three scholars, whose names, rather than the names of its schools or cities, are well-known. They are Socrates (ca. 469–399 BCE), Plato (ca. 427–347 BCE), and Aristotle (ca. 384–322 BCE). Although Socrates, as far as it is known, never wrote anything, Plato and Xenophon are the main sources of his teachings. From Xenophon comes the information that Socrates' cosmogony begins with the adoption of the νοῦς—intelligent cause—as proposed by Anaxagoras, and that from it he formulated the principle that has accompanied the cosmogonic argument during the subsequent centuries, which asserts, "whatever exists for a useful purpose must be the work of an intelligence."³⁴ From this principle most students of Socrates have established "not just that the universe is a product of divine design, but that its design is *human-serving* and, hence, must be a product of a Maker operating out of the best of philanthropic intentions."³⁵ Therefore, Forbes seems to have been right when he affirms that Socrates regarded the world as the "handiwork of some wise artifice,"³⁶ that is to say, created. Nevertheless, Socrates proposed that this world was destined to endure forever, because for him, the nature of the cosmos had nothing in common with other physical entities with a limited lifetime.³⁷ On the other hand, as Alon asserts, Socrates could have followed Anaximenes' view regarding cosmogony, because, he affirms, Socrates maintained, "according

---

33. This assertion can be supported since Pellegrin for instance states, "the ancients themselves regarded Plato and Aristotle as the two greatest philosophers who had ever lived. This evaluation has endured into modern times, as witnessed by the judgment of Coleridge cited in the Introduction to this volume, among many others. Aristotle, in fact, initiated a "style of thought" that has deeply marked the history of philosophy to the present day; and, of the two "greats" in question, he has indisputably exercised the deeper and more lasting historical influence on western thought." Pellegrin, "Aristotelian Way," 235. Carr also stated some years ago, "Greek philosophy, as influential in our modern life, is represented mainly by Socrates, Plato, and Aristotle." Carr, "Greek Elements in Modern Religious Thought," 117.

34. Turner, *History of Philosophy*, 79, 82. Xenophon is the source for this deduction, because this teleological argument, as far as can be ascertained, was never asserted by Socrates, nevertheless it can be implied from his extensive anthropological and moral arguments. See Xenophon, *Mem.* 1.4.2–19; 4.3.14–17.

35. McPherran, *Religion of Socrates*, 282.

36. Forbes, *Socrates*, 213–17.

37. Solmsen, "Aristotle and Presocratic Cosmogony," 265.

to an Arab author who quotes Plutarch, that there are three principles: the efficient cause or agent, which is God; Substance, which is the first substratum; and Form, which is a bodiless essence."[38]

The second, and perhaps the main, personality of this period is Aristocles,[39] commonly known as Plato, whose cosmogony was more popular for a long time, also in the first century. The theory of ideas is the essence of Plato's cosmogony, but must be understood that for Plato, the "ideas are neither physical nor mental; they are outside space and time. Ideas are real; the physical world is but a poor imitation."[40] To him all ideas are summed up in the one ultimate idea, which he calls the idea of the *good*—the principle of perfection—but we must not confuse this impersonal law with the personal biblical God—even the Platonic "World Soul" is not the biblical Supreme Being.[41] The cosmogony of Plato can mainly be found in the *Timaeus*, where he "presents an elaborately wrought account of the formation of the universe." But this document has been interpreted in different ways, probably because it was built on the ideas of his predecessors.[42]

Even though Plato's thoughts were very well-developed and sometimes misconstrued,[43] the cosmogony of Plato, which stated that this

38. Alon, "Socrates in Arabic Philosophy," 326.

39. As Turner affirms, the exact year of his birth is unknown, but 427 or 428 BCE is the most probable date. His father's name was Aristo and his mother's name Perictione, and he was descended from Dropides, a near relative of Solon. His original name is Aristocles, but was better known by his nickname, Plato—Πλάτων—a nickname that was given to him by his master in gymnastics on account of his broad build. See Turner, *History of Philosophy*, 93.

40. Ferguson, *Backgrounds of Early Christianity*, 313.

41. As Ferguson states, "The World Soul is intermediate between the intelligible and sensible worlds." Ferguson, *Backgrounds of Early Christianity*, 333.

42. Long states that although Plato primarily focused on the ethical questions and that his methodology has been taken from Socrates' distinctive legacy, he also affirms that his thoughts have been developed on his study of Heraclitus, Protagoras, the Pythagoreans, and the Eleatics. Long, "Scope of Early Greek Philosophy," 15. It is also possible to include several other names, listed above herein.

43. After the death of Plato in 347 BCE, his academy went through three stages that were commonly named: 1) the Old Academy, 2) the Sceptical Academy, and 3) the Eclectic Academy. Speusippus (347–339 BCE), designated by Plato to be the head of academy after his death, Xenocrates (339–314 BCE), Polemon (314–270 BCE), and Crates (270–268 BCE) were heads in the Old academy. When Arcesilas (268–241 BCE) assumed the head of the academy, this changed, and from that time the academy is called the Sceptical Academy, and they returned to that which has been referred to as the "real Socrates." But from the time of Philo of Larissa (110–80 BCE) the academy became the Eclectic academy. Philo of Larissa "claimed that Plato, Aristotle and the

world is only a shadow, indicates the existence of a real, perfect and eternal world. But the physical world is not perfect or eternal, because he teaches that everything that is physical is imperfect and has a start in time. He also stated that everything—as seen today—came by actions of a demiurge—δημιουργός—the "craftsman," who, in the cosmogony of Plato "is not a divine intelligence or a personal ruler, but a manual laborer."[44] Thus the demiurge of Plato does not create *ex nihilo*, but rather he used the fire and earth—solid elements—and air and water—liquid elements. So the demiurge orders the cosmos out of chaotic elemental matter, but in order to do so, the demiurge chose the *idea*—not physical—present in the Living Being,[45] nevertheless since he is limited for the fact that his primary substance consists of matter, the final result is not perfect or eternal. Thus, to Plato this world is temporal and cannot be eternal. Moreover, when the demiurge fashioned the universe, he also created a moving image of eternity.[46] But in order to create time, it was necessary that the demiurge brought into being the Sun, Moon, and five other stars called "wanderers"—planets. Therefore, Plato's cosmogony did not propose creation *ex nihilo*, as was stated by Brickhouse and Smith,

> Plato's [d]emiurge does not create ex nihilo, but rather orders the cosmos out of chaotic elemental matter, imitating the eternal Forms. Plato takes the four elements, fire, air, water, and earth (which Plato proclaims to be composed of various aggregates of triangles), making various compounds of these into what he calls the Body of the Universe.[47]

Stoics taught the same things, so one should select their common points" and he also states that the real successor of Plato was the Stoics group and not the Sceptical Academy. Thus Plato's academy was moving toward Stoicism, and this development contributed to the rise of Middle Platonism and Neo-Platonism. Ferguson, *Backgrounds of Early Christianity*, 317, 333–38.

44. Vlastos nevertheless states that this task of creating is not a drudge, because the demiurge—manual laborer—is an artist, not like the "inventor of new form, but the imposer of pre-existing form on as yet formless material." He also states "That the supreme god of Plato's cosmos should wear the mask of a manual worker is a triumph of the philosophical imagination over ingrained social prejudice." Vlastos, *Plato's Universe*, 26–27.

45. Vlastos, *Plato's Universe*, 27.

46. Plato taught that "time is a number, according to which the image of eternity moves." Cohen states that "On this reading, it is the cosmos that is the 'moving image of eternity,' and time is the number that measures the change in the cosmos." Cohen, "Plato's Cosmology: The Timaeus."

47. Brickhouse and Smith, *Plato (427—347 Bce)*.

But it is also important to recognize that since Plato's time, disagreements about Plato's cosmogony have arisen. Some Platonists stated that this world was ἀγένητος (not created) whereas others maintain it was γενητός (created).[48] Plato's writings are apparently not without some contradictions.

The last personality during this period is the most prominent student of Plato, viz. Aristotle (ca. 384–322 BCE),[49] and he shows a cosmogony very similar to that of his master. About God—the creator—Aristotle, like his master Plato, did not have a clear or even coherent concept;[50] and about the world, he stated that it is the center of the cosmos.[51] It is widely accepted that Aristotle believed the world did not have a beginning,[52] and also that it is eternal, because time, motion, and matter are eternal,[53] that is to say, it will have no ending.[54] And according to Philo, Aristotle believed that the κόσμος is ἀγένητος and ἄφθαρτος—indestructible.[55]

Nevertheless, and apparently contradictory, the world according to Aristotle has been caused, or was created.[56] That is why Brentano believes that Aristotle taught the doctrine of creation *ex nihilo*,[57] while Augus-

48. Winston states that there was some disagreement among the Platonists as to the precise formulation of the Platonic theory of cosmogony. Some were willing to assert that according to Plato the world was in reality ἀγένητος (uncreated) but could, for pedagogical reasons, be characterised as γενητός (created). Others, however—such as Crantor (ca. 340–290 [276] BCE) and his followers—insisted that according to Plato the world was γενητός, though this was not to be understood in a temporal sense. Proclus (412–485 CE), for example, attacked Platonists like Xenocrates and Speussippus for asserting that, according to Plato, the world was γενητός only κατ᾽ ἐπίνοιαν (to the conception), or was feigned to be so for σαφηνείας ἕνεκα διδασκαλικῆσ (for the sake [because] of clearness of instruction). From reading Timaeus, Proclus asserts the existence of the maker from the premise that the world is γενητός, but if the premise is merely conceptual, the demiurge must be so too. Winston also asserts: "Proclus therefore, prefers to say that the world is γενητός, though in the sense that it is ἀεὶ γιγνόμενον καὶ γεγενημένον, ever being produced and in a state of having been produced (*In Plat, Tim.* 290.3–25)." Winston, *Philo of Alexandria*, 14.

49. Aristotle considers himself as Platonist. See Aristotle, *Met.* 992a.10–14.

50. Turner, *History of Philosophy*, 143.

51. Aristotle, *Cael.* 296.2.5–14.

52. Adamson, "98—For a Limited Time Only."

53. Aristotle, *Ph.* 251.2.10–20.

54. Aristotle, *Ph.* 252.1.1–4.

55. Philo, *Aet.* 10.

56. Aristotle, *Ph.* 251.1.20–34

57. Franz Brentano's *Die Psychologie des Aristoteles*, quoted in Turner, History of Philosophy, 143.

tine (354–430 CE) and Aquinas (1225–1274 CE) saw no contradiction in maintaining that a being may be eternal and yet created.[58] Maybe the best phrase in which Aristotle summarizes his cosmogony which posits a kind of incipient evolution theory is when he wrote,

> What I mean is this: that the matter and the seed and the thing which is capable of seeing, which are potentially a man and corn and seeing, but are not yet so actually, are prior in time to the individual man and corn and seeing subject which already exist in actuality. But prior in time to these potential entities are other actual entities from which the former are generated; for the actually existent is always generated from the potentially existent by something which is actually existent . . . there is always some prime mover; and that which initiates motion exists already in actuality.[59]

Third Period: Cosmogonic Exclusion.

With the death of Aristotle, the Golden Age of Greek philosophy began to decline, and a new period started, here referred to as cosmogonic exclusion. During this period, six schools of thought existed:

1. The Stoics;
2. The Epicureans;
3. The Sceptics;
4. The Eclectics;
5. The Scientific Movement; and
6. The Philosophy of the Romans.

Since most of these schools were present in the first century, I will only deal briefly with those that will not be examined in the next section of this chapter. Therefore, the cosmogony of only the Sceptics, the Eclectics and the Scientific Movement will be discussed here.

---

58. Augustine, *Conf.* 11.10; 12.9, 12, 15, 29. Augustine also asserts "For if time has not existed for all time, it would follow that there was a time when there was no time. And [even] the most complete fool would not say that" *De civ.D.* 12.16. Cf. 2. 4; Cf. Aquinas, *STh.* I.Q.44.a.1-a.4.

59. Aristotle, *Met.* 1049b.15-24.

Pyrrho (ca. 365–275 BCE), the main scholar among the Sceptics (ca. 365 BCE–200 CE), left no writings and hence his cosmogony can only be built on the basis of secondary resources[60]—however, these resources contain nothing directly related to cosmogony or cosmology. The only thing that can therefore be declared is that for the Sceptics real things are not really as they are perceived, they are inaccessible[61] and no science is right in any respect. Eclecticism (ca. 266–68 BCE), meanwhile, is merely another aspect of Skepticism which resulted from the exhaustion of speculative thought.[62] As far as can be ascertained, it is impossible to formulate arguments regarding its cosmogony.

The last group, rightly called the Scientific Movement, or Mathematicians and Astronomers, had as its main representatives Hicetas (ca. 400–335 BCE), Aristarchus (ca. 310–230 BCE), Archimedes (ca. 287–212 BCE), Euclid (ca. 300 BCE) and Ptolemy (90–168 CE). Even though we do not have a clear theory of cosmogony from this school, what is known is that they developed a system of astronomy which was far superior to the astronomical theories contemplated by Plato and Aristotle.[63] Also, Aristarchus of Samos advanced the hypothesis that the earth moves around the sun,[64] and also that it rotates about its axis. They further asserted that there are other planets which are part of the much larger universe, and they also measured the distance between planets and between the sun and the earth.[65] It is possible that the Scientific Movement could have had an elaborate cosmogony, but it is today virtually unknown. Besides, it seems that during this period the scholars were focused on topics other than cosmogony. With this background begins the first century, the time during which Hebrews—the text being studied—was written.

Cosmogonic Thoughts in the First Century

It is necessary to open this section by asserting with Klauck that "in the early imperial period, the classical philosophical schools continued

---

60. Diogenes Laertius, Eusebius, and later Skeptics.

61. See Diogenes, *Vit. Phil.* 9.61.

62. Turner, *History of Philosophy*, 184–87.

63. Cicero, *Acad.* 39.

64. Furley, "Cosmology," 412.

65. More information about the cosmology and cosmogony of this period can be found in Krebs and Krebs, *Groundbreaking Scientific Experiments*, 33–60; Lovell, *Emerging Cosmology*, 32–46.

to exist, with some modification, and indeed even experienced in part a new momentum."[66] Hebrews was written in a complex and pluralistic society, and the cultural and intellectual milieu from which its ideas and themes derive have been long sought among the Greek-Roman culture, inside which Hebrews was written.

The first century is an extension of the Hellenic period (323–31 BCE),[67] which was referred to as "Third period: cosmogonic exclusion" above. It is also necessary to assert that the Hellenization project[68] started with Alexander—who commanded everyone to consider the cosmos as his own country—and lasted until the Roman period.[69] This period is characterized by the presence of diverse philosophical schools, along with the traditional academy or lyceum. As has already been asserted, Hebrews' elegant language, elevated rhetoric, and its use of language and metaphors confirm the Hellenistic Greek-Roman culture in which it was written. However, many scholars have contended that the influence of the author's cultural environment might not only have been seen in his/her rhetoric and vocabulary but also in his/her values and understanding of the world. Therefore, this section will show the main thoughts concerning cosmogony in the first century, so that in the next chapters, the degree of influence of Hellenistic thought in Hebrews can be assessed.

---

66. Klauck, *Religious Context of Early Christianity*, 332.

67. The Hellenic period, for most academics, is considered as the period from the death of Alexander the Great (323 BCE) to the defeat of Cleopatra and Mark Anthony by Octavian in 31 BCE. See *COEDLE*, s.v. "Hellenic." The death of Alexander the Great (323 BCE) undoubtedly caused big changes in the political world, but the death of Aristotle (322 BCE) also caused big changes in the philosophical world.

68. The Hellenic period came with Hellenization as it emerged in the mind of Alexander, to be continued by his successors. They established the government's Greek model (democratic) in every city, they also imposed their language as the official language in the imperium, and probably the most important action regarding Hellenisation, was the establishing of the Gymnasia (Greek schools). Thus, even some of the Jewish high priests took Greek names, and furthermore it is important to remember that in this age the Scriptures of Israel was translated. The Septuagint became the most popular translation used both inside and outside of Judea.

69. Johnson and Penner remind us that, although Hellenism is given a new frame by the Roman Empire, beginning with the accession of Augustus in 31 BCE, Hellenistic civilisation continued well through the time of the early empire, so that we can accurately designate the most encompassing symbolic world of the New Testament as Greco-Roman culture. Johnson and Penner, *Writings of the New Testament*, 23.

Cosmogony in Stoicism

This philosophical school, founded in Athens by Zeno of Citium (ca. 335–263 BCE), held that the entire universe was a living creature,[70] animated by the divine λόγος—reason or mind. This λόγος, for them, is the same as God, Fate, and Zeus—because God is one[71]—and they also stated that every person is a slave of this ruling λόγος.[72] To the Stoics all things have a genesis and a purpose, and in that, the λόγος plays an important role, because it is the seminal reason—λόγος—of the universe that is able to adapt matter to itself with a view to the next stage of creation.[73] Thus, the λόγος for them is not only the driving force, but also the soul of the world or god. Therefore, Turner is right when he labels Stoicism as pantheism.[74] They also considered active and passive principles, which are divinity and matter respectively,[75] as well as of the *god-logos* and also of the *logos-fire*. Stoics also argued that everything will be dissolved by fire,[76] that is to say,

---

70. Hahm notes that the Stoics seem to have begun with the widespread, venerable, ancient idea that the cosmos is a living being and that its origin was a birth exactly like the birth of living things. For the details of the birth of the cosmos they turned to one of the most recent authorities on the subject of reproduction. It was from Aristotle's biology that they derived the kernel of their doctrine of ἀρχαί as well as the inspiration to give the ἀρχαί the fundamental role of bringing the cosmos into existence. See Hahm, *Origins of Stoic Cosmology*, 47.

71. Diogenes, *Vit. Phil.* 7.135.

72. Perkins, "Stoicism," 993.

73. Diogenes, *Vit. Phil.* 7.136, 138.

74. Turner, *History of Philosophy*, 161. Also, Torres notes that the Stoics defended a kind of pantheism in which the λόγος extends over all things, "including the most despicable," wrote Clement of Alexandria. Also, Tatian concludes that the vision of Stoics compels them to think of God "as the author of evil deeds, and living in sewers, on earthworms and disgustingly lewd individuals." Mas Torres, *Historia de la Filosofía Antigua*, 220. cf. *SVF* 1:159.

75. Diogenes affirms that the Stoics "hold that there are two principles in the universe, the active principle and the passive. The passive principle, then, is a substance without quality, i.e., matter, whereas the active is the reason inherent in this substance, which is God. For he is everlasting and is the artificer of all things throughout the whole extent of matter." Diogenes, *Vit. Phil.* 7.134.

76. Gauli states that "Whereas the world on the whole, according to the Stoics, will last forever, the existing world order, which is sometimes called διακόσμησις, to distinguish it from the eternal κόσμος, is bound to dissolve into pure fire. This ἐκπύρωσις (conflagration), which is repeated at certain intervals, is not conceived as the destruction of the world, but as a reconstitution of the best possible state of the world, since all individual bodies are thereby transformed into divine fire." Gauli, "Cosmology and Natural Philosophy," 370.

they asserted that the world is one and finite, and that it must come to an end, inasmuch as it had a beginning.[77] They believed that matter—an unqualified substance—was composed of four elements: "fire being the hot element, water the moist, air the cold, and earth the dry."[78]

It is also important to note that the term κόσμος—universe or cosmos—was used by the Stoics in three senses: (1) the divine being; (2) the heavenly bodies as such; and (3) the whole of which these two are part. Therefore, the κόσμος is constituted by all things, namely heaven, earth, nature, gods, men, women and so on.[79] Moreover, Chrysippus (ca. 279–206 BCE) taught that the λόγος is not only like fire, but also like air. He also taught that this matter can be transformed into the other substances present in everything, land and water. To him these four elements form two pairs, one active—fire and air—and the other passive—land and water.[80] Plutarch stated, however, that Chrysippus also has evident contradictions in his writings; for example, when he affirms that the world was engendered by fire, but that it is not nourished, and also that the soul of the world increases continually until it has consumed all matter into itself.[81] Alongside this criticism, Hahm also shows up a difference between Zeno and Cleanthes, in which one has water as an essential element without a circular cycle while the other has earth as a bridging element in a circular cycle. Finally, Posidonius (ca. 135–51 BCE), as a former Stoic,

> recognized two principles in the cosmos, one active and one passive: god and matter, respectively. In this he was following Plato's doctrine of the mixing bowl, as put forth in the *Timaeus*. . . . , Posidonius posited . . . a bipartite cosmos consisting of a supra-lunar and a sub-lunar realm. He considered the supra-lunar realm to be imperishable, and the sub-lunar perishable, dissolving into the void (kenon) outside the cosmos during the conflagration (ekpurôsis), after which it is reconstituted anew.[82]

It is clear that there was no unified theory of cosmogony among the Stoics.

77. Diogenes, *Vit. Phil.* 7.140, 141.
78. Diogenes, *Vit. Phil.* 7.137.
79. Diogenes, *Vit. Phil.* 7.138.
80. Mas Torres, *Historia de la filosofía antigua*, 204.
81. See Plutarco, *Stoi. Repug.* 39.
82. Moore, "Middle Platonism."

First-Century Cosmogony 51

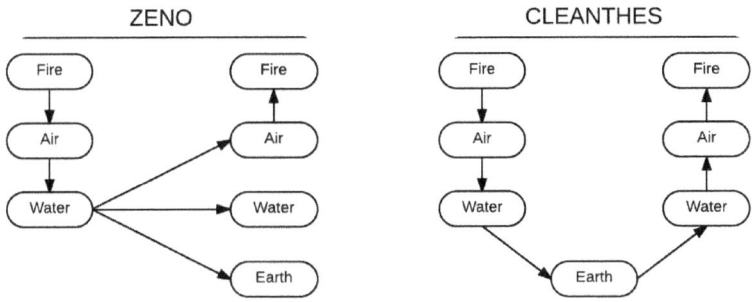

Figure 3.1 Stoics' cosmogony: its contradictions.[83]

Cosmogony in Epicureanism

The teachings of Epicurus (ca. 341–270 BCE), as Long states, is "a strange mix of stubborn empiricism, speculative metaphysics and rules to achieve a peaceful life."[84] The cosmogony of Epicurus states that all things arise from the pre-existent, and that nothing is lost in the non-being, therefore, we must conclude that all things or our reality, as a whole, always was and always will be as it is now.[85] Epicurus believed that the κόσμος was formed from atoms that fell from space,[86] violently and forcefully connecting with one another. Epicurus also believed that there are different shapes of the worlds[87] that are in continuous evolution and that there are unlimited numbers of cosmoses—κόσμοι—some coming into existence while others are passing out of existence permanently,[88] because as Gregory affirms,

---

83. The idea of this figure was taken from Hahm, *Origins of Stoic Cosmology*, 90.

84. Long, *La Filosofía Helenística*, 30.

85. Mas Torres, *Historia de la Filosofía Antigua*, 196.

86. Turner notes that the Epicurus accepted without modification the atomism of Democritus as well as the Democritean idea of a *vacuum*. Turner, *History of Philosophy*, 178.

87. Diogenes, *Vit. Phil.* 10.74.

88. Lucretius argues the same that there is not only one human being, also it is impossible to think that there is only one heaven, earth, sun, or moon. Diogenes, *Vit. Phil.* 10.89.

Epicurus and Lucretius are consistent in their application of their physical principles, and clearly take the view that there should be no difference between the processes which form *kosmoi* and the processes which are active in the *kosmos* today. That is evident from the fact that they take *kosmos* formation to be an ongoing process.[89]

Thus, Epicurus understood the κόσμος as self-contained, as a product of nature, perishable, subject to change and also supported—ἐποχέομαι—on air.[90] He put reason and nature as the most important elements in the formation of the world,[91] and he also believed that the sun, moon, stars, earth and sea began to take form and grow together.[92] He made some changes on the old Atomistic School, and probably the most significant addition was chance, because in Epicurus' cosmogony the world came into existence by chance,[93] without purpose and without any intervention from some supernatural being[94]—that is to say, the world was not created. And even though this idea is now largely accepted, Lactantius (ca. 240–320 CE) called Epicurus a crazy man who desired to discover novelties and found a sect in his own name.[95]

Cosmogony in Middle Platonism

Middle Platonism, according to More and Ritzema, begins with Antiochus of Ascalon (ca. 130–68 BCE)—who headed the Academy around 90–80 BCE—and ended with Plotinus (204–270 CE) when he recognized

---

89. Gregory, *Ancient Greek Cosmogony*, 182.
90. Diogenes, *Vit. Phil.* 10.73.
91. Erler, "Epicurus," 88.
92. Diogenes, *Vit. Phil.* 10.91. Cf.
93. Mas Torres, *Historia de la Filosofía Antigua*, 200.
94. Lactantius, *De Ira D.* 4.
95. Lactantius noted that more important philosophers held, as an acknowledged and undoubted fact, that God created the world, "until many ages afterwards the crazy Epicurus lived, who alone ventured to deny that which is most evident, doubtless through the desire of discovering novelties, that he might found a sect in his own name. And because he could find out nothing new, that he might still appear to disagree with the others, he wished to overthrow old opinions. But in this all the philosophers who snarled around him, refuted him. It is more certain, therefore, that the world was arranged by providence, than that matter was collected by providence." Lactantius, *Inst.* 2.9; Cf. 3.17; *Epit.* 70.

himself as a faithful follower of Plato (ca. 250 CE).⁹⁶ Among its main characters are Antiochus of Ascalon, Eudorus of Alexandria (*fl.* ca. 50 BCE–25 CE), Philo of Alexandria (ca. 30 BCE–45 CE), Plutarch of Chaeronea (ca. 45–125 CE), and Numenius of Apamea (*fl.* ca. 150–176 CE). Since the focus of this research is the first century, there are only three personalities relevant to this research. However, inside Middle Platonism there is a conglomeration of different thoughts as well as a mix of them, because as Losin clearly asserts:

> This [Middle Platonism] was an uneasy synthesis of a variety of influences: Aristotelian, Stoic, Pythagorean, Hebrew, Zoroastrian, and Gnostic, among them. Plato's Forms were now conceived as Ideas in the mind of God, who was, in turn, an amalgam of Aristotle's Prime Mover and the God of the Hebrew and Christian Scriptures; matter and soul were opposed; several "grades" of reality were distinguished; and genuine knowledge or understanding was often taken to require a divine "spark" or illumination.⁹⁷

Since Philo is not only a main character of Middle Platonism but also of Alexandrian Judaism, his cosmogony will be examined later in this chapter. However, here it must be asserted that Plutarch—who defended the free will as well as the immortality of the soul—sought to show that the divine being, in order to create the world, transformed matter into the receptacle of evil, but also in his discussion about the quantity of the κόσμος argued that the benevolence of god must have led him to produce more than one cosmos—κόσμοι.⁹⁸ Regarding time, Plutarch thought that there is only a formless matter of time prior to the space—κόσμος—and denied that this is time.⁹⁹

The main concern in Middle Platonism about cosmogony was focused on Plato's views on the creation of time—χρόνος—and the κόσμος in the *Timaeus*, whether they are metaphorical or not. As Gregory shows, on the basis of Taurus, Alcinous, and Diogenes Laertius (180–240 CE),

---

96. Casiday asserts that Middle Platonism is generally dated among the first century BCE to the late second century CE and Neoplatonism, which is associated particularly with the work of the philosopher Plotinus. See Casiday, "Platonism," 391–92. Cf. Ritzema, "Platonism"; Moore, "Middle Platonism."

97. Losin, "Plato and Platonism," 125.

98. Plutarch, *De Defect.* 22.

99. Plutarch, *Plat.* 8.4.

this time was characterized by debate on Plato's views and not by the development of some specific cosmogony.[100]

Cosmogony in Jewish Sects

At the beginning of the Roman Period, various sects existed among the Jews. Aside of Samaritanism,[101] Judaism—mainly based in Jerusalem, a Hellenistic city at the turn of the century[102]—was widely divided. According to Scott, there are at least four main sources from which information can be found about the variety of sects in first-century Judaism: Josephus, Hegesippus, Justin Martyr and the New Testament, and from it, he draws fourteen different groups or sects. But he also claims that there were many other minor groups reaching back to Intertestamental Judaism, like the Essenes,[103] and it is possible that these thoughts were also present in the first century, alongside other minority groups such as

---

100. The main concern was if Plato envisaged a beginning in time for the cosmos—κόσμος—or if the time and cosmos begins together. See Gregory, *Ancient Greek Cosmogony*, 218–19.

101. The Samaritan Pentateuch was significantly different from that of many other Jews. Some scholars argue that the Samaritan text represents an independent tradition which may, in part, better represent the original than does the Masoretic text of the Jews. Montgomery, *Samaritans*, 207; Gaster, *Samaritans*, 180; Scott, *Jewish Backgrounds of the New Testament*, 198. About the relation between Samaritanism and Judaism, it must be asserted that they were probably the two greatest and oldest branches relating to the Mosaic religion. See Scott, *Jewish Backgrounds of the New Testament*, 196.

102. Grabbe affirms that the Jews were placed in various Hellenistic cities in the Greek and Roman world, but that the most important Hellenistic city for Jews in the ancient world was Jerusalem itself. Grabbe, "Hellenistic City of Jerusalem," 6. Hellenism had a considerable effect on the totality of the Jews, including even the Maccabees and also the Essenes. The extensive influence of Hellenism can be seen in the Jews of that time, their writings, the names of the common people, and also some historical events reveal this reality. See Scott, *Jewish Backgrounds of the New Testament*, 30; Hengel, *Judaism and Hellenism*, 60.

103. The New Testament shows evidence about Pharisees, Sadducees, Zealots, Sicarii (Acts 21:38), Samaritans, Hellenists, Galileans, Herodians, Scribes, and Disciples of John the Baptist. Josephus wrote about the Fourth Philosophy, which could be the Zealots of the New Testament, but did not include any information about the Herodians and Scribes. Hegesipuus, even though does not mention Zealots, Sicarii, Hellenists, Herodians, Scribes, and Disciples of John the Baptist, he adds to the list the Hemerobaptists and the Masbotheans. Finally, Justin Martyr mentions eight groups and among them he mentions two that are not mentioned in any other source, the Meristae and Genistae. Scott, *Jewish Backgrounds of the New Testament*, 195–218.

Therapeutae, and Magical Judaism.[104] But also, during the first century, even though there was not an abundance of writings as there is today, there were numerous world views.[105] Clearly, it is almost impossible to cover every possible cosmogony present in the first century that may have influenced Hebrews' cosmogony, and that is why only the main and more well-known groups are discussed here.

Palestinian Judaism

Although the Hellenistic project resulted in big changes among the Jewish people, these changes had no effect on the accuracy of the Scriptures of Israel's text, but rather changed the presuppositions in the minds of the Jewish interpreters.[106] Thus, the Sadducees did not believe in a future reward and punishment, nor in the future existence of the being. The Pharisees, on the contrary, believed that there was a future life of some sort. Some of them believed in a type of resurrection and others in reincarnation.[107] From these two ideas we can deduce that their cosmogony is not the same, because one group apparently believed in the eternity and indestructibility of the being, and the other group believed in the total destruction of the being, ideas that are always linked with cosmogonic presuppositions. On this topic, Josephus is right when identifying the Sadducees with the Epicureans and the Pharisees with the Stoics.[108]

But even though the focus of the Jews was not on the method of creation[109]—because according to them, this world came into being by

---

104. Scott, *Jewish Backgrounds of the New Testament*, 229–30.

105. The sources present in this time generated many world views. These resources can be divided into Hebrew and Aramaic Sources (Mishnah, Baraita, Tosefta, Talmud, Midrashim, Halakah, Haggadah, Tannaim and Amoraim), and Greek and Latin sources (Philo of Alexandria, Josephus, Nicholas of Damascus, Strabo, Ptolemy, Pliny the Elder, Tacitus, the New Testament), among others as Archaeological Sources. See Safrai and Stern, *Jewish People in the First Century*, vol. 1.

106. During this period "The Jewish approach to the past during the third and second centuries BCE, should be examined against the background of historical writings in the Hellenist Near East. When so many writers were using the past in the service of the present, the Jews could not stay out of the picture. Hence much of their literature in the Hellenistic period shows how aware they were of the 'grand debate' occurring at the time between the various ethnē." Mendels, *Identity, Religion and Historiography*, 364.

107. Scott, *Jewish Backgrounds of the New Testament*, 228.

108. Ingalese and Ingalese, *Cosmogony and Evolution*, 173.

109. Mas Torres, *Historia de la Filosofía Antigua*, 190.

the will, action and power of God, and most of them recognized God as creator and holder of the created order—Jewish cosmogony in the first century was influenced by Greek philosophy.[110] Perhaps the most illustrative instance of this—regarding cosmogony—is the Sepher Yetzirah.[111]

Although the date this book was written is under debate, it is accepted what is stated by Reitzenstein,[112] i.e., that the Sepher Yetzirah was present, and maybe widely studied, in the first century. In order to harmonize the Old Testament cosmogony with Greek thought, the Sepher Yetzirah assumes a double creation—one ideal and the other real. It is also very interesting to observe the use of the numbers and the primordial elements in the Sepher Yetzirah's cosmogony. This document can be seen as a syncretic cosmogony of the Hebrew and Greek thought, because Platonic and Pythagorean Thought, as well as the Ionic School, can be recognized in it. For instance, the Sepher Yetzirah 1:2, 10–12, states that the twenty-two letters of the Hebrew alphabet were one of God's first creations and with the ten Sephiroth—the ten attributes or emanations in Kabbalah, through which The Infinite reveals himself and continuously creates both the physical and metaphysical realms—composed the foundation of all things.[113]

On the other hand, among the Apocrypha and Pseudepigrapha of the Old Testament, the book Wisdom of Solomon is considered to have been written by an anonymous orthodox Jew who had been strongly

---

110. Ferguson, *Backgrounds of Early Christianity*, 314–15.

111. The Book of Formation, in Hebrew ספר יצירה—*sēpher yaṣîrâh*—is a speculative text concerning God's creation of the world. Its authorship, ascribed to the biblical patriarch, Abraham, shows the high esteem which it enjoyed for centuries. Gilbert, quoting Scholem asserts that this is "a book, small in size but enormous in influence." Gilbert, Forward to *Sepher Yetzirah*, v.

112. Kaplan notes that "So ancient is this book that its origins are no longer accessible to historians. We are totally dependent on traditions with regard to its authorship. The earliest source to which Sefer Yetzirah is attributed is the Patriarch Abraham. [nevertheless] It seems highly probable that the Sefer Yetzirah was already in its present form when the Mishnah was redacted in the year 204 CE" Kaplan, *Sefer Yetzirah*, ix, xii, xviii. For instance, Benton states "However, the grammatical form of the Hebrew used in the text places its origin closer to the period of the Mishna than at the very start of the Jewish people." Benton, "An Introduction to the Sefer Yetzirah," The Maqon Journal for Studies in Rabbinic Literature, Past Maqom Journal Articles, no 27., 1. http://www.maqom.com/journal.html. However, according to Kohler and Ginzberg, the date of Sepher Yetzirah is accordingly placed by Reizenstein in the second century BCE. Kohler and Ginzberg, "Yeẓirah, Sefer," 12:603.

113. Häberl stated it on the basis of Drover's affirmation. See Häberl, "Iranian Scripts for Aramaic Languages," 53.

First-Century Cosmogony

influenced by Hellenistic culture and philosophy, most likely in Alexandria between 100 BCE and 40 CE,[114] and affirms:

> For your hand, which is all powerful
> and created the world out of formless matter,
> lacked nothing to send a horde of bears or fierce lions upon them.
> (Wis 11:17)

The Apocalypse of Baruch, which is a composite work written in the latter half of the first century CE,[115] presents a different account on the cosmogonic topic:

> 'O you that have made the earth, hear me, that have fixed the firmament by the word, and have made firm the height of the heaven by the spirit, that have called from the beginning of the world that which did not yet exist, and they obey you. (2 Bar. 21:4; cf. 2 En. 24:2)

On the other hand, Hillel's (ca. 70 BCE–7 CE)[116] cosmogony is not clear, but he asserted that man's duty is to care for his own body, since they were created in the image of God. Akiva ben Joseph (ca. 40–137 CE), widely known as Rabbi Akiva—even though it is very likely that he was too young during the time of composition of Hebrews—stated that

---

114. *EBD*, s.v. "Wisdom of Solomon." Even though most scholars will assert that Wisdom of Solomon was written in Alexandria, Grabbe asserts that "there is no reason why a book like the Wisdom of Solomon could not have been written in a variety of places in the ancient Near East. The Hellenistic world encompassed the entire eastern part of the Mediterranean. It included Palestine as well as Asia Minor, Syria, and Egypt. We know of Jewish Hellenistic literature produced in Palestine, so it is theoretically possible that the the Wisdom of Solomon was written even in Jerusalem, the heart of Judaism itself." See Grabbe, *Wisdom of Solomon*, 90. On this basis and for the purpose of this research this book will be considered under "Palestinian Judaism."

115. Charles, *Pseudepigrapha of the Old Testament*, 470.

116. Hillel (הלל), born in Babylon traditionally deemed ca. 32 BCE and died 7 CE in Jerusalem, Allen asserts that he was a "rabbinic sage and a determinant force in the development of the oral law. A Babylonian native of Davidic descent . . . Tradition describes Hillel as a skilled teacher characterized by patience, humility, and piety, who was tolerant and conciliatory toward his opponents. His seven rules for interpretation of Scripture were highly influential in Pharisaic and Talmudic hermeneutics . . . Hillel is generally regarded as the grandfather of Gamaliel I, Paul's teacher, although some sources would make him his father." Allen, *The Eerdmans Bible Dictionary*, 488–89. He was also known as the Elder Hillel and is one of the most important figures in Jewish Philosophy. On the other hand, the French philosopher, Ernest Renan, proposed that he was the teacher of Jesus Christ. See Renan, *Vida de Jesús*, 121.

humankind was not created in the image of God—בְּצֶלֶם אֱלֹהִים—but after an image, a primordial type, namely, after an *idea*.

Alexandrian Judaism

Hurst states that since the mid-seventeenth century it has been argued that to understand Hebrews one needs to know the works of Philo of Alexandria.[117] It has also been sustained that Philo is one of the main personages of Middle Platonism, but due to his origin, ought to be considered the more representative character of Alexandrian Judaism. Philo's cosmogony is perhaps the best example of Jewish-Greek syncretism, namely of Jewish Hellenism,[118] as he asserts that human beings belong to two worlds, to the ὁρατός (visible) and to the ἀόρατος (invisible) and therefore his cosmogony asserts the existence of two worlds, one visible and the other invisible.[119] To Philo the κόσμος was created,[120] and the creator is also identified as father (πατρός), creator (ποιητής),[121] and the divine reason—θεῖος λόγος—in whom the ideas are contained,[122] but also as a good Being. Apparently for Philo the creator was alone when he created everything,[123] and he also declares that the creator can chafe (χαλεπαίνω) and became angry (ὀργή) with his creation.[124] Also, the creator is a real being, only one, and in order to make his creation he resembles himself in his singleness; he employs all existing essence—ὕλη—in the creation of the universe, and he exerts his providence—προνοέω—for the benefit

---

117. Hurst, *Epistle to the Hebrews*, 7.

118. On Philo syncretism see Ladd, *Pattern of New Testament Truth*, 25–31.

119. Philo, *Opif.* 135.

120. Philo, *Opif.* 12. Philo taught that there are three opinions about the reality of this world. According to him, 1) some affirm that the world is ἀΐδιος (eternal), ἀγένητος (uncreated), and ἀνώλεθρος (indestructible) while others say 2) that the world is γενητός (created) and φθαρτός (destructible or perishable). It is important to note that he does not use the term ὄλεθρος (destruction) as is expected. But, 3) others taught that there is a mix of both who taught that the world is γενητός (created) and ἄφθαρτος (indestructible). See Philo, *Aet.* 7, 10, 75; *Opif.* 7.

121. Philo, *Opif.* 7.

122. Philo, *Opif.* 20.

123. Philo, *Opif.* 19–23. Philo uses the plural only in the creation of humankind in order to explain from what sources the blameless intentions and actions of man came, and he identifies the other assistant as bearing the imputation of these bad characteristics. See Philo, *Opif.* 72, 75.

124. Philo, *Opif.* 156.

of the world. Finally, Philo shows the constructor—δημιουργός—and the Creator—θεός—as the same person.[125]

Philo's cosmogony asserts that the creation did not come from nothing but from something,[126] and according to him, when the Creator had decided "to create this visible world, previously having formed the one which is perceptible only by the intellect,"[127] He used the active and passive cause—the active cause being the intellect of the universe while the passive cause being "something inanimate and incapable of motion by any intrinsic power of its own."[128] Regarding the purpose of the creation, Philo affirms that the human being was created to live, not to die,[129] and it also seems that Philo believed that everything was made for the enjoyment of humankind.[130]

Philo also asserts that there is only one world,[131] and argues that this creation came to existence through the invisible (ἀόρατος), spermatic (σπερματικός), technical (τεχνικός), divine word (θεῖος λόγος) which shall most properly be dedicated to the Father.[132] He further states that the world is composed of four elements: earth (γῆ), water (ὕδωρ), air (ἀήρ), and fire (πῦρ),[133] and if one among them is more fundamental, it must be the earth (γῆ), which by force of some process became water, which became air and which then became fire. When they disappear, he maintains they must go back in the reverse order until they become earth (γῆ) again.[134] Thus according to Philo, the cosmos is not eternal and is liable to destruction.

Regarding the time of creation, Philo declares the beginning (ἀρχή) does not refer to some point in time (χρόνος), but it makes reference to the beginning of time (χρόνος). That is why he asserts that time was created (ἐποίησεν), either at the same moment as the cosmos (κόσμος), or

---

125. Philo, *Opif.* 170–71.
126. Philo, *Aet.* 1–15.
127. Philo, *Opif.* 16.
128. Philo, *Opif.* 8–9.
129. Philo, *Aet.* 97.
130. Philo, *Opif.* 78.
131. Philo knows that there are some persons who believe that there are many worlds, but he believes that God used all in order to create the world. Philo, *Opif.* 171.
132. Philo, *Her.* 191.
133. Philo, *Aet.* 107.
134. Philo, *Aet.* 110.

after it.¹³⁵ And even though Philo did not make a specific assertion about the age of the cosmos, he states that the cosmos and human beings share the time of their existence.¹³⁶ Philo also asserts that the work of creation took some time,¹³⁷ and that the earth, as if it had for a long time been pregnant and travailing, produced every sort of seed, and every sort of tree, and also fruit, in unspeakable abundance, immediately (αὐτίκα) it was commanded.¹³⁸ It appears that Philo believed in an instantaneous creation and at the same time believed in a prolonged time of preparation for this event. In summary, Philo believed in three steps in the process of creation with the first step being the creation of the model of the world, before time.¹³⁹ The second step was to create the incorporeal (ἀσώματον) things from the model perceptible only by intellect, which happened on the first day.¹⁴⁰ And the third step was to create the corporeal things,¹⁴¹ which happened from the second day until the sixth day. But he stated that the days must not be taken literally, because the creation was in reality an instantaneous event that did not take place in time, "for time was not there before there was a world."¹⁴²

This corporeal cosmos, according to Philo, is also indestructible (ἄφθαρτος),¹⁴³ but if it would have to be destroyed, only God can do it; however, according to Philo, this is impossible, due to the nature of God.¹⁴⁴

---

135. Philo, *Opif.* 26–27. But in apparent contradictions, Philo also wrote that the first thing that must be created is the time, because, he states, it is impossible to put the world into a sphere without time. Namely, Philo wrote that God created the time and immediately, almost simultaneously, God created the world. See Philo, *Opif.* 24–26.

136. But Philo also wrote that it is absurd to calculate the age of the cosmos from the existence of humankind, since all men who have made discoveries in different branches of science and are remembered, can only be traced scarcely a thousand years. See Philo, *Aet.* 130, 145.

137. Philo, *Opif.* 28.

138. Philo, *Opif.* 64.

139. Philo, *Opif.* 29.

140. Philo, *Opif.* 19, 25, 29.

141. Philo, *Opif.* 29.

142. Winston, *Philo of Alexandria*, 11. See Philo, *Opif.* 26, 67; *Leg.* 1.2; *Sacr.* 65.

143. Philo asserts that the stoics claim that the cosmos (κόσμος) has been created (γενητός) and it is destructible (φθαρτός), but to him it is indestructible, and in coherency with it he believes that the humankind is mortal only in his visible structure, but immortal in his invisible component. Cf. Philo, *Opif.* 135; *Aet.* 8, 19.

144. Philo, *Aet.* 106.

Thus, the cosmos is indestructible, but—perhaps—also eternal, because Philo posits an idea in this sense when he declares,

> For this entity was in itself without arrangement, quality, life, distinctive character, and full of all disorder and confusion; but it received a change and transformation to what is opposite to this condition, and most excellent, being invested with order, quality, life, resemblance, identity, arrangement, harmony, and everything which belongs to the more excellent idea.[145]

Although it seems contradictory, Philo posited that the creation has different levels of perfection; for instance, he asserted that the human was created with a more perfect sand and not with a common one. He further stated that the first human was perfect because of his creator—God—but the actual human being is not fully perfect because s/he is the creation of other humans.[146]

But in order to better understand the cosmogony of Philo it is imperative to understand the intermedium reality in Philo's thought. According to Philo, the intermedium reality is divided into various entities;[147] among them, the λόγος—as the Divine Reason (τὸν θεῖον λόγον)—has prominence,[148] but it must also be mentioned that most of them—entities present in the intermedium reality—share characteristics with the λόγος. Therefore, even if they are listed separately, and Philo states that they are different beings, they can be identified with the λόγος as they have virtually the same characteristics. Moreover, for Philo, the λόγος existed in the world of forms as the beginning of the created order.[149] It created man in

---

145. Philo, *Opif.* 22.

146. Philo, *Opif.* 137–40.

147. Among other intermediaries we can mention: 1) the oldest being the unit and the Monad, 2) the generative substance, 3) the operating power, creator and organizer, 4) the power called lord or real power by the demiurge which governs the world—both powers come from the λόγος as a source, 5) the power called benefactor, auspicious power from operating power , 6) the power called punitive, legislative power, the real power, 7) the principle (ἀρχή) which symbolized the world apprehended by intelligent agencies or individuals forms. See Philo, *QE* 2, 68. But within them we also must consider the following: 1) The Wisdom (σοφία) divine, 2) The spirit (πνεῦμα), 3) The divine powers, 4) The angels or messengers, 5) The world of exemplary forms (ἰδέα), 6) The "man of God."

148. See Philo, *Opif.* 20.

149. See Philo, *Opif.* 19–26; *Leg.* 1.31.

the image of God (cf. Gen 1:26), and it is also God.[150] On the other hand, the Greek term κόσμος in his writings could mean:

1. A single system, containing the heaven, stars, earth, and all the animals and plants which are upon it;

2. Merely the heaven; and

3. A certain admirably-arranged essence that extends to the period of conflagration.

Philo states that in *De aeternitate mundi*, he will use the term κόσμος in its first sense.[151] It is important to take that into account, because when he speaks about eternity of the κόσμος he does not necessarily speak about the earth.

But it must also be stressed that when Philo uses κόσμος with the article and also in the nominative case, he always refers to the cosmos in its first sense—system, containing the heaven, stars, earth, and all the animals and plants which are upon it. And regarding the possible (φθορά) destruction of the κόσμος in its first sense, as has already been affirmed, Philo held that this destruction is impossible, but yet Philo agreed with Euripides, who asserted that nothing perishes, but only decomposes to form another entity.[152]

Finally, Philo's cosmogony stated that this κόσμος was built on pre-existent matter, which, as asserted, is described as "having of itself nothing lovely," and "being without order, quality, homogeneity, and full of discord and disharmony."[153] But Philo also seems to show support of the *ex nihilo* creation[154] particularly when he declares,

> And besides all this, as when the sun rises, it discovers hidden things, so also does God, who created all things, not only to bring them all to light, but also brought into being *that which*

---

150. Winston, *Philo of Alexandria*, 7.
151. Philo, *Aet.* 4.
152. Philo, *Leg.* 1.7. Cf. Philo, *Aet.* 5, 30, 140.
153. Philo, *Opif.* 22.

154. Winston asserts that since no explicit theory of creation *ex nihilo* had ever been formulated either in Jewish or Greek tradition before Philo, we should expect an emphatic and unambiguous statement from Philo on this matter, if that were indeed his position. Winston, *Philo of Alexandria*, 7. Particularly if it is considered that in 2 Maccabees 7:28 there is also a glimpse of creation ex-nihilo, a document that very likely comes from the second century BCE.

did not exist before (ἃ πρότερον οὐκ ἦν), not being only their *artificer* (δημιουργὸς), but also their *creator* (κτίστης).[155]

Thus, as stated above, Philo's cosmogony is not clear. Some of his ideas seem to show an *ex nihilo* creation, but this contradicts Philo's explicit statement, "nothing comes into being from the non-existent and nothing is destroyed into the non-existent."[156] This idea is also repeated later, "for nothing is made to disappear into nonexistence; whence it came in the beginning, thither will it return in the end."[157]

Therefore, Philo's cosmogony is a mix of ideas,[158] but this was probably not exclusive to his writings, since in reality, this can be asserted of most of the Hellenistic Jews of his time, and also to most of society of the first century CE. For this reason, Philo can also be identified with the Sceptics, since he has no clear beliefs—maybe he does not believe in anything—and also argues with both the philosophers who lived before his time as well as his contemporaries. But, Philo can also be seen as an important eclectic among the Jewish people because he gathered information from the different schools of thought, both from before his time as well as from his contemporaries.

Cosmogony in Apostolic Writings

According to Gregory, the idea of creation *ex nihilo* was taken seriously and adopted for the first time in Christianity, but he also notes that the early Christians adopted a variety of opinions on the nature of creation. Gregory further maintains that the Christian *ex nihilo* differs in several important aspects from the sort of creation *ex nihilo* proposed by others such as Parmenides for example.[159] Nevertheless, he also asserts that

---

155. Philo, *Somn.* 1.76.

156. Philo, *Aet.* 5.

157. Philo, *Spec.* 1.226.

158. Winston affirms that Philo represents a form of Judaism which had come to terms with a high degree of social-cultural and political assimilation and acculturation, and also represents people that try to accommodate Judaism to the dominant culture via practices such as allegorical interpretation without abandoning its distinctive traditions and practices. See Winston, *Philo of Alexandria*, 12.

159. Gregory, *Ancient Greek Cosmogony*, 203. Gregory affirms that the Christians are the first group that talks about creation *ex nihilo* because he does not see in any place in the Old Testament, nor in the apocryphal or pseudepigraphal literature, the idea of creation *ex nihilo*. However, it is also important to remember what was already

in the Bible—New and Old Testament—he does not "find any clear-cut evidence for this view."[160] What is clear is that the great majority of the Church Fathers understood creation as *ex nihilo*. On the other hand, Copan and Craig set out to establish and defend the doctrine of creation *ex nihilo*,[161] while others try to hold onto or develop different views on creation from biblical text.[162] What is evident today is that even though the content of Old Testament cosmogony seems to be assumed in numerous parts of the New Testament—e.g., in which it mentions the origin of the world (4:3 cf. John 1:24; Matt 25:24; Luke 11:50; Eph 1:4; 1 Pet 1:20), the creation of humanity (Matt 19:4–6; Acts 17:24–26; 1 Tim 2:13), God's rest (4:4; cf. John 5:17), and God's power to create (Matt 11:25; Luke 10:21; Acts 17:24; 1 Cor 8:6; Rom 11:36; Eph 4:6; Rev 4:11), as well as how the creation came to happen (1:2; 11:3; cf. John 1:3; Acts 14:17; Rom 1:20; Col 1:15–18)—the interpretations of these texts are diverse. Therefore, and since this research deals with Hebrews'—an exceptional, early Christian document—cosmogony, besides asserting that the interpretations of cosmological and cosmogonic texts of the New Testament are not unanimous among biblical scholars, the conclusions of Pennington and McDonough about cosmogony in *Cosmology and New Testament Theology* will only be summarized here:[163]

1. The New Testament texts do not offer enough information to reconstruct a clear and perhaps uniform view of its cosmology and cosmogony.

---

asserted, that the cosmogony of Parmenides is more a kind of pantheistic cosmogony—Eleatic School. While Gregory says that "the idea of creation *ex nihilo* was taken seriously and adopted for the first time in Christianity" the idea of creation *ex nihilo* nevertheless seems to have existed already in the second century BCE, as attested by 2 Macabees 7:28.

160. Gregory, *Ancient Greek Cosmogony*, 204.

161. Copan and Craig, *Creation out of Nothing*.

162. Today it is widely recognized that cosmogonic theories abound; not only are there creation and evolution, but there are different views of creation and different views of evolution. In Christendom, it seems that the Bible is the source from which these different views arise: Theistic Evolution, Gap Theory, Day-Age Theory, Apparent-Age Theory, Punctuated 24-Hour Theory, Scientific Creationism, Historical Creationism, amongst others. Gulley as well as Gromacki wrote enlightened articles about this topic, see Gulley, "Basic Issues between Science and Scripture," 195–229; Gromacki, "Genesis, Geology and the Grand Canyon," 26–68.

163. Pennington and McDonough, *Cosmology and New Testament Theology*, 189–92.

2. Even though there are intimations that the writers were in touch with the intellectual currents around them, there is nothing to indicate that any given author adopted such a system *in toto*.

3. The Old Testament is authoritative for the New Testament writers, especially on their theological assessment of the created order.

4. Paul's cryptic mention of the "third heaven" in 2 Corinthians 12:2 seems to be indebted to early Jewish speculation, but precisely what he meant by the term is still difficult to determine.

5. The most extended meditation on cosmic structures in the New Testament is the book of Hebrews, which is also generally seen as the most Hellenized book in the New Testament.

6. The possible dependence of 2 Peter 3:5, 7, 10–12 on Stoic cosmogonic and cosmological theory remains obscure, imprecise and unlikely.

7. Although the New Testament presents heaven and earth in sharp opposition to each other, in the end, these two join in harmonious union.

What can be asserted from Pennington and McDonough which is pertinent to this research is that the New Testament, and particularly Hebrews, holds a cosmogony that is not easy to understand, since it seems to be built on presuppositions that are not part of its philosophical context. This problem has caused different approaches to the cosmogony of the New Testament since early times.

Cosmogony in Gnosticism

Since Hebrews was linked with gnostic thoughts,[164] some concerning cosmogony will be examined here. But it must also be stated that it is impossible to speak about proper Gnosticism in the first century already—it is very likely proto-Gnosticism that is present in the context of Hebrews. That is why only a short paragraph will suffice.

---

164. Even though it is not a very popular position and there is no clear and direct link between Hebrews and Gnosticism, from 1922 when Scott spoke of Hebrews as "gnosis," and others, without using the term, paved the way for a gnostic interpretation of Hebrews, the first thorough exposition was that of E. Kaseman in 1939, and, as far as can be ascertained, the only document that holds this view. See Käsemann, *Wandering People of God*; Scott, *Epistle to the Hebrews*. More information about Hebrews and its relation with Gnosticism can be found in Hurst, *Epistle to the Hebrews*, 67–74.

Gnosticism has an anti-cosmic perspective, namely a dualism between the soul as good and the material world as evil,[165] and gnostics also believed in the eternity of matter.[166] As Cornford sustained, the Gnosticism teaching is a mixture of the philosophies of Philo and Plotinus with certain elements of Christianity: they maintained an origin of the cosmos by emanation from God, "of numberless *aeons*, the sum of which is the Pleroma; and the final return of all things to God by a universal redemption."[167] Finally, it can be asserted that the divine being of Gnosticism did not create nothing, that the creation in its view is an imperfect entity, since the creation is the work of an half-maker—$\delta\eta\mu\iota o\upsilon\rho\gamma\acute{o}\varsigma$—who imagined himself to be the ultimate and absolute divine being, and who created everything in the image of his own flaw. So this false and bad creator is responsible for the present corrupt state of the world.[168]

Chapter Conclusion

Cosmogony in the first century could be called a plethoric mixture of thoughts, and it is in this context that Hebrews was written. The purpose of this chapter was, firstly, to show the more common cosmogonic vocabulary present in the first century, and, secondly, to expose the main cosmogonic presuppositions present in first-century philosophies. These achievements will be evaluated in further chapters, but first, the main cosmogonic presuppositions present in the first century will be shown here.

As already asserted, these presuppositions were constituted by the different thoughts which originated with the Ionians, Pythagoreans, Eleatics, Atomists, Skeptics, Stoics, Epicureans, the Scientific Movement, Middle Platonism, Jewish Sects and even—perhaps—with a kind of insipient proto-Gnosticism, as well as in personalities such as Socrates, Plato, and Aristotle. Consequently, as already asserted, in first-century philosophy the cosmogonic presuppositions are diverse and even contradictory.

For the purpose of this research, they will be organized into the periods within which they occur and the theories or presuppositions

---

165. Cf. *Auth. Teach.* VI, 22:34: 223:17–20; 32:16–33
166. Gregory, *Ancient Greek Cosmogony*, 211.
167. Turner, *History of Philosophy*, 219.
168. An excellent explanation about Gnosticism and the consequences of its interaction with Christianity can be found in Wright, *Creation, Power and Truth*, 6–34. More information about Gnosticism can be found in Pearson, *Ancient Gnosticism*; Pearson, *Gnosticism, Judaism, and Egyptian Christianity*; Brakke, *Gnostics*.

First-Century Cosmogony

will focus mainly on the following topics: creator, procedure, sources, time, creation and its development, and fate, which can be seen in Tables 3.1–3.5.

Representatives		Theories	Main Vocabulary
Schools	Persons		
Skeptics Scientific Movement	Pyrrho Hicetas Aristarchus Archimedes Euclid Ptolemy	The origin of everything is something inaccessible, and the real things are not really as they are perceived, because the real things are also inaccessible.	κόσμος, γῆ, ὕδωρ, ἀήρ, πῦρ, νοῦς, ὁμοιομέρειαι, κόσμοι, ἄτομος.
		There is no science nor any approach regarding the origin of everything that can be right in any respect, therefore in order to attain a tranquil mind it is necessary to suspend judgement.	
		The earth and the other planets are in motion and they move around the sun and also the earth rotates about its axis; they are part of a much larger universe than anyone believes possible, and there are distances between planets and the earth and the sun.	

Table 3.1 Main cosmogonic presuppositions present in cosmogonic exclusion.

As already asserted, all of these achievements will be evaluated in further chapters, but the main vocabulary present in first-century cosmogony will be especially useful for the purpose of the next chapter in which the main cosmogonic vocabulary of Hebrews will be established. So it can be asserted—but not conclusively—that from the different literature that has been presented in this chapter, this vocabulary is constituted by seventy-one words in total, which can be divided into three categories: twenty-one verbs, thirty nouns—the plural κόσμοι belongs to the lemma κόσμος[169]—and twenty adjectives, as can be seen in Table 3.6.

169. In Table 3.6 κόσμοι and κόσμος can be found under the category of nouns;

Representatives		Theories and Presuppositions	Main Vocabulary
Schools	Persons		
Ionian	Heraclitus	The creation is not the work of some creator, but it is the eternal mind, which are natural laws, who formed it. So the creation is the unlimited, infinite, immobile, eternal, and immutable divine being.	κόσμος, ἀρχή, λόγος, ἐκπύρωσις, γῆ, ὕδωρ, ἀήρ, πῦρ, πάσχω, νοῦς, ὁμοιομέρειαι, κόσμοι, θεός, ἄτομος, μεταβάλλω, νοέω.
	Anaxagoras	The creation is a cyclic reality that develops from physical elements such as a multitude of tiny, pure, invisible, indestructible, and indivisible particles called atoms or *homoeomeries* or from the eternal fiery seed, i.e., it is not what it is but what it will be, since it is in constant transformation.	
Pythagorean	Pythagoras	The creation is constituted by three regions: 1) the region of the elemental fire, which is pure, perfect, and does not admit change or movement; 2) the region of the heavenly bodies, where movement is present; and 3) the earthly region, which includes the moon and its immediate surroundings.	
Eleatic	Xenophanes of Colophon, Parmenides, Zeno of Elea,	The creation is a living entity and it is a divine being; it is constituted by an infinite number of cosmos and exists from eternity. Some also taught that it is a structure built on numbers.	
		The creation came into existence due to the constant movement; matter cannot be destroyed, it can only be changed from one form to another, following natural laws, which develop new creations.	
Atomistic	Leucippus, Democritus of Abdera.	The creation came into existence because the divine being can fragment himself or because the atoms are brought together by their equal weight and not by any incorporeal agency or by chance.	
		The sources from which everything comes into existence are water, fire, air, and land, or they can be a multitude of tiny particles like seeds, the eternal fiery seed, the divine being, or the atoms.	
		The developing of the creation is controlled by the universal and eternal law, so some cosmoses are at their peak and some are in the process of disintegration.	
		The fate of the creation is to be fire again, and its destruction will happen when it comes into collision with another cosmos.	

Table 3.2 Main cosmogonic presuppositions present in cosmogonic speculation.

---

apparent duplication occurs due to the significance of this word—in plural and singular—for the purpose of this research.

First-Century Cosmogony

Representative Persons	Theories and Presuppositions	Main Vocabulary
Socrates	The creation is the handiwork of some wise artifice who can be defined as the intelligent cause or the supreme idea of good; nevertheless, although the physical world is but a poor imitation of a real and superior world, it is the center of the cosmos.	ἀπόλλυμι, ἀγένητος, γενητός, δημιουργός, νοῦς, νόος, ἡ τοῦ παντός ψυχή, ἄφθαρτος, ἰδέα, ἰδεῖν, ἡ τοῦ ἀγαθοῦ ἰδέα, ἀΐδιος, ἀιδής, ἀΐδιος, ἀνώλεθρος, προγίγνομαι, ἀλλάσσω, κτίσις
	Everything that exists for a useful purpose must be the work of an intelligence. So there are three principles that rule the creation: 1) The efficient cause or agent, which is the creator; 2) The substance, which is the first substratum; and 3) The form, which is a bodiless essence.	
	The ideas are real while the physical world is but a poor imitation, and everything that is physical has a start in time while the idea is eternal and timeless. So the creation must be temporal and cannot be eternal, since time was also created.	
	The cosmos is uncreated and indestructible, therefore the cosmos does not have a beginning and will not have an end, because time, motion, and matter are eternal.	
Plato	In order to develop the cosmos, the creator used an intermediary agent, the demiurge who is not a divine intelligence or a personal ruler, but a manual laborer. The demiurge used fire and earth—solid elements—and air and water—liquid elements, in order to fashion the cosmos out of this chaotic elemental matter.	
Aristotle	The things being seen now are the result of previous things that the actual entity cannot see, however the current entity is also the base for another future entity. So the things came from a kind of evolution or development.	
	The source or sources from which everything came into existence is unknown but there must be a source which must be eternal and indestructible. Or perhaps the source of everything is the pattern which is a real, perfect, and eternal world. Or perhaps the source is constituted by eternal and physical elements such as fire, earth, air, and water.	
	The creation was made for a useful purpose and to be a moving image of the unmoving eternity, whose fate is to endure forever, or perhaps it will end in some future moment.	

Table 3.3 Main cosmogonic presuppositions present in cosmogonic contemplation.

Representatives		Theories and Presuppositions	Main Vocabulary
Schools	Persons		
Stoicism, Epicureanism, Middle Platonism, and Gnosticism	Zeno of Citium, Chrysippus, Posidonius, Epicurus, Antiochus of Ascalon, Eudorus of Alexandria, Plutarch of Chaeronea, Numenius of Apamea, and Plotinus	The creation depends on active—divinity—and passive—matter—principles, it is divine in essence, since the active principle can be fire and air and the passive earth and water which are also divine transformations, so the creation is a living creature.	ἐκπύρωσις, ἐποχεῖσθαι, λόγος, προγίγνομαι, κόσμοι, κενός, κόσμος, κτίσις, γῆ, ὕδωρ, ἀήρ, πῦρ, δημιουργός
		The creation is animated by the divine λόγος—the seminal reason which is fire and air and can transform itself into earth and water—which is the same as god, fate, and Zeus.	
		The creation is a bipartite cosmos which is constituted by the supra-lunar realm which is imperishable and the sub-lunar realm which is perishable and is part of an unlimited number of cosmos.	
		The creation always was and always will be as it is now, since everything arose from the preexistent and nothing is lost in the non-being, and so what exists appeared by chance or perhaps by action of natural and physical laws.	
		The atoms fell violently and forcefully connecting with one another, so sun, moon, stars, earth and sea began to take form and grow together, so it is self-contained and it is a product of nature, perishable, subject to change and also supported on air.	
		The source for everything is the divine being who transformed matter into the receptacle of evil, or it can be the four elements: fire the hot element, water the moist, air the cold, and earth the dry. Or maybe everything came from fire, or maybe from atoms that fell from space.	
		The creation and time have a simultaneous origin, since all things have a genesis and sometime in the past the atoms began to fall, and it was made for a useful purpose or maybe without any purpose, since the creation is going to its end—it is in continuous development, but in the direction of its total auto destruction.	
		The creation will be dissolved by fire and consequently it will become fire; i.e., it will be dissolved into the void during the conflagration after which it will be reconstituted anew.	
		The creation is an emanation of the divine being but the work of half-maker—δημιουργός—who believes himself to be the ultimate and absolute divine being, so he is a false and bad creator and responsible for the bad state of the world.	

Table 3.4 Main cosmogonic presuppositions present in Greek-Roman philosophy.

First-Century Cosmogony

Representatives		Theories and Presuppositions	Main Vocabulary
Schools	Persons		
Jewish Sects	Samaritans Sadducees Pharisees Philo of Alexandria.	God is the creator and there is a double creation: one ideal and the other real, which came into existence through a complex process which included the creation of physical and incorporeal things, in which either the ten Sephiroth, the powerful hand, the word and the Spirit could have been used, or all of them.	ἀπόλλυμι, ἀγένητος, γενητός, δημιουργός, νοῦς, νοὸς ἡ τοῦ παντός ψυχή, ἄφθαρτος, ἰδέα, ἰδεῖν, ἡ τοῦ ἀγαθοῦ ἰδέα, ἀΐδιος, ἀιδής, ἀΐδιος, ἀνώλεθρος, προγίγνομαι, ἀλλάσσω, κτίσις
		God created first the twenty-two letters of Hebrew alphabet and he was alone when he created everything through an instantaneous event in which also time was created; on the other hand, humanity is not the image of God but the image of the Idea and it—humanity—belongs to two worlds, the visible and the invisible.	
		The procedure followed by the creator in order to create was to use the divine λόγος as an intermedium reality who brought everything into existence following three steps: 1) Creation of model before time; 2) Creation of incorporeal things from the model; and 3) Creation of corporeal things. Or maybe the earth became water, which in turn became air, and air became fire.	
		The source for everything was a formless matter, namely an all-existent and preexistent essence since it must be an active and passive cause, and if the passive cause was there in creation then the matter is eternal. But also, the source could be nothing or maybe a pattern which is the Idea.	
		The creation could be temporary or an eternity and an indestructible entity; if temporary, it is not eternal and could be destroyed. On the other hand, there are different levels of perfection and there are numberless creations.	
		The purpose of the creation is to exist forever or maybe it could be to end in the future or it could be changed into another entity. Or perhaps it will never change nor will it be destroyed due to the nature of God.	

Table 3.5 Main cosmogonic presuppositions present in Jewish cosmogony.

No	VERBS	NOUNS	ADJECTIVES
1	ἐποχέομαι (be carried upon)	ἀήρ (air)	ἀγένητος (uncreated)
2	κτίζω (create, to found)	ἐκπύρωσις (conflagration)	ἀΐδιος or ἀϊδής or ἀίδιος (eternal)
3	μεταβάλλω (change)	ἰδέα (idea)	ἀνώλεθρος (indestructible)
4	προγίγνομαι (pre-exist)	κόσμοι (cosmoses)	ἀσώματον (incorporeal)
5	προνοέω (provide for, care for)	κτίστης (creator, founder)	ἄτομος (indivisible, atom)
6	ἀλλάσσω (change, exchange)	νοῦς or νόος (mind, god)	ἄφθαρτος (imperishable)
7	ἀπόλλυμι (destroy, perish)	ὁμοιομερεία (homoeomeries)	γενητός or γεννητός (generated)
8	βλέπω (see, observe, perceive)	ποιητής (doer, maker)	κενός (void, empty, vain)
9	γεννάω (beget, produce)	ὕλη (existing essence)	ὁρατός (visible, to be seen)
10	γίνομαι or γίγνομαι (to become)	χάος (chaos)	σπερματικός (power to generate)
11	δεῖ (it is necessary, inevitable)	ἄνθρωπος (humanity, man)	τεχνικός (artistic, skilful)
12	δηλόω (reveal, make clear)	ἀρχή (beginning, ruler)	φθαρτός (perishable, corruptible)
13	εἰμί (be, exist, happen)	γῆ (earth, land, ground)	αἴτιος (cause, source)
14	καταπαύω (rest, stop, cease)	δημιουργός (crafts worker)	ἀόρατος (invisible, unseen)
15	κατασκευάζω (build, prepare)	δύναμις (power)	ἕβδομος (seventh, seventh day)
16	μένω (remain, stay, persist)	εἰκών (mental representation)	ἴδιος (one's own, particular)
17	νοέω (understand, perceive)	ἔργον (work, deed, action)	μέγας (large, great, big)
18	πάσχω (suffer, endure)	λόγος (word, message)	πᾶς (every, all, everything)
19	πήγνυμι (pitch a tent, build, fix)	ὄνομα (name, title)	πρῶτος (first, before, earliest)
20	ποιέω (make, do, manufacture)	πατήρ (father, forefather)	τέλειος (perfect, mature)
21	φαίνω (shine, become visible)	πῦρ (fire)	ἡμέρα (day, time)
30	κτίσις (creation, creature)	στοιχεῖον (primary principle)	θεός (God, deity, goddess)
	πόλις (city, town)	τεχνίτης (designer, artisan)	κόσμος (world, order, cosmos)
	χείρ (hand)	ὕδωρ (water)	οὐρανός (heaven, sky)

Table 3.6 Main cosmogonic vocabulary present in first-century philosophy.

4

Text-Linguistic Analysis in Hebrews' Cosmogony

To HAVE A BETTER understanding of Hebrews' cosmogony it is necessary to understand its text and, more specifically, its cosmogonic text; consequently, this chapter will analyze the main constituent of Hebrews, i.e., its text, through text-linguistic strategies in order to find the specific literary component of Hebrews' cosmogony.

Chapter Introduction

Text-linguistic analysis or literary analysis is a close examination of the text,[1] to see how it affects the whole, which in this case will be the comprehension of Hebrews' cosmogony. It includes a grammatical analysis, but, this will be tackled in the next chapter. This chapter will emphasize the literary characteristics of Hebrews' text by referring to elements such

---

1. George Guthrie uses the phrase "text-linguistic analysis" when he does the analysis of Hebrews' text in order to find its structure, but he also recognizes that the "literary analysis" is a very close analysis related to his approach to the Hebrews' text. Here, the phrase is used because it can imply a broader field of action, which could include grammatical, semantical, and textual analysis of Hebrews' text, and even of its genre, as well as its historical and contextual analysis. And since Hebrews' text is the main component under analysis in this research, and since through it Hebrews portrays its cosmogony, this kind of analysis is indispensable to this research. More about this issue can be found in Guthrie, *Structure of Hebrews*, 45–58; Zuck, *Basic Bible Interpretation*, 98–122; Trotter, *Interpreting the Epistle to the Hebrews*, 145–63.

as structure, rhetorical figures, aspects of style, genres, repetitions, vocabulary, and linguistic issues, amongst other particular features that are pertinent to this study, with the main goal being to define the literary component of Hebrews' cosmogony. Consequently, this chapter will be divided into specific sections, namely: the literary component of Hebrews' cosmogony; its structural analysis; the genre analysis; the textual dependence; and the linguistic analysis of Hebrews' cosmogony.

Literary Component of Hebrews' Cosmogony

This first section will establish the literary component of Hebrews' cosmogony, i.e., it will examine Hebrews, not in order to find its central theme, but rather to find the most prominent texts which form the core points around which a cosmogonic discourse of Hebrews is presented. Neeley presents four principles for developing a more concise outline of Hebrews:

1. Deletion;

2. Combination;

3. Simplification; and

4. Special linguistic indications of prominence.[2]

These principles form the basis on which the principles that will be used here in order to determine the literary component of Hebrews' cosmogony have been developed, which are:

1. Identification;

2. Exclusion;

3. Simplification; and

4. Organization.

---

2. The four principles set out by Neeley are useful for identifying the central theme of any extensive text, however, in order to find the main texts on a specific topic, some modification to these four principles must be made. Therefore, since the purpose of this research is different to Neely's purpose, i.e., to determine the literary component of Hebrews' cosmogony and not to identify the central theme of Hebrews, these principles only form the basis on which the principles that will be used here have been developed in order to determine the literary component of Hebrews' cosmogony. More about Neeley's four principles can be found in Neeley, "Discourse Analysis of Hebrews," 27–29.

Identification

There are two specific linguistic strategies that will be used in order to identify the key Hebrews' texts—phrases or sentences—on cosmogony. The first of these strategies will be called (1) correspondence between Hebrews' text and its external context; and the second, (2) pragmatic evaluation of Hebrews' text with emphasis on its cosmogony. The first will help to identify the keywords of first-century cosmogony present in Hebrews, and the second will help to identify Hebrews' verses with cosmogonic perspectives. To employ the first strategy, all keywords of first-century cosmogony used in the text of Hebrews will be identified, and then some principles of intertexture will be applied.[3] To employ the second, four strategies of reading that have been proven to increase comprehension and understanding of text, will be used, i.e., predicting, making connections, summarizing, and questioning,[4] along with some principles of the inner texture.[5]

---

3. Intertexture and inner texture, amongst other terminology, are part of the vocabulary used in Socio-rhetorical criticism. Robbins explains that intertexture deals with the phenomena that lie outside the text but that are in some way present in the text. Which could be specific use of language in other texts and people's use of language in daily speech—oral-scribal intertexture—but also with social intertexture, cultural intertexture, and historical intertexture. So the emphasis here will be on the application of principles that lead the scribal intertexture, which are recitation, recontextualisation, reconfiguration, narrative amplification, and thematic elaboration. Nevertheless, the principle of recitation will mainly be applied. Inner texture, meanwhile, according to Robbins, deals with the phenomena that lie inside the text, namely features like repetitions, and particular ways in which the words present the arguments and topic, which in this case is the cosmogony. Robbins, *Exploring the Texture of Texts*, 3, 40.

4. Küçükoğlu shows six strategies of reading (predicting, visualising, making connections, summarising, questioning, inferring), but some of them are not pertienent to the purpose of this research. Küçükoğlu, "Improving Reading Skills," 710–11.

5. According to Robbins, the socio-rhetorical interpretation is a multi-dimensional approach to texts guided by a multi-dimensional hermeneutic. Rather than being one more method for interpreting texts, for him socio-rhetorical interpretation is an approach that evaluates and reorients its strategies—this means that it invites methods and creates new strategies to read the text using insights from sociolinguistics, semiotics, rhetoric, ethnography, literary studies, social sciences, and ideological studies. Consequently, Robbins states, "socio-rhetorical interpretation enacts an interactive interpretive analytic that juxtaposes and interrelates phenomena by drawing and redrawing boundaries of analysis and interpretation." Robbins, "Socio-Rhetorical Interpretation," 192.

Correlation between Hebrews' Text and Its External Cosmogonic Context

As can be seen in the previous chapter, the main cosmogonic vocabulary in the first century has particular words and thoughts that characterize it. It can therefore be expected to find some of them in Hebrews' cosmogony, and here, the words will be the focus—the thoughts will be tackled in later chapters. As already shown in the conclusion of the previous chapter, the main cosmogonic vocabulary present in the first century is constituted by seventy-one words—see Table 3.6. Not all of these seventy-one words are present in Hebrews however—of these, eight adjectives, twenty nouns, and sixteen verbs, can be found in Hebrews, distributed throughout. The specific words used in Hebrews can be seen in Table 4.1 and are marked with the symbol ◉. On the other hand, their distribution in Hebrews is shown in Figure 4.1.[6]

As can be seen, of the seventy-one keywords of first-century cosmogony, only forty-four are present in Hebrews; however, as can be seen in Figure 4.1, the presence of these forty-four words are not significant in Hebrews' text, since every mark (|) represents only one word and not the total verse. Nevertheless, this analysis, which is the first step in determining the literary component of Hebrews' cosmogony, reveals that among Hebrews' thirteen chapters and 303 verses,[7] some information about cosmogony can be found in 130 verses,[8] since 130 verses of Hebrews contain some keyword(s) of first-century cosmogony.

---

6. In order to find the correlation between Hebrews' text and its external cosmogonic context, the lemmas of both texts were used, and therefore, the roots can be shared for more than one word. Nevertheless, it must be mentioned that in Figure 4.1 only six verbs appear, mainly due to space, but these six verbs can be considered the most representative since the other verbs mostly appear together with these six main verbs.

7. The *kephalaia*, a system of chapter divisions used in the ancient Greek manuscripts, however, considers Hebrews as a document divided into twenty-two sections: 1 (1:1–4), 2 (1:5—2:8), 3 (2:9–18), 4 (3:1–19), 5 (4:1–10), 6 (4:11—5:10), 7 (5:11—6:12), 8 (6:13-20), 9 (7:1–10), 10 (7:11—8:6), 11 (8:7—9:10), 12 (9:11—10:4), 13 (10:5–23), 14 (10:24–31), 15 (10:32–39), 16 (11:1–40), 17 (12:1–11), 18 (12:12–17), 19 (12:18–29), 20 (13:1-8), 21 (13:9–19), 22 (13:20-25). Cf. Aland et al., *Greek Bible Text From*, 85. Guthrie asserts that the most common conjunctions appearing at the beginning of *kephalaia* sections are γάρ and δέ, each appearing five times. Other conjunctions or particles used are οὖν, διό, καί, τοιγαροῦν, and ὅθεν. None appear at 5:11, 13:1, and 13:9. Guthrie, *Structure of Hebrews*, 3.

8. See the following Hebrews' texts: 1:1–5, 7, 10; 2:2–4, 6, 12; 3:2–4, 8–10, 13–14; 4:2–4, 7–8, 10, 12–14; 5:1, 5, 7, 9, 11–14; 6:1–3, 5, 7, 10, 13, 16; 7:2–3, 8, 10, 16, 26–28; 8:1–2, 5, 7–13; 9:1–2, 6, 8–9, 11–12, 14–15, 18, 23–24, 26–27; 10:1, 5, 7, 9, 11, 16,

Hebrews' Cosmogonic Presuppositions

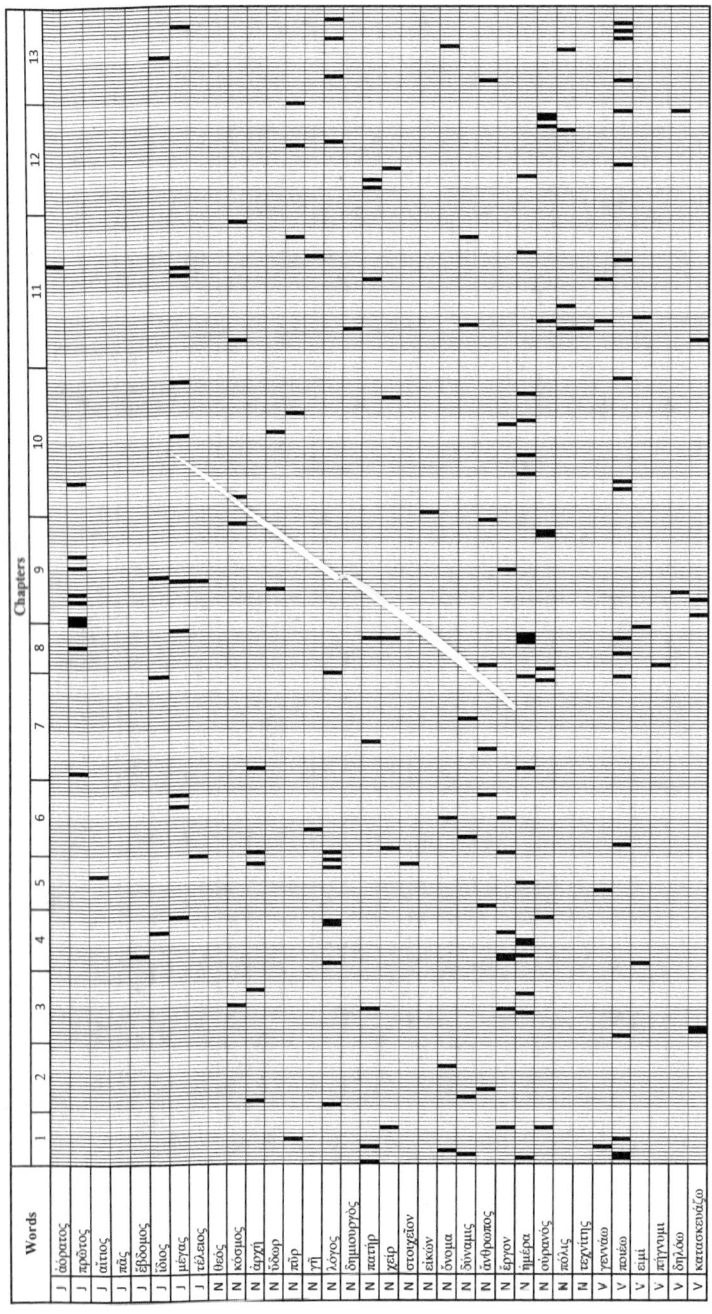

Figure 4.1 Keywords of first-century cosmogony present in Hebrews.

Text-Linguistic Analysis in Hebrews' Cosmogony

No	VERBS	NOUNS	ADJECTIVES
1	μεταβάλλω (change)	ἀήρ (air)	ἀγένητος (uncreated)
2	ἐπόχέομαι (be carried upon)	ἐκπύρωσις (conflagration)	ἀΐδιος or ἀϊδής or ἀΐδιος (eternal)
3	κτίζω (create, to found)	ἰδέα (idea)	ἀνώλεθρος (indestructible)
4	προγίγνομαι (pre-exist)	κόσμοι (cosmoses)	ἀσώματον (incorporeal)
5	προνοέω (provide for, care for)	κτίστης (creator, founder)	ἄτομος (indivisible, atom)
6	⊙ ἀλλάσσω (change, exchange)	νοῦς or νόος (mind, god)	ἄφθαρτος (imperishable)
7	⊙ ἀπόλλυμι (destroy, perish)	ὁμοιομερεία (homoeomeries)	γενητός or γεννητός (generated)
8	⊙ βλέπω (see, observe, perceive)	ποιητής (doer, maker)	κενός (void, empty, vain)
9	⊙ γεννάω (beget, produce)	ὕλη (existing essence)	ὁρατός (visible, to be seen)
10	⊙ γίνομαι or γίγνομαι (to become)	χάος (chaos)	σπερματικός (power to generate)
11	⊙ δεῖ (it is necessary, inevitable)	⊙ ἄνθρωπος (humanity, man)	τεχνικός (artistic, skilful)
12	⊙ δηλόω (reveal, make clear)	⊙ ἀρχή (beginning, ruler)	φθαρτός (perishable, corruptible)
13	⊙ εἰμί (be, exist, happen)	⊙ γῆ (earth, land, ground)	⊙ αἴτιος (cause, source)
14	⊙ καταπαύω (rest, stop, cease)	⊙ δημιουργός (crafts worker)	⊙ ἀόρατος (invisible, unseen)
15	⊙ κατασκευάζω (build, prepare)	⊙ δύναμις (power)	⊙ ἕβδομος (seventh, seventh day)
16	⊙ μένω (remain, stay, persist)	⊙ εἰκών (mental representation)	⊙ ἴδιος (one's own, particular)
17	⊙ νοέω (understand, perceive)	⊙ ἔργον (work, deed, action)	⊙ μέγας (large, great, big)
18	⊙ πάσχω (suffer, endure)	⊙ λόγος (word, message)	⊙ πᾶς (every, all, everything)
19	⊙ πήγνυμι (pitch a tent, build, fix)	⊙ ὄνομα (name, title)	⊙ πρῶτος (first, before, earliest)
20	⊙ ποιέω (make, do, manufacture)	⊙ πατήρ (father, forefather)	⊙ τέλειος (perfect, mature)
21	⊙ φαίνω (shine, become visisble)	⊙ πῦρ (fire)	⊙ ἡμέρα (day, time)
	⊙ κτίσις (creation, creature)	⊙ στοιχεῖον (primary principle)	⊙ θεός (God, deity, goddess)
30	⊙ πόλις (city, town)	⊙ τεχνίτης (designer, artisan)	⊙ κόσμος (world, order, cosmos)
	⊙ χείρ (hand)	⊙ ὕδωρ (water)	⊙ οὐρανός (heaven, sky)

Table 4.1 Correlation between Hebrews' text and first-century cosmogony.

21–22, 24–25, 27, 31–32, 35–36; 11:7, 10–13, 16, 23–24, 26–30, 34, 38; 12:7, 9–10, 12–13, 18–19, 22–23, 25–27, 29; 13:6–7, 12, 14–15, 17, 19–22.

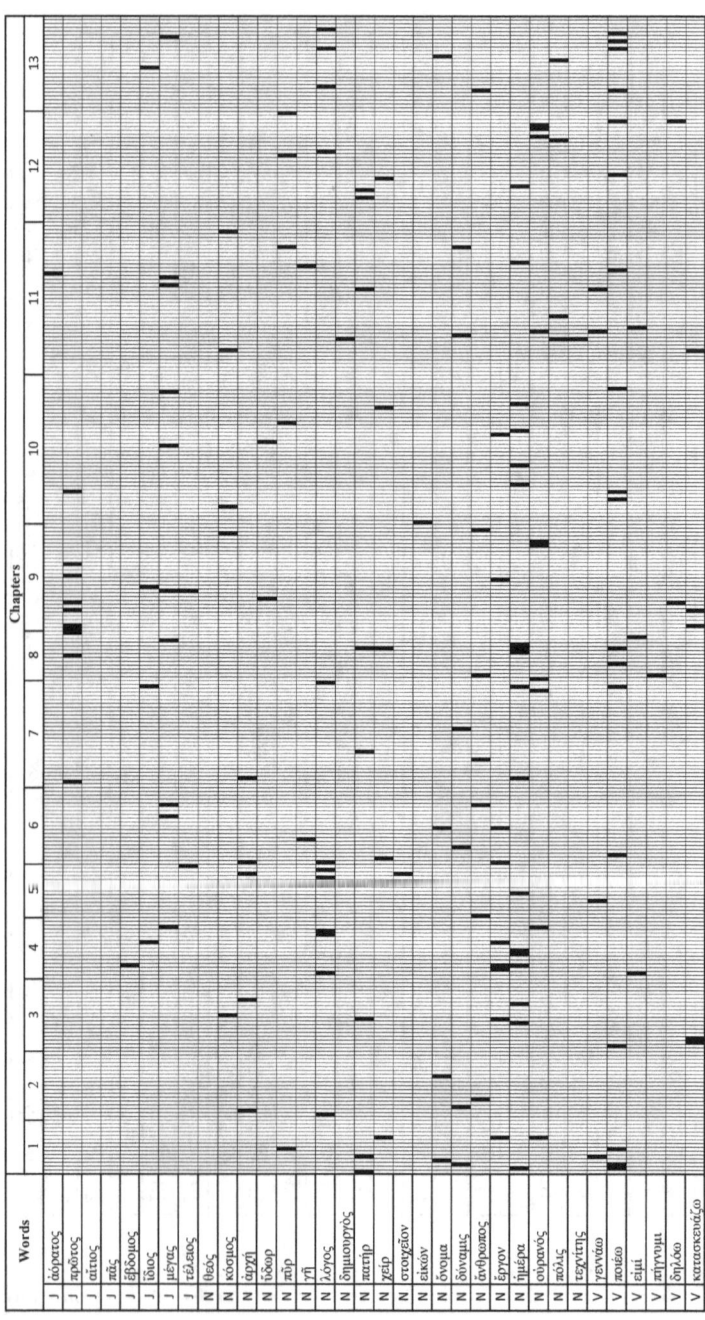

Figure 4.1 Keywords of first-century cosmogony present in Hebrews.

Pragmatic Evaluation of Hebrews' Text with Emphasis On Its Cosmogony

In order to identify all Hebrews' texts with cosmogonic insights, i.e., to establish all the texts that could be part of the literary component of Hebrews' cosmogony, a pragmatic evaluation[9] was done, since it includes some principle of inner texture analysis.[10] The focus was on the 130 verses in Hebrews that have some keyword of first-century cosmogony, as well as on verses where some allusion or echo of the cosmogonic topic may be found.[11] In order to do this evaluation, Hebrews was studied verse by verse in seven different versions in English and four versions in Spanish, along with the NA[28].[12] In this process it was found that Hebrews' verses can be classified in three levels on the basis of their pertinence to the cosmogony topic. Level 1: the word is not used in a context related to cosmogony; level 2: the word is used in a context indirectly related to cosmogony; and level 3: the word is used in a context which is directly related to cosmogony. The results of this analysis can be seen in Figure 4.2.

---

9. The pragmatic evaluation in context consists in the application of four strategies of reading adapted to our purpose. 1) Predicting: which consists of setting a purpose for the reading by a written document in which there must be some ideas or words that the reader expects to find in the document—in this case it was the conclusion of previous chapter; 2) making connections: which consists of connecting ideas in the text with the prior knowledge of the reader and also connecting ideas of some part of the text with some other part of the text; 3) summarizing: which consists of determining the main idea(s) of every verse, and 4) questioning: which consists of using some predetermined question(s) that must be asked during the process of reading every sentence.

10. Information about inner texture analysis can be found in footnotes 3 and 5 from current chapter.

11. The search for allusions and echoes forms part of cultural intertexture analysis which in turn forms part of the Socio-rhetorical criticism. Allusion is a statement that presupposes a tradition that exists in textual form, but the text being interpreted is not attempting to "recite" the text. Therefore, the general knowledge of first-century cosmogony of the researcher was used here, in order to find some arguments, ideas or phrases that could be selected. Echo is a word or phrase that evokes, or potentially evokes, a concept from cultural tradition, in this case from the cosmogony of the first century. More about allusion and echo can be found in, Robbins, *Exploring the Texture of Texts*, 58–60; deSilva, *Introduction to the New Testament*, 800–806; Roncace et al., "Dictionary of Socio-Rhetorical Terms."

12. The seven versions in English were NKJV, ESV, NASB95, NIV, CJB, LEB, HCSB, and the versions in Spanish were RV60, BTX, LBLA, and the NTV.

Number	Chapter	Verse	Level 1	Level 2	Level 3	Number	Chapter	Verse	Level 1	Level 2	Level 3	Number	Chapter	Verse	Level 1	Level 2	Level 3	Number	Chapter	Verse	Level 1	Level 2	Level 3
1	1	1	x			34	5	11	x			66	9	6	x			98	11	16	x		
2		2		x		35		12		x		67		8	x			99		23	x		
3		3	x			36		13	x			68		9		x		100		24	x		
4		4	x			37		14	x			69		11			x	101		26	x		
5		5	x			38	6	1	x			70		12	x			102		27		x	
6		7		x		39		2	x			71		14	x			103		28	x		
7		10			x	40		3		x		72		15	x			104		29	x		
8	2	2	x			41		5	x			73		18	x			105		30	x		
9		3	x			42		7		x		74		23	x			106		34	x		
10		4	x			43		10	x			75		24			x	107		38	x		
11		6		x		44		13	x			76		26			x	108		7	x		
12		12	x			45		16	x			77		27	x			109		9	x		
13	3	2	x			46	7	2	x			78	10	1	x			110		10	x		
14		3	x			47		3		x		79		5		x		111		12	x		
15		4			x	48		8	x			80		7	x			112		13	x		
16		8	x			49		10	x			81		9	x			113		18	x		
17		9	x			50		16	x			82		11	x			114	12	19	x		
18		10		x		51		26	x			83		16	x			115		22		x	
19		13	x			52		27	x			84		21		x		116		23	x		
20		14	x			53		28	x			85		22	x			117		25		x	
21	4	2	x			54	8	1		x		86		24	x			118		26		x	
22		3			x	55		2			x	87		25	x			119		27			x
23		4			x	56		5		x		88		27		x		120		29		x	
24		7	x			57		7	x			89		31	x			121	13	6	x		
25		8	x			58		8	x			90		32	x			122		7	x		
26		10			x	59		9	x			91		35	x			123		12	x		
27		12	x			60		10	x			92		36	x			124		14		x	
28		13		x		61		11	x			93		7	x			125		15	x		
29		14		x		62		12	x			94		10			x	126		17	x		
30	5	1	x			63		13	x			95	11	11	x			127		19	x		
31		5	x			64	9	1	x			96		12	x			128		20	x		
32		7	x			65		2	x			97		13	x			129		21	x		
33		9	x															130		22	x		

Figure 4.2 Classification of Hebrews' verses with presence of first-century cosmogony keywords.[13]

From Figure 4.2, it can be observed that there are ninety-four verses in level 1, twenty-four verses in level 2, and twelve verses in level 3. Therefore, according to this analysis, in order to find the cosmogonic presuppositions in Hebrews in its first-century philosophical context—the main aim of this research—the focus of this research must be on the verses that belong to level 3, which are 1:2, 10; 3:4; 4:3–4, 10; 8:2; 9:11, 24, 26; 11:10;

13. For the keywords referred to here, see Figure 4.1 and Table 4.1, since due to space it is impossible to put all the keywords present in all the verses of Hebrews.

Text-Linguistic Analysis in Hebrews' Cosmogony   81

12:27. The verses in level 2 will also be considered, but since the verses in this category are used in a context indirectly related to cosmogony, the focus will not be on theses verses.

Nevertheless, the pragmatic evaluation in context has revealed some other verses in Hebrews' text with cosmogonic insights, which do not contain any word(s) belonging to the main vocabulary of first-century cosmogony. Figure 4.3 shows what is being asserted here. So, as has already been asserted, all verses falling in levels 2 and 3 have one or more words that belong to the main vocabulary of first-century cosmogony, which are marked with (x) in Figure 4.3. But it is also very important to note that although some Hebrews' verses, marked with (■) in Figure 4.3, do not have any words belonging to the main vocabulary of first-century cosmogony, they still provide some perspectives on cosmogony.

Number	Chapter	Verse	Level 1	Level 2	Level 3	Number	Chapter	Verse	Level 1	Level 2	Level 3	Number	Chapter	Verse	Level 1	Level 2	Level 3	Number	Chapter	Verse	Level 1	Level 2	Level 3
1	1	1		x		18	3	6		■		34	6	8		■		50	11	37		■	
2		2			x	19		10	x			35		19		■		51		3			■
3		3		x		20		11				36	7	3		x		52		4			
4		6		■		21		12				37		1		x		53		5			
5		7		x		22		18		■		38	8	2			x	54		6			
6		8		■		23		3			x	39		4		■		55		10			x
7		9		■		24		4			x	40		5		x		56		16		x	
8		10			x	25	4	10			x	41		9		x		57		27		x	
9		11			■	26		13		x		42		11			x	58		40		■	
10		12			■	27		14		x		43	9	24			x	59		22		x	
11		5				28		16		■		44		26			x	60		25		x	
12		6		x		29		8		■		45		28		■		61	12	26		x	
13	2	7				30	5	10		■		46		5		x		62		27			x
14		8				31		12		x		47	10	21		x		63		28		■	
15		9				32	6	3		x		48		27		x		64		29		x	
16		10				33		7		x		49		34		■		65	13	8		■	
17	3	4			x													66		14		x	

Figure 4.3 Hebrews' texts with cosmogony perspectives.

Thus, in level 2, there are twenty-five more verses than those presented in Figure 4.2. And in level 3, which is the level of special consideration in this research, there are four verses more than those presented in Figure 4.2. Therefore, it can be stated that in Hebrews there are sixteen key-verses—i.e., level 3 verses—that play an important role in achieving the purpose of this research, i.e., tracing the document's cosmogonic presuppositions. However, there are also fifty other verses that can help one to understand the cosmogony of Hebrews better, along with the other 237 verses of Hebrews, i.e., the full book. Therefore, each of these sixteen key-verses must be studied in their context—the full document—and not as isolated verses.

Exclusion

In order to find the most prominent material which forms the core points around which a cosmogonic discourse of Hebrews can be presented, it is necessary to exclude some texts. The texts will be deleted in two stages, in their macro and microstructure, for two reasons: first, if the syntactic structure of Hebrews does not include the verse or verses as part of the key-verses of Hebrews' cosmogony; and second, if some part or parts of the syntactic structure of the key-verses has information that is semantically not pertinent to the cosmogony.

Exclusion in Macrostructures

In this first step, the evaluation of the syntactic structure of Hebrews, i.e., the evaluation of sentences and clauses, was made on the basis of previous works in this respect. Porter, O'Donnell, Reed, and Tan argued for the presence of 366 sentences—which they call primary sentences—in Hebrews,[14] while Lukaszewski, Dubis, and Blakley argued for the presence of 178 sentences.[15] Leedy, meanwhile, asserts that there are 181 sentences in Hebrews[16] and Andi and Tan believed that Hebrews is composed of 247 sentences.[17] The analysis of the sixteen key-verses inside of these four scholarly works shows some differences and similarities as can be seen in Figure 4.4.

As can be observed, Lukaszewski and Leedy consider that the sixteen key-verses are part of thirteen sentences which begin and end in the same place. But Porter and Andi show some significant differences. Due to the purpose of this section, it is only necessary to highlight here that from Figure 4.4 it can be asserted that some of the key-verses in Hebrews' cosmogony can be considered as full sentences while others are part of a

---

14. Porter et al., *Syntactically Analyzed Greek New Testament*. It is possible to find also this information in OpenText.org, under http://www.opentext.org/texts/NT/Heb.html.

15. Lukaszewski et al., *Lexham Syntactic Greek New Testament*.

16. Leedy, *New Testament Diagrams*.

17. Wu and Tan, *Cascadia Syntax Graphs*.

Text-Linguistic Analysis in Hebrews' Cosmogony 83

sentence. Therefore, it is possible to exclude all the texts in Hebrews that are not present in Figure 4.4, since only these verses can be considered as key-sections to the literary component of Hebrews' cosmogony. Thus, twelve key-sections remain: 1:1–4, 10–12; 2:10; 3:3–4; 4:3–5, 10; 8:1–2; 9:7b–12, 24–26; 11:3, 9–10; 12:27.

Chapter	Verse	Sentences				Chapter	Verse	Sentences			
		Porter	Lukaszewski	Leedy	Andi			Porter	Lukaszewski	Leedy	Andi
1	2	1:1-3	1:1-4	1:1-4	1:1-4	4	4	4:4a	4:4-5	4:4-5	4:4
								4:4b			
							10	4:10	4:10	4:10	4:10
	10	1:10a			1:10	8	2	8:2	8:1-2	8:1-2	8:1-2
		1:10b									
	11	1:11a			1:11a-b		11	9:7b-12			
		1:11b									
		1:11c	1:10-12	1:10-12		9			9:11-12	9:11-12	9:11
	12	1:12a			1:11c-12a-b		24	9:24a			9:24
		1:12b									
		1:12c			1:12c-d		(25)	9:24b-26a	9:24-26	9:24-26	9:25-26a
		1:12d					26	9:26b			9:26b
2	10	2:10	2:10	2:10	2:10	11	3	11:3	11:3	11:3	11:3
3	4	3:4a	3:3-4	3:3-4	3:3		10	11:10	11:9-10	11:9-10	11:10
		3:4b			3:4						
4	3	4:3	4:3	4:3	4:3	12	27	12:27	12:27	12:27	12:27

Figure 4.4 Key-verses within syntactic structure of Hebrews' cosmogony.

Exclusion in Microstructures

In order to be more precise in the selection of the literary component of Hebrews' cosmogony it is necessary to see the internal syntactic structure of these twelve key-sections, since the verses can carry more than one topic and not only the cosmogonic theme. Thus, from these twelve key-sections, some information which is semantically not pertinent to cosmogony will be deleted, but in order to achieve this purpose, first it is necessary to determine the beginning and ending of each sentence of the twelve key-sections. The reasons for the final establishment of the sentences inside which there are essential components of Hebrews' cosmogony will be provided later in this chapter and supplemented in the next chapter. However, the decision of where each sentence begins and ends is shown in Figure 4.5—i.e., column *B. Rojas* shows the decision of the author of this research—since it is fundamental to this research and to this section. Further, only the words that have a direct relation with cosmogony must be taken from each sentence.[18]

Chapter	Key-verse	Sentences			
		Porter	Lukaszewski & Leedy	Andi	B. Rojas
1	2	1:1-3	1:1-4	1:1-4	1:1-4
	10	1:10a 1:10b		1:10	
	11	1:11a 1:11b 1:11c	1:10-12	1:11a-b	1:10-12
	12	1:12a 1:12b 1:12c 1:12d		1:11c-12a-b 1:12c-d	
2	10	2:10	2:10	2:10	2:10
3	4	3:4a 3:4b	3:3-4	3:3 3:4	3:3 3:4
4	3	4:3	4:3	4:3	4:3
	4	4:4a 4:4b	4:4-5	4:4	4:3-5

Chapter	Key-verse	Sentences			
		Porter	Lukaszewski & Leedy	Andi	B. Rojas
4	10	4:10	4:10	4:10	4:10
8	2	8:2	8:1-2	8:1-2	8:1-2
9	11	9:7b-12	9:6-10 9:11-12	9:6-10 9:11	9:6-10 9:11-12
	24	9:24a		9:24	
	(25)	9:24b-26a	9:24-26	9:25-26a	9:24-26
	26	9:26b		9:26b	
11	3	11:3	11:3	11:3	11:3
	10	11:10	11:9-10	11:9 11:10	11:9 11:10
12	27	12:27	12:27	12:27	12:25-27

Figure 4.5 Key-sentences with literary component of Hebrews' cosmogony.

In order to extract the relevant words the following process will be followed:

1. The subject, verb, and its complement will be taken from the primary clause (PC)[19] of the sentence.

---

18. Here a sentence is considered as the text found between two major marks—they can be rhetorical marks or punctuation marks in modern Greek texts of the New Testament—that is a single unit of language that contains a single proposition, assertion, negation, query or suggestion. The sentence can also be one primary clause but usually it is composed of more than one clause, i.e., it can be divided into multiple independent clauses which are joined by conjunctions or by asyndeton. More information can be found in Wallace, *Greek Grammar Beyond the Basics*; Porter, *Idioms of the Greek New Testament*; Robertson, *Grammar of the Greek New Testament*.

19. Primary clause—PC will be the abbreviation for primary clause in this document—is an independent clause which has a subject, verb, and complement, and sometimes some of its parts can be presented in a tacit way. Also, it must be noted that I consider that only one primary clause can be found in one sentence, as well as that the finite verb—mainly the indicative—is usually present in the primary clause. More information can be found in, Wallace, *Greek Grammar Beyond the Basics*; Porter,

2. If there are secondary clauses (SC)[20] in the sentence, the subject, verb, and its complement, if pertinent to cosmogony, will be taken.

3. If there are adjuncts (AJ)[21] in the sentence—either in primary, secondary, or embedded clauses—those that are pertinent to cosmogony will be taken.

4. If there are embedded clauses (EC)[22] in the sentence—either in clauses or adjuncts—the subject, verb, and complement, if pertinent to cosmogony, will be taken.

5. If there are words, phrases, or clauses in apposition, they will be considered as part of the literary component of Hebrews' cosmogony only if they are extremely relevant.

6. From all the supplements (SP),[23] only those extremely pertinent to the cosmogony topic will be considered.

Idioms of the Greek New Testament; Robertson, *Grammar of the Greek New Testament*.

20. Porter asserts that the secondary clause—SC will be the abbreviation for secondary clause in this document—"is a clause that depends on another clause, and this dependency is usually indicated by the presence of certain particles or conjunctions which are traditionally referred to as subordinating particles. Common secondary clauses are relative clauses and clauses beginning with words such as ὡς, καθώς and ὅτε, ὅταν. Non-embedded participle and infinitive clauses are also classified as secondary clauses." Porter et al., *Syntactically Analyzed Greek New Testament*.

21. According to Porter, the adjunct—AJ will be the abbreviation for adjunct in this document—"is a word group or the word groups that modify the predicator—verb—providing an indication of the circumstances associated with the process that carries on the verb." Porter et al., *Opentext.Org: Glossary*.

22. According to Porter, an embedded clause—EC will be the abbreviation for embedded clause in this document—is a clause that occurs inside a component—subject, predicator, complement, adjunct—of another clause. "Frequently the predicator of embedded clauses are non-finite (i.e. participal and infinitive clauses), but finite clauses can also be embedded." Porter et al., *Opentext.Org: Glossary*.

23. Supplement—SP will be the abbreviation for supplement in this document—referenced by only numbers in the diagrams, is the name that is given in this document to any word, phrase, or sentence that is adding some meaning to the subject, complement, or adjunct—never directly to the verb—of one sentence. This group of words are usually referred to as qualifiers, identifiers, modifiers, determiners, specifiers, etc., in biblical Greek grammars. See for instance Robertson, *A Grammar of the Greek New Testament*; Wallace, *Greek Grammar Beyond the Basics*; Porter, *Idioms of the Greek New Testament*.

Key-Section 1: Hebrews 1:1–4

As can be seen in Figure 5.1—for all the key-sections [1–12], the figures can be seen in the section entitled "Grammatical Analysis"—this key-section is only one sentence long. For the purpose of this section, it is enough to state that only the SC2 has information pertinent to cosmogony, while the other parts of this sentence are more relevant to topics such as Christology, theology, soteriology, etc. Therefore, in the first key-section of Hebrews' cosmogony, the PC—ὁ θεὸς ἐλάλησεν ἡμῖν ἐν υἱῷ—and the SC2—δι' οὗ καὶ ἐποίησεν τοὺς αἰῶνας—will be considered in order to determine the more specific literary component of Hebrews' cosmogony.

Key-Section 2: Hebrews 1:10–12

As can be seen in Figure 5.3, this key-section is only one sentence with six ECs. Here it is only necessary to assert that the EC3 and the EC6 do not have essential content on cosmogony. Therefore, these two clauses will not be considered in determining the more specific literary component of Hebrews' cosmogony. They will not be discussed, since they are more closely related to Christology than cosmogony. However, the EC1—σὺ κατ' ἀρχάς κύριε, τὴν γῆν ἐθεμελίωσας καὶ ἔργα τῶν χειρῶν σού εἰσιν οἱ οὐρανοί—and the EC2—αὐτοὶ ἀπολοῦνται—and the EC4—καὶ πάντες ὡς ἱμάτιον παλαιωθήσονται καὶ ὡσεὶ περιβόλαιον ἑλίξεις αὐτούς—as well as the EC5—ὡς ἱμάτιον[24] καὶ ἀλλαγήσονται—will be considered in order to determine the more specific literary component of Hebrews' cosmogony.

Key-Section 3: Hebrews 2:10

As can be seen in Figure 5.4, this key-section is only one sentence. The complex subject constituted by the EC1 shows content that is more closely related with topics such as Christology or soteriology, and consequently they will not be considered in determining the more specific literary component of Hebrews' cosmogony. Therefore, only the verb—ἔπρεπεν—the

---

24. But as can be seen in Figure 5.3, the words ὡς ἱμάτιον are not present in the EC5. This phenomenon happens due the conclusion of the linguistic analysis of Hebrews' cosmogony—see section "Textual Dependence of Hebrews' Cosmogony" in chapter 4—namely the evaluation to the textual witnesses of 1:10–12 can permit to do that.

complement—αὐτῷ—and the SP1—δι' ὃν τὰ πάντα καὶ δι' οὗ τὰ πάντα—will be considered.

Key-Section 4: Hebrews 3:3–4

As can be observed in Figure 5.5, this key-section has two sentences. In sentence 1, the PC as well as its AJ and its EC1 and EC2 has no content that is essential to cosmogony, and consequently they will not be considered in determining the more specific literary structure of Hebrews' cosmogony. However, in sentence 2, the PC—πᾶς οἶκος κατασκευάζεται—and the SC1—θεός—which has as its complement the EC1—ὁ πάντα κατασκευάσας—have relevant information about cosmogony, and therefore they will be considered in determining the more specific literary component of Hebrews' cosmogony.

Key-Section 5: Hebrews 4:3–5

As can be seen in Figure 5.6, this key-section is one complex sentence, and in it the AJ2—καίτοι τῶν ἔργων ἀπὸ καταβολῆς κόσμου γενηθέντων—which belongs to the PC—εἰσερχόμεθα—and the SC2—εἴρηκεν—the EC6—κατέπαυσεν ὁ θεὸς—and the AJ7—ἐν τῇ ἡμέρᾳ τῇ ἑβδόμῃ—and the AJ8—ἀπὸ πάντων τῶν ἔργων αὐτοῦ—have content that could be essential to cosmogony. Therefore, only the words in these phrases will be considered in order to determine the more specific literary component of Hebrews' cosmogony.

Key-Section 6: Hebrews 4:10

As can be observed in Figure 5.7, this key-section is one sentence, and in it only the SC1—ὁ θεός—which naturally belongs to the PC—αὐτὸς κατέπαυσεν—and its AJ, namely the AJ3—ἀπὸ τῶν ἰδίων—have content that could be pertinent to cosmogony. Therefore, only these phrases will be considered in determining the more specific literary component of Hebrews' cosmogony.

Key-Section 7: Hebrews 8:1–2

As can be seen in Figure 5.8, this key-section is one sentence. The PC—κεφάλαιον—which is a nonverbal clause, has as its indirect object the EC1—ἔχομεν ἀρχιερέα—which is constituted by two SCs and one AJ. Among them, only the SC2—τῶν ἁγίων λειτουργὸς καὶ τῆς σκηνῆς τῆς ἀληθινῆς, ἣν ἔπηξεν ὁ κύριος, οὐκ ἄνθρωπος—is pertinent to the cosmogonic topic. Therefore, only these phrases will be considered in order to find the literary component of Hebrews' cosmogony.

Key-Section 8: Hebrews 9:6–12

As can be noted, in this key-section there are two sentences. The first sentence has no content that is essential to cosmogony, consequently it will not be considered as part of the literary component of Hebrews' cosmogony. As can be seen in Figure 5.9, the second sentence of this key-section is a complex sentence and inside of its PC—Χριστὸς εἰσῆλθεν—the AJ1—διὰ τῆς μείζονος καὶ τελειοτέρας σκηνῆς οὐ χειροποιήτου, τοῦτ' ἔστιν οὐ ταύτης τῆς κτίσεως—is relevant to the cosmogonic topic. Therefore, only these phrases will be considered in determining the more specific literary component of Hebrews' cosmogony.

Key-Section 9: Hebrews 9:24–26

As can be observed in Figure 5.10, this key-section has only one complex sentence. The PC—εἰσῆλθεν Χριστός—has three complex AJs, but only the AJ1—οὐ εἰς χειροποίητα ἅγια ἀντίτυπα τῶν ἀληθινῶν ἀλλ' εἰς αὐτὸν τὸν οὐρανόν—and the AJ3—οὐδ' ἵνα πολλάκις προσφέρῃ ἑαυτόν ὥσπερ ὁ ἀρχιερεὺς εἰσέρχεται εἰς τὰ ἅγια κατ' ἐνιαυτὸν ἐν αἵματι ἀλλοτρίῳ ἐπεὶ ἔδει αὐτὸν πολλάκις παθεῖν ἀπὸ καταβολῆς κόσμου—are pertinent to the cosmogonic topic. Therefore, only these phrases will be considered in determining the more specific literary component of Hebrews' cosmogony.

Key-Section 10: Hebrews 11:3

As can be seen in Figure 5.11, this key-section is one sentence. In this case, the whole sentence, i.e., the entire verse—πίστει νοοῦμεν κατηρτίσθαι τοὺς αἰῶνας ῥήματι θεοῦ, εἰς τὸ μὴ ἐκ φαινομένων τὸ βλεπόμενον γεγονέναι—which, incidentally, is a special key-verse on Hebrews' cosmogony, will be considered in determining the more specific literary component of Hebrews' cosmogony.

Key-Section 11: Hebrews 11:9–10

As can be observed in Figure 5.12, this key-section has two sentences. Sentence 1 has no content that is essential to cosmogony, and consequently it will not be considered as part of the literary component of Hebrews' cosmogony. However, sentence 2—ἐξεδέχετο γὰρ τὴν τοὺς θεμελίους ἔχουσαν πόλιν ἧς τεχνίτης καὶ δημιουργὸς ὁ θεός—has relevant information about cosmogony, and therefore, it will be considered in determining the more specific literary component of Hebrews' cosmogony.

Key-Section 12: Hebrews 12:25–27

As can be seen in Figure 5.13, this key-section is only one complex sentence. But in the PC—βλέπετε—only the SC2—τὸ δὲ ἔτι ἅπαξ δηλοῖ τὴν τῶν σαλευομένων μετάθεσιν ὡς πεποιημένων ἵνα μείνῃ τὰ μὴ σαλευόμενα—has some information about cosmogony. Therefore, only these two clauses will be considered in determining the more specific literary component of Hebrews' cosmogony, while the other elements will not be considered for this purpose.

Simplification

In order to determine the more specific literary component of Hebrews' cosmogony, i.e., to find the keywords or the main vocabulary and sentences about cosmogony in Hebrews, it is further necessary to simplify all the information already established in the previous steps, for greater clarity and conciseness.

Methodology of Simplification

There are some principles that will be used in order to simplify the Hebrews' text that has been selected in order to determine the more specific literary component of Hebrews' cosmogony. The application of these principles can be seen in Figure 4.6. As can be seen in Image-1 inside Figure 4.6, there are some elements in the PC as well as in the SC2 that are obscuring the cosmogonic component of this text, while in Image-2 inside Figure 4.6, the cosmogonic component of the text is showing with absolute clarity and simplicity. In order to produce this simplification, principles congruent with the morphology and syntax of Koine Greek were applied.

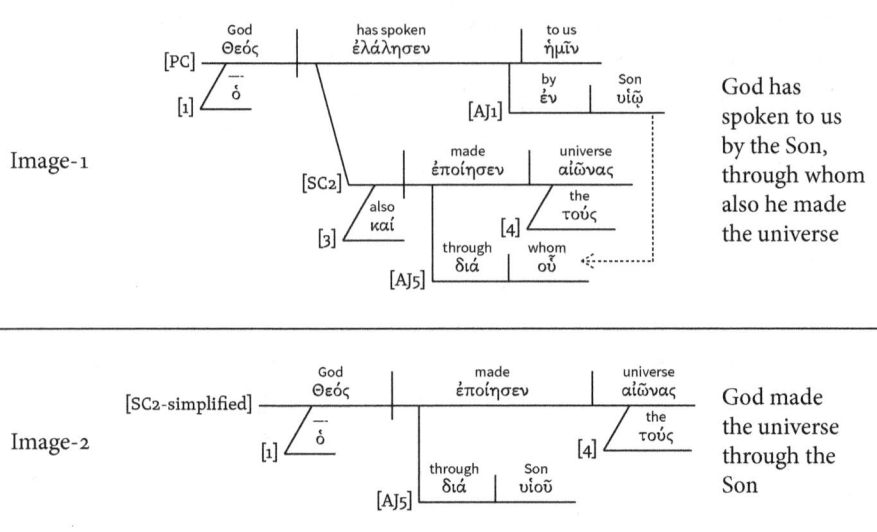

Figure 4.6 Simplification of Hebrews 1:1–4.

These principles will be explained using key-section 1 (cf. 1:1–4) as an example. As can be seen in Figure 5.1, this section is only one sentence, and as already stated only the PC—ὁ θεὸς ἐλάλησεν ἡμῖν ἐν υἱῷ—and the SC2—δι' οὗ καὶ ἐποίησεν τοὺς αἰῶνας—have been considered in determining the more specific literary component of Hebrews' cosmogony.

As can be observed, the PC ὁ θεὸς ἐλάλησεν ἡμῖν ἐν υἱῷ (God has spoken to us by the Son) is not pertinent to the cosmogonic topic, but it was considered in the previous step since the SC2 δι' οὗ καὶ ἐποίησεν τοὺς αἰῶνας (also he made the universe through whom) needs the PC in order to be completely understandable. Therefore, since only the PC was considered for its contribution to some parts of the clause—i.e., SC2—that are directly related to cosmogony, these two clauses will be simplified by replacing some parts in the SC2 and deleting the unnecessary parts. Thus for instance, in this illustration, the PC contributes with the subject—ὁ θεός—and with the object of the AJ1—υἱῷ—to the SC2. Therefore, in the first place, the subject of the PC has been placed in the place of the subject of the SC2, an action that is grammatically and syntactically correct. When this happens, the adverb καί loses its function, since it is there in order to communicate that ὁ θεός is the subject of this sentence, therefore it must be deleted. In the second place, the pronoun οὗ in the AJ5 which belongs to the SC2 must be replaced with the noun υἱῷ, since it is making reference to this noun. But even though the exchange will be done between the prepositional objects of the AJ1 and AJ5, it is necessary to change the case of the noun υἱός from the dative to genitive—i.e., from υἱῷ to υἱοῦ—since the pronoun οὗ is in the genitive case. After this process, which allows simplification without loss of essential ideas and words it is possible to have the SC2 simplified, which can be seen in Image-2 inside Figure 4.6.

This process, which allows the simplification of some text which does not need to be considered as the literary component of Hebrews' cosmogony, is based in grammatical and syntactical principles, and maintains the structure of the text but does not allow for changing the main ideas of the text. And it is indispensable for the purpose of this research, since one of the main principles on which the conclusions of this research will be developed is "comparison." In further chapters the main vocabulary of first-century cosmogony will be compared with the main vocabulary used in Hebrews in order to address its cosmogony.

Simplification of the 12 Key-Sections

After having applied the above-mentioned process of simplification to all twelve key-sections of Hebrews' cosmogony, main sentences, words, and phrases have been identified which must be considered as the literary component of Hebrews' cosmogony. The summary shows the more relevant words in Hebrews' cosmogony as well as the words that Hebrews shares with the literary frameworks—i.e., main vocabulary—of first-century cosmogonies. The result of this process of simplification can be seen in Table 4.2, where the first column enumerates the key-sentence (KS), the second and third show a current Greek and English text, and the last shows the biblical verses from which the clause was developed.

KS	Text simplified based in NA²⁸	Translation based in ESV	Texts
1	ὁ θεὸς δι' υἱοῦ ἐποίησεν τοὺς αἰῶνας.	God through His Son created the world.	1:1–2
2	σὺ κατ' ἀρχάς κύριε τὴν γῆν ἐθεμελίωσας καὶ ἔργα τῶν χειρῶν σού εἰσιν οἱ οὐρανοί αὐτοὶ ἀπολοῦνται καὶ πάντες ὡς ἱμάτιον παλαιωθήσονται καὶ ὡσεὶ περιβόλαιον ἑλίξεις αὐτούς καὶ ἀλλαγήσονται.	You, Lord, laid the foundation of the earth in the beginning, and the heavens are the work of your hands; they will perish, they will all wear out like a garment, like a robe you will roll them up, they will be changed.	1:10–12
3	Ἔπρεπεν αὐτῷ δι' ὃν τὰ πάντα καὶ δι' οὗ τὰ πάντα.	It was fitting for whom and by whom all things exist.	2:10
4	ὁ πάντα κατασκευάσας θεός.	The builder of all things is God.	3:4
5	καίτοι τῶν ἔργων ἀπὸ καταβολῆς κόσμου γενηθέντων κατέπαυσεν ὁ θεὸς ἐν τῇ ἡμέρᾳ τῇ ἑβδόμῃ ἀπὸ πάντων τῶν ἔργων αὐτοῦ.	Although his works were finished from the foundation of the world, God rested on the seventh day from all his works.	4:3–5
6	κατέπαυσεν ἀπὸ τῶν ἔργων ὁ θεός	God has rested from his works.	4:10
7	ἔχομεν τῶν ἁγίων λειτουργὸς καὶ τῆς σκηνῆς τῆς ἀληθινῆς ἣν ἔπηξεν ὁ κύριος οὐκ ἄνθρωπος.	We have a minister in the holy places in the true tent that the Lord set up, not man.	8:1–2
8	Χριστὸς διὰ τῆς μείζονος καὶ τελειοτέρας σκηνῆς οὐ χειροποιήτου, τοῦτ' ἔστιν οὐ ταύτης τῆς κτίσεως εἰσῆλθεν.	Christ entered through the greater and more perfect tent not made with hands, that is, not of this creation.	9:11
9	οὐ εἰς χειροποίητα εἰσῆλθεν ἅγια Χριστός ἀντίτυπα τῶν ἀληθινῶν, ἀλλ' εἰς αὐτὸν τὸν οὐρανόν οὐδ' ἵνα πολλάκις προσφέρῃ ἑαυτόν ἐπεὶ ἔδει αὐτὸν πολλάκις παθεῖν ἀπὸ καταβολῆς κόσμου.	Christ has entered, not into holy places made with hands, which are copies of the true things, but into heaven itself. Nor to offer himself repeatedly, for then He would have had to suffer repeatedly since the foundation of the world.	9:24–26

KS	Text simplified based in NA[28]	Translation based in ESV	Texts
10	Πίστει νοοῦμεν κατηρτίσθαι τοὺς αἰῶνας ῥήματι θεοῦ εἰς τὸ μὴ ἐκ φαινομένων τὸ βλεπόμενον γεγονέναι.	By faith we understand that the universe was created by the word of God, so that what is seen was not made out of things that are visible.	11:3
11	ἐξεδέχετο τὴν πόλιν ἧς τεχνίτης καὶ δημιουργὸς ὁ θεός.	He was looking forward to the city, whose designer and builder is God.	11:10
12	τὸ ἔτι ἅπαξ δηλοῖ τὴν τῶν σαλευομένων μετάθεσιν ὡς πεποιημένων ἵνα μείνῃ τὰ μὴ σαλευόμενα.	This phrase, "Yet once more," indicates the removal of things that are shaken—that is, things that have been made—in order that the things that cannot be shaken may remain.	12:25–27

Table 4.2 Key-sentence or literary component of Hebrews' cosmogony.

Thus, it can be asserted that the basic literary component of Hebrews' cosmogony is constituted by 174 words, which form twelve clauses.

Organization

The twelve clauses that constitute the basic literary component of Hebrews' cosmogony are, in turn, constituted by words, and these words can be organized by their morphology, grammatical function, accidence, semantic, or some other feature. Since this research will compare Hebrews' cosmogony with first-century cosmogonies—and in so doing will also compare their main vocabularies—it is more useful for this purpose to organize these words by their morphology.

Although there are eleven categories[25] in biblical Greek morphology, the 174 words in the literary component of Hebrews' cosmogony can be organized into nine morphological categories only. Among them, the article is the most used morphological form, even though by its grammatical function it can also function as a pronoun.[26] The organization

25. Adverbs, conjunctions, articles, interjections, adjectives, nouns, prepositions, pronouns, particles, verbs, and indeclinable words.

26. Mounce for instance affirms that the article in Greek is much more than just

of the 174 words by their morphology can be seen in Table 4.3, which shows the 174 words which represent eighty-six lemmas, organized into nine morphological categories—among them, three are most significant to the purposes of this research, namely, the nouns, verbs, and adjectives.

The nouns and pronouns show the main entities that are present in the cosmogony of Hebrews, the verbs and adverbs show the main actions, and the adjectives show the main features. Therefore, understanding these words, and how they function inside of Hebrews, is indispensable in order to understand the cosmogony of Hebrews. In addition, understanding how these words are used in first-century philosophies is important for the purpose of this research, and this will be done in further chapters.

Structural Analysis in Hebrews' Cosmogony

Understanding the structure of the document under scrutiny is crucial to a right understanding of its message, but in the case of Hebrews, it seems impossible to reach agreement on this issue.[27] However, since the structural analysis[28] aims to expose the overall pattern by which any writer will develop its ideas, with main and supporting arguments in a series of connected thoughts,[29] four different attempts at outlining the structure

---

the word "the," that "it can perform as a demonstrative ("that"), a relative ("who"), or even a personal pronoun ("he," "one")," i.e., even though the article is not a true pronoun in Koine Greek it can function semantically in the place of a pronoun. See Mounce, *Basics of Biblical Greek*, 87.

27. A very illustrative research about the problem on the structure of Hebrews during history can be found in Guthrie, *Structure of Hebrews*, 3–41.

28. It is important to highlight the structural analysis based on the linguistic theories of A. J. Greimas, Ferdinand de Saussure, and others, which try to discern the "deep structures" that underlie the biblical passage. As Gugliotto affirms, "Frequently these deep structures will reveal ideas that are polar opposites which are then mediated by a third idea. The assumption is that the larger act of verbal communication has a grammar to it just as do the sentences and paragraphs that constitute a literary work." Gugliotto, *Handbook for Bible Study*, 33. Therefore, in this research structural analysis must be understood as the syntactical structure of written works, namely, how words function in phrases, how phrases function in sentences, how sentences function in paragraphs, etc. But some of this work will be incorporated in this research, in an attempt towards better interpretation of the text.

29. Gugliiotto states that the analysis of the structure of some documents must be done "without disturbing the original context or stripping the writer's original intent from a single word." Gugliotto, *Handbook for Bible Study*, 33.

of Hebrews are shown in Figure 4.7. Figure 4.7 also serves as a kind of illustration that allows the realization of how difficult it is to construct a comprehensible structure of Hebrews.

Nouns		
1	θεός	6
2	ἔργον	3
3	αἰών	2
4	ἱμάτιον	2
5	καταβολή	2
6	κόσμος	2
7	κύριος	2
8	οὐρανός	2
9	σκηνή	2
10	Χριστός	2
11	ἄνθρωπος	1
12	ἀρχή	1
13	γῆ	1
14	δημιουργός	1
15	ἡμέρα	1
16	λειτουργός	1
17	κτίσις	1
18	μετάθεσις	1
19	περιβόλαιον	1
20	πίστις	1
21	πόλις	1
22	ῥῆμα	1
23	τεχνίτης	1
24	χείρ	1
	TOTAL:	39

Verbs		
1	γίνομαι	2
2	εἰμί	2
3	ποιέω	2
4	σαλεύω	2
5	εἰσέρχομαι	2
6	καταπαύω	2
7	ἀλλάσσω	1
8	ἀπόλλυμι	1
9	βλέπω	1
10	δηλόω	1
11	ἐκδέχομαι	1
12	ἑλίσσω	1
13	θεμελιόω	1
14	καταρτίζω	1
15	κατασκευάζω	1
16	πάσχω	1
17	ἔχω	1
18	προσφέρω	1
19	δεῖ	1
20	μένω	1
21	νοέω	1
22	παλαιόω	1
23	πήγνυμι	1
24	φαίνω	1
25	πρέπω	1
	TOTAL:	31

Adjectives		
1	πᾶς	5
2	χειροποίητος	2
3	ἅγιος	2
4	ἀληθινός	2
5	ἀντίτυπος	1
6	ἕβδομος	1
7	ἴδιος	1
8	μέγας	1
9	τέλειος	1
	TOTAL:	16

Adverbs		
1	οὐ	3
2	μή	2
3	πολλάκις	2
4	ἅπαξ	1
5	καί	1
6	ἔτι	1
	TOTAL:	10

Conjunctions		
1	καί	7
2	ὡς	2
3	ἵνα	2
4	ἀλλά	1
5	καίτοι	1
6	ἐπεί	1
7	οὐ	1
8	ὡσεί	1
	TOTAL:	16

Pronouns		
1	αὐτός	6
2	ὅς	5
3	οὗτος	2
4	σύ	2
5	ἑαυτοῦ	1
	TOTAL:	16

Prepositions		
1	ἀπό	4
2	διά	4
3	εἰς	3
4	ἐκ	1
5	ἐν	1
6	κατά	1
7	ὡς	1
	TOTAL:	15

Article		
1	ὁ	30

Particle		
1	οὐδέ	1

CATEGORIES:	9
LEMMAS:	86
WORDS:	174

Table 4.3 Morphological organization of the literary component of Hebrews' cosmogony.

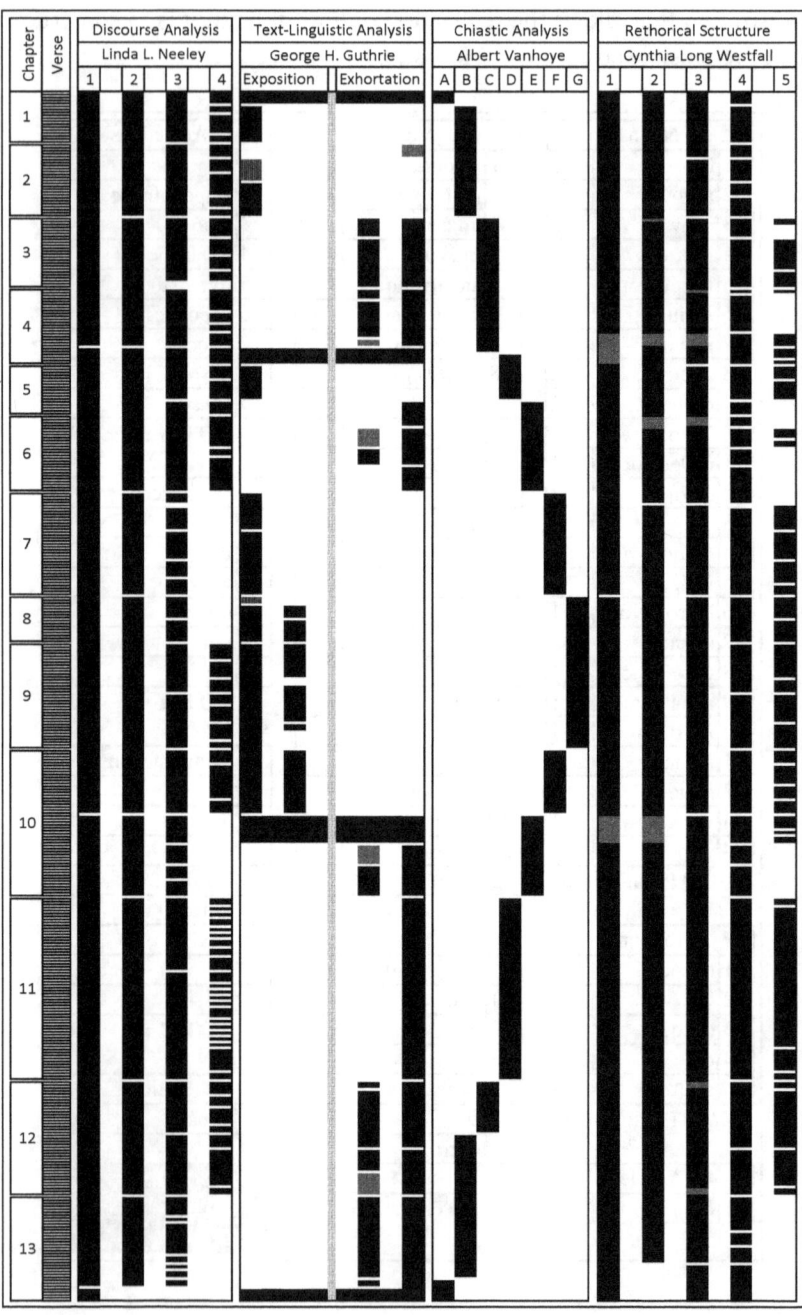

Figure 4.7 Different structure proposals for Hebrews.

Since the purpose of this research is not to determine the structure of Hebrews, these different structures will only be used here as attempts to illustrate a better understanding of Hebrews' texts. However, it is important to note that all of these different structures, used without trying to dogmatize any of them—i.e., representing one of them as an undeniable truth—could bring a better understanding of Hebrews' text.[30]

From Figure 4.7, important conclusions can be inferred. First: verses 1:1–4 function as an introductory part, with verses 1:5—4:14 being the first important section, and verses 4:16—10:18 the second important section, and from 10:19 the third major section begins. However, there is no agreement regarding the conclusion, since for Neeley it is constituted by the verses 13:20–21 and the last four verses he considers as *finis*, and for Guthrie it is constituted by verses 13:22–25, while for Vanhoye verses 13:20–25, and for Westfall verses 13:17–25, constitute the conclusion. Regarding the third section, variations also exist.[31]

Second: Some order and clarity can be observed in two of them—Neeley and Vanhoye—while there is a sort of confusion and complication in the other two—Guthrie and Westfall. Since this issue is pertinent and will be useful and helpful in the interpretation of Hebrews, the proposals

---

30. As Bateman rightly notes, every kind of approach on the structure of Hebrews has its pros and cons, thus for instance the thematic arrangement describes and explains the content of Hebrews divided into blocks based upon its major themes but it ignores repetitions, significant literary shifts, and thus it does little to reveal the author's flow of thought. On the other hand, the rhetorical arrangement gives attention to the literary devices in Hebrews, is sensitive to its oral features and it is consistent with the strongly pastoral character of Hebrews—if this is true, thus it highlights the flow of thought from one section to another. However, the rhetorical arrangement is not easy to categorize into any form of ancient Greek rhetorical speech, it does not provide an easy way in order to follow the thought of the author and it seems that the author used one kind of complex structure in order to conceal something in its document. The same problem can be mentioned about the text-linguistic literary arrangement, but it incorporates the best features of rhetorical and chiastic arrangements, emphasizes its parts, and draws attention to the literary and thematic relationship between paragraphs. Finally, chiastic literary arrangement is useful since it identifies aspects of style, genre shifts, repetition and vocabulary, and is more concerned with the interpretation of the text and less concerned with Greek rhetorical developments. Nevertheless, it ignores the linear manner in which Hebrews' author moves from the beginning to the end, and it misses some of the intertwining and the repetition of themes prominent throughout Hebrews. See more about it in Bateman, *Charts on the Book of Hebrews*, 51–52.

31. The documents consulted to do this evaluation as well as to develop Figure 4.7, are the following: Neeley, "Discourse Analysis of Hebrews"; Westfall, *Discourse Analysis*; Guthrie, *Structure of Hebrews*; Vanhoye, *Structure and Message*.

of Guthrie and Westfall will be shown here in more detail,[32] because, as will be seen, the twelve key-sentences of the literary component of Hebrews' cosmogony are placed in some very specific locations according to these two different structures.

Cosmogony in Guthrie's Structure

In the structure elaborated by Guthrie, some of the twelve key-sentences of the literary component of Hebrews' cosmogony have some specific placements. Key-sentence 1 (1:2) is part of the general introduction, which has a "majestic style and high concentration of programmatic topics, which the author will elaborate throughout the book,"[33] and it is entitled "God has spoken to us in his Son." Key-sentence 2 (1:10–12) and key-sentence 3 (2:10) are part of the exposition section entitled by Guthrie "The Position of the Son in Relation to the Angels" which is divided into two parts. In the first part—The Son Superior to the Angels—key-sentence 2 is part of a subtopic called "The Eternity of the Son's Reign and Relationship to the Cosmos" (1:8–12). In the second part—The Son Lower Than the Angels to Suffer for the "Sons"—key-sentence 3 alone forms the subsection entitled "The Appropriateness of the Son's Suffering (2:10)."

Key-sentence 4 (3:4) is part of the first section of exhortation, which Guthrie divided into three subsections. Key-sentence 4 is placed in the first subsection, entitled "Jesus, the Supreme Example of a Faithful Son" (3:1–6), and according to Guthrie, the prominent theme in this unit is the faithfulness of Jesus.[34] Key-sentence 5 (4:3–5) also forms part of this first section of exhortation, and it is found in the subsection entitled "The Promise of Rest for Those Who Are Faithful" (4:3–11), where key-sentence 6 (4:10) is also found. However, key-sentence 5 is specifically located in the subtopic entitled "Identification of the 'Rest'" (4:3–5),[35] while key-sentence 6 is found in the subtopic entitled "The Promise of Rest Still Stands" (4:6–11).

---

32. Even though the proposals of Neeley and Vanhoye will not be analyzed here in more detail, it does not mean that it will not be taken into account in further chapters; in fact, these two are more useful and more understandable, and therefore they will be used more in further chapters.
33. Guthrie, *Structure of Hebrews*, 119.
34. Guthrie, *Structure of Hebrews*, 128.
35. Guthrie, *Hebrews*, 151.

One of the key parts according to Guthrie is key-sentence 7 (8:1–2) of the literary component of Hebrews' cosmogony. In Guthrie's structure, this key-sentence functions as the intermediary transition between 5:1—7:28 "The Appointment of the Son as High Priest" and 8:3—10:18 "The Better Heavenly offering in the True Tabernacle," which are the two main subsections of the second exposition section (4:14—10:25). This key-sentence, according to Guthrie, makes an effective transition between the Son's appointment and the later "discourse on the heavenly high priest's superior service."[36]

"Key-sentence 8 (9:11–12) and key-sentence 9 (9:24–26) are part of the section of exposition entitled by Guthrie, "The Superior Offering of the Appointed High Priest" (8:3—10:18), and in the subsection "The Superiority of the New Covenant Offering" (9:1—10:18). Key-sentence 8 functions as a general introduction for three subtopics, "The superior blood of Christ" (9:13–22), "The heavenly tabernacle or a sacrifice in heaven" (9:23–24), and "The once for all offering" (9:25–28), while key-sentence 9, it is noted, is found in the last two subtopics.

Key-sentence 10 (11:3) and key-sentence 11 (11:10) are part of the section of exhortation entitled "The Positive Example of the Old Testament Faithful" (11:1–40). Key-sentence 10 is part of the "overture" (11:1–3) of this section of exhortation, while key-sentence 11 is part of the subtopic entitled "first examples of faith" (11:4–12).

Key-sentence 12 (12:25–27) is part of the resultant section of warning entitled "Do Not Reject God's Word!" (12:25–29), which is the fifth and final warning of the book, where the writer "uses an *a fortiori* argument, i.e., if those who rejected the voice from the mount Sinai did not escape, then those who turn away from the heavenly warning certainly will not escape."[37]

Cosmogony in Westfall's Structure

The first six key-sentences of the literary component of Hebrews' cosmogony, according to Westfall, belongs to the first part of the book entitled by her as "Jesus: the apostle of our confession" (1:1—4:16). In this section, key-sentence 1 (1:2) is found in the subsection "Let's Pay Attention to the Message of God's Ultimate Messenger" (1:1—2:4), and

36. Guthrie, *Hebrews*, 279.
37. Guthrie, *Structure of Hebrews*, 133.

more specifically it forms part of the subtopic entitled "God Has Spoken through His Son" (1:1–4), while key-sentence 2 (1:10–12) is found in the subtopic entitled "How God Speaks to the Son Compared to How He Speaks to Angels" (1:5–14).

Key-sentence 3 (2:10) is found in the subsection entitled "Jesus is a merciful and faithful high priest" (2:5–18), a passage that according to Westfall provides the basis for "Jesus' identification as high priest, and the exhortation to consider him as the high priest of our confession."[38] More specifically, it forms part of the subtopic entitled "Jesus Belongs to the Same Family as Believers" (2:10–13), where Jesus is fully identified with believers.

Key-sentence 4 (3:4) and key-sentence 5 (4:3–5) are found in the third subsection—of the first part of the book—entitled "Let's respond to Jesus' voice today and enter the rest" (3:1—4:13). According to Westfall, 3:1 functions as a summary and discourse orientation—transition—between the first and second subsections and the third subsection.[39] Key-sentence 4, however, is found in the subsection entitled "Unlike the Israelites, let's respond to his voice and enter the rest" (3:1—4:1), and more specifically in the subtopic, "We are Jesus' house, like the Israelites were Moses' house" (3:1–6), which according to Westfall can function "as a summary of the preceding co-text and introduction of the following co-text."[40] This section is comparing and contrasting Jesus and Moses, and according to her, the contrast is balanced with the comparison, since both Moses and Jesus are faithful over their houses, and both houses are built by God (cf. 3:4).[41] Key-sentence 5, meanwhile, is found in the subsection entitled "Since the promise of the rest is still open, let's try to enter" (4:1–13), and more specifically in the subtopic "There is still a Sabbath

---

38. Westfall, *Discourse Analysis*, 109.

39. The command in 3:1 concludes the first two units. The first unit (1:1—2:4) described Jesus as God's ultimate messenger, which is paraphrased in 3:1 with the title apostle. The second unit (2:5–18) presented Jesus as the believer's high priest, which is repeated. Westfall, *Discourse Analysis*, 111. However, it is important to recognise that according to Westfall, the command in 3:1 not only concludes and combines the first two units, but it is also discourse *deixis* and staging, indicating the organisation and topics of the discourse—of the whole book—since according to her the three sections of the discourse correspond with the three topics introduced in 3:1: 1) Consider Jesus as our apostle (1:1—4:16); 2) consider Jesus as our high priest (4:11—10:25); and 3) you are partners in Jesus' heavenly calling (10:19—13:25). Therefore, according to Westfall, the author is informing the readers about what they can expect in the following section in 3:1. Westfall, *Discourse Analysis*, 114.

40. Westfall, *Discourse Analysis*, 115.

41. Westfall, *Discourse Analysis*, 117.

rest for God's people" (4:2–10). But she also puts key-sentence 5 under the title "There is a Rest" (4:1–10), and as can be seen, key-sentence 6 (4:10) is also part of these sections.

Key-sentence 7 (8:1–2), key-sentence 8 (9:11–12) and key-sentence 9 (9:24–26) are part of the second section of the book entitled "Consider Jesus as the High Priest of our Confession" (4:11—10:25), and more specifically they are found in the subsection entitled "Let's draw near to God" (7:4—10:25), which in turn also has a subsection entitled "Jesus' priesthood cleanses us and qualifies us to serve as priests" (8:1—10:18). However, key-sentence 7 is found in the subsection entitled "Jesus' priesthood, covenant, tabernacle and sacrifice" (8:1–13), and more specifically in the subtopic entitled "We Have a High Priest Who Serves in a Tabernacle and Offered a Sacrifice" (8:1–6).[42] Key-sentence 8 (9:11–12), in the subsection entitled "Jesus' ministry in the tabernacle cleanses the conscience of the believer" (9:1–14) is, according to Westfall, focusing on the arrangement of the Holy of Holies and in the high priest's limited access to it.[43] Key-sentence 9 (9:24–26), meanwhile, is found in the subsection entitled "Jesus' death inaugurated the new covenant and removed sins once for all" (9:15–28), which in the first part (9:15–18) focuses on the requirement—death—for the inauguration of a covenant, while in the second part (9:19–22) focuses on the inauguration of the first covenant,[44] and in the third subtopic (9:23–28) focuses on the heavenly tabernacle and on its sacrifice.

Key-sentence 10 (11:3), key-sentence 11 (11:10) and key-sentence 12 (12:25–27) are part of the section which, according to Westfall, affirms that "we are partners in Jesus' heavenly calling" (10:19—13:25). However, only key-sentences 10 and 11 belong to the subsection entitled "Let's run the race" (10:19—12:2), and in it, key-sentence 10 (11:3) is part of the subsection entitled "Faith is modelled by action-events in the lives of people from the past" (11:1–40), and more specifically it opens the subtopic entitled "Actions of Faith" (11:3–31), and key-sentence 11 (11:10) also belongs to this section. Key-sentence 12 (12:25–27), meanwhile, belongs to the subsection entitled "Let's serve God as priests in heavenly Jerusalem" (12:1–29), and more specifically to the subtopic which shows the contrast between life and service in the Heavenly Jerusalem with life

---

42. Westfall, *Discourse Analysis*, 190.
43. Westfall, *Discourse Analysis*, 198.
44. Westfall, *Discourse Analysis*, 210.

and service in the earthly Jerusalem. The first contrast is between Mount Sinai and Mount Zion (12:18–24), the second contrast is between the Israelites and the recipients of Hebrews (12:25), while the third contrast is between Mount Sinai and the Kingdom.[45]

Genre and Figures of Speech in Hebrews' Cosmogony

As already shown in the section entitled "Genre of Hebrews," the genre of Hebrews as a book has provoked different conclusions among scholars—theories involve seeing the genre as that of a letter, sermon, sermonic letter, rhetorical sermon, epistle, synagogue homily, Midrash in rhetorical prose, or Christian church homily, amongst others. The focus here will be on the literary component of Hebrews' cosmogony and not on the book as a whole.

Section 1:1–14 can be considered as an expositional argument,[46] namely a text that interprets various Old Testament passages in service of a larger theological argument, while key-sentence 1 (1:2) is evidently an allusion to the Old Testament literature, and key-sentence 2 (1:10–12) is clearly a quotation from the Old Testament. Likewise key-sentence 3 (2:10) is part of an expositional argument (2:5–18), but it can more specifically be considered as an assertion also.[47] Key-sentence 4 (3:4), key-sentence 5 (4:3–5) and key-sentence 6 (4:10), as already mentioned, are part of the exhortation section (3:1—4:16) and more specifically, they must be considered as assertions. But key-sentence 4 and key-sentence 6 must also be considered as an allusion to the Old Testament literature, while key-sentence 5 is a quotation from the Old Testament.

Key-sentence 7 (8:1–2), key-sentence 8 (9:11–12) and key-sentence 9 (9:24–26), meanwhile, are part of the expositional argument (7:1—10:18), as already mentioned. But key-sentence 7, more specifically, must

---

45. Westfall, *Discourse Analysis*, 267–69.

46. The literary genre of expository argument as well as poetry and narrative, are not arbitrary categories, since these genres are natural expressions of the different ways in which human beings 'make sense' of their experience. The expository argument is centred in idea or argument language, while poetry is centred in image language, and narrative is centred in story language. cf. Jensen, *Envisioning the Word*, 136.

47. An assertive speech is one where a speaker makes an assertion or a statement, providing information to the hearer or audience which is then accepted by them. The assertive speech is generally less forceful than the directive speech—for instance the Decalogue or the Sermon on the Mount. See Schnabel, "Scripture," 39.

be considered as an assertion and allusion to the Old Testament literature, while key-sentence 8 can be considered as an interpretation[48] placed in a sort of parallelism.[49] Finally, key-sentence 9 can also be considered as an assertion and support literature, since it is serving to reinforce the preceding point.

Key-sentence 10 (11:3), key-sentence 11 (11:10) and key-sentence 12 (12:25–27), as already shown, are part of the exhortation section; however, key-sentence 10 must also be considered as an allusion to the Old Testament literature, while key-sentence 11 must be considered as an allusion to Old Testament literature and also as an assertion. Key-sentence 12, however, can also be considered as exposition literature and as an allusion and quotation of the Old Testament literature, but in addition, as Koester also considered, it could be defined as the transitional digression—warning and encouragement[50]—of the third series of arguments (11:1—12:27) of Hebrews.

Textual Dependence of Hebrews' Cosmogony

In order to interpret the document, it is essential to determine the origin of the cosmogony-related words, sentences, and phrases present in Hebrews. As already noted, the sources—physical, philosophical, technical, etc.—that were used by the author of Hebrews to write his document are widely debated. For instance, Spicq has carefully cataloged an impressive

---

48. Even though the interpretation style is usually used in the study of the literature of the Scriptures of Israel, it can be applied here since the text implies that the author is doing an interpretation of events—Christ's life—in relation to the Scriptures of Israel's texts about priest's duties.

49. Even though the parallelism is used in Hebrew Bible literature, and since Hebrews is very deeply influenced by the Hebrew Bible, some kind of parallelism can be seen in its texts in this section, as can be seen in Figure 5.9, there is a sort of parallelism, especially in the AJ1. In this case it can be considered as a kind of semantic parallelism. More about it can be found in Gugliotto, *Handbook for Bible Study*, 35–40; Trotter, *Interpreting the Epistle to the Hebrews*, 180–84.

50. The transitional digression must be defined as a text that does not directly advance the main argument but contributes to the persuasive quality of the speech by warnings and words of encouragement, and according to Koester, Hebrews presents this kind of literature three times (2:1–4; 5:11—6:20; 10:26–39; 12:25–27). Koester, *Hebrews*, 89.

list of parallels between Philo and Hebrews,[51] but regarding this issue Williamson affirms in his monumental study:

> There is nothing that has been said by Spicq (or by Carpzov or by anyone else) that constitutes overwhelming proof, on linguistic grounds, that the Writer of Hebrews was familiar with the words and works of Philo. . . . There are, of course, words and phrases common to the two writers, but in every case, as we tried to show, there is an explanation of such verbal similarities. . . . What our examination of the evidence has, we hope, succeeded in showing is that even where the two writers use identical words or expressions they use them in different ways. The difference in our view, lies in the fact that the vocabularies of Philo and the Writer of Hebrews are instruments in the service of fundamentally different views on a wide range of basic concepts. . . . [But] it is also true that "Words are . . . the counters we employ in the exchange of impressions and ideas, and no single one of them has precisely the same value, or connotation or boundaries in your mind and in mine." We must beware, therefore, of constructing a theory of the Philonism of the Epistle to the Hebrews on the basis of the linguistic evidence alone.[52]

Consequently, I will not here try to establish the mindset of Hebrews regarding cosmogony on the basis of linguistic evidence, I am only trying to establish the main literary resource that could have been used when the sentences about cosmogony were written. Today it is widely accepted that the main source used by the author of Hebrews was some Greek text of the Scriptures of Israel,[53] since the writer quotes it more frequently than any other New Testament author.[54] It is easy to recognize

---

51. Spicq, *Hébreux Introduction*, 39–91.

52. Williamson, *Philo and the Epistle to the Hebrews*, 134.

53. As Lane asserts, the character of the text that the author of Hebrews has used continues to be debated. "The importance of the debate was signalled over 150 years ago when F. Bleek argued in his commentary that Paul could not have written Hebrews because he used a Greek text similar to Codex Vaticanus (B), while the writer of Hebrews seems to have had access to a Greek text similar to Codex Alexandrinus (A)." The writer of Hebrews used a form of the Greek text to which s/he enjoyed access, and it is more probable that it was the local form of the text used by the community of which s/he was a part. Lane, *Hebrews 1–8*, cxviii.

54. If the comparison is done by taking into account allusions, echoes, citations, and quotations, then Hebrews will rank after Revelation, Acts, Matthew, and Luke. But since allusions and echoes are quite imprecise, it is better to do the comparison only with quotations and citations, and in the combination of these two kinds of uses of the Scriptures of Israel, Matthew can be placed first, followed by Hebrews or Romans.

that his/her thinking was saturated with the Scriptures of Israel narration, persons, entities, types, and other Jewish particularities. According to Lane, Hebrews uses the Scriptures of Israel in 104 places: thirty-one explicit quotations, four implicit quotations, thirty-seven allusions, nineteen instances where some segments of the Scriptures of Israel are summarized, and thirteen more where a biblical name or topic is cited without reference to a specific context.[55] Although it could be true, Lane himself declares that there is no common agreement "even on the number of quotations from the OT text in Hebrews."[56] But on one thing most of the commentators agree, that the writer develops his/her arguments on the basis of the Scriptures of Israel, from which s/he used mainly two books: the Psalms and Genesis.

As mentioned above, when counting Scriptures of Israel quotations and citations, Hebrews holds the second place among the New Testament documents, but with the most references to Genesis 1–3 and creation in general. Hebrews has 1031 Greek lemmas and 139 of them can be found in Genesis 1–3, but more relevant is Hebrews' thematic allusions to the narrative of Genesis 1–3. For instance, Hebrews reads "God, having spoken in former times" (1:1, ISV), while Genesis 1–3 is the first place where it was noted that God had spoken with humankind (cf. Gen 1:28; 2:16; 3:9). Therefore, the cosmogony of Hebrews has a special connection with the cosmogony of Genesis.

But apart from that, as has also been asserted by Cockerill, there are "some commonalities between the distinctive character of Hebrews and the particular emphases of other NT writers,"[57] particularly with Luke and Paul. Therefore, even though the Pauline authorship of Hebrews was argued in the past, the existence of "some form of preliterary contact between Paul and the author of Hebrews . . . is certainly possible"[58] particu-

---

55. Lane himself affirms: Longenecker suggested that there are thirty-eight quotations in Hebrews; Caird found only twenty-nine; Spicq identified thirty-six; and Michel only thirty-two. Lane, *Hebrews 1–8*, cxvi. In *New Testament Use of the Old Testament*, Logos Edition, ninety-three references in Hebrews to the Old Testament, thirty-five allusions, thirty quotations, twenty-one citations, and seven echoes can be found. See Jackson and Brannan, *New Testament Use of the Old Testament*. Voorwinde, meanwhile, found 40 places where Hebrews uses the Scriptures of Israel in three different ways: 17 exact quotations, 17 close quotations, and six paraphrases, see. Stephen Voorwinde, "Hebrews' Use of the Old Testament," *VR* 73 (2007): 75–77.

56. Lane, *Hebrews 1–8*, cxiv.

57. Cockerill, *Epistle to the Hebrews*, 24.

58. Lane, *Hebrews 1–8*, cx. Hurst meanwhile asserts: "In the three motifs

larly if the existence of some relative early document is assumed.[59] One thing is undeniable, there is abundant evidence that points to a possible dependence or interdependence between Hebrews and the other New Testament writings. For instance, the theme of Christ as the creator, with different shades of meaning, is common to Hebrews and other New Testament writers (1:2 cf. John 1:3; 1 Cor 8:6; Eph 3:9; Col 1:16; Rev 4:11), as well as the theme of Jesus' actions regarding the creation (1:3; cf. 1 Cor 8:6; Col 1:17; Rev 3:14), in addition to other themes.[60] Depending on the date given for the writing of Hebrews and for the writing of other

---

considered there is evidence that in Hebrews one finds a similar development of some central themes of Pauline theology. In some cases, this is seen in the same ideas being expressed by a different deployment of the same terms; in others these ideas are expressed in different language and imagery. Such unity and diversity are what one would expect if both writers are engaging in a deep interaction with the same traditions. Whether this points to the common pool of Christian tradition or to a form of pre-literary contact with Paul himself must remain an exercise of subtle scholarly judgment. What cannot be evaded is that Hebrews appears to relate to Paul in a way quite unlike Qumran, Philo, Gnosticism or the other non-Christian backgrounds" See Hurst, *Epistle to the Hebrews*, 124.

59. The existence of some relative early collection can be assumed, because as Saul Lieberman, an expert in Talmudic literature, asserts, "Now the Jewish disciples of Jesus, in accordance with the general rabbinic practice, wrote the sayings which their master pronounced *not* in form of a book to be published, but as notes in their *pinaces*, codices, in their note-books (or in private small rolls). They did this because otherwise they would have transgressed the law." Lieberman, *Hellenism in Jewish Palestine*, 205, emphasis original. Without quoting Lieberman, Hurst explains that Luke—if Stephen is associated with Hebrews—could have used some early collections of traditions which supplied a starting point for special emphases one finds in Hebrews, especially the inferiority of the earthly cult and the dangers of repeating past patterns of disobedience. Hurst, *Epistle to the Hebrews*, 105. On the basis of Hurst's assertion, it is possible to assume that Stephen's speech (cf. Acts 7) could also have been a written document, perhaps by himself.

60. Ellingworth claims that with different shades of meaning, the theme of shame suffered by Christians is common to Hebrews (11:26; 13:13) and Paul (Rom 15:3). The metaphor of spiritual milk (5:12) is common also to Paul (1 Cor 3:2). The theme of Christ as the—great—Shepherd (13:20; cf. 1 Pet 2:25) goes back through the Gospels (Mark 6:34; 14:27; John 10:2, 11) to the Old Testament image of God as his people's shepherd (Ps 23; Ezek 34). Likewise, he asserts that Hebrews and First Peter draw on common doctrinal tradition in speaking of the purifying power of Christ's sacrificial blood once offered (9:28; cf. 1 Pet 3:18). Both writings use the language of sprinkling (12:24; cf. 1 Pet 1:2) and of taking away sins (9:28; cf. 1 Pet 2:24). In both, the readers are urged to respond by offering their own spiritual sacrifices (13:15; cf. 1 Pet 2:5). Images such as that of believers' "inheritance" (1:2, 4; cf. 1 Pet 1:4; 3:9) are a common Christian reminder of Hebrew Bible language. See Ellingworth, *Epistle to the Hebrews*, 16–18.

New Testament documents, the above conclusions can also imply some dependence on New Testament literature, too, and not only on Old Testament literature. However, due to the purpose of this research it is important to highlight the more specific relationship between the literary component of Hebrews' cosmogony and the Old Testament.

Thus, among quotations, citations and allusions a close relationship can be found between key-sentence 1 (1:2) and Psalm 2:8, and also between key-sentence 2 (1:10–12), Psalm 102:25–27 and Isaiah 48:13. Key-sentence 3 (2:10) is also related to Proverbs 16:4 and Isaiah 43:21, while key-sentence 4 (3:4) has an allusion to Numbers 12:7. Key-sentence 5 (4:3–5), meanwhile can be related to Psalm 95:11, and key-sentence 6 (4:10) to Genesis 2:2, while key-sentence 7 (8:1–2) shows a form of allusion to Psalm 110:1 and Numbers 24:6, and in a similar way key-sentence 8 (9:11–12) could be related to Exodus 25:8–9 and Daniel 9:24. Key-sentence 9 (9:24–26) also shows a form of allusion to Genesis 3:19, Exodus 24, and Leviticus 16, while in key-sentence 10 (11:3) some connection can be found with Genesis 1:1 and Psalm 33:6, 9. Key-sentence 11 (11:10) meanwhile is connected with Genesis 12–17, and finally, key-sentence 12 (12:25–27) is without doubt connected with Haggai 2:6, 21, Exodus 19:18, Judges 5:5, and Psalm 68:8.[61]

Linguistic Analysis of Hebrews' Cosmogony

It is well known that there is no one *autographa* of any New Testament document, there are only copies with slight differences between them, and Hebrews is no exception. According to the Institute for New Testament Textual Research there are 240 documents in Greek that can function as textual witnesses for Hebrews.[62] And, although all the Hebrews'

61. It is important however to mention that more connections between the Hebrew Bible and the literary component of Hebrews' cosmogony can be found, as suggested in Guthrie, "Hebrews," 919–93; deSilva, "Hebrews," 199–256. And also in Smith, *New Treasury of Scripture Knowledge*, 1442–64.

62. The mss. listed in the NT.VMR 2.0 that have some content of Hebrews in Greek are the following. The clave is as follows [name or number of the ms. / possible date of scripture / page(s) or paragraphs in the ms.]; they are arranged in chronological order: [P12 / III (E) / 1 Frg], [P13 / III or IV / 2 Frg], [P17 / IV / 1 Frg], [P46 / III (A) / 86], [P79 / VII / 1 Frg], [P89 / IV / 1 Frg], [P114 / III / 1 Frg], [P116 / VI or VII / Frg], [P126 / IV / Frg], [01 / IV / 148], [02 / V / 144], [03 / IV / 142], [04 / V / 145], [06 / VI / 533], [010 / IX / 136], [015 / VI / 1], [018 / IX / 288], [020 / IX / 189], [044 / IX or X / 261], [048 / V / 21], [056 / X / 381], [075 / X / 333], [0122 / IX / 2], [0142 / X / 381], [0227 / V / Frg], [0228 / IV / Frg], [0243 / X / 2], [0250 / VIII / 33], [0252 / V / Frg], [0272 / IX

texts determined as its cosmogonic literary component are not present

/ 3], [0278 / IX / 120], [0280 / VIII / 1], [0285 (+081) / VI / 20], [0319 / IX / 177], [1 / XII / 297], [3 / XII / 451], [5 / XIII / 342], [6 / XIII / 235], [18 / XIV / 444], [33 / IX / 143], [35 / XI / 328], [38 / XII / 300], [42 / XI / 303], [43 / XI / 388], [61 / XVI / 455], [69 / XV / 213], [81 / XI / 282], [82 / X / 246], [88 / XII / 123], [90 / XVI / 480], [93 / X / 270], [103 / XII / 333], [131 / XIV / 233], [133 / XI / 332], [141 / XIII / 400], [142 / XI / 324], [149 / XV / 179], [172 / XIII or XIV / 234], [175 / X or XI / 247], [177 / XI / 225], [203 / XII / 149], [205 / XV / 80], [209 / XIV / 381], [218 / XIII / 138], [223 / XIII / 376], [234 / XIII / 315], [250 / XI / 379], [263 / XIII / 294], [319 / XII / 303], [321 / XII / 293], [322 / XV / 134], [323 / XII / 374], [326 / X / 206], [330 / XII / 287], [336 / XV / 268], [337 / XII / 375], [339 / XIII / 200], [365 / XII / 356], [367 / XIV / 349], [378 / XIII / 221], [383 / XIII / 181], [384 / XIII / 132], [398 / X / 251], [424 / XI / 353], [429 / XIV / 185], [452 / XII / 327], [453 / XIV / 295], [454 / X / 244], [456 / X / 377], [457 / X / 294], [462 / XI or XII / 240], [465 / XI / 157], [467 / XV / 331], [468 / XIII / 200], [506 / XI / 240], [517 / XI or XII / 201], [606 / XI / 373], [613 / XII / 174], [614 / XIII / 276], [616 / XV / 164], [619 / X / 342], [620 / XII / 150], [622 / XII / 270], [623 / XI / 187], [627 / X / 187], [629 / XIV / 265], [630 / XII or XIII / 215], [664 / XV / 233], [676 / XIII / 344], [794 / XIV / 269], [824 / XIV / 366], [869 / XII / 245], [876 / XII / 282], [891 / XIV / 474], [909 / XII / 268], [915 / XIII / 237], [919 / XI / 265], [922 / XII / 405], [945 / XI / 347], [1003 / XV / 305], [1072 / XIII / 411], [1075 / XIV / 348], [1100 / XIV / 244], [1127 / XII / 345], [1140 / 1242 / 208], [1149 / XIII / 461], [1161 / XIII / 253], [1175 / X / 202], [1240 / XII / 277], [1241 / XII / 193], [1243 / XI / 281], [1244 / XI / 279], [1315 / XII / 355], [1319 / XII / 216], [1354 / XIV / 237], [1424 / IX or X / 337], [1448 / XII / 256], [1495 / XIV / 263], [1503 / XIV / 263], [1505 / XIII / 273], [1509 / XIII / 332], [1611 / X / 312], [1617 / XV / 362], [1637 / XIV / 294], [1642 / XIII / 321], [1652 / XVI / 506], [1661 / XIV / 173], [1678 / XIV / 334], [1718 / XII / 124], [1725 / XIV / 229], [1728 / XIII / 134], [1729 / XV / 209], [1732 / XIV / 193], [1734 / XI / 233], [1739 / X / 102], [1740 / XII / 307], [1751 / XV / 168], [1757 / XV / 183], [1769 / XIV / 209], [1770 / XI / 93], [1771 / XIV / 105], [1818 / XII / 155], [1832 / XIV / 220], [1837 / X / 181], [1841 / IX or X / 204], [1855 / XIII / 209], [1857 / XIII / 198], [1862 / IX / 429], [1865 / XIII / 315], [1870 / XI / 298], [1874 / X / 191], [1875 / X / 181], [1876 / XV / 276], [1879 / XI / 357], [1880 / X / 241], [1889 / XII / 140], [1893 / XII / 166], [1894 / XII / 263], [1897 / XII or XIII / 186], [1900 / IX / 270], [1903 / XVII / 250], [1905 / X / 251], [1912 / X / 170], [1916 / XI / 177], [1917 / XII / 249], [1920 / X / 285], [1929 / XIV / 381], [1933 / XI / 273], [1948 / XV / 187], [1957 / XV / 9], [1963 / XVI / 262], [1976 / XIII / 143], [1978 / XV / 529], [1991 / XIII / 204], [1997 / X / 268], [1998 / X / 181], [2003 / XV / 189], [2004 / XII / 158], [2005 / XIII / 100], [2007 / XI / 392], [2080 / XIV / 278], [2127 / XII / 1], [2138 / XI / 398], [2191 / XI / 1], [2200 / XIV / 286], [2201 / XV / 245], [2221 / XV / 376], [2243 / XVII / 103], [2344 / XI / 61], [2374 / XIII or XIV / 252], [2400 / XIII / 207], [2401 / XII / 152], [2431 / XIV / 239], [2492 / XIV / 178], [2495 / XV / 222], [2516 / XIII / 278], [2523 / XV / 266], [2554 / XIV / 382], [2587 / XI / 237], [2596 / XI / 54], [2625 / XII / 290], [2626 / XIV / 178], [2674 / XVII / 158], [2716 / XIV / 197], [2718 / XII / 236], [2723 / XI / 360], [2736 / XV / 290], [2762 / XII / 1], [2774 / XIII or XIV / 349], [2805 / XII or XIII / 155], [2817 / XI / 387], [2865 / XII / 219], [2886 / XV / 54], [2889 / XIV / 439], [2892 / X / 170], [2893 / XIII / 15], [2903 / XII or XIII / 108], [2926 / XVI / 74], [l 895 / XIII / 134]. Cf. http://ntvmr.uni-muenster.de/manuscript-workspace. To visualize the manuscripts, it is necessary to use the Full Search button and select *Hebrews* in the selection criteria.

in all the textual witnesses,[63] it must be stated that it is not the purpose of this research to evaluate all the witnesses where they are present. Nevertheless, in order to reconstruct the most accurate text of the literary component of Hebrews' cosmogony, the critical apparatus of NA[28] will be used, and Alford, Tischendorf, the SBL edition, and the UBS,[5] as well as the "A Textual Guide to the Greek New Testament,"[64] will also be consulted. And only the textual issues that are directly related to the literary component of Hebrews' cosmogony will be taken into account.

Textual Issues of Hebrews' Cosmogony

In the twelve identified key-sections of the literary component of Hebrews' cosmogony there are only six key-sections that present textual issues—i.e., intentional or unintentional variations in diverse Hebrews' manuscripts which can influence its translation and interpretation[65]—which are shown in Table 4.4.

---

63. The texts are presented in the following number of manuscripts: 1:1 (181 mss.); 1:2 (169 mss.); 1:10 (123 mss.); 1:11 (121 mss.); 1:12 (120 mss.); 2:10 (105 mss.); 3:4 (107 mss.); 4:3 (103 mss.); 4:4 (101 mss.); 4:10 (102 mss.); 8:1–2 (94 mss.); 9:11–12 (93 mss.); 9:24 (93 mss.); 9:25 (95 mss.); 9:26 (94 mss.); 11:3 (93 mss.); 11:10 (93 mss.); 12:27 (99 mss.).

64. Omanson, *Textual Guide*; Alford, *Alford's Greek Testament*; Tischendorf, *Novum Testamentum Graece Apparatum Criticum*; Holmes, *Greek New Testament: SBL Edition*; Aland et al., *Greek New Testament: Apparatus*.

65. Even though the phrase "textual issues" can imply different problems that arise during the study of some ancient text, here it is used mainly to identify the problem of variations among different manuscripts of the same document—Hebrews. So it is important to clarify that, as Widder clearly states, the *translation* issues will not be tackled here, since they do not belong to *textual* issues, which are more concerned with variations and with the quality of the manuscripts. See Widder, *Textual Criticism*, 5. More information about textual issues can be found in, Comfort, *Encountering the Manuscripts*, 255–88; Porter, *How We Got the New Testament*, 77–146; Wegner, *Student's Guide*, 204–65.

KS	Textual Issues and Evaluation in UBS⁵	Alternative Readings[66]	
1	ὁ θεὸς δι' οὗ °καὶ [∅] ⌜ἐποίησεν τοὺς αἰῶνας⌝ [∅]	ὁ θεὸς δι' οὗ ° ⌜ἐποίησεν τοὺς αἰῶνας⌝	ὁ θεὸς δι' οὗ °καὶ ⌜τοὺς αἰῶνας ἐποίησεν⌝
2	σὺ κατ' ἀρχάς, κύριε, τὴν γῆν ἐθεμελίωσας, καὶ ἔργα τῶν χειρῶν σού εἰσιν οἱ οὐρανοί· αὐτοὶ ἀπολοῦνται, πάντες ὡς ἱμάτιον παλαιωθήσονται, καὶ ὡσεὶ περιβόλαιον ⌜ἑλίξεις [A] αὐτούς, ⸂ὡς ἱμάτιον⸃ [B] καὶ ἀλλαγήσονται	σὺ κατ' ἀρχάς, κύριε, τὴν γῆν ἐθεμελίωσας, καὶ ἔργα τῶν χειρῶν σού εἰσιν οἱ οὐρανοί· αὐτοὶ ἀπολοῦνται, πάντες ὡς ἱμάτιον παλαιωθήσονται, καὶ ὡσεὶ περιβόλαιον ⌜ἀλλάξεις αὐτούς, ⸂ὡς ἱμάτιον⸃ καὶ ἀλλαγήσονται	σὺ κατ' ἀρχάς, κύριε, τὴν γῆν ἐθεμελίωσας, καὶ ἔργα τῶν χειρῶν σού εἰσιν οἱ οὐρανοί· αὐτοὶ ἀπολοῦνται, πάντες ὡς ἱμάτιον παλαιωθήσονται, καὶ ὡσεὶ περιβόλαιον ⌜ἑλίξεις αὐτούς, ⸂ ⸃ καὶ ἀλλαγήσονται
4	ὁ ᵀ [∅] πάντα κατασκευάσας θεός.	ὁ ᵀ τὰ πάντα κατασκευάσας θεός.	
7	τῶν ἁγίων καὶ τῆς σκηνῆς τῆς ἀληθινῆς ἔπηξεν ὁ κύριος, ᵀ [∅] οὐκ ἄνθρωπος	τῶν ἁγίων καὶ τῆς σκηνῆς τῆς ἀληθινῆς ἔπηξεν ὁ κύριος, ᵀ καὶ οὐκ ἄνθρωπος	
10	Πίστει νοοῦμεν κατηρτίσθαι τοὺς αἰῶνας ῥήματι θεοῦ, εἰς τὸ μὴ ἐκ φαινομένων ⌜τὸ βλεπόμενον⌝ [∅] γεγονέναι.	Πίστει νοοῦμεν κατηρτίσθαι τοὺς αἰῶνας ῥήματι θεοῦ, εἰς τὸ μὴ ἐκ φαινομένων ⌜τὰ βλεπόμενα⌝ γεγονέναι.	

66. The space here does not allow every textual witness to be shown that can support these readings, for as can be seen in footnote 62 from current chapter, there are more than 100 textual witnesses for these texts. Since the NA[28] fulfils this purpose satisfactorily, the Critical Apparatus of the NA[28], as well as of the UBS5, can be used in order to verify the textual witnesses for these texts. The symbols are also the same as used in the NA[28].

KS	Textual Issues and Evaluation in UBS⁵		Alternative Readings[66]
12	τὸ δὲ ἔτι ἅπαξ δηλοῖ ⌜[τὴν] τῶν σαλευομένων⌝ [Ø] μετάθεσιν ὡς πεποιημένων, ἵνα μείνῃ τὰ μὴ σαλευόμενα.	τὸ δὲ ἔτι ἅπαξ δηλοῖ ⌜τῶν σαλευομένων⌝ τὴν⌝ μετάθεσιν ὡς πεποιημένων, ἵνα μείνῃ τὰ μὴ σαλευόμενα.	τὸ δὲ ἔτι ἅπαξ δηλοῖ ⌜τῶν σαλευομένων⌝ μετάθεσιν ὡς πεποιημένων, ἵνα μείνῃ τὰ μὴ σαλευόμενα.

Table 4.4 Textual issues in the literary component of Hebrews' cosmogony.

Table 4.4 shows these textual issues alongside their alternative readings, with critical signs in order to aid identification of the variation. Also in Table 4.4, the evaluation of the editors of the UBS⁵ on these issues can be seen. The symbol [Ø] is used to show where the UBS⁵ does not show indications of its decision regarding which variant of the text is the more probable original text. It is important to highlight here that the text of the UBS⁵ and the text of the NA²⁸ are the same. Consequently, if there is no evaluation in the UBS⁵, it means that its editors fully agree with the decision of the NA²⁸. So, after considering the evaluation presented in the UBS⁵, it can be asserted that in the literary component of Hebrews' cosmogony there is only one key-section—key-section 2 (1:10–12)—which shows considerable issues which must be evaluated.

In key-section 2 there are two textual issues, the first[67] ⌜ has been evaluated in the UBS⁵ with the letter A, which indicates that the text is certain.[68] However, it is important to underline that ἑλίξεις—VFAI2S[69] of ἑλίσσω (you will roll up)—is replaced by ἀλλάξεις—VFAI2S of ἀλλάσσω (you will change)—in ℵ* D* t vg^(cl.ww); Ath, and also that it is the word present in the LXX (Ps 101:27 LXX [102:26]). Nevertheless, since ἑλίξεις has

---

67 ⌜ This critical sign means that the next word in the text is transmitted with variants.

68. Aland et al., *Greek New Testament: Apparatus*, 8.

69. For the purpose of morphological analysis, the abbreviation provided by The Lexham Analytical Lexicon to the Greek New Testament as well as to the Septuagint will be used, See "Logos Bible Software Greek Morphology Codes" in Brannan, *Lexham Analytical Lexicon*; Hoogendyk, *Lexham Analytical Lexicon*. Also all the abbreviations used here are in the section of abbreviations of this document.

the most support—it is used in nearly all manuscripts[70]—the word that will be accepted as the more probable original text here will be ἑλίξεις.

The second textual issue[71] ⸆ has been evaluated in the UBS⁵ with the letter B, which indicates that the text is almost certain.[72] However, it is important to underline that even though the phrase ὡς ἱμάτιον—C and NASN of ἱμάτιον (like a garment)—present in the NA²⁸ has strong manuscript support—𝔓⁴⁶ ℵ A B D* 1739 vg^mss—the support for the absence of the phrase is also robust, abundant—D¹ K L P Ψ 0243. 0278. 33. 81. 104. 365. 630. 1175. 1241. 1505. 1881. 2464. l 249 𝔐 lat sy sa^ms bo; Ath—and strong, since most of these manuscripts are considered as 'consistently cited witnesses' in the NA²⁸ and among them there are also some early manuscripts supporting this reading.[73] On the other hand, it is important to consider that the 𝔓⁴⁶—as well as ℵ A B D* 1739 vg^mss—is not always an accurate witness to Hebrews (cf. 1:2, 3, 4, 8; 2:6, 8; 3:6, 18; 4:6, 11, 5:1, 6, 11, 12, etc.), and it is also important to note that the words ὡς ἱμάτιον are not present in the LXX[74] (cf. Ps 101:26 LXX [102:26]) document that is cited here. It is also less probable that Hebrews uses the same construction twice as it evidently tried to avoid repetitions. In addition, as will be shown later, the cosmogonic thoughts of Hebrews, as well as the syntaxes of this key-section (1:10–12), fit better without the presence of the words ὡς ἱμάτιον. Consequently, its internal and external evidence compels the deletion of this phrase[75] and it will therefore be removed from the identified key-section 2, which is part of the literary component of Hebrews' cosmogony.

70. Omanson, *Textual Guide*, 454.

71 ⸆ This critical sign means that words enclosed between ⸆ and ⸆ in the text are omitted.

72. Aland et al., *Greek New Testament: Apparatus*, 8.

73. The probable date of each of these manuscripts is shown in footnote 62 from current chapter. It can also be found in the introduction to the Greek version of the New Testament and on the webpage of the Institute for New Testament Textual Research.

74. Omanson asserts that ὡς ἱμάτιον καί is not in the passage being quoted from the Septuagint, however it is true that in some manuscripts of the LXX the καί is present, therefore in the LXX only the phrase ὡς ἱμάτιον is absent. Cf. Omanson, *Textual Guide*, 454; Bacon, "Heb 1:10–12," 280–85; Tan et al., *Lexham Greek-English Interlinear Septuagint*.

75. In the external evidence, there are four principles that are usually used in order to determine the value of the variance: 1) The date and character of the witnesses; 2) the geographical distribution of the witnesses that support a variant; 3) the genealogical relationship of texts and families of manuscripts; and 4) manuscripts are to be weighed rather than counted. In the internal evidence two principles are usually

Chapter Conclusion

This chapter began with the purpose of finding the specific literary component of Hebrews' cosmogony, since in order to have a better understanding of Hebrews' cosmogony it is necessary to focus the study on specific Hebrews' texts without, however, disregarding or ignoring its wider literary context. It must be kept in mind, however, that it is not right to focus on the wider literary context only, disregarding the more specific texts about the topic under study. In order to achieve this purpose, strategies of text-linguistic analysis were applied to the text, and from these analyses, some important findings can be asserted.

1. The literary component of Hebrews' cosmogony is constituted by 174 words which represent eighty-six lemmas and nine morphological categories, which form twelve sentences that in turn belong to twelve key-sections of Hebrews' text (cf. 1:1–4, 10–12; 2:10; 3:3–4; 4:3–5, 10; 8:1–2; 9:11–12, 24–26; 11:3, 9–10; 12:25–27).

2. Hebrews' structure is useful in order to have a better understanding of its topics, but its complexity warns to not build studies and conclusions mainly on this basis.

3. Even though Hebrews' genre as a book is difficult to define, what is clear is that the twelve identified key-sections are predominantly linked with the Scriptures of Israel, since they could be considered as expositional arguments (1:1–4; 2:10; 8:1–2; 9:11–12, 24–26; 12:25–27), allusions (1:2; 3:4; 4:10; 8:1–2; 11:3, 10; 12:25–27), quotations (1:10–12; 4:3–5; 12:25–27), assertions (2:10; 8:1–2; 9:24–26; 11:10), exhortations (3:4; 4:3–5, 10; 11:3, 10; 12:25–27) or interpretations (9:11–12) of the Scriptures of Israel.

4. Hebrews' cosmogony—in accordance with the previous assertion—is deeply dependent on the Scriptures of Israel, particularly Genesis 1–3.

5. Apart from the identified key-section 1:10–12, there are no significant textual issues in Hebrews' cosmogonic texts that can influence the comprehension of the whole of Hebrews' view of this topic.

---

used to determine the value of the variance: 1) Transcriptional probabilities; and 2) intrinsic probabilities. More information about it can be found in Omanson, *Textual Guide*, xxx; Wegner, *Student's Guide*, 204–65. Besides them, the work of Widder has an excellent presentation about textual criticism of the New Testament and he also lists several important resources for the New Testament textual criticism. See Widder, *Textual Criticism*, 109–54.

The next chapter can be considered a continuation of this chapter, since as already asserted, text-linguistic analysis or literary analysis includes the grammatical analysis. The grammatical analysis will be done in the next chapter on the basis of the main findings of this chapter, and, as will be seen, this chapter is in part developed further in some findings of the next chapter, i.e., these two chapters are deeply connected.

5

Grammatical Analysis of Cosmogonic Hebrews' Text

THE COSMOGONY OF HEBREWS must be present in its text, therefore an analysis of the text itself by conducting a grammatical analysis—which, as already asserted, belongs to the text-linguistic analysis—is imperative, since responsible interpretation of the text, as Hagner asserts, is possible only when the scholar has "control of the grammatical data of a passage."[1]

Chapter Introduction

Following on from—and in harmony with—the previous chapter, this chapter will only tackle the grammatical analysis of the twelve identified key-sections which are concerned with the cosmogony topic. On the other hand, it must be asserted that the purpose of this chapter is the

---

1. Nevertheless, Hanger also asserts that the assumption that a mechanical, grammatical analysis, i.e., believing that some particular point such as a tense, mood of a verb, a case, or even the root of a Greek word, by itself settles the meaning of a passage conclusively, is not correct. So Hanger will also assert, "a grammatical point is most convincing when it is in accord with the evidence of the other aspects of exegesis such as context and historical/cultural background." Hagner, *New Testament Exegesis and Research*, 5. Therefore, the grammatical analysis must include a semantic, syntactic, contextual, and morphological analysis. Finally, the grammatical analysis must also be part of the broader text-linguistic analysis, since an interpretation can only be developed from a combination of all these insights.

same as that of *The Baylor Handbook on the Greek New Testament*,[2] or of many other grammatical commentaries on the Greek New Testament, i.e., to provide the foundational analysis of the Greek text upon which interpretation may then be established in further chapters. Therefore, this chapter will present insights arising from a syntactic, morphological, contextual, and semantic analysis of the literary component of Hebrews' cosmogony which can assist in the comprehension of its cosmogony.

Methodology and Procedure

This analysis, as it is logical, will focus on the key-sections, sentences, phrases, and words—in this order—of the literary component of Hebrews' cosmogony, i.e., analysis of the sentence will progress to the interpretation of the separate concepts and words.[3] Therefore, the grammatical analysis of Hebrews' cosmogony will be developed in two steps: firstly, the syntactic structure analysis of the twelve identified key-sections; and secondly, the morpho-syntactic analysis of the twelve established key-sentences which form the literary component of Hebrews' cosmogony. The syntactic structural analysis will have the goal of indicating how the words are organized in the key-sections, and consequently, in order to achieve this purpose, each key-section will be diagrammed, since it will serve as the primary tool for clarifying the relationships between words and groups of words in a biblical text.[4]

On the other hand, the morpho-syntactic analysis of the key-sentence—the process that constitutes a union between the morphological

---

2. Martin M. Culy in the introduction to the series of *The Baylor Handbook on the Greek New Testament* states that this handbook provides readers of the New Testament with a foundational analysis of the Greek text upon which interpretation may then be established, i.e., it displays the mechanics of the Greek text and the more perplexing grammatical issues. See Campbell, *Colossians and Philemon*, ix.

3. Berkhof affirms that in "the study of the text the interpreter can proceed in a twofold way. He [sic] can begin with the sentence, with the expression of the writer's thought as a unity, and then descend to particulars, to the interpretation of the separate words and concepts; or he [sic] can begin with the latter, and then gradually ascend to a consideration of the sentence, of the thought as a whole. From a purely logical and psychological point of view, the first method deserves preference." Berkhof, *Principles of Biblical Interpretation*, 67.

4. More information about grammatical diagramming can be found in Guthrie and Duvall, *Biblical Greek Exegesis*, 27; Harrison et al., *Biblical Criticism*; Schreiner, *Interpreting the Pauline Epistles*; Parker, *Learning New Testament Greek*; Long, *Kairos: A Beginning Greek Grammar*; Kantenwein, *Diagrammatical Analysis*.

and syntactic analysis—seeks to assist in determining the meaning of the text[5] by ascertaining four things:

1. The part of speech to which the word belongs, since, for instance, the same word could function as an adjective, noun, verb, or adverb.[6]

2. The morphology of the word, since the form in which the words are inflected—namely, the case, number, genre, etc.—influences their meaning.

3. The lexicology of the word, since to know its etymology and usage in the document as well as in other documents is helpful in understanding the meaning of the text.

4. The syntax of the word, since understanding the relationship of the words is also very important in order to determine the right meaning of the text.[7]

5. It is believed that the morpho-syntactic analysis can assist in the process of determining the meaning since, as Cotterell asserts, the meaning is not determined in the grammatical analysis, because "the past tenses do not always signify the past, imperative forms are not always commands, interrogative particles do not always signal questions, and meaning is to be found not in the word, still less in the morpheme, but in the context within which language is being used." Cotterell, "Review of Linguistics for Students," 28. Also, Mastora, Kapidakis, and Monopoli show that the morpho-syntactic analysis of the actual Greek by electronic tools are deficient to a high degree. See Mastora et al., "Failed Queries." These results can also be applied to the morpho-syntactic analysis of the Bible text, provided by electronic tools, since the grammatical and syntactic determination of the words are deeply linked with the presuppositions of the researcher.

6. In English, one word can belong to different parts of speech—for instance, the word "above" could be a preposition, adverb, adjective, or noun—since it is the function or use that determines to which part of speech a particular word belongs. So, even though it is not common, it is possible, for instance, to find in the Bible the same word fulfilling different functions or which has been used for different parts of speech. For instance, the Greek word ἀκούσας, which by its morphology is usually identified as VAAP-SNM, can be identified with different parts of speech by its function in a sentence: for instance, in Luke 6:49 it can function as a noun since it is the subject of a sentence, but in Matthew 2:2 it must be identified as an adverb, while in John 6:45 it functions as a verb and in John 12:29 as an adjective. Although these assertions can be debated, other examples are widely accepted, for instance, that the word καί can be identified as a conjunction or as an adverb. Among morphological categories of Greek words, the participle can be considered the more versatile type of word in this sense. More information about how the participle can be identified with different parts of speech can be found in Porter, *Idioms of the Greek New Testament*, 181–90.

7. More information about these four steps can be found in Zuck, *Basic Bible Interpretation*, 100; Osborne, *Hermeneutical Spiral*; Trotter, *Interpreting the Epistle to the Hebrews*, 115–85.

These four steps will assist in finding sufficient information in Hebrews' text which will be used in the following chapters to advance the main goal of this research, i.e., to determine the cosmogonic presuppositions of Hebrews in its first-century philosophical context.

Grammatical Analysis

Key-Section 1: Hebrews 1:1–4

The Greek text that will be used in this section[8] and its translation—a dynamic translation—follows, with words previously selected as forming part of the literary component of Hebrews' cosmogony appearing in bold.

Greek Text	Translation
Πολυμερῶς καὶ πολυτρόπως πάλαι **ὁ θεὸς λαλήσας** τοῖς πατράσιν ἐν τοῖς προφήταις ἐπ' ἐσχάτου τῶν ἡμερῶν τούτων **ἐλάλησεν ἡμῖν ἐν υἱῷ** ὃν ἔθηκεν κληρονόμον πάντων **δι' οὗ καὶ ἐποίησεν τοὺς αἰῶνας** ὃς ὢν ἀπαύγασμα τῆς δόξης καὶ χαρακτὴρ τῆς ὑποστάσεως αὐτοῦ φέρων τε τὰ πάντα τῷ ῥήματι τῆς δυνάμεως αὐτοῦ [δι' εαυτοῦ] καθαρισμὸν τῶν ἁμαρτιῶν [ἡμῶν] ποιησάμενος ἐκάθισεν ἐν δεξιᾷ τῆς μεγαλωσύνης ἐν ὑψηλοῖς τοσούτῳ κρείττων γενόμενος τῶν ἀγγέλων ὅσῳ διαφορώτερον παρ' αὐτοὺς κεκληρονόμηκεν ὄνομα.	God, who spoke to the fathers, at various times and in various ways, long ago, by the prophets, has spoken to us, in these last days, by the Son. God appointed the Son as heir of all things, and He also made the universe through Him. Who is the radiance of His glory and the exact image of His essence, and who upholds all things by the power of His word. He sat down at the right hand of the Majesty on high, to make purification of our sins by Himself, and He has obtained a more excellent name than any name, having become so much better than the angels.

---

8. It is important also to note that this text is not too similar to the NA[28], since the words in brackets—[]—are not present in the NA[28]; however, the evaluation of the textual witnesses allows some insertions, since δι' εαυτοῦ is present in D2 Hc K L 0243. 104. 630. 1241. 1739. 1881 𝔪 ar bvgms sy sa bo, and δι αυτου is present in 𝔓[46] D* 0278. 365. 1505. On the other hand, ἡμῶν is present in ℵ D1 H 33. 2464 and in a different order in K L 104. 365. 630. 1241. 1505. 1881 𝔪 sy.

Syntactic Structure Analysis of Key-Section 1

As can be seen in Figure 5.1, this key-section has five indicative verbs and is a complex sentence.[9] The PC is constituted by two SCs, which are asyndeton, and two AJs. The subject of the PC—θεός—has one SP and the EC1 working as its apposition.[10] On the other hand, the AJ1—ἐν υἱῷ—has the EC2 and the EC3 working as its apposition,[11] which share the subject ὅς, and two finite clauses, which are the SP9 and the SP10, since they are giving supplementary information about υἱῷ. The SP9 is expressing the locative issue, while its indirect object, which is constituted by the EC6, has a descriptive function in a way similar to the SP10, while its AJ10, constituted by the EC7, expresses the reason or cause for which the action is done, i.e., it fundamentally addresses a causative issue.

Even though it is not necessary to explain every part of speech in the whole section since it can be seen in Figure 5.1,[12] it must be highlighted that this section can be divided into two parts. In the first part, which has four clauses—PC, SC1, SC2, EC1—the subject is θεός, while in the second part, which has six clauses—EC2, EC3, EC4, EC5, EC6, EC7—the subject is υἱός. All of these ten clauses are asyndeton, and among them the two

---

9. Most of the scholars assert that there is a chiastic structure here, and very few of them consider verse 4 to be part of the next pericope.

10. The EC1, which is a participial clause and has an implicit subject, and λαλήσας—VAAP-SNM of λαλέω (He spoke)—as its verb, and πατράσιν—NDPM of πατήρ (to the fathers)—as its complement, is explaining the identity of the subject of the PC. The AJ3 in this clause is showing when God spoke and in this time, how He spoke. For this reason, this participial clause is considered an appositional element to θεός, i.e., θεός is the one who spoke to the fathers in former times, and He is the one who has spoken to us by the Son.

11. The two participial sentences linked by the conjunction τε are defining the υἱῷ, i.e., the υἱῷ is the ἀπαύγασμα and the χαρακτὴρ of θεός, but He is also the one who φέρων of τὰ πάντα. Here it is important to highlight that VPAP-SNM φέρων carries on with the sense of bringing (cf. John 19:39) and also of being (cf. Wis 18:16; Isa 30:17; 2 Macc 4:25; 7:39; 11:1 LXX). Therefore, this sentence could also be transmitting the idea that the Son is the source of everything or that the Son is He who brings everything into existence; however, it seems that the final idea of the verse is that the Son was and is the support for the existence of everything.

12. Information about how the horizontal, vertical, or diagonal lines address different parts of sentences, which in turn will help with the identification of the part of speech to which the individual word belongs, can be found in Schreiner, *Interpreting the Pauline Epistles*, 69–95; Kantenwein, *Diagrammatical Analysis*, 17–85. Nevertheless, it can be observed that the horizontal lines identify sentences here, while content held by vertical lines identifies adjuncts that add information to the verbs, and diagonal lines identify supplements that can add information to subjects or complements.

120   Hebrews' Cosmogonic Presuppositions

SCs are very special ones, because they are linked to the primary clause by their subjects, but also by their use of the relative pronouns, ὅν and οὗ in their predicates. However, only the SC2 is pertinent to this research, because it contains important information about cosmogony. Therefore, since the focus of this research is cosmogony, the analysis of this key-section will be focused in the SC2 and in the elements that have a more direct relation with this clause.

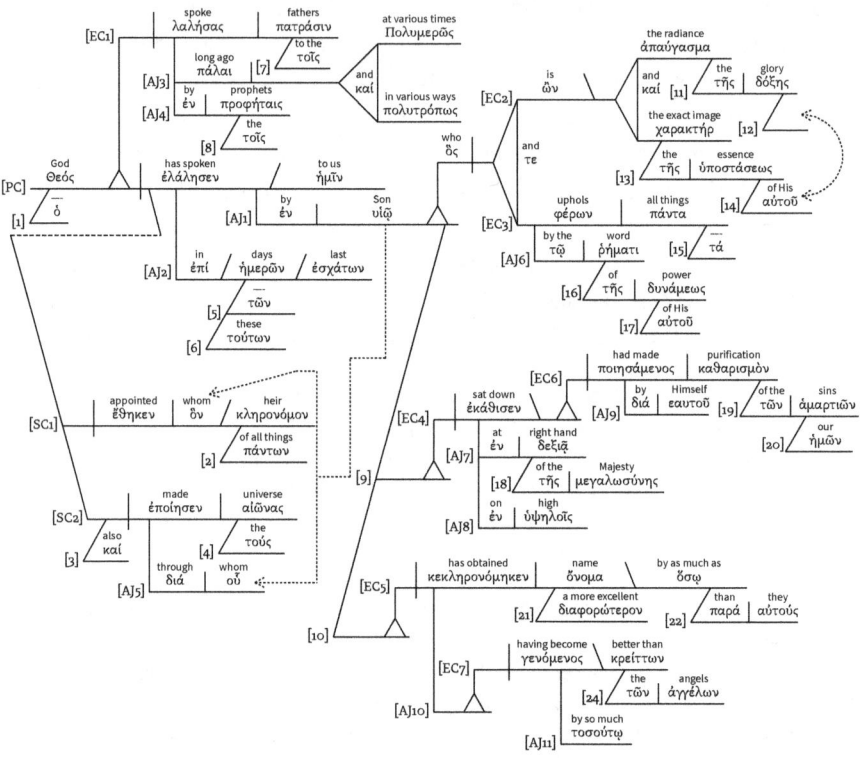

Figure 5.1 Line diagram of key-section 1: Hebrews 1:1–4.

Morpho-Syntactic Analysis of Key-Sentence 1

As has already been determined, key-sentence 1 is constituted by the following words: ὁ θεὸς δι' υἱοῦ [υἱῷ] ἐποίησεν τοὺς αἰῶνας. This clause can be considered an asyndeton clause, since the SC2 from which this clause is developed is asyndeton also. However, as already noted, the analysis here will be done in the SC2 and also in the elements taken from the PC to develop key-sentence 1. As already asserted, in order to do so, the proposal of *The Baylor Handbook on the Greek New Testament*[13] will be followed, since the goal of this analysis is to provide a foundational analysis of the Greek text upon which interpretation may then be established.

ὁ θεὸς: DNSM and NNSM from θεός, a noun which is used 4009 times in the LXX, 2397 times in Philo, 1343 times in the New Testament, and sixty-eight times in Hebrews.[14] It is the subject of the verb ἐποίησεν, i.e., he is the one who performs the action of the verb.[15] It is also important to highlight that wherever the nominative θεός is present, it is accompanied by its article.[16] The article is never meaningless in Greek,[17] according to Wallace, it fulfills three main functions: it conceptualizes, identifies, and definitizes.[18] Robertson, meanwhile, states that the article serves to emphasize a specific entity that is commonly used as a common name.[19] Winer, however, asserts that the use of the article points to well-known facts, arrangements, doctrines, persons, or to something previously

---

13. See footnote 2 from current chapteR.

14. Depending on the version of the LXX and if the alternate text is included in the counting, as well as the Greek version of the New Testament, the number of times the word is used can change; for instance, θεός is used sixty-nine times in the Byz. text.

15. It is important to highlight here that in Hebrews the noun θεός is found twenty-nine times in genitive case, and twenty-four times in nominative case. So, in Hebrews it is predominantly in relation to something.

16. This is for all the cases where the nominative θεός is presented in Hebrews, and not only in the literary component of Hebrews' cosmogony.

17. The article is a crucial element to unlock the meaning of nuances in the Greek text of the New Testament. Osborne affirms "the presence or absence of the article is an important interpretive device." Osborne, *Hermeneutical Spiral*, 75. Robertson points out "The article is never meaningless in Greek, though it often fails to correspond with the English idiom." Robertson, *Grammar of the Greek New Testament*, 756. More information about the article can be found in Wallace, *Greek Grammar Beyond the Basics*, 206–90.

18. Wallace asserts that the article 1) conceptualizes, because it turns "any part of speech into a noun and, therefore, a concept;" 2) identifies, because it stresses the identity of an individual or class or quality; 3) definitizes, i.e., whenever it is used, the term it modifies must, of necessity, be definite. See Wallace, *Greek Grammar Beyond the Basics*, 209–10.

19. Robertson, *Grammar of the Greek New Testament*, 755, 59.

mentioned,[20] and Porter asserts "the presence or absence of an article does not make a substantive definite or indefinite."[21] Consequently, the use in Hebrews of this nominative articular noun ὁ θεός and particularly in its cosmogony, points to the fact that this popular noun—in the first century—is used in Hebrews to identify some well-known entity previously mentioned. That is, the writer of Hebrews has already spoken to his/her audience about this ὁ θεός—in previous meetings since ὁ θεός is used in 1:1—or s/he is referring to the plural Hebrew well-known noun, אֱלֹהִים of the Old Testament.[22] The latter is almost certain, thus in Hebrews and especially in its cosmogony, the singular ὁ θεός really carries on the plural sense of אֱלֹהִים.

ἐλάλησεν: VAAI3S from λαλέω, used 1191 times in the LXX, sixty times in Philo, 296 times in the New Testament, and sixteen times in Hebrews. Verb intransitive with perfective aspect due to its tense,[23] but non-stative, which implies a summary *aktionsart*, namely, this aorist simply expresses that something happened, without further specification.[24]

ἡμῖν: RP1DP from ἐγώ, used 12603 times in the LXX, 1584 times in Philo, 2589 times in the New Testament, and sixty-six times in Hebrews. Dative of indirect object and interest—advantage—namely for the benefit of the insider group or at least for the readers of the document.

ἐν υἱῷ: P and NDSM from υἱός, a noun which is used 5201 times in the LXX, 276 times in Philo, 377 times in the New Testament, and twenty-four times in Hebrews. The anarthrous dative υἱῷ has a particular use here, since the NDSM υἱῷ—this specific accidence—is used only fifteen times in the New Testament and only twice it is used to introduce someone other than Jesus (cf. Luke 12:53; John 4:5); from the other thirteen times, twelve times are used with the article, and only here it is used without the article. According to Bultmann, the article is omitted with abstract terms in apothegmatic sentences, in general adverbial adjuncts,

---

20. Winer, *Treatise on the Grammar*, 132.

21. Porter, *Idioms of the Greek New Testament*.

22. θεός is the more common word used in the LXX to translate the Hebrew words אֵל, אֱלוֹהַּ and אֱלֹהִים. See Kittel et al., *Theological Dictionary of the New Testament*, 3:79; Mcguire-Moushon, "Divine Beings"; Schmidt, "אֵל," 116.

23. The perfective is the aspect of the Aorist tense of the Greek verb, and according to Campbell this is the aspect that perceives "an action or state from the outside," i.e., it is the external viewpoint or the view of the whole event, and thus it does not express the details of the action or how it unfolds. Campbell, *Basics of Verbal Aspect*, 83.

24. Campbell, *Basics of Verbal Aspect*, 86.

with words individualized by the context, and with quasi-proper names.[25] Since in Hebrews the noun υἱός is used twenty-four times and from this, thirteen times it is used in direct or indirect apposition to Jesus—a proper name—here it is very probable that the omission of the article is due to the writer considering it as a proper name of the person in reference, i.e., Jesus. Besides, this prepositional phrase, i.e., ἐν υἱῷ, is used only once in Philo in a cosmogonic context when he affirms that it is impossible that a son can contain the being that brought the universe into existence.[26] Also, it is used once by Ignatius to make reference to God the Son,[27] and twice in the LXX to make reference to David, the son of Jesse (3 Kgdms 12:26 [1 Kgs 12:26]; 2 Chr 10:16 LXX). Therefore, in this prepositional phrase the noun must be a dative of agency, while the preposition could be an adverbial ἐν or a modal ἐν.[28] Nevertheless, it must be recognized that the grammar of the text can allow different interpretations such as those who posit the prepositional phrase as an instrumental or causal expression.

δι' οὗ: P and RR-GSM from ὅς, a pronoun which is used 4943 times in the LXX, 5823 times in Philo, 1407 times in the New Testament, and seventy-four times in Hebrews. The preposition is expressing not "the efficient means, but the ultimate cause; not instrumentality, but sole agency." Also, this same construction with the same use can be found in 2:10 where God the Father is designated the sole cause—see the judgement of δι' οὗ τὰ πάντα in Harris[29]—of everything. The use of the definite anaphoric—i.e., relative—pronoun οὗ shows that the emphasis in Hebrews' introduction (1:1–4) is not in the nominative θεός but in the dative υἱῷ,[30] which means that υἱός is the main personality in Hebrews.

καί: B, even though it is used here as an adverb, καί is the word used more often, mainly as a conjunction in old Greek literature. Here it is more probable that it is being used as an adverb. Its omission in some textual witnesses—e.g., 𝔓[46] 0150 sa[mss]—as well as its context, since it is between asyndeton clauses—seven to be exact—gives support to this assertion.

25. Bultmann, *Grammar of the New Testament Greek*, 88–89.

26. Philo, *Migr.* 193.

27. Ignatius, *Magn.* 13.1.

28. The instrumental and the modal are closely related, while the adverbial ἐν expresses the manner in which the action of the main verb is performed. Harris, *Prepositions and Theology*, 119–20.

29. Harris, *Prepositions and Theology*, 70.

30. Westfall, *Discourse Analysis*, 91.

ἐποίησεν: VAAI3S from ποιέω, is used 3386 times in the LXX, 618 times in Philo, 568 times in the New Testament, and nineteen times in Hebrews. It is a transitive verb with perfective aspect which can imply a punctiliar *aktionsart* or a summary *aktionsart*,[31] but since determining which is more accurate is almost the main objective of this research—especially when the subject is God—further discussion will follow later.

τοὺς αἰῶνας: DAPM and NAPM from αἰών, a noun which is used 749 times in the LXX, seventy-three times in Philo, 122 times in the New Testament, and fifteen times in Hebrews. The article is working as a simple identifier, while the noun is an accusative direct object. However, it is important to clarify that although the masculine noun αἰών is used eleven times in Hebrews in the accusative case (cf. 1:2, 8; 5:6; 6:20; 7:17, 21, 24, 28; 11:3; 13:8, 21) and four times in the genitive case (cf. 1:8; 6:5; 9:26; 13:21), it is only used twice in the literary component of Hebrews' cosmogony in the accusative case. The interesting point here is the accusative case in plural number, given that it appears twice in the literary component of Hebrews' cosmogony in accusative plural (cf. 1:2; 11:3). Therefore, there are six times—i.e., in plural—in which αἰών appears in Hebrews that are useful in understanding its use in its cosmogonic context, as can be seen in Figure 5.2, building on the basis of the text present in the NA[28].

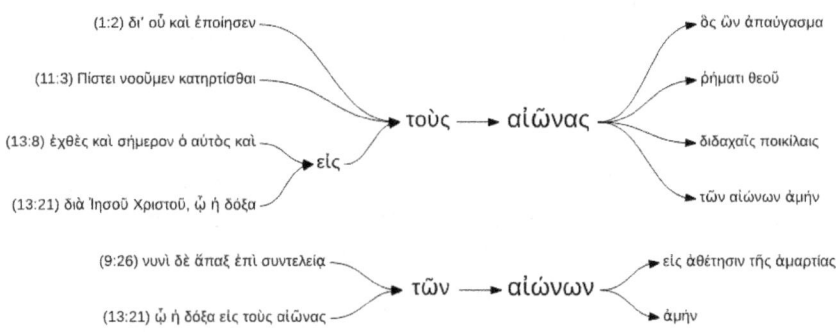

Figure 5.2 Use of αἰών in Hebrews' cosmogonic literary context.

Nevertheless, from the image it can be seen that in all six cases αἰών appears with its article and its two appearances in the literary component of Hebrews' cosmogony (1:2; 11:3) do not form part of the prepositional

---

31. If ἐποίησεν is considered as a transitive punctiliar lexeme it can imply a punctiliar *aktionsart*, but if ἐποίησεν is considered as a transitive non-punctiliar lexeme it can imply a summary *aktionsart*. Campbell, *Basics of Verbal Aspect*, 86–87.

phrase opening with εἰς. Of the 122 times that αἰών is used in the New Testament, it is used seventy-two times with the preposition εἰς, but these texts are not relevant to this research.³² Therefore, the use of αἰών fifty times in the New Testament seems to be more relevant to this research.³³ However, besides noting that αἰών is used without the preposition εἰς, it is also important to note that it is used in a clear connection with a verb in the literary component of Hebrews' cosmogony. And of the fifty occurrences, this configuration appears twice only, besides those in Hebrews: Luke 20:35 and Romans 12:2, but in both these cases they are singular, and one is genitive and the other is dative. So, it can be stated that these Hebrews' uses of αἰών in 1:2 and 11:3 are unique in the New Testament. On the other hand, the εἰς with the articulated noun αἰών is broadly used in the LXX and consistently translated as "into the ages,"³⁴ while Philo only uses this arrangement of words twice although not in a cosmogonic context.³⁵ However, the LXX never uses the plural accusative in connec-

---

32. These texts are not relevant to this research, since they follow a strict pattern which could be considered an idiomatic phrase which carries a temporal sense. Thus, the accusative plural, present thirty times in the New Testament, twenty-six times with the structure εἰς τοὺς αἰῶνας and eighteen of these times are followed by the genitive plural τῶν αἰώνων, which verses are marked [*] (13:8; 13:21*; cf. Luke 1:33; Rom 1:25; 9:5; 11:36; 16:27; 2 Cor 11:31; Gal 1:5*; Phil 4:20*; 1 Tim 1:17*; 2 Tim 4:18*; 1 Pet 4:11*; 5:11; Rev 1:6*, 18*; 4:9*, 10*; 5:13*; 7:12*; 10:6*; 11:15*; 15:7*; 19:3*; 20:10*; 22:5*), are not relevant to this research. However, it is used four times in accusative plural, with a different configuration (1:2; 11:3; cf. Jude 25; Rev 14:11), and nine times in the genitive plural (twenty-seven times used in the New Testament), also with a different configuration (9:26; cf. 1 Cor 2:7; 10:11; Eph 3:9, 11, 21; 1 Tim 1:17; Col 1:26; Rev 14:11). The accusative singular, meanwhile, is used thirty-one times in the New Testament, twenty-eight times in the structure εἰς τὸν αἰῶνα (1:8; 5:6; 6:20; 7:17, 21, 24, 28; cf. Matt 21:19; Mark 3:29; 11:14; Luke 1:55; John 4:14; 6:51, 58; 8:35, 51, 52; 10:28; 11:26; 12:34; 13:8; 14:16; 1 Cor 8:13; 2 Cor 9:9; 1 Pet 1:25; 1 John 2:17; 2 John 2), and therefore they are not relevant to this research. However, in three verses it has a different configuration (cf. Eph 2:2; 2 Tim 4:10; Jude 13).

33. All these texts use the noun αἰών without following some extensive pattern (1:2, 8; 6:5; 9:26; 11:3; cf. Matt 24:3; 28:20; 12:32; 13:22, 39-40, 49; Mark 4:19; 10:30; Luke 1:70; 16:8; 18:30; 20:34-35; John 9:32; Acts 3:21; 15:18; Rom 12:2; 1 Cor 1:20; 2:6-8; 3:18; 10:11; 2 Cor 4:4; Gal 1:4; Eph 1:21; 2:2, 7; 3:9, 11, 21; Col 1:26; 1 Tim 1:17; 6:17; 2 Tim 4:10; Titus 2:12; 2 Pet 3:18; Jude 13, 25; Rev 14:11) and among them are the two uses of αἰών that form part of the literary component of Hebrews' cosmogony.

34. However, in the LXX the prepositional phrase εἰς τοὺς αἰῶνας τῶν αἰώνων appears three times (Ps 83:4; 4 Macc 18:24; Tob 14:15 LXX), but the phrase is never used in Philo or in any other ancient writer. It was, however, used at least thirteen times by the apostolic Fathers.

35. See Philo, *Gig.* 19 (quotation of Gen 6:3); *Prov.* 2.19.

tion with some verb—as happens in 1:2 and 11:3. Moreover, there are only ten times where the plural accusative of αἰών is used and not one of these cases is in a cosmogonic context. In all of these cases the LXX shows the eternity of God or the repercussions of his actions.[36] Therefore, the LXX also leaves the use of αἰών in 1:2 and 11:3 without parallels as to its right understanding. So, it can be stated that from a morphological analysis it is almost impossible to determine the meaning of αἰών in 1:2 and 11:3, and since the determination of its meaning is basically the main objective of this research, its meaning will be further explored in succeeding chapters.

Key-Section 2: Hebrews 1:10–12

The Greek text that will be used for this section[37] and its translation—a dynamic translation—follows, with words *not* previously selected as forming part of the literary component of Hebrews' cosmogony appearing in bold.

Greek Text	Translation
καί σὺ κατ' ἀρχάς, κύριε τὴν γῆν ἐθεμελίωσας καὶ ἔργα τῶν χειρῶν σού εἰσιν οἱ οὐρανοί αὐτοὶ ἀπολοῦνται **σὺ δὲ διαμένεις** καὶ πάντες ὡς ἱμάτιον παλαιωθήσονται καὶ ὡσεὶ περιβόλαιον ἑλίξεις αὐτούς [] καὶ ἀλλαγήσονται **σὺ δὲ ὁ αὐτὸς εἶ καὶ τὰ ἔτη σου οὐκ ἐκλείψουσιν.**	And God says, Lord, You laid the foundation of the earth in the beginning and the heavens are the work of your hands; they will perish but You remain. Namely, Lord, all things will grow old like garments, and You will fold them up like a cloak, also they will be changed but You are the same and Your years will fail not.

36. Depending on the particular version of the LXX in which the counting is realized, the number of this configuration can differ—i.e., verb + article + αἰών—but also if the alternate texts are considered in the counting (cf. Exod 15:18; Tob 6:17; Odes Sol. 1:18; Wis 13:9; 14:6; Isa 57:15; Bar 3:3; Dan 5:4; [alternate texts Tob 3:2; 14:7; Dan 12:7] Pss. Sol. 9:18; Enoch 9:6; 22:14 LES). On the other hand, in some versions only Enoch 9:6 has the inscription τὰ μυστήρια καὶ ἀπεκάλυψε τῷ αἰῶνι τὰ ἐν οὐρανῷ (and He has revealed the mysteries of the ages that are in the heaven), but in other versions there is only the phrase τὰ μυστήρια τοῦ αἰῶνος τὰ ἐν οὐρανῷ (the mysteries of the ages that are in the heaven). Here too therefore, there is no absolute correlation with Hebrews' use of αἰών in 1:2 and 11:3. cf. Rick Brannan et al., *Lexham English Septuagint*; Ken and Heiser, *Old Testament Greek Pseudepigrapha with Morphology*.

37. It is important to also note that this text is not similar to the NA[28], since there are some words omitted here, and these are represented by the brackets—[ὡς ἱμάτιον]. For the reason for their omission, see "Textual issues of Hebrews' cosmogony" in chapter 4.

Grammatical Analysis of Cosmogonic Hebrews' Text 127

Syntactic Structure Analysis of Key-Section 2

As can be observed in Figure 5.3, this key-section has nine indicative verbs and it is one complex sentence. The PC has its subject and verb as tacit elements—θεός λέγει—but its complement is constituted by six ECs. The EC2 and the EC5 are asyndeton, while the EC1, the EC4 and the EC6 each have one SC. Also, there are two AJs, one in the EC1 and the other in the EC4. The AJ1 contains a temporal reference while the AJ2 contains a modal reference. Among them, the EC3 and the EC6, connected with the previous clauses by the conjunction δέ, have an adversative function,[38] and they are therefore in contrast with their previous ECs, and have no essential content on cosmogony.

Although it is not necessary to explain each phrase of the entire section, since it can be seen in Figure 5.3, it must be highlighted that the complement of the PC could be organized in a kind of chiasmic structure, since the EC1 with the EC4 address the same topic—the subjugation of the creation—while the EC3 and the EC5 are referring to the fragility of the creation. The EC3 and the EC6 also correspond with each other, because they are describing the vocative κύριε, and they therefore only have collateral information about cosmogony, since they are contrasting the creator with his creation.

Morpho-Syntactic Analysis of Key-Sentence 2

As already determined, key-sentence 2 is constituted by the following words: καί σὺ κατ' ἀρχάς, κύριε τὴν γῆν ἐθεμελίωσας καὶ ἔργα τῶν χειρῶν σού εἰσιν οἱ οὐρανοί αὐτοὶ ἀπολοῦνται καὶ πάντες ὡς ἱμάτιον παλαιωθήσονται καὶ ὡσεὶ περιβόλαιον ἑλίξεις αὐτούς καὶ ἀλλαγήσονται. Therefore, the morpho-syntactic analysis will be done on this clause in order to provide the foundational analysis of the Greek text upon which interpretation may then be established.

καί: C, is being used here as a coordinating conjunction, linking this sentence with the next, which are both PCs.

σὺ: RP2NS from σύ, used 14027 times in the LXX, 884 times in Philo, 2906 times in the New Testament, and sixty times in Hebrews.

---

38. The adversative function of these two clauses is evident due to its semantic content as well as the use of the conjunction δέ as their connector, which has the adversative function as its main function.

Here it seems that it has been used as a nominative of emphasis, involving some sort of contrast, with subject focus.[39]

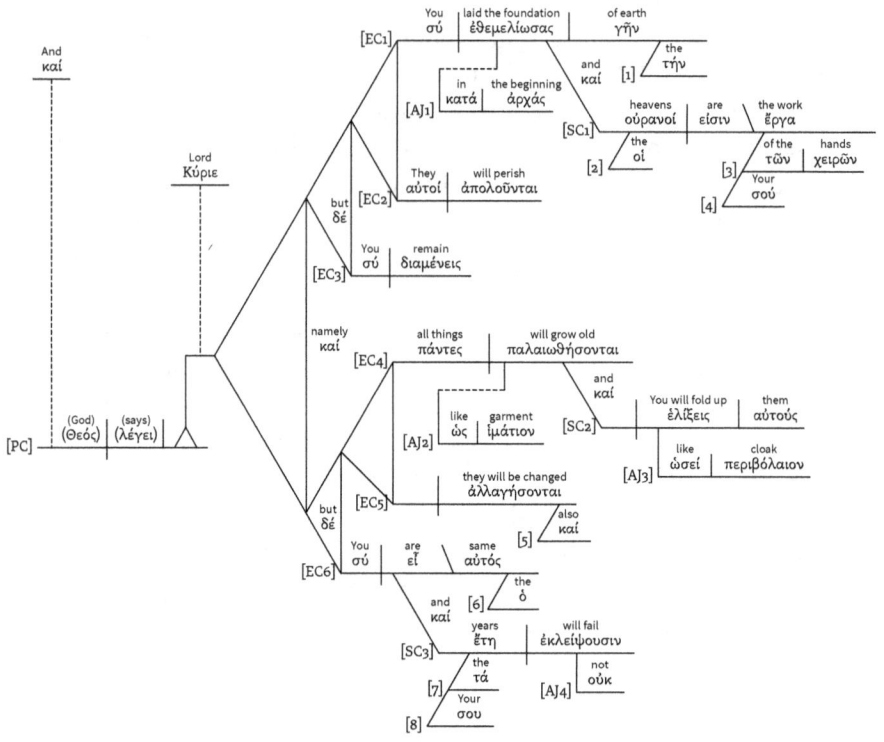

Figure 5.3 Line diagram of key-section 2: Hebrews 1:10–12.

κατ' ἀρχάς: P and NAPF from ἀρχή, a noun which is used 236 times in the LXX, 505 times in Philo, fifty-five times in the New Testament, and six times in Hebrews. ἀρχή is only used four times in the New Testament (1:10; Luke 12:11; Eph 6:12; Col 2:15) with this accidence—NAFP—but with the exception of Hebrews, the other three times it has a sense of principality. On the other hand, here ἀρχή is used without the article and as the object of the preposition κατά, which arrangement is found only

---

39. Wallace asserts that "the nominative personal pronoun is most commonly used for emphasis, . . . [which] may involve some sort of contrast." Namely, the implied subject is in contrast to the second subject. But in this case, the contrast is not clear whether it is of kind—i.e., antithetical—or degree—i.e., comparison. Wallace, *Greek Grammar Beyond the Basics*, 321–23.

once in the New Testament (1:10), twice in the LXX (Ps 101:26; 118:152 LXX), and eight times in Philo.[40] However, it is only used once in Philo in an indirect cosmogonic context, when he is talking about the very beginning of the human race.[41] Besides, the LXX—which uses ἀρχή to translate various words—significantly[42] uses the noun ἀρχή to translate the Hebrew noun רֵאשִׁית in Genesis 1:1. This noun is also used to translate פָּנֶה in Psalms 102:25 (101:26 LXX), text with a clear cosmogonic connotation, and also to translate the noun קֶדֶם in Psalms 119:152 (118:152 LXX). Therefore, it is possible that ἀρχή in the cosmogony of Hebrews in all likelihood refers to Genesis 1.

κύριε: NVSM from κύριος, used 8608 times in the LXX, 479 times in Philo, 715 times in the New Testament,[43] and 16 times in Hebrews. Even though κύριος is here working as a vocative of simple address,[44] it is important to highlight that this masculine noun,[45] used twice in the liter-

---

40. See Philo, *Leg.* 3.92; *Det.* 118; *Ios.* 225; *Praem.* 63, 68; *Contempl.* 63; *Flacc.* 11, 138.

41. Philo, in his treatment of the rewards for obedience and punishments for disobedience concerning the law written by Moses, holds, "ἐγένετό τις κατ' ἀρχὰς εὐθύς, ὅτ' οὔπω τὸ τῶν ἀνθρώπων γένος ἐπλήθυνεν (at the very beginning when the human race had not yet multiplied)." cf. *Praem.* 68.

42. The adverb "significantly" is used here in order to emphasize the quality and the fact that in the first sentence of the Scriptures of Israel, the translators of the LXX chose the noun ἀρχή which has important usage in the New Testament in order to translate the Hebrew noun רֵאשִׁית. It is also important to note that the Hebrew noun רֵאשִׁית is used forty-nine times in the Old Testament and only seventeen times ἀρχή is used to translate it, and in all of these instances it portrays a clear temporal sense. But also, as Lust, Eynikel, and Hauspie asserts, ἀρχή is a stereotypical rendition of רֵאשִׁית in the LXX. See "ἀρχή" in Lust et al., *Greek-English Lexicon of the Septuagint*. Therefore, since Hebrews' cosmogony is deeply influenced by Genesis 1–3 it is more probable that its use in a cosmogonic context has some sort of dependence on the Hebrew noun רֵאשִׁית.

43. As already affirmed, there are some differences between the different Greek versions in the usage of the words, and here the NA[28] is used, however these variations are usually only in respect of very few words. Nevertheless, in the case of the noun κύριος the difference is quite significant, since, for instance the Byz. text uses the word κύριος 748 times.

44. Wallace asserts that the substantive in the vocative is used to direct a statement to the addressee, predominantly without some special significance but obviously with great emotion in the utterance. Wallace, *Greek Grammar Beyond the Basics*, 67.

45. The etymology of the word shows that this word was inititally an adjective, which means that it can be understood as a kind of title which conveys features of the noun and adjective. Nevertheless, even though this use—as an adjective—can be found in the first century, it is very unlikely that the New Testament uses it thus in

ary component of Hebrews' cosmogony (1:10; 8:2), is the noun which in the LXX has largely mainly been used for the translation of the Hebrew יהוה, i.e., the more important, divine name in the Scriptures of Israel. On the other hand, in Hebrews, κύριος is used mostly in a sort of appositional way to θεός (cf. 7:21; 8:8, 9; 10:30), but it can also be seen in a sort of appositional way to the person of Jesus (7:14). Therefore, the noun κύριος in Hebrews is used to identify יהוה in the Scriptures of Israel, as well as the θεός and the χριστὸν Ἰησοῦν (3:1 Byz.) in Hebrews.

τὴν γῆν: DASF and NASF from γῆ, a noun which is used 3174 times in the LXX, 823 times in Philo, 250 times in the New Testament, and 11 times in Hebrews. For the article, see the analysis of ὁ θεὸς in key-section 1 above. The noun γῆ, which here functions as the direct object, is a feminine noun used abundantly both in the New Testament and elsewhere. Its sense is principally spatial, i.e., it refers to some specific area or the whole earth, which includes the sea,[46] particularly in Hebrews where θάλασσα is used only twice to identify some area that belongs to the dry land (cf. 11:12, 29).

ἐθεμελίωσας: VAAI2S from θεμελιόω, is used 41 times in the LXX, twice in Philo, five times in the New Testament, and only once in Hebrews. This transitive verb has a punctiliar lexeme, while the aorist tense has a perfective aspect, therefore it expresses an action—to lay the foundations—that is once-occurring and instantaneous, namely a punctiliar *aktionsart*.[47]

καὶ: C, here it is used as a connective conjunction, because it is used to add an additional element or an additional idea to the train of thought.[48]

---

reference to Jesus. As Spicq states, the substantive κύριος, was formed in the fourth century BCE from the substantivised adjective τὸ κύριον, which has as its first meaning "having power or being master of a city and governing it," or as describing a successful politician and particularly someone that is head of an estate. Spicq, *Theological Lexicon of the New Testament*, 2:341.

46. Even though some believe that the word γῆ is restricted to the totality of solid land only, cf. Kittel et al., *Theological Dictionary of the New Testament*, 1:678. It is important to note that in the cosmogonic context this division is irrelevant, since in it God only created the heavens and the earth (cf. Gen 1:1), and the sea appears as a result of the organization of this creation.

47. However, it must be clarified that, according to Campbell, the same accidence, i.e., the aorist indicative with punctiliar lexeme, can also imply a gnomic *aktionsart* or a present or future aorist. Campbell, *Colossians and Philemon*, xxiv.

48. Wallace, *Greek Grammar Beyond the Basics*, 671.

ἔργα: NNPN from ἔργον, is used 591 times in the LXX, 446 times in Philo, 169 times in the New Testament, and nine times in Hebrews. Here it is functioning as a predicate nominative.[49] In Hebrews ἔργον is used seven times in the genitive case (cf. 4:3, 4, 10; 6:1, 10; 9:14; 10:24), once in accusative (3:9) and once in nominative (cf. 1:10). In the literary component of Hebrews' cosmogony, it is used three times; twice in the genitive case with the article (cf. 4:3, 4) and once in the nominative case without the article (cf. 1:10). In all the forms in which ἔργον appears in Hebrews, it is linked with human beings four times (cf. 6:1, 10, 9:14; 10:24) and the other five times it is linked with deity. The LXX, meanwhile, uses ἔργον to translate 162 מְלָאכָה times, a noun that occurs 167 times in the Old Testament. It is significant that the first three times the word מְלָאכָה is used is in Genesis 2:2–3, in an evidently cosmogonic context. In these verses the LXX uses ἔργον twice in the genitive and once in the accusative, very similar to its use in Hebrews' literary component of cosmogony—i.e., with the article. Therefore, ἔργον in the cosmogony of Hebrews is most likely linked with Genesis 2:2–3, and hence with Genesis 1, particularly given the genitive cases of the word. And since the article is used with ἔργον here and in Genesis, it is very likely that ἔργον in the cosmogony of Hebrews is not referring to one of the innumerable acts of God, but to the work of God, namely his action of creating.

τῶν χειρῶν: DGPF and NGPF from χείρ, a noun which is used 1945 times in the LXX, 252 times in Philo, 177 times in the New Testament, and five times in Hebrews. Here it seems to be acting as an attributive genitive, more specifically as a genitive of quality,[50] and thus it can be translated with the adjective: handmade. It is also important to note that in its abundant use, this noun has various senses, such as: (1) human hand; (2) power; (3) right side; (4) God's activity; and (5) the medium through which the power is transferred—i.e., the laying on of hands.[51] However, it is also well-known that in all of these uses, there is an implication of a personal and direct intervention, and therefore it must also be understood in this sense in Hebrews.

σοῦ: RP2GS from σύ, here it functions as a possessive genitive.[52]

---

49. As Chapman and Shogren state, the copulative verbs (εἰμί, γίνομαι, ὑπάρχω) do not take a direct object; in their predicate, they take a nominative. Chapman and Shogren, *Greek New Testament Insert*, 18.

50. Robertson, *Grammar of the Greek New Testament*, 496.

51. See Kittel et al., *Theological Dictionary of the New Testament*, 9:424–34.

52. The possessive genitive is the word that reveals some sort of dependent or

εἰσιν: VPAI3P from εἰμί, used 6829 times in the LXX, 6834 times in Philo, 2462 times in the New Testament, and fifty-five times in Hebrews. It is an intransitive verb with a stative lexeme and with an imperfective aspect, therefore its use here implies a stative *aktionsart*, i.e., it expresses a state of being rather than a process.[53]

οἱ οὐρανοί: DNPM and NNPM from οὐρανός, a noun which is used 682 times in the LXX, 425 times in Philo, 273 times in the New Testament, and ten times in Hebrews. The article is working as a simple identification, while the noun is the subject of εἰσιν, a finite verb. In Hebrews οὐρανός is consistently translated as heaven, and it seems that in most cases it is referring to the habitat of God (cf. 8:1; 9:23, 24) and also to the place where the heavenly bodies are placed, which is between the habitat of God and the habitat of human beings (cf. 4:14; 7:26; 11:12). It is never used with the sense of divinity, and in this, Hebrews departs from Philo's and other Greek usages of the word. Also, it is well-known that the LXX consistently uses the articular οὐρανός to translate the Hebrew שָׁמַיִם in Genesis 1–2; apparently, only in Genesis 1:8 the LXX uses οὐρανός without the article—καὶ ἐκάλεσεν ὁ θεὸς τὸ στερέωμα οὐρανόν—and their God is naming the στερέωμα—רָקִיעַ—as οὐρανός. Here it is important to note that the Hebrew רָקִיעַ has a sense of a large solid surface, because it is the word used to describe the barrier between the waters above and below (Gen 1:6–7).[54] Therefore, οὐρανός in the literary component of Hebrews has a clear union with the meaning of שָׁמַיִם and רָקִיעַ in Genesis 1–2, and it is also important to note that οὐρανός is used in Genesis 1:1 LXX in parallel and as a complement of γῆ, i.e., both words are used in a kind of hendiadys.

αὐτοί: RP3NPM from αὐτός, used 29390 times in the LXX,[55] 4522 times in Philo, 5596 times in the New Testament, and fifty-five times in Hebrews. Here, as can be seen in Figure 5.3, it is functioning as the subject of ἀπολοῦνται, a finite verb, and its referents are οὐρανός and γῆ.

---

derivative status for the main term in relation to the word in genitive. Here it seems to be a possessive genitive without doubt, even though, according to Porter, in some cases it is difficult to distinguish between the possessive and the subjective genitive. Porter, *Idioms of the Greek New Testament*, 93. Chapman also states that "the subjective genitive can be difficult to distinguish from the possessive genitive." Chapman, *New Testament Greek Notebook*, 61.

53. Campbell, *Basics of Verbal Aspect*, 64.
54. Lookadoo, "Celestial Bodies."
55. It must be clarified that in the LXX it is not clear when its use is on the basis of αὐτός or of αὑτός, however it is clear that the use of this pronoun is abundant.

ἀπολοῦνται: VFMI3P from ἀπόλλυμι, used ninety-three times in the LXX, forty-one times in Philo, ninety times in the New Testament, and only once in Hebrews. This intransitive lexeme[56] has a perfective aspect, therefore it can imply a summary or an ingressive *aktionsart*, but since here the context sets a new direction, it must be portraying an ingressive *aktionsart*, i.e., it depicts the beginning of a new state or action.[57] On the other hand, the middle voice shows that "the subject is acting in relation to himself somehow,"[58] which here are οὐρανός and γῆ through the pronoun αὐτοί.

καὶ: C, here it is used as an explanatory conjunction because it is used to give additional information about what is being described.[59]

πάντες: JNPM from πᾶς, used 6821 times in the LXX, 3554 times in Philo, 1243 times in the New Testament, and fifty-three times in Hebrews. Here it has a substantive function—it is a noun—and it is the subject of the finite verb παλαιωθήσονται, and since here it is an *anarthrous noun*, it can mean all creatures or all the things that have been created, but that are also visible for the human being.[60] However, it is important to highlight that the word πᾶς carries the sense of all, any, total, whole, every kind of; and in some special constructions it can mean "since all times" (πρό παντὸς τοῦ αἰῶνος), "forever" (εἰς παντὰς, τοὺς αἰῶνας, τῶν αἰώνων), and "through all" (διὰ παντός) with a sense of periodical occurrence or permanent occurrence.[61] However, it seems that in a biblical cosmogonic

---

56. This verb however, can be considered as a verb that can be either transitive or intransitive—depending on the context, it may act upon an object in some situations or it may not act upon an object in other situations. These lexemes are best labeled "ambitransitive," because they can go either way. Campbell, *Basics of Verbal Aspect*, 56–57. Here it seems that this verb is performing an intransitive action since it does not have a direct object.

57. Campbell, *Basics of Verbal Aspect*, 97.

58. Robertson asserts that "the only difference between the active and middle voices is that the middle calls especial attention to the subject. In the active voice the subject is merely acting; in the middle the subject is acting in relation to himself somehow." Robertson, *Grammar of the Greek New Testament*, 804. Also, Wallace states that "The difference between the active and middle is one of emphasis. The active voice emphasises the *action* of the verb; the middle emphasises the *actor* [subject] of the verb." Wallace, *Greek Grammar Beyond the Basics*, 415.

59. Wallace, *Greek Grammar Beyond the Basics*, 671.

60. More explanation about the difference of the use of πᾶς with the article or without the article can be seen in Kittel et al., *Theological Dictionary of the New Testament*, 5:888–90.

61. Louw and Nida, *Greek-English Lexicon*, 1:588, 596, 612, 630, 639, 640–41, 646, 662, 690; 2:190.

context it is used to make reference to Genesis 2:2–3, since in the LXX and also in Philo the use of πᾶς with the preposition διά or ἀπό is almost always referring directly or indirectly to the completed creation as it is shown in Genesis 2:2–3.[62] Also, the articulate πᾶς, abundantly used in the LXX and in other documents, is almost always related with everything, even the things that are not perceptible to the human being.

ὡς: P,[63] used 2055 times in the LXX, 2386 times in Philo, 504 times in the New Testament, and twenty-two times in Hebrews. Here ὡς is answering the question how, i.e., it is working in a comparative sense,[64] and it is working as AJ of παλαιωθήσονται, and it has as its object the noun ἱμάτιον. Nevertheless, it must be conceded that the grammar also allows it to be considered as a preposition of manner.

ἱμάτιον: NNSN from ἱμάτιον, used 223 times in the LXX, 20 times in Philo, 60 times in the New Testament, and twice in Hebrews.[65] Here it is working as the object of the preposition ὡς which is used to make

---

62. For instance, Philo when trying to explain the superiority of the numbe seven, quotes Gen 2:2–3. Cf. Philo, *Leg.* 1.16, 18; *Post.* 64. In the LXX very similar uses can be seen that are present in the cosmogony of Hebrews, for instance in 2 Macc 12:21, where the indirect reference is the completed creation.

63. Ninety-nine times the New Testament uses ὡς as a preposition, therefore here, due to the syntactic context, it must be considered as a preposition also, as in 3:5, 6; 6:19; 12:16.

64. There are not many studies about the use of this preposition, but it seems that this preposition can be used with the nominative (thirty-nine times), accusative (nineteen times) and genitive (six times) case. And since the adverbs and the preposition are closely related, it can also be asserted that ὡς is functioning as an adverb of comparison, since it is amplifying the verbal idea, particularly since the ending—ως is very common and frequently occurring in the adverbs. Porter, *Idioms of the Greek New Testament*, 125. On the other hand, Wallace affirms that "Prepositions are, in some respects, extended adverbs. That is, they frequently modify verbs and tell how, when, where, etc. But, unlike adverbs, they govern a noun and hence can give more information than a mere adverb can. 'Christ dwells in you' is more specific than 'Christ dwells inside.'" Wallace, *Greek Grammar Beyond the Basics*, 356. In addition, Harris states "In each Greek preposition, it seems, there is an inherent, foundational meaning that is further defined by a particular context." Harris, *Prepositions and Theology*, 27.

65. In the NA[28] there are only two times where ἱμάτιον is used in Hebrews, and in both cases they are used with the conjunction ὡς, in the literary component of Hebrews' cosmogony (1:11–12). However, as already mentioned, the second instance when the noun ἱμάτιον appears in Hebrews was omitted since the linguistic analysis allows it—see the section entitled "Textual Issues of Hebrews Cosmogony." It is also important to state that in the NA[28] the first is nominative and the second is accusative, perhaps following the morphology of περιβόλαιον present in other textual witnesses, since the form of ἱμάτιον is the same in the nominative and accusative case.

comparisons, as can be seen in Figure 5.3. In any event, the meaning of this noun is not complex, as the word is used to refer to clothing in a general sense,[66] as is widely attested in first-century literature.

παλαιωθήσονται: VFPI3P from παλαιόω, used 28 times in the LXX, once in Philo, four times in the New Testament, and three times in Hebrews. It is an intransitive verb—non-punctiliar lexeme—with a tense that carries on a perfective aspect. Therefore, here it implies a summary *aktionsart*, i.e., it simply expresses that something is happening, without further specification. The passive voice, meanwhile, indicates that the subject receives the action,[67] which here is πάντες.

καί: C, here it is used as a connective conjunction, because it is used to add an additional element or an additional idea to the train of thought.

ὡσεί: B,[68] used 204 times in the LXX, 12 times in Philo, 21 times in the New Testament, and only once in Hebrews. Here it is working in union with περιβόλαιον to modify the meaning of the verb ἑλίξεις.

περιβόλαιον: NASN from περιβόλαιον, used 11 times in the LXX, three times in Philo, twice in the New Testament, and only once in Hebrews. Here it could be a direct object of an adverbial clause but it is better to regard it as the object of the adverb, which is working in a very similar way to the object of the preposition. It must be highlighted that this is a compound word—περι + βαλλω—and that in all the uses of this word in the LXX, it is never found in a cosmogonic context (cf. Exod 22:26; Deut 22:12; Judg 8:26; Ps 101:27; 103:6; Job 26:6; Isa 50:3; 59:17; Jer 15:12; Ezek 16:13; 27:7 LXX). Philo, meanwhile, who uses the word only three times, also never uses it in a cosmogonic context.[69] In all cases

---

66. Smith, "Clothing."

67. Wallace asserts that "the most common use of the passive voice is to indicate that the subject receives the action;" he also affirms, "no implication is made about cognition, volition, or cause on the part of the subject. This usage occurs both with and without an expressed agent." See Wallace, *Greek Grammar Beyond the Basics*, 439.

68. The word ὡσεί is mostly considered as a conjunction, however, it is also possible to consider it as an adverb, cf. Liddell et al., *Greek-English Lexicon*; Thomas, *New American Standard*. An adverb can be "a word or phrase that modifies the meaning of an adjective, verb, or other adverb." See *COEDLE*, s.v. "Adverb." Usually it expresses manner, place, time, or degree, and here this adverb is working in union with the noun περιβόλαιον to modify the meaning of the verb ἑλίξεις. However, it is important to clarify that its meaning does not change if it is considered as a preposition—due to its relation with ὡς—or a conjunction, but if it is a conjunction the accusative περιβόλαιον must be a direct object of a sentence with a tacit subject and verb, and this is less probable.

69. See Philo, *Somn.* 1.92, 101, 107.

where the word is used it has the sense of covering or cloak, and it is in this sense that it must be understood in Hebrews.

ἑλίξεις: VFAI2S from ἑλίσσω, used twice in the LXX, never used in Philo, twice in the New Testament, and only once in Hebrews. This transitive verb has a perfective aspect and a non-stative lexeme, therefore it implies an ingressive *aktionsart*, which simply depicts an ingressive action, in which the beginning of the state or action is in view.[70] The active voice, meanwhile, as the voice that is the least semantically weighted, simply states that the agent acts in the event,[71] i.e., the κύριος will fold up all things.

αὐτούς: RP3APM from αὐτός, as can be seen in Figure 5.3, is working as the direct object of the finite verb ἑλίξεις, in the SC2, and has as its referent the word πάντες, which is working as the subject of the EC4.

καί: B, here it is an emphatic modifier of the verb ἀλλαγήσονται, and means 'also'.

ἀλλαγήσονται: VFPI3P from ἀλλάσσω, used 42 times in the LXX, 26 times in Philo, six times in the New Testament, and only once in Hebrews. This transitive verb has a perfective aspect and a non-stative lexeme, therefore it implies an ingressive *aktionsart* that simply depicts an ingressive action, in which the beginning of the state or action is in view. The passive voice, meanwhile, indicates that the subject receives the action, i.e., πάντες will be changed.

Key-Section 3: Hebrews 2:10

The Greek text that will be used for this section[72] and its translation—a dynamic translation—follows, with words that were previously selected as the literary component of Hebrews' cosmogony appearing in bold.

Greek Text	Translation
ἔπρεπεν γὰρ **αὐτῷ δι' ὃν τὰ πάντα καὶ δι' οὗ τὰ πάντα** πολλοὺς υἱοὺς εἰς δόξαν ἀγαγόντα τὸν ἀρχηγὸν τῆς σωτηρίας αὐτῶν διὰ παθημάτων τελειῶσαι.	It was fitting for Him, for Whom all things are and by Whom all things are, to make perfect the ruler of their salvation through suffering, in order to bring many sons to glory.

---

70. Campbell, *Basics of Verbal Aspect*, 97.
71. Porter, *Idioms of the Greek New Testament*, 63.
72. In this case the text is the same as the NA[28].

Syntactic Structure Analysis of Key-Section 3

As can be seen in Figure 5.4, this key-section has only one indicative verb and, consequently, it forms one sentence. The PC—ἔπρεπεν αὐτῷ—is linked to the previous sentence through the conjunction γάρ, and has a complex subject, which is the EC1—τὸν ἀρχηγὸν τῆς σωτηρίας αὐτῶν τελειῶσαι—which in turn is constituted by the AJ1—διὰ παθημάτων— and the SC1—πολλοὺς υἱοὺς ἀγαγόντα—which is asyndeton and has the AJ2—εἰς δόξαν—as its modifier. On the other hand, the complement of the PC—αὐτῷ—is constituted by the SP1 which in turn is constituted by two prepositional phrases and each of them has one EC with implicit verbs.

Morpho-Syntactic Analysis of Key-Sentence 3

As already determined, key-sentence 3 is constituted by the following words: ἔπρεπεν γὰρ αὐτῷ δι' ὃν τὰ πάντα καὶ δι' οὗ τὰ πάντα. Therefore, the morpho-syntactic analysis will be done on this clause in order to provide the foundational analysis of the Greek text upon which interpretation may then be established.

ἔπρεπεν: VIAI3S from πρέπω, used ten times in the LXX, thirty-five times in Philo, seven times in the New Testament, and only twice in Hebrews. This impersonal verb[73] has an imperfective aspect—i.e., remoteness—due to its tense, and a stative lexeme, and the context also allows stativity, so it can imply a stative *aktionsart*. It expresses a state of being rather than a process. On the other hand, the imperfect tense shows that the clause is going to provide supplementary information that describes, characterizes, or explains, previous ideas.[74] The subject of this impersonal verb is "it"—αὐτός—and it has an action, not a noun, as its referent, i.e., the verb which is present in the EC1—τελειῶσαι—and with it the verb of the SC1—ἀγαγόντα—i.e., to complete, to finish or to perfect, and to bring, all actions which are fitting only for him.

---

73. Porter states that an impersonal verb is one in which the subject is not specified either explicitly or implicitly, and it is usually confined to the third person singular, although some have posited that under Semitic influence the plural could be used in this way as well. Porter, *Idioms of the Greek New Testament*, 77–78.

74. Campbell asserts that the difference between aorist and imperfect verbs is that the aorist verbs "typically provide the skeletal structure of the narrative mainline," while the imperfect verbs "provide supplementary information that describes, characterises, or explains." Campbell, *Basics of Verbal Aspect*, 62.

138 Hebrews' Cosmogonic Presuppositions

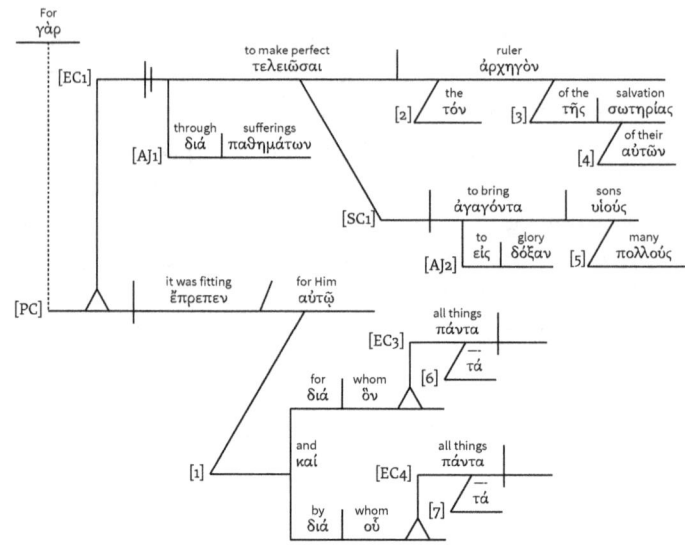

Figure 5.4 Line diagram of key-section 3: Hebrews 2:10.

γάρ: C, used 1548 times in the LXX, 5728 times in Philo, 1041 times in the New Testament, and ninety-one times in Hebrews. Even though this conjunction is linking two PCs, i.e., two sentences, here it has an explanatory function, which, according to its composition, γέ and ἄρα, is essentially a particle that posits an affirmation and conclusion, meaning *"truly therefore, verily as the case stands,* the thing is first affirmed by the particle γέ, and then is referred to what precedes by the force of the particle ἄρα."[75]

αὐτῷ: RP3DSM from αὐτός, here it is an instance of the oblique case, that is to say, it is there "in the place of a noun or other nominal. This use of the pronoun is usually called *anaphoric*, in that it refers back to its antecedent,"[76] which in this case is ὁ θεός.

δι' ὅν: P and RR-ASM from ὅς, here it is expressing purpose or ultimate goal, therefore, it must mean "for the sake of whom."[77]

τὰ πάντα: DNPN and JNPN from πᾶς, here it is used with the article and as a noun. As can be seen in Figure 5.4, it is functioning as the subject of the EC3, and with the article has an implicative or summative

75. Thayer, *Greek-English Lexicon*, 109.
76. Wallace, *Greek Grammar Beyond the Basics*, 324.
77. Harris, *Prepositions and Theology*, 76.

significance, i.e., it can imply the universe as a whole, including the things that are not perceptible.[78]

καὶ: C, here it is a coordinating conjunction, i.e., a conjunction used to express coordination between two sentential elements.

δι' οὗ: P and RR-GSM from ὅς, here this prepositional phrase is not expressing "the efficient means but the ultimate cause, not instrumentality but sole agency," i.e., θεός is designated the sole cause[79] of everything.

τὰ πάντα: DNPN and JNPN from πᾶς, subject of the EC4, which means "everything, or all the universe."[80]

Key-Section 4: Hebrews 3:3–4

The Greek text that will be used for this key-section[81] and its translation—a dynamic translation—follows, with words previously selected as the literary component of Hebrews' cosmogony appearing in bold.

Greek Text	Translation
Πλείονος γὰρ οὗτος δόξης παρὰ Μωϋσῆν ἠξίωται καθ' ὅσον πλείονα τιμὴν ἔχει τοῦ οἴκου ὁ κατασκευάσας αὐτόν πᾶς γὰρ οἶκος κατασκευάζεται ὑπό τινος, **ὁ δὲ πάντα κατασκευάσας θεός**.	For this One is considered worthy of greater glory than Moses inasmuch as he who builds the house has greater honor than the house. For every house is built by someone but **God is Who built everything**.

78. Kittel et al., *Theological Dictionary of the New Testament*, 5:888–89. Also, Salmond affirms that τὰ πάντα explains "the widest possible and most comprehensive universality, including the sum total of created objects, wherever found, whether men or things." Nicoll, *Expositor's Greek Testament*, 3:262.

79. Harris asserts that sometimes, διά with the genitive expresses not "the efficient means but the ultimate cause, not instrumentality but sole agency, as in Romans 11:36, where God the Father is designated the source (ἐκ) sole cause (διά) and goal (εἰς) of all things." Similarly, ὁ θεός, δι' οὗ ἐκλήθητε (1 Cor 1:9); κληρονόμος διὰ θεοῦ (Gal 4:7); ἔπρεπεν γὰρ αὐτῷ ... δι' οὗ τὰ πάντα (2:10). Harris, *Prepositions and Theology*, 70.

80. Thayer states that τὰ πάντα means all things, the totality of created things, the whole universe, the things in all places. Thayer, *Greek-English Lexicon*, 493.

81. In this case the text is the same as the NA[28].

140 | Hebrews' Cosmogonic Presuppositions

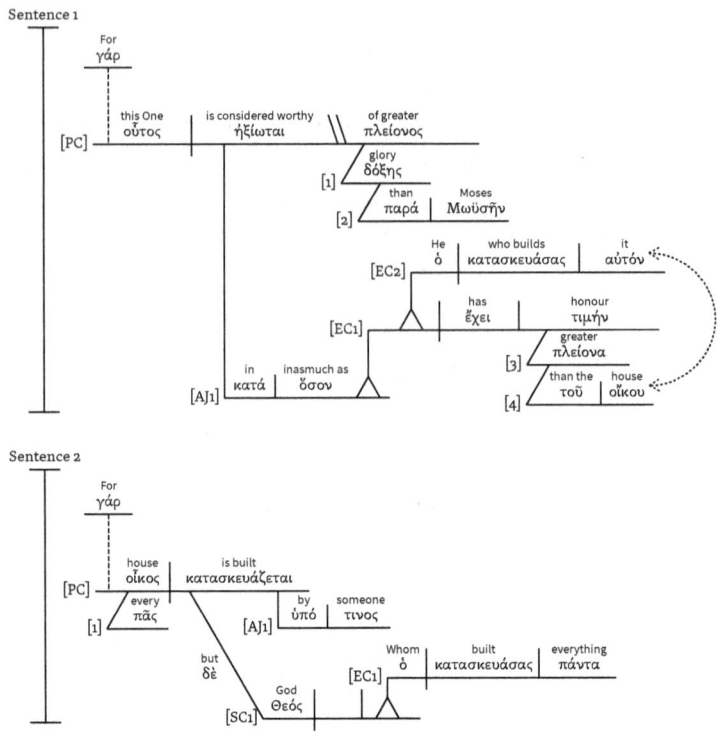

Figure 5.5 Line diagram of key-section 4: Hebrews 3:3–4.

Syntactic Structure Analysis of Key-Section 4

In this key-section there are three indicative verbs and as can be seen in Figure 5.5, it consists of two sentences. Verse 4 is not a dependent clause of verse 3, since the coordinating conjunction γὰρ, which has an explanatory function, is linking these two sentences. Sentence 1, which belongs to verse 3, has only collateral information about cosmogony, while sentence 2, which belongs to verse 4, is more pertinent to the cosmogony of Hebrews. In sentence 2 the PC—πᾶς οἶκος κατασκευάζεται—has a transitive finite verb and has no complement; in addition, this PC is constituted by the AJ1—ὑπό τινος—and by the SC1—θεός—which has a tacit verb, and its complement is constituted by the EC1—ὁ πάντα κατασκευάσας— which has as its verb a nominative participle which is also functioning as a finite verb. The PC and the SC1 are linked by the conjunction δὲ that here has an emphatic function.

Morpho-Syntactic Analysis of Key-Sentence 4

As already determined, key-sentence 4 is constituted by the following words: ὁ δὲ πάντα κατασκευάσας θεός. Therefore, the morpho-syntactic analysis will be done on this clause, in order to provide the foundational analysis of the Greek text upon which interpretation may then be established.

ὁ: DNSM, here it is working as a demonstrative pronoun and it is functioning as the subject of the EC1 in sentence 2.[82]

δὲ: C, used 4905 times in the LXX, 11166 times in Philo, 2791 times in the New Testament, and seventy-one times in Hebrews. Here it is functioning as an adversative conjunction, i.e., "a coordinating conjunction that suggests a contrast or opposing thought to the idea to which it is linked."[83]

πάντα: JAPN from πᾶς, here it is working as a direct object in the EC1 and means "everything." However, it is important to note that in other textual witnesses—C³ D² L P Ψ 0278. 81. 104. 365. 630. 1175. 1241. 1505. 2464 𝔐—this adjective is accompanied by its article, and can therefore carry the sense of the whole universe.

κατασκευάσας: VPPI3S from κατασκευάζω, used twenty-eight times in the LXX, 155 times in Philo, eleven times in the New Testament, and six times in Hebrews. This transitive verb has a non-punctiliar[84] and non-stative lexeme, and due to its tense has an imperfective aspect, and therefore it expresses a process or action in progress, i.e., an ingressive *aktionsart*.[85]

---

82. More information about the article and its function as a pronoun can be found in Wallace, *Greek Grammar Beyond the Basics*, 211–16; Robertson, *Grammar of the Greek New Testament*, 693–94.

83. A more comprehensive definition of the term can be found in Heiser and Setterholm, *Glossary of Morpho-Syntactic Database Terminology*; Lukaszewski, *Lexham Syntactic Greek New Testament Glossary*.

84. Even though to build (κατασκευάζω) must be a non-punctiliar lexeme, in the case of God who is performing the action it can be punctiliar, since punctiliar action is performed on an object and is instantaneous in nature. Campbell, *Basics of Verbal Aspect*, 57.

85. Although it is too early to make conclusions at this point, it is important to highlight here that perhaps Hebrews is trying to portray God's continuous intervention in his creation in order to create life or to allow that the life can continue in

θεός: NNSM from θεός, here it is the subject of the SC1, i.e., the element of the clause, which performs or causes the main verbal action.[86]

Key-Section 5: Hebrews 4:3–5

The Greek text that will be used for this key-section[87] and its translation—a dynamic translation—follows, with words previously selected as the literary component of Hebrews' cosmogony appearing in bold.

Greek Text	Translation
Εἰσερχόμεθα γὰρ εἰς τὴν κατάπαυσιν οἱ πιστεύσαντες καθὼς εἴρηκεν ὡς ὤμοσα ἐν τῇ ὀργῇ μου εἰ εἰσελεύσονται εἰς τὴν κατάπαυσίν μου **καίτοι τῶν ἔργων ἀπὸ καταβολῆς κόσμου γενηθέντων** εἴρηκεν γάρ που περὶ τῆς ἑβδόμης οὕτως καὶ **κατέπαυσεν ὁ θεὸς ἐν τῇ ἡμέρᾳ τῇ ἑβδόμῃ ἀπὸ πάντων τῶν ἔργων αὐτοῦ** καὶ ἐν τούτῳ πάλιν εἰ εἰσελεύσονται εἰς τὴν κατάπαυσίν μου.	For we—who have believed—enter into the rest, since His works were finished from the foundation of the world, although, in another place, He said: I swore in My wrath they shall not enter in My rest. Because, He had spoken in one place about the seventh day, even so: And God rested on the seventh day from all of His works, then, in turn, this one place can mean: they shall enter in my rest.

Syntactic Structure Analysis of Key-Section 5

In this key-section there are seven indicative verbs, four in verse 3, two in verse 4, and one in verse 5, although, as can be seen in Figure 5.6, this key-section is only one sentence. The PC—εἰσερχόμεθα—has as its subject the EC1—οἱ πιστεύσαντες—with the AJ1—εἰς τὴν κατάπαυσιν—and the AJ2—καίτοι τῶν ἔργων ἀπὸ καταβολῆς κόσμου γενηθέντων—as its modifiers, while its SC1—καθὼς εἴρηκεν ὡς ὤμοσα ἐν τῇ ὀργῇ μου εἰ εἰσελεύσονται εἰς τὴν κατάπαυσίν μου—and its SC2—γάρ που περὶ τῆς ἑβδόμης οὕτως καὶ κατέπαυσεν ὁ θεὸς ἐν τῇ ἡμέρᾳ τῇ ἑβδόμῃ ἀπὸ πάντων

---

existence. It could also be referring to his capacity of creating whatever he wants, wherever, and whenever he decides to do it.

86. Lukaszewski, *Lexham Syntactic Greek New Testament Glossary*. The presence of the article ὁ, working as demonstrative pronoun, morphologically and grammatically connected with θεός, can be seen in this clause.

87. In this case the text is the same as the NA^{28}.

τῶν ἔργων αὐτοῦ καὶ ἐν τούτῳ πάλιν εἰ εἰσελεύσονται εἰς τὴν κατάπαυσίν μου—are subordinate clauses, offering nuance to the PC.[88]

In this clause, the AJ2, particularly its EC2, which is a genitive absolute, and, in the SC2, the EC6—καὶ κατέπαυσεν ὁ θεὸς ἐν τῇ ἡμέρᾳ τῇ ἑβδόμῃ ἀπὸ πάντων τῶν ἔργων αὐτοῦ—are most pertinent to this research. But it must also be noted that the SC1 and the SC2 have some sort of adversative relation, given their use of the conjunctions: ὡς and εἰ, in the SC1, and the conjunctions: οὕτως and εἰ, in the SC2.[89] This assertion is also supported by the use of the same verb—εἴρηκεν—in the SC1 and the SC2, as well as by the use of the same words in the EC4 and the EC8—εἰ εἰσελεύσονται εἰς τὴν κατάπαυσίν μου.

Morpho-Syntactic Analysis of Key-Sentence 5

As already determined, key-sentence 5 is constituted by the following words: καίτοι τῶν ἔργων ἀπὸ καταβολῆς κόσμου γενηθέντων κατέπαυσεν ὁ θεὸς ἐν τῇ ἡμέρᾳ τῇ ἑβδόμῃ ἀπὸ πάντων τῶν ἔργων αὐτοῦ. Therefore, the morpho-syntactic analysis will be done on this clause, in order to provide the foundational analysis of the Greek text upon which interpretation may then be established.

καίτοι: C, used four times in the LXX,[90] 148 times in Philo, twice in the New Testament, and only once in Hebrews. Its use here is difficult to determine, but since it appears to be introducing a genitive absolute clause,[91] it must be considered as an adverb with a concessive function. In addition, the combination of καί and the particle τοι (then) gives support

---

88. Lukaszewski, *Lexham Syntactic Greek New Testament Glossary*.

89. The uses of these conjunctions can imply a sort of adversarial relation between the two clauses, since εἰ is a marker of a condition—real or hypothetical, actual or contrary to fact—that can be used to contradict the fact, but it can also be used to affirm the fact. See Louw and Nida, *Greek-English Lexicon of the New Testament*, 1:785. Also, the use of the conjunctions ὡς and οὕτως which are usually translated as "so" and "even so" can contribute to this conclusion.

90. Only used in 4 Macc 2:6; 5:18; 7:13; 8:16.

91. The genitive absolute is usually placed at the beginning of the clause, but here it is placed in the middle of it, and, as Wallace states, it is always adverbial, i.e., dependent on some verb, and usually temporal. Here it is evidently temporal, since it provides information about when the rest is available to humanity. Wallace, *Greek Grammar Beyond the Basics*, 644–55.

for this assertion (cf. 4 Macc 8:1 LXX [4 Macc 7:24]), and therefore it can mean 'so also' or preferably, "since."[92]

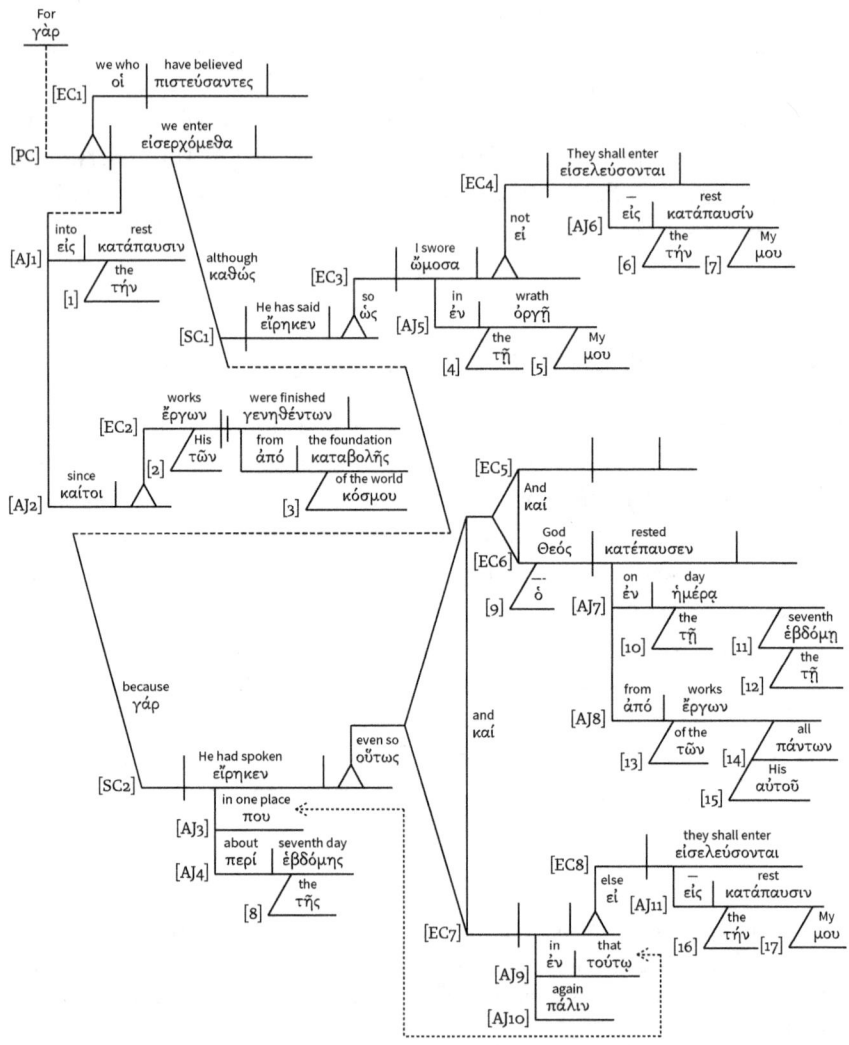

Figure 5.6 Line diagram of key-section 5: Hebrews 4:3–5.

92. Although there are not many more treatises about the use of καίτοι, some information about this word can be found in Thayer, *Greek-English Lexicon*, 319; Liddell et al., *Greek-English Lexicon*, 860; Louw and Nida, *Greek-English Lexicon*, 1:785.

τῶν ἔργων: DGPN and NGPN from ἔργον, here the article is functioning as a possessive pronoun, while the noun is functioning as the subjective genitive—the subject of γενηθέντων—even though it can also be seen as the objective genitive.[93]

ἀπὸ καταβολῆς: P and NGSF from καταβολή, a noun which is used once in the LXX, seven times in Philo, eleven times in the New Testament, and three times in Hebrews. Here the prepositional phrase, in harmony with the genitive absolute clause, has a temporal sense. It is also important to state that καταβολή is almost always used with the masculine noun κόσμος and, in two instances, in the genitive case (cf. 4:3; 9:26), with the only exception to this in 11:11.[94] The LXX, meanwhile, uses the term only once and there it means "structure of the house."[95] In the pseudepigrapha of the Old Testament, the word is used seven times, and only two of these seven times is not in relation to κόσμος. Josephus and Philo also use this word but never in connection with κόσμος, and Josephus never uses it in a cosmogonic context.[96] Philo, meanwhile, uses καταβολή seven times, and in all of these cases it carries the sense of seed or the foundation that gives origin to something, such as life, disease, plants, and so on, i.e., something like the original seed.[97] On the other hand, more recent researchers have noted that the use of καταβολή

---

93. As Wallace asserts, when the genitive "is related to a verbal noun, then, it is probably objective or subjective"; the difference however, is that with the objective genitive the equative—γίνομαι in this case—verb is a participle in the genitive case rather than a finite verb. On the other hand, Wallace also asserts that "the genitive substantive functions semantically as the subject of the verbal idea" and that the objective genitive function "as the *direct object* of the verbal idea." Therefore, even though in this case there is no main noun present, which is usually expected, it can be affirmed that the genitive ἔργων is more likely a subjective genitive. This assertion can also be supported if it is considered that the genitive participle γενηθέντων could be considered syntactically as a verbal noun. Wallace, *Greek Grammar Beyond the Basics*, 82, 102, 113, 116.

94. Here its use is confusing: "αὐτὴ Σάρρα στεῖρα δύναμιν εἰς καταβολὴν σπέρματος ἔλαβεν ('with Sarah he received the ability to procreate' [LEB] or 'Sarah herself received strength to conceive seed' [NKJV])." This phrase seems to be incoherent, because, as Thayer states, it seems that 11:11 is saying that Sarah receives power to conceive seed, but since this power belongs to the male—καταβάλλειν τὸ σπέρμα—not to the female, this interpretation cannot stand. See Thayer, *Greek-English Lexicon*, 330.

95. The text says, "τῆς καινῆς οἰκίας ἀρχιτέκτονι τῆς ὅλης καταβολῆς φροντιστέον (the master builder of a new house must take heed of the whole structure)" (2 Macc 2:29).

96. See Josephus. *Ant.* 12.64; 18.163, 164, 274; *J.W.* 2.260, 409, 417.

97. See Philo, *Opif.* 132; *Sobr.* 45; *Her.* 115; *Mos.* 1.279; *Spec.* 3.36; *Legat.* 54, 125.

expresses a temporal idea related to the beginning of all things.[98] Therefore, καταβολή in Hebrews conveys a temporal sense, which posits the time when the κόσμος—in this case—appears in its first moment, i.e., the time when the founding of the κόσμος is at hand.

κόσμου: NGSM from κόσμος, used seventy-two times in the LXX, 617 times in Philo, 186 times in the New Testament, and five times in Hebrews. Here it is functioning as an attributed genitive.[99] Also, since it is the first appearance of κόσμος in this analysis, it must be mentioned that it is used twice in the literary component of Hebrews' cosmogony (4:3; 9:26). In both of these cases, it is used in the prepositional phrase ἀπὸ καταβολῆς κόσμου, used only once outside of the New Testament,[100] and never used in the LXX, Philo, or Josephus. In the New Testament, κόσμος is almost always translated as "world,"[101] while in the LXX it conveys two senses, i.e., "ornament" and "world." Although the senses in which κόσμος is used in the New Testament can be debated, in Hebrews κόσμος definitely conveys a spatial sense, i.e., a physical entity (cf. 4:3; 9:26; 10:5; 11:7, 38). However, its use in Hebrews seems to differ from its common use in first-century Judaism, since Hebrews seems to use κόσμος to portray the spatial habitat of the human being and not the totality of the cosmic system in the sense of the universe.[102]

---

98. The temporal idea can make reference to the origin of the plan of salvation or the "pretemporality" of the divine action, but the use of the word "pretemporality" here could be wrong, since it can imply that God had acted in a moment when time was non-existent, and that is impossible. More information about καταβολή and its temporal use can be found in Kittel et al., *Theological Dictionary of the New Testament*, 3:620–21; Arndt et al., *Greek-English Lexicon*, 515.

99. This use happens when the main noun, rather than the genitive, conveys the attributive sense, but the use of the genitive implies a more emphatic and a stronger force than that of the main noun. See Wallace, *Greek Grammar Beyond the Basics*, 89.

100. "ἔτι δὲ καὶ τοῦτο, ἀδελφοί μου εἰ ὁ κύριος ὑπέμεινεν παθεῖν περὶ τῆς ψυχῆς ἡμῶν, ὢν παντὸς τοῦ κόσμου κύριος ᾧ εἶπεν ὁ θεὸς ἀπὸ καταβολῆς κόσμου ποιήσωμεν ἄνθρωπον κατ' εἰκόνα καὶ καθ' ὁμοίωσιν ἡμετέραν πῶς οὖν ὑπέμεινεν ὑπὸ χειρὸς ἀνθρώπων παθεῖν (And also in addition to this, my brothers if the lord endured to suffer for our souls being Lord of all the world, to whom God says *since the foundation of the world*, "Let us make humankind according to our image and according to our likeness, how therefore, did he endure to suffer under the hand of humanity?)." *Barn.* 5.5.

101. The only exception is found in 1 Pet 3:3, where κόσμος carries the meaning of adornment or external beauty. This means that κόσμος kept its primary meaning even in the first century.

102. A very good study on the word κόσμος can be found in Kittel et al., *Theological Dictionary of the New Testament*, 3:868–95.

γενηθέντων: VAPP-PGN from γίνομαι, used 2222 times in the LXX,[103] 1721 times in Philo, 668 times in the New Testament, and twenty-nine times in Hebrews. This participle, due to its tense, has a perfective aspect, which can imply an action that is antecedent to its leading verb, or an action that is temporally subsequent to its leading verb—although this is rare—or an action that is contemporaneous to the action of the main verb.[104] Here, due to its context, an action that is antecedent to its leading verb must be implied, i.e., before someone can enter—εἰσερχόμεθα—into God's rest, His works were finished—γενηθέντων.

κατέπαυσεν: VAAI3S from καταπαύω, used sixty-seven times in the LXX, nine times in Philo, four times in the New Testament, and three times in Hebrews. This intransitive verb, due to its context, does not have a stative lexeme,[105] and due to its tense has a perfective aspect, i.e., an external viewpoint of the facts. The context, meanwhile, permits the entry into a new direction or state. Therefore, here this verb can imply an ingressive *aktionsart*, i.e., the beginning of a new action.

ὁ θεός: DNSM and NNSM from θεός, here it is functioning as the subject who performs the action of κατέπαυσεν.

ἐν τῇ ἡμέρᾳ: P, DDSF and NDSF from ἡμέρα, this noun is used 2573 times in the LXX, 421 times in Philo, 389 times in the New Testament, and eighteen times in Hebrews. Here this prepositional phrase—ἐν τῇ ἡμέρᾳ τῇ ἑβδόμῃ—has a temporal sense, in that it means "during this day." It is important to note also that ἡμέρα in the LXX mainly means "day," the period of twenty-four hours,[106] especially in a cosmogonic context. It is used in the same sense in 4:4 and in key-verses of the cosmogony of the Old Testament (cf. Gen 2:2; 5:1; Exod 20:10–11). Therefore, ἡμέρα, in this

---

103. It must be clarified that the LXX (Rahlfs, Alfred) use the lemma γίγνομαι in place of γίνομαι.

104. Campbell, *Basics of Verbal Aspect*, 94.

105. A stative lexeme can be seen in the verb καταπαύω, since the rest can be seen as a state; however, the context of Hebrews shows that the work—the action prior to the rest—of God is not a state, because he works and after it he rests, therefore his rest—καταπαύω—also ought to be considered as an action leading to a new action.

106. In Genesis 1 ἡμέρα is the totality of the period of darkness and light in each day of the creation. As Gerhard von Rad asserts, the ancient Hebrew day consisted of day and night, and according to the cultus it officially began in the evening (Exod 12:18; Lev 23:32), and in this, he affirms, the creation narrative harmonises well with this cultic usage, since the text says, "There was an evening, and there was a morning: one day." (Gen 1:5 CSB). See Kittel et al., *Theological Dictionary of the New Testament*, 2:943–47.

prepositional phrase,[107] can mean "the evening and the morning," i.e., the chronological day.

τῇ ἑβδόμῃ: DDSF and JDSF from ἕβδομος, an adjective which is used 134 times in the LXX, 139 times in Philo, nine times in the New Testament, and twice in Hebrews. Here it is working with the noun in an attributive position and with a locative function, thus it is a modifier of ἡμέρᾳ in that it still forms part of the prepositional phrase—ἐν τῇ ἡμέρᾳ τῇ ἑβδόμῃ—and it is specifying which day was the day when God rested from all his works, i.e., the seventh day.

ἀπὸ: P, it is a modifier of the verb κατέπαυσεν, and has as its object the words πάντων τῶν ἔργων αὐτοῦ. The basic force of ἀπό in classical Greek was "separation from,"[108] and since this preposition can function here as a preposition of separation, it must convey the sense of "away from." Nevertheless, it must be recognized that this preposition could also introduce the cause or reason for the main verb action, but in this case it seems unlikely.

πάντων: JGPN from πᾶς, here it is working as a SP of ἔργων, i.e., God rested from all his works and not from some of his works.

τῶν ἔργων: DGPN and NGPN from ἔργον, here it is a descriptive genitive[109] even though it is functioning as the object of the preposition ἀπό which indicates that God rests because he separates himself from his action of creating. However, it must be highlighted that Hebrews does not assert that God will never perform the action of creating again, i.e., this separation must be considered as circumstantial or incidental but not as a permanent state, which could be better understood as a genitive of separation. On the other hand, it must be remembered that the genitive of separation, as Wallace posits, "is determined by the lexical meaning of the word to which the genitive is related,"[110] and not necessarily by the presence of the preposition.

---

107. More about the use of this preposition in connection with ἡμέρα can be found in Harris, *Prepositions and Theology*, 119.

108. Wallace, *Greek Grammar Beyond the Basics*, 368.

109. The descriptive genitive is a special use of the genitive and, as Wallace asserts, "this is the category one should appeal to when another slot cannot be found. The title is descriptive not of the genitive, but of the feeling one has in the pit of his/her stomach for having spent so much time on this case and coming up with nothing." Wallace, *Greek Grammar Beyond the Basics*, 79.

110. Wallace states that only if the head word of the genitive, which in this case will usually be "a verb connotes motion away from, distance, or separation can the genitive be one of separation." Wallace, *Greek Grammar Beyond the Basics*, 108.

αὐτοῦ: RP3GSM from αὐτός, here it is functioning as a possessive genitive and as a SP of ἔργων, and it has as its reference the noun θεός, the subject of this clause—see the EC6 in Figure 5.6.

Key-Section 6: Hebrews 4:10

The Greek text that will be used for this key-section[111] and its translation—a dynamic translation—follows, with words that were previously selected as the literary component of Hebrews' cosmogony appearing in bold.

Greek Text	Translation
ὁ γὰρ εἰσελθὼν εἰς τὴν κατάπαυσιν αὐτοῦ καὶ αὐτὸς **κατέπαυσεν** ἀπὸ τῶν ἔργων αὐτοῦ ὥσπερ **ἀπὸ τῶν ἰδίων ὁ θεός**	For he who has entered into His repose, also has ceased from his works, just as God has ceased from His own.

Syntactic Structure Analysis of Key-Section 6

In this key-section there is only one indicative verb and as can be seen in Figure 5.7, this key-section has only one sentence. The PC—αὐτὸς κατέπαυσεν—has a complex subject which is constituted by the EC1—ὁ εἰσελθὼν εἰς τὴν κατάπαυσιν αὐτοῦ—which is functioning as the apposition of the pronoun αὐτός. On the other hand, the AJ1—καὶ—and the AJ2—ἀπὸ τῶν ἔργων αὐτοῦ—are specifying the way in which the verbal action is being modified. The SC1—ὥσπερ ἀπὸ τῶν ἰδίων ὁ θεός—meanwhile, which is a nonverbal clause as can be seen in Figure 5.7, which demands the finite κατέπαυσεν as its verb, could be considered as an explanatory or correlative clause.

Morpho-Syntactic Analysis of Key-Sentence 6

As already determined, key-sentence 6 is constituted by the following words: κατέπαυσεν ἀπὸ τῶν ἔργων ὁ θεός. However, as was also mentioned, the analysis here will be done in the SC1 and also in the elements that were taken from the PC to develop key-sentence 6. Therefore, the

---

111. In this case the text is the same of the NA^{28}.

morpho-syntactic analysis will be done on this clause, in order to provide the foundational analysis of the Greek text upon which interpretation may then be established.

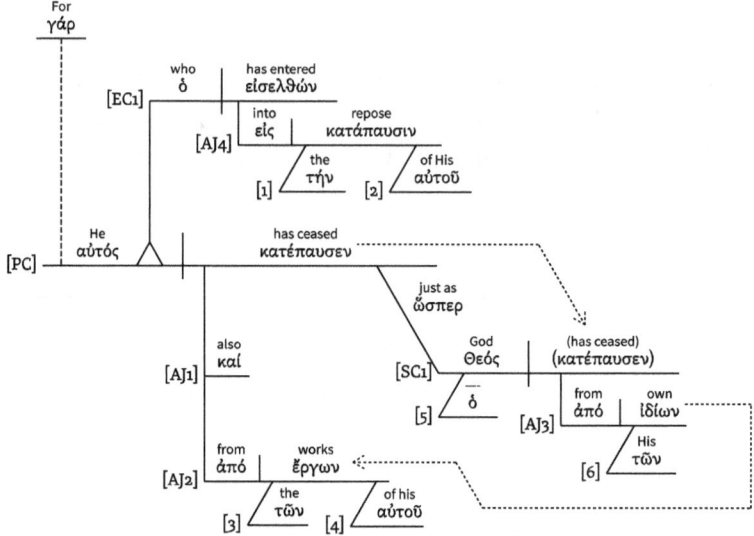

Figure 5.7 Line diagram of key-section 6: Hebrews 4:10.

κατέπαυσεν: VAAI3S from καταπαύω, as already asserted, this verb can imply an ingressive *aktionsart*, namely the beginning of a new action.

ὥσπερ: C, used 263 times in the LXX, 562 times in Philo, thirty-six times in the New Testament, and three times in Hebrews. It is functioning as an adverbial conjunction with comparative force, which amplifies the verbal idea and introduces a subordinate clause.[112] Therefore, here it means "just as" or "in the same way," particularly if it is considered in the broad theological context of Hebrews.

ἀπὸ τῶν ἰδίων: P, DGPN and JGPN from ἴδιος, which is used seventy-nine times in the LXX, 402 times in Philo, 114 times in the New Testament, and four times in Hebrews. Here the adjective ἴδιος is working as a relative pronoun because it is pointing to τῶν ἔργων, while the prepositional phrase can be a partitive preposition, preposition of direction, preposition of separation or preposition of reference.[113] However, in

112. Wallace, *Greek Grammar Beyond the Basics*, 675.
113. Lukaszewski et al., *Lexham Syntactic Greek New Testament*, Heb 4:10.

Grammatical Analysis of Cosmogonic Hebrews' Text 151

harmony with the cosmogonic context of Hebrews, this preposition must be a preposition of separation, and therefore it must convey the sense of 'away from'.

τῶν ἔργων: DGPN and NGPN from ἔργον. Here it is a descriptive genitive,[114] and it is functioning as the object of the preposition ἀπό, i.e., God rests because he separates himself from his action of creating.[115]

ὁ θεός: DNSM and NNSM from θεός, here it is the subject of SC1.

Key-Section 7: Hebrews 8:1–2

The Greek text that will be used for this key-section[116] and its translation—a dynamic translation—follows, with words that were previously selected as the literary component of Hebrews' cosmogony appearing in bold.

Greek Text	Translation
κεφάλαιον δὲ ἐπὶ τοῖς λεγομένοις τοιοῦτον **ἔχομεν** ἀρχιερέα ὃς ἐκάθισεν ἐν δεξιᾷ τοῦ θρόνου τῆς μεγαλωσύνης ἐν **τοῖς οὐρανοῖς** τῶν ἁγίων λειτουργὸς καὶ τῆς σκηνῆς τῆς ἀληθινῆς ἣν ἔπηξεν ὁ κύριος οὐκ ἄνθρωπος.	Now, the main point on the things that we are saying is that we have such a High Priest in the heavens, who is seated at the right hand of the throne of the Majesty, a minister of the sanctuary and of the tabernacle which the Lord erected, not man, the true one.

Syntactic Structure Analysis of Key-Section 7

This key-section has three indicative verbs and they form only one complex sentence. The subject—κεφάλαιον—of the PC, which is a nonverbal clause, as can be seen in Figure 5.8, has as its modifier the SP1 which is constituted by the preposition ἐπί, which has as its object the EC2—τοῖς λεγομένοις. On the other hand, the PC has a complex complement, which is constituted by the EC1—τοιοῦτον ἔχομεν ἀρχιερέα—which is constituted by the AJ1—ἐν τοῖς οὐρανοῖς—which is providing spatial information

---

114. See footnote 109 from current chapter.

115. The phrase τῶν ἔργων is replacing the object of the preposition ἀπό which is τῶν ἰδίων, since the adjective ἴδιος is serving almost as a pronoun with reference to the noun ἔργων.

116. In this case the text is the same as the NA[28].

and so it is addressing the locative issue. The SC1—ὃς ἐκάθισεν—meanwhile, is a relative clause, which has as its modifier the AJ2—ἐν δεξιᾷ τοῦ θρόνου τῆς μεγαλωσύνης—which is also providing spatial information and so it is expressing the locative issue. All of them—the SC1 and SC2 with their AJs and SPs—are providing information about the complement—ἀρχιερέα—which is functioning as a direct object of the EC1.

The SC2, which is a nonverbal clause, is functioning as an explanatory clause[117] and it is constituted by the complex SP6, which is modifying its complement—λειτουργός. The SP6, in turn, is constituted by the phrase τῶν ἁγίων καὶ τῆς σκηνῆς (of the sanctuary and of the tabernacle) which is also modified by the SP7—ἥν—which is constituted by the EC3—ἔπηξεν ὁ κύριος—and the EC4—οὐκ ἄνθρωπος—which are in an adversative position.

Morpho-Syntactic Analysis of Key-Sentence 7

As already determined, key-sentence 7 is constituted by the following words: ἔχομεν τῶν ἁγίων λειτουργὸς καὶ τῆς σκηνῆς τῆς ἀληθινῆς ἣν ἔπηξεν ὁ κύριος οὐκ ἄνθρωπος. Therefore, the morpho-syntactic analysis will be done on this clause, in order to provide the foundational analysis of the Greek text upon which interpretation may then be established.

ἔχομεν: VPAI1P from ἔχω, used 501 times in the LXX, 1104 times in Philo, 708 times in the New Testament, and thirty-nine times in Hebrews. This transitive verb, due to its context, has a stative lexeme, and due to its tense, has an imperfective aspect, i.e., an internal or very close viewpoint of the facts, and the context, meanwhile, allows stativity. Therefore, here this verb can imply a stative *aktionsart*, i.e., this verb describes a state of being rather than a process or transitive action,[118] and thus it expresses the fact of having.

τῶν ἁγίων: DGPN and JGPN from ἅγιος, an adjective which is used 831 times in the LXX, 128 times in Philo, 233 times in the New Testament, and nineteen times in Hebrews. It is important to note that the plural τῶν ἁγίων in the LXX is used consistently in relation to the Jewish sanctuary, as its name (cf. Exod 26:33, 34; Lev 10:4; 19:30; 26:2; Jdt 4:13;

---

117. A subordinate clause offering an explanation of some aspect of the immediate sentence or paragraph context, i.e., it "expresses further clarification of the author's intended meaning—this occurs most often epexegetically and is therefore marked as appositional." See Lukaszewski, *Lexham Syntactic Greek New Testament Glossary*.

118. Campbell, *Basics of Verbal Aspect*, 64.

16:20; Ezek 42:20; 43:21; 44:1, 15; 45:7; 47:12; 48:10, 18 LXX), and as the translation of the Hebrew קֹדֶשׁ, which in the Scriptures of Israel is frequently used to name the Jewish sanctuary. Philo also uses the phrase τῶν ἁγίων to refer to the Jewish sanctuary.[119] Therefore, and due to its context, here this adjective functions as a noun and more specifically as the noun referring to the Jewish sanctuary.

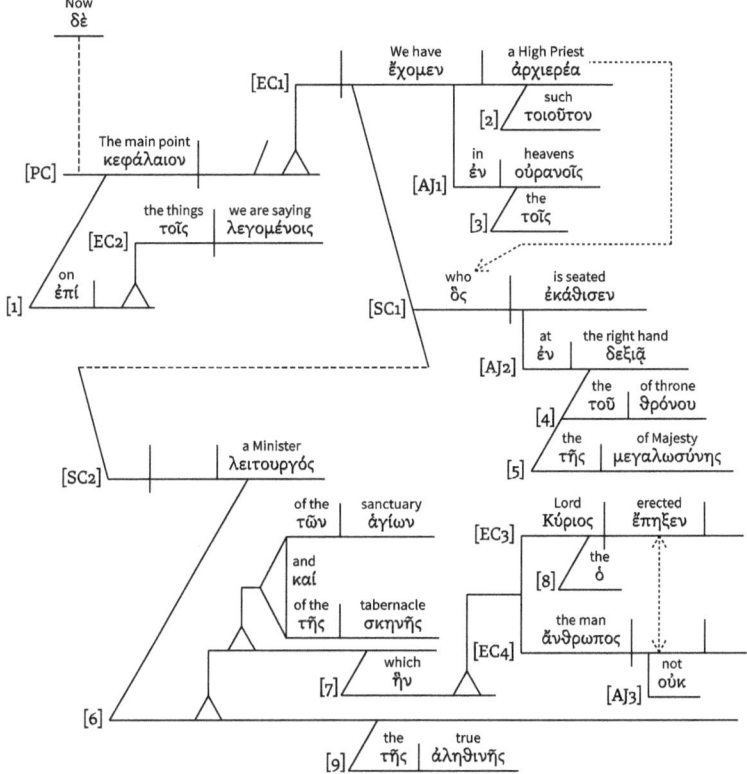

Figure 5.8 Line diagram of key-section 7: Hebrews 8:1–2.

λειτουργὸς: NNSM from λειτουργός, used fourteen times in the LXX, eleven times in Philo, five times in the New Testament, and twice in Hebrews. Here it is working as the complement of the SC2. In the LXX this word is used in the context of cultic legislation and in reference to the

---

119. Even though Philo does not use the phrase τῶν ἁγίων on its own very often, but mostly alongside with the τὰ ἅγια, there is one instance when he uses only τῶν ἁγίων to refer to the sanctuary. cf. Philo, *Fug.* 93.

priestly ministry, therefore it can be stated that here it is used to identify the heavenly ministry of Jesus Christ with the high-priestly ministry.[120]

καὶ: C, is a coordinating conjunction, namely a conjunction used to express coordination between two sentential elements of the same value.

τῆς σκηνῆς: DGSF and NGSF from σκηνή, a noun which is used 436 times in the LXX, seventy-four times in Philo, twenty times in the New Testament, and ten times in Hebrews. This feminine noun is only used twice in the literary component of Hebrews' cosmogony (cf. 8:2; 9:11) and is only used once in Hebrews outside of its connection with the tabernacle built by Moses (cf. 11:9). Also significant is its use to translate the word מִשְׁכָּן in Exodus 25:9 (25:8, LXX) and accordingly, it can be asserted that the second-most common use in the LXX, Philo, and Josephus makes reference to the tabernacle built by Moses as the physical place which was considered to be the residence of God. Therefore, it seems that Hebrews uses the word—particularly in its cosmogonic context—to refer to the physical place where God dwells; its context here supports this assertion.

τῆς ἀληθινῆς: DGSF and JGSF from ἀληθινός, an adjective which is used fifty times in the LXX, eighteen times in Philo, twenty-eight times in the New Testament, and three times in Hebrews. Here it is functioning as a modifier of the SP6, as can be seen in Figure 5.8, and indirectly, it is also modifying the direct object of the SC2—λειτουργὸς—i.e., this minister is the true minister, as well as the place where he develops his ministry.[121]

ἣν: RR-ASF from ὅς, here it is working as a sort of adverb,[122] as can be seen in Figure 5.8, since it is working as a hinging word between the SP6—which is the modifier of λειτουργὸς—and its specifier, constituted by the SP7, which in turn is constituted by the EC3 and the EC4. Therefore, this relative pronoun refers to the place where Jesus is ministering, i.e., to the true τῆς σκηνῆς and τῶν ἁγίων erected by the Lord.

ἔπηξεν: VAAI3S from πήγνυμι, used forty-one times in the LXX, sixty-eight times in Philo, and once in the New Testament, only in Hebrews. This transitive verb is a *hapax legomena* in the New Testament

---

120. Kittel et al., *Theological Dictionary of the New Testament*, 4:215–16, 229–31.

121. As Bultmann asserts, in relation to divine things the word ἀληθινός has the sense of that which truly is, or of that which is eternal, Kittel et al., *Theological Dictionary of the New Testament*, 1:250–51. But also it is possible, that these two nuances of the text can be combined in the word ἀληθινός in relation to divine things, i.e., ἀληθινός can mean in this context, truly eternal thing.

122. More information about the different possible uses that have the relative pronoun ὅς can be found in Wallace, *Greek Grammar Beyond the Basics*, 336–43.

Grammatical Analysis of Cosmogonic Hebrews' Text 155

and, due to its context, has a punctiliar lexeme, and, due to its tense, has a perfective aspect, i.e., an external or distant viewpoint of the facts—and the context, meanwhile, is a general statement about reality. Therefore, here this verb can imply a gnomic *aktionsart*, i.e., this verb depicts a timeless and universal action.[123] Thus it means that this true sanctuary and tabernacle was erected in some undefined moment.

ὁ κύριος: DNSM and NNSM from κύριος, here it is functioning as the subject of the EC3 as can be seen in Figure 5.8.

οὐκ: B, from οὐ, used 6569 time in the LXX, 4596 times in Philo, 1624 times in the New Testament, and sixty-six times in Hebrews. This adverb of negation is denying the EC4, which is nonverbal but which must be, due to its context, the verb ἔπηξεν.

ἄνθρωπος: NNSM from ἄνθρωπος, used 1426 times in the LXX, 1111 times in Philo, 550 times in the New Testament, and ten times in Hebrews. Here it is functioning as the subject of EC4. Its meaning as "human being" is not questioned.[124] However, it is interesting to note that the LXX uses the singular of ἄνθρωπος consistently in Genesis 1–2 to translate the generic noun אָדָם which means "humanity." Therefore, in the literary component of Hebrews' cosmogony, ἄνθρωπος must be read with this background, particularly in each place where it appears in the singular (cf. 2:6; 8:2; 13:6).

Key-Section 8: Hebrews 9:6–12

In this key-section there are two sentences, and only the second sentence is relevant to this research, which is constituted by verses 11 and 12, therefore the Greek text that will be used for this key-section[125] will only be from verses 11 and 12. The text and its translation—a dynamic translation—follows, with words previously selected as the literary component of Hebrews' cosmogony appearing in bold.

---

123. Campbell, *Basics of Verbal Aspect*, 135.
124. More information about the uses and meaning of the word ἄνθρωπος can be found in Kittel et al., *Theological Dictionary of the New Testament*, 1:364–66.
125. In this case the text is the same as the NA[28].

Greek Text	Translation
Χριστὸς δὲ παραγενόμενος ἀρχιερεὺς τῶν γενομένων ἀγαθῶν **διὰ τῆς μείζονος καὶ τελειοτέρας σκηνῆς οὐ χειροποιήτου τοῦτ' ἔστιν οὐ ταύτης τῆς κτίσεως** οὐδὲ δι' αἵματος τράγων καὶ μόσχων διὰ δὲ τοῦ ἰδίου αἵματος **εἰσῆλθεν** ἐφάπαξ εἰς τὰ ἅγια αἰωνίαν λύτρωσιν εὑράμενος.	But Christ, whom has become High Priest of the good that have come, entered, in the tabernacle—the greater and more perfect not made with hands, that is not of this creation—once for all, and not with blood of goats and calves but with his own blood, in the most holy place. Thus He obtained eternal redemption.

Syntactic Structure Analysis of Key-Section 8

In this extensive key-section there are only five indicative verbs, with one present in every verse with the exception of verses 8 and 10. The use of conjunctions is significant here in order to determine the sentences.[126] So for instance, the conjunction δέ is used at the beginning of verse 11 in an adversative sense, which usually points to the beginning of one new independent clause or sentence,[127] and therefore verses 11 and 12 can be considered as one sentence. Besides, verses 11 and 12 are linked with the conjunction οὐδέ, which usually has a continuative sense,[128] thus these two verses are combined into one complex sentence, as can be seen in Figure 5.9. Only this sentence will be analyzed here.

The PC—Χριστὸς εἰσῆλθεν—is constituted by four AJs, the SC1—αἰωνίαν λύτρωσιν εὑράμενος—and two ECs. The EC1—παραγενόμενος ἀρχιερεὺς τῶν γενομένων ἀγαθῶν—is functioning as a sort of appositional clause to the subject of the PC. The AJ1—διὰ τῆς μείζονος καὶ τελειοτέρας σκηνῆς οὐ χειροποιήτου τοῦτ' ἔστιν οὐ ταύτης τῆς κτίσεως—and the AJ4—εἰς

---

126. The conjunction δέ is used in the beginning of verse 6 in a transitional sense, in the beginning of the verse 7 in an adversative sense, at the beginning of the verse 11 also in an adversative sense, and in verse 12 in an emphatic or continuative sense. The use of δέ in a transitional and adversative sense usually points to the beginning of one independent clause or sentence, therefore verses 6–10 can be considered one sentence, or verse 6 and then verses 7–10 can be considered two different sentences.

127. Wallace affirms that "the function of an independent clause is usually determined by the "logical" function of the coordinating conjunction introducing the clause." Among them, the conjunction δέ can have a connective, contrastive, correlative or transitional function. Wallace, *Greek Grammar Beyond the Basics*, 657–58.

128. Robertson, *Grammar of the Greek New Testament*, 1185.

τὰ ἅγια—meanwhile, are portraying the location, i.e., they are expressing the locative issue. As the AJ2—ἐφάπαξ—is providing temporal information about the verbal action, and the AJ3—οὐδὲ δι' αἵματος τράγων καὶ μόσχων διὰ δὲ τοῦ ἰδίου αἵματος—is providing information about the key used in order to execute the verbal action, it can be stated that the AJ3 is fundamentally causative, although it could also be understood as supportive.

Morpho-Syntactic Analysis of Key-Sentence 8

As already determined, key-sentence 8 is constituted by the following words: Χριστὸς διὰ τῆς μείζονος καὶ τελειοτέρας σκηνῆς οὐ χειροποιήτου, τοῦτ' ἔστιν οὐ ταύτης τῆς κτίσεως εἰσῆλθεν. Therefore, the morpho-syntactic analysis will be done on this clause, in order to provide the foundational analysis of the Greek text upon which interpretation may then be established.

Χριστὸς: NNSM from Χριστός, used fifty times in the LXX,[129] never used in Philo, 529 times in the New Testament, and twelve times in Hebrews. Here it is functioning as the subject of the PC. Of the fifty times it is used in the LXX, it is used only once (cf. Hab 3:13, LXX) to make clear reference to the Anointed that will bring salvation, but the New Testament uses the word to identify Jesus with the מָשִׁיחַ, and thus it was used to emphasize the fulfilment of the Old Testament, announced in his person.[130] Therefore, the noun Χριστός is used in Hebrews in a form of apposition to Ἰησοῦς and υἱός (cf. 3:6; 13:8).

διὰ: P: here introduces a complex prepositional genitive spatial phrase, and, due to its context (cf. 8:1–2), it is better translated as "in."[131]

τῆς: DGSF of ὁ, here it is functioning as the SP of σκηνῆς.

μείζονος: JGSF from μέγας, used 913 times in the LXX, 895 times in Philo, 243 times in the New Testament, and ten times in Hebrews. Here it is functioning as the SP of σκηνῆς. Semantically, this is a comparative adjective, which has as its main function to direct attribution of qualities or characteristics to a substantive,[132] and since the adjective here is between

---

129. It is necessary to clarify that the noun Χριστός only appears two times in the LXX (Odes Sol. 13:14, 27 LXX) but as an adjective χριστός appears fifty times in the LXX.

130. Cross and Livingstone, *Oxford Dictionary of the Christian Church*, 335.

131. Even though διά is usually translated as "by, through or because of," there are some instances in the New Testament where the context impels its translation with the word "in" (cf. Matt 26:61; Acts 16:9; 2 Cor 11:33; 2 Thess 3:14; 2 Pet 3:5).

132. Porter, *Idioms of the Greek New Testament*, 116.

the article and the noun—with the noun at the end—the adjective must receive greater emphasis than the substantive.[133]

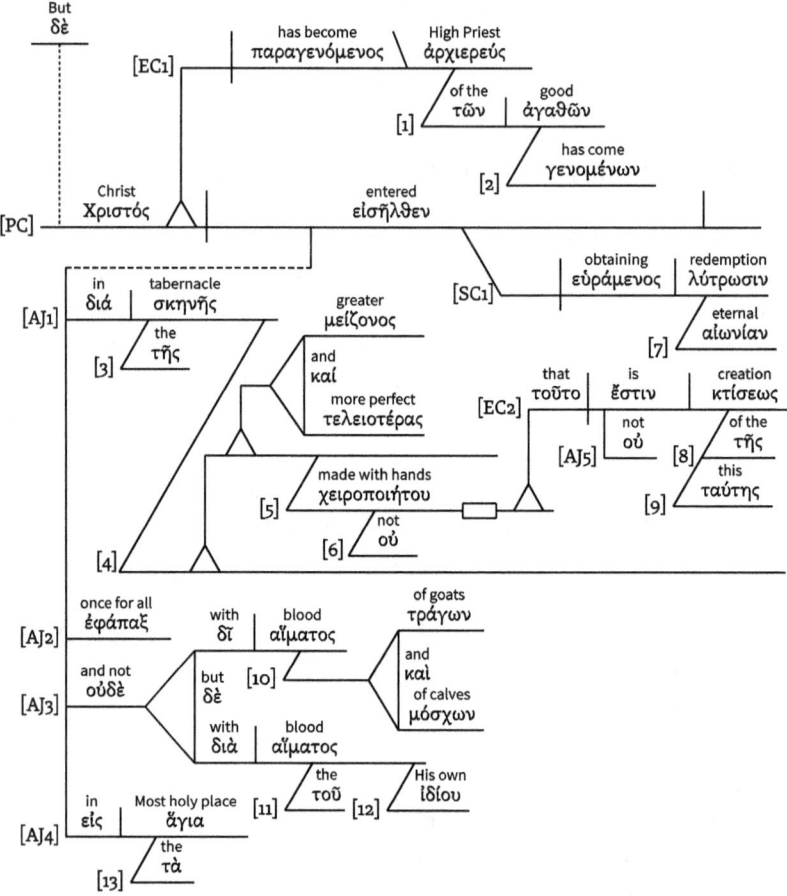

Figure 5.9 Line diagram of key-section 8: Hebrews 9:11–12.

καί: C, here it functions as a copulative conjunction, i.e., a conjunction used to bind two words together in a close logical relationship.

---

133. Robertson and Wallace note that when the sequence "article-adjective-noun" occurs, the emphasis is on the adjective, and this configuration is usually called "the first attributive position." See Robertson, *Grammar of the Greek New Testament*, 776; Wallace, *Greek Grammar Beyond the Basics*, 306.

τελειοτέρας: JGSF from τέλειος, used nineteen times in the LXX, 439 times in Philo, nineteen times in the New Testament, and twice in Hebrews. It is functioning as the SP of σκηνῆς, and, since it is an adjective comparative, semantically it must receive the same emphasis as μείζονος. Its translation, along with its related words, must be "the greater and more perfect," as a type of hendiadys.

σκηνῆς: NGSF from σκηνή, here it is functioning as the object of the preposition διὰ, and means "tabernacle."

οὐ: B, from οὐ, this adverb of negation is the SP of χειροποιήτου here.

χειροποιήτου: JGSF from χειροποίητος, used fifteen times in the LXX, sixteen times in Philo, six times in the New Testament, and twice in Hebrews. Here, as can be seen in Figure 5.9, it is the SP which is modifying σκηνῆς indirectly and the phrase μείζονος καὶ τελειοτέρας directly. Therefore, since adjectives are words used primarily to modify nouns,[134] which is the case here, it could be translated as "handmade,"[135] i.e., the greater and more perfect tabernacle is not handmade.

τοῦτ': RD-NSN from οὗτος, used 4401 times in the LXX, 3438 times in Philo, 1387 times in the New Testament, and forty-three times in Hebrews. It is functioning as the subject of the EC2.[136]

ἔστιν: VPAI3S from εἰμί, this intransitive verb with stative lexeme and with a perfective aspect implies a stative *aktionsart*, i.e., it expresses a state of being rather than a process.

οὐ: B, from οὐ, this adverb of negation is the SP of ἔστιν, i.e., it is denying the EC2.

ταύτης: RD-GSF from οὗτος, it is modifying the genitive κτίσεως.

τῆς κτίσεως: DGSF and NGSF from κτίσις, which is used sixteen times in the LXX, once in Philo, nineteen times in the New Testament, and twice in Hebrews. As can be seen in Figure 5.9, this word is functioning as the complement—direct object—in the EC2. It is notable that the word is identifying one creation—by the use of the article—and it

---

134. Porter, *Idioms of the Greek New Testament*, 115.

135. This is more probable if the etymology of the word is considered, since χειροποιήτου comes from χείρ and ποιέω which literally can mean: made by the hand, and was applied to describe the skills of humans. See Thayer, *Greek-English Lexicon*, 668.

136. It must be noted that the form τοῦτο can also be RD-ASN, i.e., it can function as the direct object of the clause. However, here its context and particularly its union with ἔστιν impels one to consider it as nominative and as the subject of the clause. τοῦτ' ἔστιν is a very common phrase and can also be considered as an adverbial clause, a mark of some appositional clause or the introduction of some explanatory clause. See Robertson, *Grammar of the Greek New Testament*, 399, 411–12, 705.

consequently implies the existence of other creations. Besides, as already shown, this word is only used once in Philo, outside of a cosmogonic context,[137] while the LXX always uses it in a cosmogonic context (cf. Jdt 9:12, 16:14; Tob 8:5, 15; 3 Macc 2:2, 7; 6:2; Wis 2:6; 5:7; 16:24; 19:6; Sir 16:17; 43:25; 49:16), as does the Pseudepigrapha (cf. Pss. Sol 8:7), where it mainly describes the whole creation, which includes those things visible to humans, but also the things that are outside of the environment of humanity, i.e., things that are not visible to them.

εἰσῆλθεν: VAAI3S from εἰσέρχομαι, used 709 times in the LXX, seventy-two times in Philo, 194 times in the New Testament, and seventeen times in Hebrews. This intransitive verb, due to its context, has a non-stative lexeme, and its context is a general statement about reality. Therefore, this verb can imply a gnomic *aktionsart*, i.e., this verb depicts a timeless and universal action.[138] Thus it means that the time or moment when the action of entering into the tabernacle occurs is not defined.

Key-Section 9: Hebrews 9:24–26

The Greek text that will be used for this key-section[139] and its translation—a dynamic translation—follows, with words that were previously selected as the literary component of Hebrews' cosmogony appearing in bold.

Greek Text	Translation
οὐ γὰρ εἰς χειροποίητα εἰσῆλθεν ἅγια Χριστός ἀντίτυπα τῶν ἀληθινῶν, ἀλλ' εἰς αὐτὸν τὸν οὐρανόν νῦν ἐμφανισθῆναι τῷ προσώπῳ τοῦ θεοῦ ὑπὲρ ἡμῶν **οὐδ' ἵνα πολλάκις προσφέρῃ ἑαυτόν** ὥσπερ ὁ ἀρχιερεὺς εἰσέρχεται εἰς τὰ ἅγια κατ' ἐνιαυτὸν ἐν αἵματι ἀλλοτρίῳ **ἐπεὶ ἔδει αὐτὸν πολλάκις παθεῖν ἀπὸ καταβολῆς κόσμου** νυνὶ δὲ ἅπαξ ἐπὶ συντελείᾳ τῶν αἰώνων εἰς ἀθέτησιν τῆς ἁμαρτίας διὰ τῆς θυσίας αὐτοῦ πεφανέρωται.	For Christ entered into the sanctuary not made with hands—a copy of the true one—but into heaven itself, now to appear, on our behalf, in the presence of God, but He entered not in order to offer Himself many times as the high priest enters into the most holy place every year, with the blood of another—since it would have been necessary for Him to suffer many times since the foundation of the world. So He appeared now, once, at the end of the ages, for the removal of sin through the sacrifice of Himself.

---

137. See Philo, *Mos.* 2.51.
138. Campbell, *Basics of Verbal Aspect*, 135.
139. In this case the text is the same of the NA[28].

Syntactic Structure Analysis of Key-Section 9

This key section can be considered as one complex sentence with four indicative verbs and two infinitive clauses—EC1 and EC3—as can be seen in Figure 5.10. The PC—εἰσῆλθεν Χριστός—is constituted by the complex AJ1—οὐ εἰς χειροποίητα ἅγια ἀντίτυπα τῶν ἀληθινῶν, ἀλλ' εἰς αὐτὸν τὸν οὐρανόν—which is portraying the locative matter.

The complex AJ2—νῦν ἐμφανισθῆναι τῷ προσώπῳ τοῦ θεοῦ ὑπὲρ ἡμῶν—and the complex AJ3—οὐδ' ἵνα πολλάκις προσφέρῃ ἑαυτόν ὥσπερ ὁ ἀρχιερεὺς εἰσέρχεται εἰς τὰ ἅγια κατ' ἐνιαυτὸν ἐν αἵματι ἀλλοτρίῳ ἐπεὶ ἔδει αὐτὸν πολλάκις παθεῖν ἀπὸ καταβολῆς κόσμου—are fundamentally causative, since they express the reason or cause for the verbal action. The SC1—νυνὶ δὲ ἅπαξ ἐπὶ συντελείᾳ τῶν αἰώνων εἰς ἀθέτησιν τῆς ἁμαρτίας διὰ τῆς θυσίας αὐτοῦ πεφανέρωται—meanwhile, is functioning as an explanatory clause, since it gives additional information about what is being described.[140]

Morpho-Syntactic Analysis of Key-Sentence 9

As already determined, key-sentence 9 is constituted by the following words: οὐ εἰς χειροποίητα εἰσῆλθεν ἅγια Χριστός ἀντίτυπα τῶν ἀληθινῶν, ἀλλ' εἰς αὐτὸν τὸν οὐρανόν οὐδ' ἵνα πολλάκις προσφέρῃ ἑαυτόν ἐπεὶ ἔδει αὐτὸν πολλάκις παθεῖν ἀπὸ καταβολῆς κόσμου. Therefore, the morpho-syntactic analysis will be done on this clause, in order to provide the foundational analysis of the Greek text upon which interpretation may then be established.

οὐ: from οὐ, this adverb of negation is the SP of εἰς, i.e., it is denying the first part of this prepositional phrase.

εἰς: P, used 7472 times in the LXX, 2360 times in Philo, 1767 times in the New Testament, and seventy-four times in Hebrews. Here εἰς is used as a spatial preposition, i.e., it introduces the phrase that expresses the locative issue or rather, in this case, the spatial realm where Χριστός is not present. It is part of the AJ1 and has as its object the adjective ἅγια with its SPs.

χειροποίητα: JAPN from χειροποίητος. Here, as can be seen in Figure 5.10, it is the SP which is modifying ἅγια. Therefore, since the adjectives

---

140. Wallace asserts that the conjunctions usually used to connect explanatory clauses are: γάρ, δέ, εἰ and καί. Wallace, *Greek Grammar Beyond the Basics*, 673.

are words used primarily to modify nouns,[141] ἅγια must be considered as a noun which is a handiwork, i.e., the earthly one.

εἰσῆλθεν: VAAI3S from εἰσέρχομαι. Here it is functioning as the verb of the PC. This intransitive verb, due to its tense, has a perfective aspect, due to its context has a non-stative lexeme, and its context is a general statement about reality. Therefore, here this verb can imply a gnomic *aktionsart*, i.e., the time or moment when the action of entering into heaven occurs is not defined.

ἅγια: JAPN from ἅγιος. Here it is functioning as the object of the preposition εἰς. Due to its context, it must be considered as the translation of the Hebrew מִקְדָּשׁ, usually used to name the Jewish sanctuary. Therefore, and due to its context, here this accusative adjective has the function of a noun and refers to the Jewish Sanctuary.[142]

Χριστός: NNSM from Χριστός. Here it is functioning as the subject of the PC. And as already asserted, this noun is used to identify Jesus with the מָשִׁיחַ, i.e., it is used in Hebrews in a sort of apposition to Ἰησοῦς and υἱός (cf. 3:6; 13:8).

ἀντίτυπα: JAPN from ἀντίτυπος, never used in the LXX, used three times in Philo, twice in the New Testament, and once in Hebrews. Here it is used in apposition to χειροποίητα. This word is used by Philo in its primary sense,[143] but in Hebrews it is used outside of the influence of neo-platonic thought,[144] and in contingence to τύπος used in the Exodus 25:40 LXX.[145] Therefore, it must be understood as the word that describes the physical representation of the heavenly sanctuary on earth.[146]

---

141. Porter, *Idioms of the Greek New Testament*, 115.

142. Vine asserts about it that the absence of the article and the plural number appears to suggest "the idea of the sanctuary with all its parts," while the singular fixes its attention on the character of the sanctuary or on a part of it. Vine et al., *Vine's Complete Expository Dictionary*, 2:546.

143. Its primary sense came from the word τύπος, derived from τύπτω "to strike," so it can mean "striking back," "sending back," then "resistant." cf. Philo, *Plant.* 133; *Conf.* 102; *Her.* 181. Other senses in which the word is used can be found in Kittel et al., *Theological Dictionary of the New Testament*, 8:246–59.

144. Arndt et al., *Greek-English Lexicon*, 90–91; Kittel et al., *Theological Dictionary of the New Testament*, 8:248.

145. The preposition ἀντί used here as a prefix of τύπος, is used to make a definite statement contingent upon something, i.e., here the author of Hebrews is trying to make his statement contingent to Exodus 25:40. Thus, it is used as a sort of apposition to ἅγια and σκηνή. Mounce, *Basics of Biblical Greek: Grammar*, 395.

146. For other possibilities see Kittel et al., *Theological Dictionary of the New Testament*, 8:246–59.

Grammatical Analysis of Cosmogonic Hebrews' Text 163

τῶν ἀληθινῶν: DGPN and JGPN from ἀληθινός. Here it is functioning as a modifier of ἀντίτυπα, i.e., it is functioning in a sort of apposition to the noun τύπος used in Exodus 25:40, LXX.

ἀλλ': C, and it is functioning as an adversative conjunction.

εἰς: P, and it is used as a spatial preposition and has as its object the noun οὐρανόν. In this case, the preposition is pinpointing the spatial realm where Χριστός is present.

αὐτὸν: RP3ASM from αὐτός. Here, as can be seen in Figure 5.10, it is functioning as the SP of οὐρανόν, and serves to emphasize and identify it.

τὸν οὐρανόν: DASM and NASM from οὐρανός. Here this noun is functioning as the object of the preposition εἰς and its article serves to identify it.

οὐδέ: B,[147] used 614 times in the LXX, 510 times in Philo, 143 times in the New Testament, and six times in Hebrews. Here it is a modifier of the verb εἰσῆλθεν and it is affirming that Christ entered—εἰσῆλθεν—that Christ offered—προσφέρῃ—himself, that Christ suffered—παθεῖν—but it is denying the temporal information about it, i.e., the emphasis of its negation is on πολλάκις.

ἵνα: C, used 620 times in the LXX, 686 times in Philo, 662 times in the New Testament, and twenty times in Hebrews. Here it is introducing a subordinate clause of purpose.[148]

πολλάκις: B, used twelve times in the LXX, 187 times in Philo, eighteen times in the New Testament, and four times in Hebrews. Here it is modifying προσφέρῃ, and it is functioning as an adverb of frequency.

προσφέρῃ: VPAS3S from προσφέρω, used 1165 times in the LXX, ninety-four times in Philo, forty-seven times in the New Testament, and twenty times in Hebrews. In the New Testament it is clear that this word has a special cultic meaning. It is used when someone was presented before Jesus to receive favor from him, and when something was presented before God as an offering. In this case, this verb, due to its tense, has an imperfective aspect—internal viewpoint—and its mood implies an activity that is temporally ongoing.[149]

---

147. As already stated, the word οὐδέ also can function as a conjunction, especially in a continuative sense, i.e., it usually serves to set a SC, but here it must be used as an adverb, due to its syntactic context. More about οὐδέ can be found in Robertson, *Grammar of the Greek New Testament*, 1185.

148. Wallace, *Greek Grammar Beyond the Basics*, 676.

149. Campbell, *Basics of Verbal Aspect*, 69.

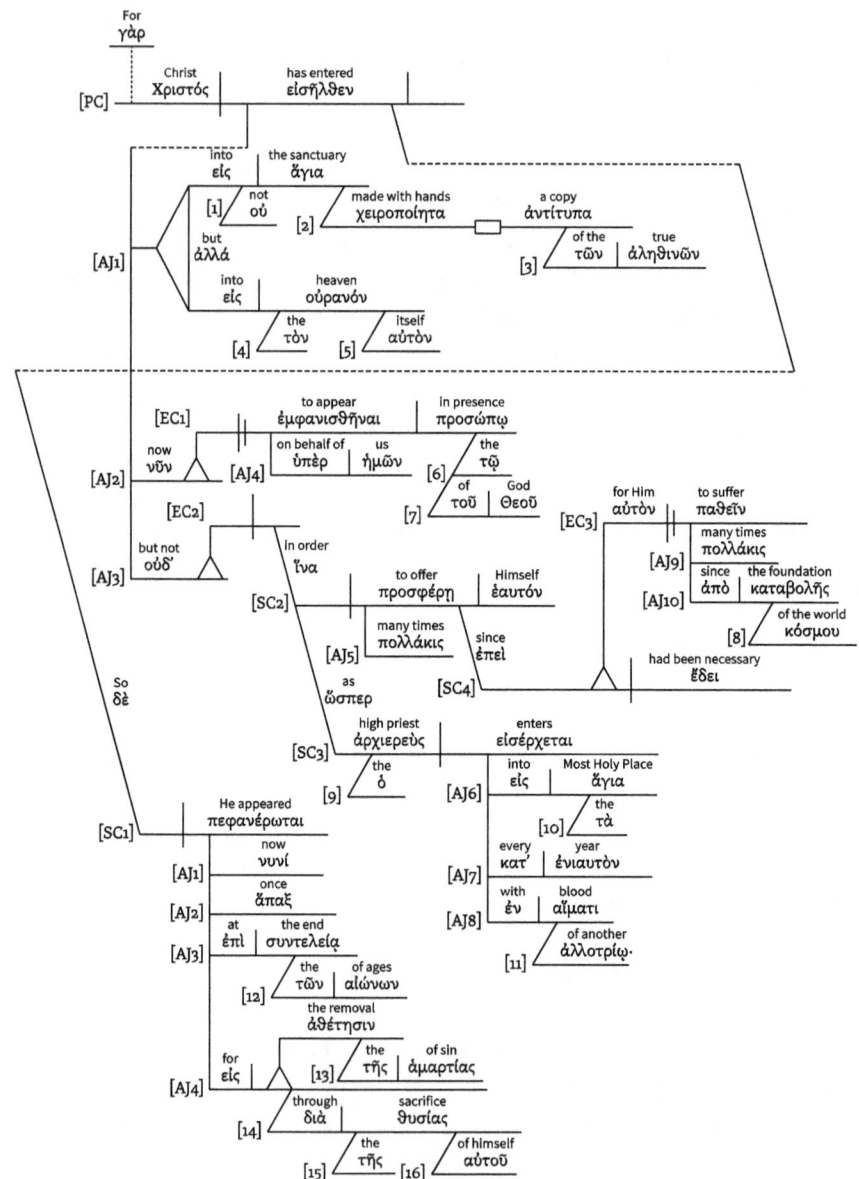

Figure 5.10 Line diagram of key-section 9: Hebrews 9:24–26.

ἑαυτόν: RF3ASM from ἑαυτοῦ, used 666 times in the LXX, 1436 times in Philo, 320 times in the New Testament, and thirteen times in Hebrews. Here it is functioning as the direct object of the SC2.

ἐπεί: C, used thirty-nine times in the LXX, 274 times in Philo, twenty-six times in the New Testament, and nine times in Hebrews. Here it is introducing a SC4 which is functioning as a subordinate causal clause.[150]

ἔδει: VIAI3S from δεῖ, used once in the LXX, once in Philo,[151] 101 times in the New Testament, and three times in Hebrews. In this case, this verb, due to its tense, has an imperfective aspect, non-stative lexeme, and its context allows repetition, therefore, it must imply an iterative *aktionsart*, i.e., the religious obligation implied in the semantic of the word—necessity or compulsion for performing religious obligations[152]— must be repeated periodically.

αὐτόν: RP3ASM from αὐτός. This anaphoric pronoun is functioning as the subject of the EC3[153] and has as its reference the noun Χριστός.

πολλάκις: B. It modifies παθεῖν and functions as an adverb of frequency.

παθεῖν: VAAN from πάσχω, used eighteen times in the LXX, 204 times in Philo, forty-two times in the New Testament, and four times in Hebrews. Here it is functioning as the verb of the EC3.[154] Due to its tense, it has a perfective aspect, which along with its infinitive mood implies an antecedent action in time in relation to its main verb, which in this case is προσφέρῃ. Therefore, the παθεῖν—to suffer—must be understood as an obligation that Christ must experience, many times—πολλάκις—before he

---

150. Wallace, *Greek Grammar Beyond the Basics*, 676.

151. The form δεῖ is used at least thirty-one times in the LXX and 185 times in Philo, but they are perhaps more related to the verb δέω; however, since the context in various cases impels a translation with the sense of necessity, perhaps in this case the lemma of the verb δεῖ is what must be considered and not the verb δέω.

152. A more complete treatise of the verb δεῖ can be found in Kittel et al., *Theological Dictionary of the New Testament*, 2:21.

153. The "anaphoric" pronoun "is one that denotes an object already mentioned or otherwise known." Robertson, *Grammar of the Greek New Testament*, 693. Wallace states that "the almost exclusive use of personal pronouns in the oblique cases (i.e., gen., dat., acc.) is simply to stand in the place of a noun or other nominal. This use of the pronoun is called *anaphoric* in that it refers back to its antecedent." On the other hand, he also mentions that the accusative can function as a substantive when it is related to an infinitive verb. Wallace, *Greek Grammar Beyond the Basics*, 324, 731.

154. Porter states that "an infinitive may be used in a predicate structure, serving the function of a finite verb such as an imperative (commanding use)" and it seems that is the case here. Porter, *Idioms of the Greek New Testament*, 201.

can offer himself, but since the emphasis of negation—due to the adverb οὐδέ—is on the temporal information, it does happen, but not many times.

ἀπὸ καταβολῆς: P and NGSF from καταβολή. Here the preposition is used in a temporal sense,[155] it is a modifier of the verb παθεῖν and has as its object the noun καταβολῆς. As already asserted, the noun καταβολή is hardly related to the beginning of all things, i.e., when the κόσμος came into being.

κόσμου: NGSM from κόσμος. Here it is a SP of καταβολῆς, it is functioning as an attributed genitive,[156] and it is part of the prepositional phrase opened with ἀπό.

Key-Section 10: Hebrews 11:3

The Greek text that will be used for this key-section[157] and its translation—a dynamic translation—follows, with words that were previously selected as the literary component of Hebrews' cosmogony appearing in bold.

Greek Text	Translation
πίστει νοοῦμεν κατηρτίσθαι τοὺς αἰῶνας ῥήματι θεοῦ εἰς τὸ μὴ ἐκ φαινομένων τὸ βλεπόμενον γεγονέναι.	Because of faith we understand that the universe was created by God via His word, so that that which can be seen came into existence from what is not visible.

Syntactic Structure Analysis of Key-Section 10

This key-section has only one indicative verb and it forms only one complex sentence. The PC—νοοῦμεν—is constituted by the SP1—πίστει—and its complex complement—direct object—which in turn is constituted by

---

155. More about the different uses of the preposition ἀπό, which according to Harris are six—temporal, causal, instrumental, adverbial, place of origin, and membership—can be found in Harris, *Prepositions and Theology*, 57–58.

156. This use happens when "the head noun, rather than the genitive, is functioning (in sense) as an attributive adjective," but the use of the noun implies a more emphatic and a stronger force than that of the adjective. See Wallace, *Greek Grammar Beyond the Basics*, 89.

157. In this case the text is the same as the NA[28].

Grammatical Analysis of Cosmogonic Hebrews' Text

an infinitive clause, which in Figure 5.11 is the EC1—κατηρτίσθαι τοὺς αἰῶνας—which in turn is constituted by the AJ1—ῥήματι θεοῦ—and the AJ2—εἰς τό. The AJ1 expresses either method or manner while the AJ2 expresses the result of the related verbal action. The AJ2 has as its object the EC2—γεγονέναι—which is functioning as the object of the prepositional phrase, which in turn has as its subject the EC3—τὸ βλεπόμενον— and the AJ3—ἐκ—which is expressing the locative or spatial issue, i.e., from which the things came into existence. More specifically, the object of the AJ3, i.e., the EC4—φαινομένων—which in turn has the AJ4—μὴ— as its modifier, is referring to the source of the creation.

Morpho-Syntactic Analysis of Key-Sentence 10

As already determined, key-sentence 10 is constituted by the following words: πίστει νοοῦμεν κατηρτίσθαι τοὺς αἰῶνας ῥήματι θεοῦ εἰς τὸ μὴ ἐκ φαινομένων τὸ βλεπόμενον γεγονέναι. Therefore, the morpho-syntactic analysis will be done on this clause, in order to provide the foundational analysis of the Greek text upon which interpretation may then be established.

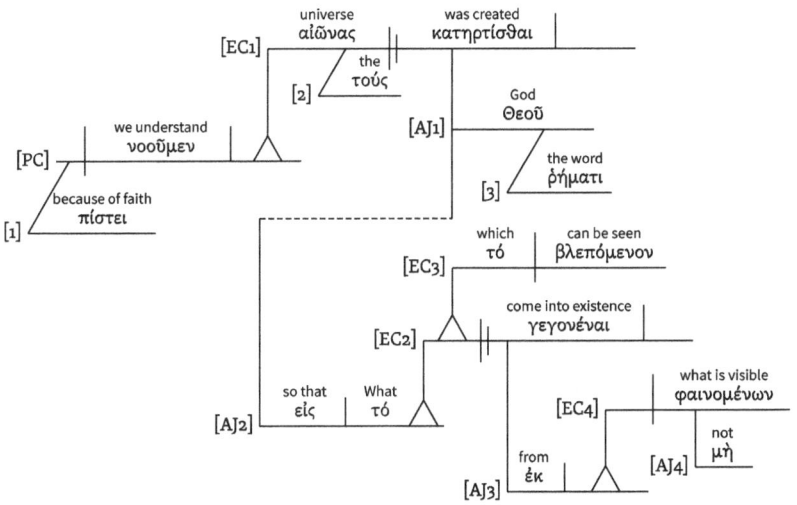

Figure 5.11 Line diagram of key-section 10: Hebrews 11:3.

πίστει: NDSF from πίστις, used fifty-nine times in the LXX, 154 times in Philo, 243 times in the New Testament, and thirty-two times in Hebrews. Here it is functioning as a dative of agency,[158] since the finite verb—νοοῦμεν—associated with πίστει is the action of faith,[159] and apparently not the action of the grammatical subject of the verb, which in this case is "we," which is the medium through which the faith can execute its action. Thus, the faith and the believer belong together. Therefore, even though this word has a large usage in the New Testament that can mean "faithfulness, assurance, proof, trust, or belief," it seems that in Hebrews, and particularly eighteen times in chapter 11—where it appears twenty-four times—it means the entity that empowers the human being to do something, even though no earthly reward is received (cf. 11:13, 39–40). Therefore, it is modifying not the verb but the subject of the verb, as can be seen in Figure 5.11.

νοοῦμεν: VPAI1P from νοέω, used thirty-one times in the LXX, sixty-three times in Philo, fourteen times in the New Testament, and once in Hebrews. This intransitive verb is functioning here as the verb of the PC and has a stative lexeme; and, due to its tense, it has an imperfective aspect—an internal or very close viewpoint of the facts—and its context allows stativity. Therefore, here this verb can imply a stative *aktionsart*, i.e., this verb describes a state of being rather than a process or transitive action,[160] and thus it means that the believer understands permanently.

κατηρτίσθαι: VRPN from καταρτίζω, used seventeen times in the LXX, never used in Philo, thirteen times in the New Testament, and three times in Hebrews. Here this infinitive verb is functioning as the verb of the EC1. Delling states that here, this word must be understood as "to order,"[161] while Arndt et al. affirms that it must be understood as "created"[162]— hence determination of its meaning is not easy. In the New Testament

---

158. This word could be also considered as dative of means, but if it is so, the faith is not the subject that performs the action but the implied subject of the verb, which is we, i.e., the believer. However, since the faith is used in a particular pattern in which not only rational subjects are involved (cf. 11:30), and in other cases the grammatical subject of the verb is not whom performs the action, it is better to consider it as a dative of agency. More about the different uses of the dative as modifier can be found in Wallace, *Greek Grammar Beyond the Basics*, 162–63.

159. For a more extensive treatment on the use of the word πίστει in Hebrews 11 see Westfall, *Discourse Analysis*, 247–53.

160. Campbell, *Basics of Verbal Aspect*, 64.

161. Kittel et al., *Theological Dictionary of the New Testament*, 1:476.

162. Arndt et al., *Greek-English Lexicon*, 526.

this verb has various nuances[163] and in the LXX it is used only in two books, Esdras B (2 Esd) and Psalms, and since its main sense in Psalms is creation of something new,[164] here—in 11:3—a document deeply influenced by Psalms, must be understood also as "to create," nevertheless it must be recognized that the grammar of the word allows the translation of "to fashion." On the other hand, as Campbell asserts, "the perfect tense-form semantically encodes imperfective aspect [a closer view of the fact, view of the inside] with the spatial value of heightened proximity",[165] i.e., it implies a close and personal intervention of the agent of creation, as well as a closer viewpoint of the writer. Meanwhile, the infinitive mood implies an antecedent action in time in relation to the main verb, which in this case is νοοῦμεν. Therefore, the κατηρτίσθαι—to create—must be an action that happens before the action of faith, which is νοοῦμεν—to understand—which is performed through the believers—we. The passive voice, meanwhile, demands that the direct object of the clause functions here as the subject of the clause, while the agent is usually only implied, since the passive voices is mostly used to regard the verbal action on the object and not in the agent or subject.[166] Here, since both the subject and the object are present in the context, it seems that the author is trying to emphasize both of them, particularly if it is considered in the general theological context of Hebrews.

τοὺς αἰῶνας: DAPM and NAPM from αἰών. Here it functions as the subject of the infinitive clause.

ῥήματι: NDSN from ῥῆμα, used 546 times in the LXX, sixty-four times in Philo, sixty-eight times in the New Testament, and four times in Hebrews. Here it is functioning as a dative of means[167] but also as a dative

---

163. Among its nuances are: to correct, to complete, to finish, to create, to equip, or to repair; a short but exhaustive treatment of the word in the New Testament can be found in Balz and Schneider, *Exegetical Dictionary of the New Testament*, 268.

164. Second Esdras basically implies restoration (cf. 2 Esd 4:12, 13, 16; 5:3; 6:14, LXX) and also the building of something new (cf. 2 Esd 5:9, 11 LXX). While Psalms implies the creation of something new (cf. Ps 8:3; 10:3; 28:9; 39:7 [due to its Hebrew origin, it must be translated as 'create']; 73:16, LXX), some other texts are not clear but could also imply creation (cf. Ps 16:5; 17:34;67:10; 79:16; 88:38, LXX).

165. Campbell, *Basics of Verbal Aspect*, 104.

166. Porter, *Idioms of the Greek New Testament*, 64.

167. This is a type of dative substantive that "is used to indicate the means or instrument by which the verbal action is accomplished", and consequently, the means or instrument that is used by the agent who performs the action. It is possible to confuse this dative with the dative of manner, which usually answers the question of how the

of agency,[168] and it is modifying θεοῦ, thus this word is functioning something like πίστει. On the other hand, it is important to note that ῥῆμα in Hebrews—twice in the dative case (cf. 1:3; 11:3), once in the accusative (cf. 6:5) and genitive (cf. 12:19)—particularly in its singular number form,[169] is working with θεός and with the noun δύναμις. Likewise, it must be noted that among the few words—i.e., θεός, κύριος, ἰσχυρός, and δύναμις—used to translate אֵל in the LXX, δύναμις is also used (Neh 5:5; Sir 46:7, 16 LXX). In addition, in the philosophical context of the first century δύναμις is linked with the deity, and further, Hebrews uses δύναμις to describe the power that is able to overcome mortality and corruption.[170] Therefore, ῥῆμα is a special noun in Hebrews which is closely linked to the deity and does not belong to the realm of human beings.

θεοῦ: NGSM from θεός. Here it is the object of a tacit preposition that is modifying the verb, i.e., it is functioning as an adverbial genitive.[171] It is the agent who performs the verbal action, and therefore it must be functioning in connection with the verb. In order to understand its use better, this genitive should be linked to the verb with a preposition, or placed between the verb and the noun. However, since there is no preposition here—it is not a prepositional phrase—there are various

---

action is realised, but as Wallace states, one key feature of the dative of means is that it usually employs concrete nouns while the dative of manner employs abstract nouns. More about the different uses of the dative as modifier can be found in Wallace, *Greek Grammar Beyond the Basics*, 161–63.

168. Even though this word could be considered as a dative of means, it also could be considered as a dative of agency, since the subject of the EC1 is not the one who performs the action of the verb, but the implied subject of the verb, which in this case must be θεός. Nevertheless, it seems that for Hebrews' author it is not θεός who performs the action but more specifically the ῥῆμα of θεός. Therefore, in this complicated syntactic configuration, it appears that ῥῆμα is the means but also the agency that performs the action of the verb καταρτίζω (created). More about the different uses of the dative as modifier can be found in Wallace, *Greek Grammar Beyond the Basics*, 162–63.

169. The dative and accusative case are singular in number, and the only genitive case in Hebrews is plural and is in a clear context that refers to the audible presence of God, and it seems that there is a kind of apposition with λόγος in this case (cf. 12:19).

170. Hebrews describes the δύναμις of the exalted Christ as a δύναμις ἀκαταλύτου ζωῆς (7:16), i.e., as a power which, having overcome mortality and corruption, is beyond the reach of mortality and corruption. Kittel et al., *Theological Dictionary of the New Testament*, 2:305.

171. "This is the use of the genitive that is similar in force to an adverb," i.e., it is used in some way as a prepositional phrase. Thus, this genitive is usually related to a verb rather than a noun. Wallace, *Greek Grammar Beyond the Basics*, 121.

possibilities—i.e., ἀπό, διά, ἐκ, ἐπί, κατά, παρά, ὑπό—which will be evaluated and determined in the next chapter.

εἰς τὸ: P and DASN. Here the preposition must be identified as an *ecbatic* εἰς, which can express results or consequences of verbal action.[172] As the article is functioning as a relative pronoun, it must be translated as "what." This prepositional phrase is the introduction of the complex AJ2, as can be seen in Figure 5.11, and is following an infinitive verb.[173]

μὴ: B from μή, used 3174 times in the LXX, 2369 times in Philo, 1042 times in the New Testament, and forty times in Hebrews. This adverb of negation is denying the EC4 here.

ἐκ: P. It can be functioning as a preposition of source or means here, but, due to its context, it is more probable that it is used here as a preposition of source. It must also be noted that this preposition is the opposite of εἰς in its basic meaning—"to the inside of." So, it is more related to a spatial idea—geography or a physical place.[174]

φαινομένων: VPUP-PGN from φαίνω, used sixty-six times in the LXX, 132 times in Philo, thirty-one times in the New Testament, and once in Hebrews. Here it is functioning as the verb of the EC4, which is the object of the preposition. The semantic of this verb is very precise: it can mean "to shine, to appear or to be seen." On the other hand, the voice of this verb, due to its context, must be a passive voice, while its tense translates an imperfective aspect, i.e., it expresses an action that is contemporaneous with its leading verb. Thus, "this present participle depicts a situation that, while antecedent in origin, becomes contemporaneous with the action of the leading verb."[175]

---

172. Therefore, this phrase can probably mean "with the result that," not "in order that"; i.e., it can be an expression of result rather than purpose. Ellingworth and Nida, *Handbook on the Letter to the Hebrews*, 253. More uses of this preposition can be found in Harris, *Prepositions and Theology*, 83–102.

173. In this case it must be understood as "in such a way that" or "so, that is to say." Zerwick, *Biblical Greek Illustrated by Examples*, 122.

174. Harris, *Prepositions and Theology*, 103.

175. It is important to note that the present participle will not usually "be found depicting an action that is completed before the action of the leading verb begins," i.e., in this case the unseeing source with which the universe was created is present—it is alive—i.e., it is not finished. Information about the present participle and its implications can be found in Campbell, *Basics of Verbal Aspect*, 72.

τὸ: DASN from ὁ. Here this article is functioning as a relative pronoun, and as a subject of the EC3, which, within the greater clausal context functions as the subject[176] of the EC2.

βλεπόμενον: VPPP-SAN from βλέπω, used 133 times in the LXX, eighty times in Philo, 131 times in the New Testament, and eight times in Hebrews. Here it is functioning as a finite verb of the EC3, and, as φαινομένων, it implicates an action that occurs at the same time as that of its leading verb. The meaning of this word can imply action such as "to see, to watch out for, to think about, to understand, to cause to happen, to face,"[177] but here, due to its context, a better translation appears to be the verb "to see."

γεγονέναι: VRAN from γίνομαι. Here it is functioning as the verb of the EC2 and as the object of the prepositional phrase led by εἰς. This word's meaning revolves around verbs such as "to come to exist," "to be," "to become," "to happen," "to move," "to belong to," "to come to be in a place," "to behave." On the other hand, the perfect-tense form semantically renders an imperfective aspect—a closer view of the fact, view of the inside—which implies a close and personal intervention of the agent of the verb. Meanwhile, the infinitive mood implies an antecedent action in time in relation to the main verb, which in this case is κατηρτίσθαι. Therefore, the γεγονέναι—come into existence—must be an action that happened before the action described with the verb κατηρτίσθαι—was created—which is performed by God. The active voice, meanwhile, highlights the agent of the action—here the implied agent is God—and not the action or the object of the action.

Key-Section 11: Hebrews 11:9–10

The Greek text that will be used for this key-section[178] and its translation—a dynamic translation—follows, with words that were previously selected as the literary component of Hebrews' cosmogony appearing in bold.

---

176. Lukaszewski et al., *Lexham Syntactic Greek New Testament*, Heb. 11:3.
177. Louw and Nida, *Greek-English Lexicon of the New Testament*, 46–47.
178. In this case the text is the same as the NA[28].

Greek Text	Translation
Πίστει παρῴκησεν εἰς γῆν τῆς ἐπαγγελίας ὡς ἀλλοτρίαν ἐν σκηναῖς κατοικήσας μετὰ Ἰσαὰκ καὶ Ἰακὼβ τῶν συγκληρονόμων τῆς ἐπαγγελίας τῆς αὐτῆς. **ἐξεδέχετο** γὰρ **τὴν** τοὺς θεμελίους ἔχουσαν **πόλιν ἧς τεχνίτης καὶ δημιουργὸς ὁ θεός**.	Because of faith he dwelt in the promised land as a stranger, in tents, dwelling with Isaac and Jacob—who were joint heirs of the same promise. For he waited for the city, which has foundations, and of which God is the builder and the maker.

Syntactic Structure Analysis of Key-Section 11

This key-section has only two indicative verbs and they form two complex sentences, as can be seen in Figure 5.12. Since the first sentence has no information about cosmogony, it is asserted here that its PC is constituted by four AJs and two ECs. The PC—ἐξεδέχετο—of the second sentence, meanwhile, has as its complement—πόλιν—which has the SP2 and the SP3 providing descriptive information about it. The SP2—τοὺς θεμελίους ἔχουσαν—is answering the question, how is the city? I.e., it is descriptive in essence, while the SP3—ἧς τεχνίτης καὶ δημιουργὸς ὁ θεός—is also providing descriptive information about the owner of the city.

Morpho-Syntactic Analysis of Key-Sentence 11

As already determined, key-sentence 11 is constituted by the following words: ἐξεδέχετο τὴν πόλιν ἧς τεχνίτης καὶ δημιουργὸς ὁ θεός. Therefore, the morpho-syntactic analysis will be done on this clause, in order to provide the foundational analysis of the Greek text upon which interpretation may then be established.

ἐξεδέχετο: VIUI3S from ἐκδέχομαι, used fifteen times in the LXX, twenty-three times in Philo, six times in the New Testament, and twice in Hebrews. Here it is functioning as the verb of the PC, and due to its tense and mood, it implies a stative *aktionsart*, i.e., it describes a state of being rather than a process or transitive action.[179] Its meaning

---

179. Campbell, *Basics of Verbal Aspect*, 75–76.

174 Hebrews' Cosmogonic Presuppositions

is always related to the intransitive action of waiting with expectation and certainty.[180]

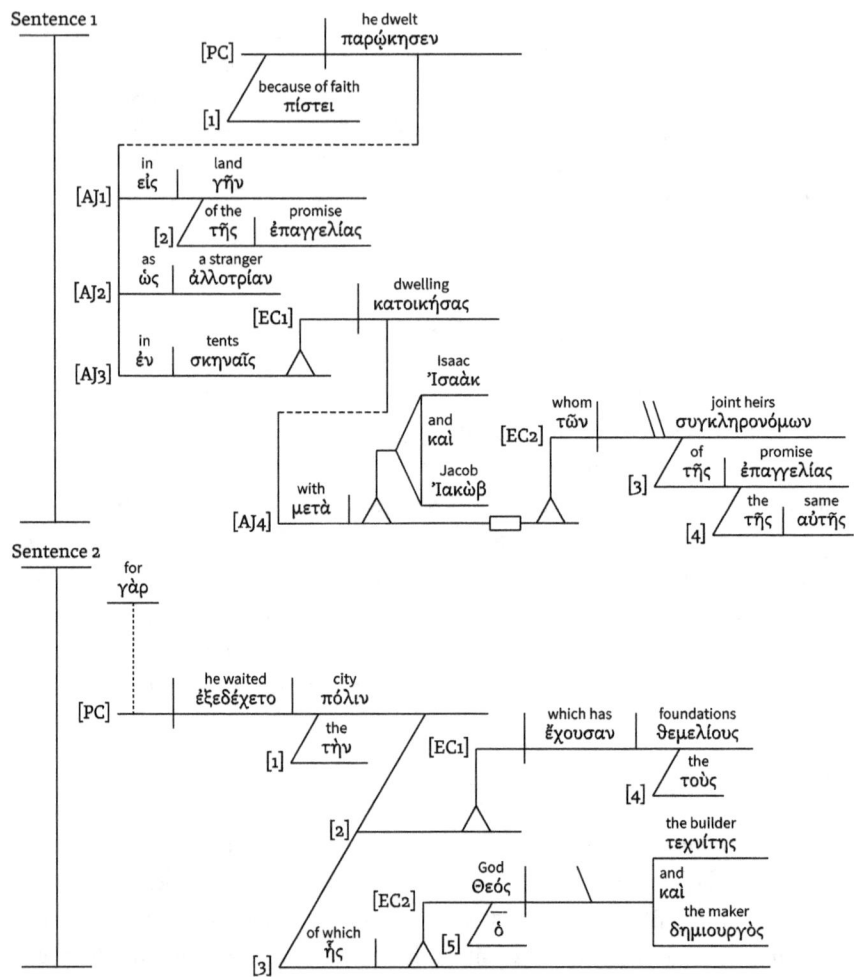

Figure 5.12 Line diagram of key-section 11: Hebrews 11:9–10.

180. There are various instances in the New Testament of this (10:13; cf. Acts 17:16; 1 Cor 11:33; 16:11; Jas 5:7). More information about the meaning of the verb ἐκδέχομαι can be found in Balz and Schneider, *Exegetical Dictionary of the New Testament*, 1:407.

τὴν πόλιν: DASF and NASF from πόλις, a noun which is used 1579 times in the LXX, 483 times in Philo, 163 times in the New Testament, and four times in Hebrews. Here the phrase is functioning as the direct object of the PC. The major uses of the word occur in Matthew twenty-seven times, in Luke thirty-nine times, in Acts forty-three times, and in Revelation twenty-seven times. In the first three it is evident that it mainly refers to some physical place, however, in Revelation it can be understood not only as a physical place, but also as some kind of illustrative or symbolic word. In Hebrews πόλις is always something that belongs to God (cf. 11:10, 16; 12:22; 13:14), and among these uses a special consideration must be given to the use of πόλις in 13:14 where, due to its context, it is clearly related to Jerusalem,[181] a physical place (cf. 12:22). Therefore, its use in Hebrews probably refers to some physical place, although not necessarily.

ἧς: RR-GSF from ὅς. Here this relative pronoun is linked to the SP3 with the noun πόλιν.

τεχνίτης: NNSM from τεχνίτης, used twelve times in the LXX, sixty-six times in Philo, four times in the New Testament, and once in Hebrews. Here it is functioning as a predicate nominative[182] of the equative verb εἰμί in the EC2. This noun, in at least three places in the New Testament, conveys the idea of craftsman (cf. Acts 19:24, 38; Rev 18:22), but in none of these places is it associated with δημιουργός. This association is only found in Philo once, where he is trying to define the πνεῦμα θεῖον (Spirit of God) as the pure knowledge, which, according to him, Bezaleel received (Exod 31:3, LXX) and was used in the creation of the world.[183] Therefore, this noun conveys the sense of some special characteristic to build or create something.

καὶ: C. Here it functions as a copulative conjunction, i.e., a conjunction used to bind two words together in a close logical relationship.

δημιουργὸς: NNSM from δημιουργός, used twice in the LXX, 112 times in Philo, and only once in the New Testament, in Hebrews. Here it

---

181. Nichol, *Seventh-Day Adventist Bible Commentary*, 7:492.

182. As Wallace states, "the predicate nominative is *approximately* the same as the subject and is joined to it by an equative verb, whether stated or implied, but the equation of subject and the predicate nominative does not necessarily or even normally imply complete correspondence... Rather, the predicate nominative normally describes a larger category or state to which the subject belongs." Wallace, *Greek Grammar Beyond the Basics*, 40. Therefore, it can function as a sort of adjective to the noun.

183. See Philo, *Gig.* 22, 23.

functions as a predicate nominative in the same way as τεχνίτης. Neither the noun δημιουργός nor the verb δημιουργεῖν is ever used for God as the Creator in the LXX (cf. 2 Macc 4:1; 10:2; 4 Macc 7:8; Wis 15:13).[184] For this reason its meaning has always been interpreted on the basis of its use in other documents, from which various likely meanings can be identified: one who works for the people, handicraftsman, maker, creator, producer, and magistrate.[185] Therefore, in order to determine the meaning of δημιουργός in Hebrews, it must be studied on the basis of its syntaxes and context, which indicates that it is working in association with the noun τεχνίτης as a kind of hendiadys and as predicate nominative in a nonverbal clause that has the noun θεός as its subject.

ὁ θεός: DNSM and NNSM from θεός. Here the noun functions as the subject of the nonverbal EC2, while the article serves to define and identify the noun. It is also important to note that since θεός is the subject of the equative nonverbal clause, His predicative nominative describes his state of being and not his actions.[186] On the other hand, this configuration shows that the subject of the clause has the nouns of the predicative nominative as its characteristics.[187]

Key-Section 12: Hebrews 12:25–27

The Greek text that will be used for this section[188] and its translation—a dynamic translation—follows, with words that were previously selected as the literary component of Hebrews' cosmogony appearing in bold.

---

184. Kittel et al., *Theological Dictionary of the New Testament*, 2:62.

185. Liddell et al., *Greek-English Lexicon*, 386.

186. Parker states that equative verbs require a nominative object, rather than an accusative object, since they describe states of being rather than action(s) taking place—this configuration is called a predicate nominative. Parker, *Learning New Testament Greek Now and Then*, 39. Robertson, however, asserts that the predicate nominative is in line with the subject nominative and that it is actually in apposition to it. Robertson, *Grammar of the Greek New Testament*, 457.

187. More about the predicative nominative can be found in Wallace, *Greek Grammar Beyond the Basics*, 40–48.

188. In this case the text is the same as the NA[28].

Grammatical Analysis of Cosmogonic Hebrews' Text 177

Greek Text	Translation
βλέπετε μὴ παραιτήσησθε τὸν λαλοῦντα εἰ γὰρ ἐκεῖνοι οὐκ ἐξέφυγον ἐπὶ γῆς παραιτησάμενοι τὸν χρηματίζοντα πολὺ μᾶλλον ἡμεῖς οἱ τὸν ἀπ᾽ οὐρανῶν ἀποστρεφόμενοι οὗ ἡ φωνὴ τὴν γῆν ἐσάλευσεν τότε νῦν δὲ ἐπήγγελται λέγων ἔτι ἅπαξ ἐγὼ σείσω οὐ μόνον τὴν γῆν ἀλλὰ καὶ τὸν οὐρανόν **τὸ δὲ ἔτι ἅπαξ δηλοῖ τὴν τῶν σαλευομένων μετάθεσιν ὡς πεποιημένων ἵνα μείνῃ τὰ μὴ σαλευόμενα.**	Beware. Do not refuse who speaks, for if they—those who refused who warned on earth—did not escape, we—those who reject who warned from heaven—much less. The voice of Him who stirred up the earth at that time, also has promised now saying: I will still do this once again, I will shake not only the earth but I will shake also the heaven. For, this "still once again" indicates the removal of what can be stirred up—because they belong to the created things—for what cannot be stirred up may remain.

Syntactic Structure Analysis of Key-Section 12

As can be seen in Figure 5.13, this key-section has five indicative verbs but forms only one complex sentence. The PC—βλέπετε—has the SC1 functioning as a sort of apposition, while the SC2 provides the reason for the warning. The SC1—παραιτήσησθε—is constituted by the AJ1—μὴ— and the SC3 which is a conditional clause, and which in turn has as its protasis the EC2—εἰ γὰρ ἐκεῖνοι οὐκ ἐξέφυγον ἐπὶ γῆς παραιτησάμενοι τὸν χρηματίζοντα. The apodosis of the SC3 is constituted by the EC3—πολὺ μᾶλλον ἡμεῖς οἱ τὸν ἀπ᾽ οὐρανῶν ἀποστρεφόμενοι. On the other hand, the protasis and the apodosis of the SC3 are constituted by two ECs and two AJs, as can be seen in Figure 5.13, and the entire SC3 is fundamentally causative since it expresses the reason why readers must not refuse the one who speaks.

The complement of the SC1 is constituted by the EC1—τὸν λαλοῦντα—which in turn is constituted by the SC4—οὗ ἡ φωνὴ τὴν γῆν ἐσάλευσεν τότε νῦν δὲ ἐπήγγελται λέγων ἔτι ἅπαξ ἐγὼ σείσω οὐ μόνον τὴν γῆν ἀλλὰ καὶ τὸν οὐρανόν—which is giving information about the action and characteristic of the voice of the one who speaks. The SC2—τὸ δὲ ἔτι ἅπαξ δηλοῖ τὴν μετάθεσιν—which is given the reason for the warning is constituted by the SC5—ἵνα μείνῃ τὰ μὴ σαλευόμενα. The complement—a direct object—of the SC2 is constituted by the SP5—τὴν—and the SP6, which in turn is constituted by the EC14—τῶν σαλευομένων—and the

EC15—ὡς πεποιημένων, with the EC15 functioning as a sort of apposition of the EC14.

Morpho-Syntactic Analysis of Key-Sentence 12

As already determined, key-sentence 12 is constituted by the following words: τὸ ἔτι ἅπαξ δηλοῖ τὴν τῶν σαλευομένων μετάθεσιν ὡς πεποιημένων ἵνα μείνῃ τὰ μὴ σαλευόμενα. Therefore, the morpho-syntactic analysis will be done on this clause in order to provide the foundational analysis of the Greek text upon which interpretation may then be established.

τὸ: DNSM from ὁ. Here this article is functioning as a demonstrative pronoun, and as a subject of the SC2, which, within the sentence, is giving the reason for the PC.[189]

ἔτι ἅπαξ: Substantive phrase which is functioning as the subject of the SC2. This phrase is composed of two adverbs: (1) ἔτι, used 550 times in the LXX, 458 times in Philo, ninety-three times in the New Testament, and thirteen times in Hebrews; and (2) ἅπαξ, used fifty-four times in the LXX, sixty-two times in Philo, fourteen times in the New Testament, and eight times in Hebrews. This phrase is never used in Philo and is only used four times in the LXX (cf. Gen 18:32; Jdg 6:39; 2 Macc 3:37; Hag 2:6). With the exception of Haggai 2:6, this phrase in the LXX implies the idea of "the last one," and therefore in Haggai and in Hebrews it must be understood in this sense.

δηλοῖ: VPAI3S from δηλόω, used thirty-seven times in the LXX, 234 times in Philo, seven times in the New Testament, and twice in Hebrews. This transitive finite verb with a punctiliar and stative or non-stative lexeme, could imply a stative *aktionsart* or an iterative *aktionsart*, namely an action that occurs repeatedly, while its semantics includes "to make known or to make clear."

τὴν: DASF from ὁ. It is an attributive article which is modifying μετάθεσιν, since it can be considered as an abstract substantive.[190]

---

189. But as Greenlee points out, some authors, such as Bloomfield, Morris, Lenski, Miller, and Kistemaker, amongst others, assert that the neuter definite article τό, "the," makes a substantive of the phrase τὸ ἔτι ἅπαξ—yet once. Greenlee, *Exegetical Summary of Hebrews*, 543.

190. More about the use of the article with abstract substantives can be found in Porter, *Idioms of the Greek New Testament*, 107. It is also important to mention that according to the NA[28] this article is not present in the following textual witnesses: 𝔓[46] D* L 0243. 323. 1739, therefore it implies that if the article is omitted the sentence must not be changed in its meaning.

Grammatical Analysis of Cosmogonic Hebrews' Text 179

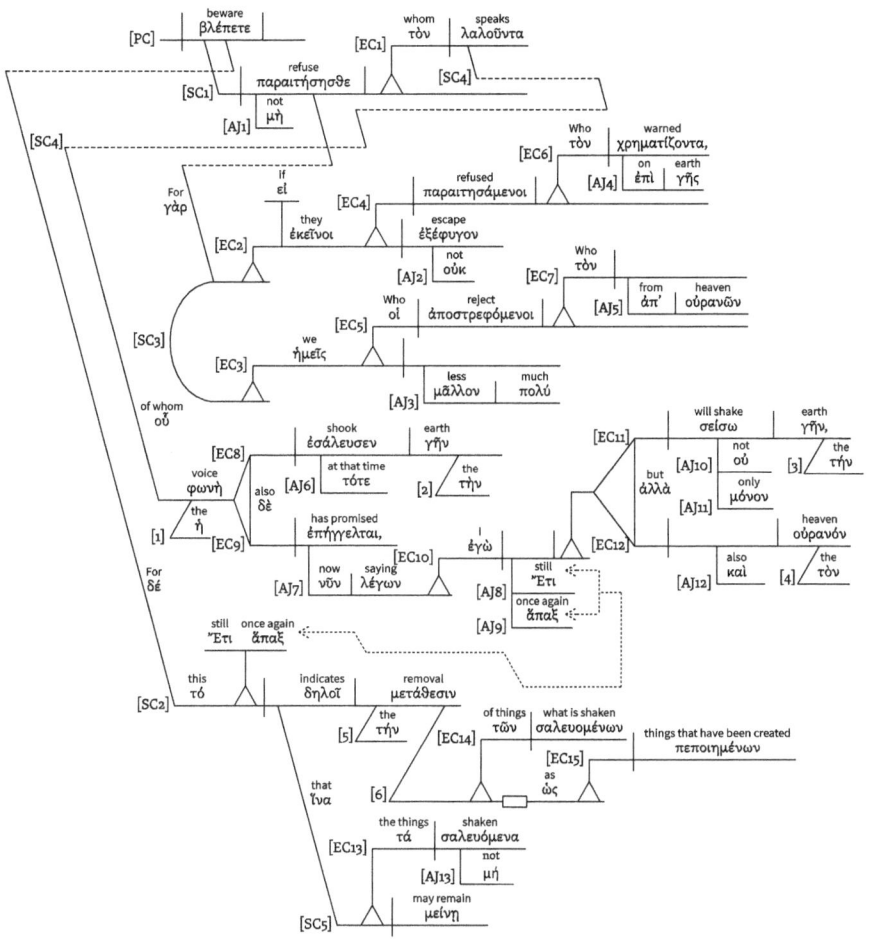

Figure 5.13 Line diagram of key-section 12: Hebrews 12:25–27.

τῶν: DGPN from ὁ. Here it is functioning in the EC14 as its subject, while in the greater SC2 context, the EC14 is functioning as an objective genitive,[191] i.e., it is the specifier of μετάθεσιν.

σαλευομένων: VPPP-PGN from σαλεύω, used seventy-eight times in the LXX, sixteen times in Philo, fifteen times in the New Testament, and three times in Hebrews. This participle is functioning here as a verb of the EC14 and, due to its tense and mood, implicates contemporaneous

---

191. Lukaszewski et al., *Lexham Syntactic Greek New Testament*, Heb. 12:27.

action, in which the action of the participle occurs at the same time as that of its leading verb. However, as it is here related to the noun μετάθεσιν, which can be considered a verbal noun since it is a noun that implies an action, it is not giving supplementary information about δηλοῖ but about μετάθεσιν, therefore σαλευομένων—to stir up—and μετάθεσιν—the removal—can be considered as appositional words.[192]

μετάθεσιν: NASF from μετάθεσις, used once in the LXX, ten times in Philo, and three times in the New Testament, all in Hebrews (cf. 7:12; 11:5; 12:27). Here it is functioning as the direct object in the SC3. The LXX uses this noun only once (cf. 2 Macc 11:24), outside of the cosmogonic context, while Philo uses it ten times[193] but only once in a cosmogonic context.[194] Philo's use of μετάθεσις in a cosmogonic context happens when he names the four principal ways in which, according to Philo, some naïve men who think that the world is everlasting use the word μετάθεσις to support their idea. Namely, these naïve men use μετάθεσις to describe the destruction of the world that is not the end of the world but only its transformation.[195] Further, Philo uses μετάθεσις with the same accidence that is used in Hebrews, and in addition, it must be emphasized that in all these cases this word conveys a sense of change of some features of an entity and not the change or removal of the entity itself. Therefore, it is in this sense that it must be understood in Hebrews' cosmogony.

ὡς: B. As already shown, this word can be considered as a preposition also, but here, due to its context, it must function as an adverb of relation or as a comparative particle.[196]

πεποιημένων: VRPP-PGN from ποιέω. Here this attributive participle—a participle used to attribute a characteristic or an action to another sentential element, usually a noun[197]—is part of the SP6, i.e., it is a modi-

---

192. But it is important to note that it seems that σαλεύω is less intense than σείω used in 12:26. Also, Vine asserts that σαλεύω means "to agitate, shake," while σείω, means "to shake to and fro." Vine et al., *Vine's Complete Expository Dictionary*, 2:567.

193. See Philo, *Gig.* 66; *Mut.* 60, 130; *Abr.* 18, 81; *Ios.* 136; *Praem.* 17.

194. See Philo, *Aet.* 113.

195. The four words used by Philo in *Aet.* 113 are: 1) πρόσθεσιν, 2) ἀφαίρεσιν, 3) μετάθεσιν, 4) ἀλλοίωσιν; translated usually as addition, subtraction, transposition, and transmutation, they literally mean: 1) addition of a part, 2) taking away, 3) change of position, transformation, and 4) alteration, change. Cf. Liddell et al., *Greek-English Lexicon*; Arndt et al., *Greek-English Lexicon*; Kittel et al., *Theological Dictionary of the New Testament*.

196. Lukaszewski et al., *Lexham Syntactic Greek New Testament*, Heb. 12:27.

197. Lukaszewski, *Lexham Syntactic Greek New Testament Glossary*.

fier of μετάθεσιν. It is functioning as a finite verb in the EC15, which is a relative clause that is in an appositional function with the EC14.

ἵνα: C. Here it is introducing a subordinate clause of purpose.[198]

μείνῃ: VAAS3S from μένω, used eighty-nine times in the LXX, 106 times in Philo, 118 times in the New Testament, and six times in Hebrews. It is the intransitive finite verb of the SC5, which as Campbell states, due to its tense and mood, reveals regular expressions of the perfective aspect, i.e., the activity implied in the verb must be considered as a summarized action, punctiliar, or concrete rather than abstract.[199]

τὰ: DNPN from ὁ. Here it is functioning in the EC13 as its subject, which in turn is the subject of the SC5, i.e., this article is functioning in a similar way to a relative pronoun.

μὴ: B. Here this adverb of negation is denying the EC13.

σαλευόμενα: VPPP-PNN from σαλεύω. This intransitive verb here is functioning as the verb of the SC5, which, due to its tense and mood, implicates contemporaneous action in which the action of the participle occurs at the same time as that of its leading verb. However, since it is functioning here as the subject of the SC5, it must be related to the verb μένω—not to δηλοῖ—i.e., the action of the verb σαλευόμενα—to stir up—as well as the action of the verb μείνῃ—to remain—happens at the same time, and they also have the same consequences.

Chapter Conclusion

This chapter started with the purpose of exposing the foundational analysis of the Greek text which constitutes the literary component of Hebrews' cosmogony. Therefore, this chapter asserted that the syntax, morphology, context, and semantic of the twelve identified key-sections and key-sentences in Hebrews portray abundant insights on its cosmogony, which will be presented in a systematic and organized way in the next chapter. Yet, it is possible to formulate some general—the more significant ones—conclusions already.

For instance, the syntactic structure analysis of the twelve identified key-sections could easily show that Hebrews does not have cosmogonic issues as its main topic. From the twelve identified key-sections, only two (cf. 1:10–12; 11:3) have the cosmogonic topic as part of their principal

---

198. Wallace, *Greek Grammar Beyond the Basics*, 676.
199. Campbell, *Basics of Verbal Aspect*, 91.

structure—PC—while the other ten have the cosmogonic topic as supplementary information for other topics. This conclusion has two main consequences: first, the cosmogony of Hebrews will rest mainly on the interpretation of two sentences (1:10–12; 11:3); and second, the identification of Hebrews' cosmogonic presuppositions, as well as its systematic organization, will compel a reading "between the line." However, this fact, instead of distorting the research, provides the reason for its main goal—i.e., to find cosmogonic presuppositions in Hebrews—since reading between the lines is the main method of finding presuppositions in a text,[200] i.e., ideas which are not always explicitly exposed in the text. Nevertheless, as asserted in the first chapter, this research tries to avoid subjectivity—i.e., it tries to be objective as far as possible—and therefore this kind of reading will be performed together with more objective methodologies.

Further, the morpho-syntactic analysis of the twelve identified key-sentences allows the interpretation of Hebrews' text to commence on the following basis: First, the part of speech to which the words of the literary component of Hebrews' cosmogony belongs was identified. Second, the morphology—case, number, genre, etc.—of the words which constitute the literary component of Hebrews' cosmogony has been defined and its implication for its comprehension in its context has also been stated. Third, the use of the more significant words, which form the literary component of Hebrews' cosmogony, was analyzed, also in other documents, and so its meaning in the cosmogonic context has been ascribed more accurately. Fourth, the relationship between the words comprising the twelve identified key-sentences has been stated.

Consequently, it is possible to determine the cosmogonic presuppositions of Hebrews from the text-linguistic analysis—which task will be performed in chapter 6—which considers not only the grammatical analysis, but also the contextual and structural analyses of Hebrews' text as well as the analysis of Hebrew's genre, textual dependence, and textual issues, which were shown in chapter 4.

---

200. As Goddard states, talking about advertising, "Presuppositions is all about reading between the lines; since this is, as it suggests, a hidden process, it is very interesting to advertisers, as we can be taking in all sorts of assumptions without consciously paying attention to them." Goddard, *Language of Advertising*, 127. However, this assertion could be applicable to any document that intends to communicate something.

6

Cosmogonic Presuppositions in Hebrews

This research began with six minor purposes, one of them being to establish the cosmogonic presuppositions in Hebrews. That purpose can only be realized after having achieved some of the other minor purposes, such as determining the cosmogonic literary component in Hebrews, and evaluating the grammatical features that can assist in extracting the cosmogonic presuppositions, purposes that were accomplished in previous chapters. So this chapter will focus on one key part of the main purpose of this research, i.e., to establish the cosmogonic presuppositions in Hebrews.

Chapter Introduction

In its simplest way, cosmogony can be defined as "the branch of science that deals with the origin of the universe, especially the solar system."[1] Therefore, in biblical science,[2] frequently called biblical

---

1. *OED*, s.v. "Cosmogony."

2. Biblical science does not mean that the documents which constitute the Bible are documents of science. However, a methodological study of the Bible—as an old document, developed in different times and cultures—recognizes that its content has different kinds of information and different types of literary styles. It also recognizes that its study must be guided for a coherent and verified methodology and therefore ought to be considered a science. This is so particularly if the definition of science is taken seriously, which says that science is a systematized knowledge of facts or principles gained by systematic study.

studies, cosmogony[3] is basically constituted by assertions about the phenomena of creation, which assertions must be labeled cosmogonic presuppositions. In some cases, these assertions could be very direct and clear—i.e., they can be understood through a simple reading of the content—but in other cases they could be almost incomprehensible. The Bible presupposes the existence of a higher, almighty, and personal power which is able to create and is mainly called "God,"[4] and Hebrews explicitly affirms that "whoever would draw near to God must believe that he exists" (11:6, ESV), so Hebrews categorically asserts that ὁ θεός is real. Consequently, the cosmogony of Hebrews, expressed through presuppositions, mainly deals with two aspects, namely with the creator and with the creation itself.[5]

On the other hand, Hebrews' cosmogony requires that Genesis 1 and 2, being text that deeply shaped its cosmogonic presuppositions, be read alongside it, since as already shown in previous chapters, there is a deep connection between Genesis 1 and 2 and the cosmogony of Hebrews. Therefore, this chapter will show more specifically what Hebrews presupposes about the creator, the procedure followed in order to create, and about the creation itself on the basis of its text-linguistic analysis,

---

3. Is there room for cosmogony in biblical science? It is a legitimate question. Cosmogony is defined as "the branch of science that deals with the origin of the universe, especially the solar system," see, *ODE*, s.v. "cosmogony." Therefore, cosmogony is usually understood as part of astronomy or physics. Nevertheless, even though these scientific fields can provide abundant insights about the origin of everything, cosmogony belongs mainly to philosophers, and more specifically to metaphysicians, philosophers of physics, and philosophers of space and time. That is why when the topic of cosmogony is mentioned, the words "theory" or "presupposition" must also be mentioned. On the other hand, in the Bible there is abundant metaphysical and philosophical information, and therefore cosmogony must also be part of biblical science. Besides, there is abundant literature that treats cosmogony as part of religious studies, and the study of the Bible, of course, forms part of it. See for instance Frazer, *Creation and Evolution*; Horwitz, *Defence of the Cosmogony of Moses*; Greenwood, *Scripture and Cosmology*; Hartnett, "Biblical Creationist Cosmogony," 13–20.

4. It is broadly accepted that the Bible presupposes the existence of God, however, an important study about the topic is found in Henry, *God, Revelation, and Authority*, 5:21–407. Another good study about God is found in Kittel et al., *Theological Dictionary of the New Testament*, 3:66–119.

5. Anderson, discussing the cosmogony of Genesis, maintains that the two first chapters "cannot be reconciled from a purely historical or scientific perspective," but they "produce a theological melody that can only be appreciated when heard together." On the other hand, he asserts that understanding these texts implies understanding Israel's view on creation and the Creator, which is applicable to Hebrews' cosmogony. Anderson, "Creation."

which has already been determined. But before showing that information, this chapter will briefly explore the differences between ancient and contemporary cosmogonic presuppositions. So, although this is not the goal of this research, the manner in which scientific developments in sciences such as physics, astronomy, sociology, or even politics, have allowed changes, if any, in the current worldview of the origin of everything in comparison to Hebrews' cosmogony must be considered.

Development of Ancient Cosmogonic Presuppositions

In 1937 Leeming exposed 213 traditions from all parts of the world regarding the origin of all things, organized them into five main presuppositions and associated them with forty-two topics.[6] What is pertinent to this research is the five main assumptions in which they were grouped by Leeming: 1) *ex nihilo* creation; 2) creation from chaos; 3) world parent creation; 4) emergence creation; and 5) Earth-diver creation. In 1963 Long amended these categories slightly and added one, and he then named the six categories: 1) emergence myths; 2) world-parent myths; 3) creation from chaos; 4) creation from a cosmic egg; 5) creation from nothing; and 6) Earth-diver myths.[7] What these assertions prove is that diversity, rather

---

6. The association made by Leeming of the 213 different cosmogonic traditions was made with the following topics and they are listed here since most of them also must be considered as cosmogonic presuppositions: 1) ages of creation; 2) ancestors in creation; 3) animals in creation; 4) animistic creation; 5) axis mundi in creation; 6) birth as creation metaphor; 7) bodily waste or fluids as creation source; 8) clay-based creation; 9) cosmic egg in creation; 10) coyote in creation; 11) creation myths as curing; 12) culture heroes in creation; 13) death origin in creation; 14) deus faber creation; 15) deus otiosus or absconditus in creation; 16) devil in creation; 17) dismemberment of primordial being as creation; 18) dreaming as creation; 19) duality in creation; 20) etiological creation myths; 21) fall from grace in creation; 22) father creators; 23) flood in creation myths; 24) four directions in creation; 25) goddess as creator; 26) imperfect or accidental creation; 27) incest in creation; 28) origin of evil in creation; 29) primordial waters in creation; 30) raven in creation; 31) sacrifice in creation; 32) separation of heaven and earth in creation; 33) sexual impulse in creation; 34) shamanism and creation; 35) sky woman descends; 36) sun in creation; 37) thought-based creation; 38) trickster in creation; 39) twins in creation; 40) two creators motif; 41) woman as source of evil; 42) word-based creation. Leeming, *Creation Myths of the World*, 301–64.

7. The six main assumptions about the origin of the cosmos and their main ideas are as follows: 1) Emergence myths or emergence creation depict the creation of the cosmos in the symbolism of gestation and birth in a "harmonious relationship among all the forms of the created order." 2) World-parent myths or world parent creation

than uniformity, is the main feature in ancient cosmogony. Namely, as Fitzgerald asserts,

> There is not one ancient [cosmogony], but rather multiple [cosmogonies] exist, each offering a different account of the universe and of humans within it. Early Christianity arises within the context of these multiple and competing [cosmogonies] and it adds its own . . . cosmogonies to the mix.[8]

On the other hand, actual theories—which could also be called myths or presuppositions—about the origin of all things are, likewise, not uniform. The more popular big bang theory for the origin of all things,[9] is challenged today, but also developed by theories such as the Stationary Universe, Inflationary Universe, and Oscillatory Universe.[10]

---

portrays creation as the result of the reproductive powers of primordial world parents, a fact that is usually portrayed as an indifferent or unconscious activity, in which the parents may even be hostile to their offspring's needs and desires. 3) Creation from chaos describes "how the creation arises out of a prior matter or stuff that is either negative or confused. The chaotic condition may be variously depicted, [but] in any case, the situation of chaos inhibits creation." 4) Creation from a cosmic egg, in which the potency for creation is contained within the form of the egg. "The symbolism of the egg also connotes a state of primordial perfection out of which the created order proceeds." 5) Creation *ex nihilo* or creation from nothing. 6) Earth-diver myths, in which the water constitutes the primordial matter of the beginning, since in it a god, cultural hero, or even an animal dives "to bring up particles of earth, mud, or sand, out of which an ordered cosmos begins to appear." Long, *Alpha*; Long, "Cosmogony," 1986–88.

8. Fitzgerald, "Cosmologies of the Ancient Mediterranean World," 6.

9. From Leeming's document it can be stated that the big bang theory also belongs to a group of myths about the origin of everything, since as he affirms, "the big bang theory, the currently accepted creation story of our scientific culture, reflects our cultural priorities; it is a record of our culture's understanding of its own place in the universe and its sense of what the universe is. It depicts a world created in a few minutes in one great explosion long, long ago. According to the theory, our solar system was organised by that explosion and has been expanding ever since. . . . [So] the big bang theory suggests that everything that exists has a common ancestry in a single primeval event, the ultimate expression of an ex nihilo creation." Leeming, *Creation Myths of the World*, 240. An apparently more scientific definition about the big bang theory is "10 billion to 20 billion years ago the entire vastness of the observable universe, including all of its matter and radiation, was compressed into a hot, dense mass just a few millimetres across. This nearly incomprehensible state is theorized to have existed for just a fraction of the first second of time. So a massive blast allowed all the universe's known matter and energy—even space and time themselves—to spring from some ancient and unknown type of energy." Greshko and Staff, "Origins of the Universe, Explained," paras. 3–4.

10. For a biblical scholar, the terminology, and even more so the equations, used in order to prove these theories can be difficult to understand or even incomprehensible.

Among them, the intelligent design theory also appears as a cosmogonic alternative and to these diverse theories the various creationist theories also need to be added. What is curious is that among the advocates of both, the new and earlier cosmogonic theories, there is a perpetual claim that the others are partially or completely unscientific because they are a-theoretical, i.e., that they have no connection with and are not founded on theory, which seems a contradiction. Nonetheless, what remains true is the assertion of the eminent physics astronomer Hughes: "Cosmogony is at a strange stage [nowadays]."[11]

The last few decades have been characterized by outstanding efforts in sciences such as physics, astronomy, sociology, and even politics, in attempting to provide a more accurate theory regarding the origin of all things.[12] However, from time to time, in some of these fields of study some

---

Nevertheless, what can be asserted is that not one of these theories are completely developed, every one of them must be concluded with the assertion "a lot of work still has to be done to verify this conclusion." Linde and Mezhlumian, "Stationary Universe," 31. The Stationary Universe is a theory developed by Edward Milne in 1935 which mainly posits that the universe does not have a beginning or an end. Inflationary Universe theory was developed in 1981 by Alan Guth which mainly proposes a period of extremely rapid—i.e., exponential—expansion of the universe during its first few moments. Oscillatory Universe theory was developed by Paul Steinhardt and basically asserts that the universe is the last one of many originated in the past after successive explosions—i.e., big bang—and contractions—i.e., big crunch—so the universe never ends, it remains forever. More information about these theories can be found in Mukhanov, *Physical Foundations of Cosmology*.

11. Hughes, "Cosmogony (the Origin of Planetary Systems)," 228.

12. No comments will be made about physics and astronomy as their contributions are widely known, and it is not the purpose of this research to deal with all of these cosmogonies and their implications. Nevertheless, current sociology and anthropology state that "we need to pay attention to the human cosmogony, the human creation of the world through contingencies, accidents, and choices," i.e., "whereas the two Genesis accounts of creation presuppose the existence of God, Hesiod [in antiquity and current sociology] presupposes the existence of humans" in the beginning of all things. Blundell, *Origins of Civilization*, 4, 9; Barrett and Srivastval, "History as a Mode of Inquiry," 231–54. Moreover, current anthropology states that cosmogony provides identity to human beings, since it gives the sense of belonging to a grander cosmos or of being part of it. On the other hand, politics and cosmogony are also interrelated but it is difficult to determine whether there is a political cosmogony, or whether the different cosmogonies can influence political science. However, it is true that, as Kim asserts, "every practical philosophy explicitly or implicitly offers at least a partial conceptual rationale for a certain type of cosmos in which social and political actions play a role." So politicians could ask "if creation begins with some sort of unity, and then proceeds to a duality and then multiplicity, what kind of relationship does the individual being, after the creation process, maintain between itself and the larger unity?" See Youngmin, "Cosmogony as Political Philosophy," 111, 19.

proponents have attempted to prove that their own perspectives hold more validity than the others, by making a distinction between what they call "a scientific approach" and "mythical assertions" regarding cosmogony. Nevertheless, regarding this problem of the religious view versus the scientific view of the cosmos, it is important to note the following assertion by Bolle:

> Contrary to popular opinion, pondering the conflicts between science and religion is not often necessary.... The idea of many long ages and periods with truly astronomical numbers and the concept of many worlds existing both in succession and simultaneously are pan-Indian.... This does not mean that the large figures of years given in the Purāṇas are figments of the imagination or betray a disregard for science. Quite the reverse is true.... On a wider scale, a comparable correction has been made with respect to the generally held opinion that prehistoric people and, in their wake, members of every nonliterate tradition were wanting in intellectual power capable of raising scientific questions. This correction has been made through the work of Alexander Marshack, who persuasively interpreted prehistoric data as records of precise astronomical observations. None of this suggests oppositions between religion and science; such oppositions are in fact a very recent phenomenon in history and are restricted to very few sciences and only to specific religious traditions.... It is certainly impossible on the basis of the cumulative evidence to regard religious and mythical views of the cosmos merely as precursors to science or as preliminary or inadequate endeavors that are discarded with the development of science. Moreover, not only from the point of view of the historian of religions but also from that of the historian of science, no single moment in history can ever be established to pinpoint the supposed fundamental change from myth to science. In fact, no such moment exists.[13]

Bolle's assertion can be corroborated in different ways and through different sources. For instance, the big bang theory supposedly developed in response to the recent scientific discovery of the expanding universe—which in turn was developed on Einstein's general relativity theory even though Einstein himself initially thought the universe was static, neither expanding nor contracting—which, in effect, was suggested at least eight hundred years ago by the renowned Torah scholar Ramban, as can be seen in Table 6.1.

---

13. Bolle, "Cosmology: And Overview," 1995.

So Hebrews' cosmogony, and particularly its presuppositions, which were considered as part of first-century cosmogony, should not be discarded; it can be added to the current worldview about the origin of all things in order to enrich it, since diversity rather than uniformity appears to be the main feature of cosmogony throughout history. In this context—i.e., the present time, in which multiple and competing cosmogonies exist, with some labelled as "old"—Hebrews' cosmogony will be presented.

Ramban Cosmogony	Scientific Cosmogony
At the briefest instant following creation all the matter of the universe was concentrated in a very small place no larger than a grain of mustard. The matter at this time was so thin, so intangible, that it did not have real substance. It did have, however, a potential to gain substance and form and to become tangible matter. From the initial concentration of this intangible substance in its minute location, the substance expanded, expanding the universe as it did so. As the expansion progressed, a change in the substance occurred. This initially thin noncorporeal substance took on the tangible aspects of matter as we know it. From this initial act of creation, from this ethereally thin pseudosubstance, everything that has existed, or will ever exist, was, is, and will be formed.	Before the big bang, the entire vastness of the observable universe, including all of its matter and radiation, was compressed into a hot, dense mass just a few millimetres across. This nearly incomprehensible state is theorised to have existed for just a fraction of the first second of time . . . a massive blast allowed all the universe's know matter and energy—even space and time themselves—to spring forth . . . after the big bang, the universe expanded with incomprehensible speed from its pebble-size origin to astronomical scope. Expansion has apparently continued, but much more slowly, over the ensuing billions of years.

Table 6.1 Old and contemporaneous cosmogonic presuppositions.[14]

The Creator in Hebrews' Cosmogony

Cosmogony can be divided into two branches: those who include in their view the presence of one or more supernatural beings; and those who do not.[15] Hebrews can be placed among the former. The first noun that

---

14. Table 6.1 was take from Friedman, *Genesis One Code*, 100.

15. The two main branches among the current human view on cosmogony are the two main views on cosmogony held by humanity since earlier times: those who see the origin of the world being a long time ago—which could also be called eternity—from the action and reaction of various natural elements—for instance the Ionian School—and those who see the origin of the world as caused by the intervention of one or more

appears in Hebrews is θεός, affirmed to be a "living God" (cf. 9:14; 10:31; 12:22), and even though Hebrews portrays other supernatural beings,[16] in Hebrews' cosmogony the title of creator can only rest upon θεός and nouns closely related with it, such as υἱός, κύριος, Χριστός and Ἰησοῦς. Therefore, this section will focus on whether the responsibility of being the creator rests in one or more beings, since even though the noun κτίστης (cf. 1 Pet 4:19) is never used in Hebrews, its sense is very present. But who is the κτίστης of Peter in Hebrews? According to Alford, the Greek Fathers understood it as the θεός,[17] and moreover, more recently κτίστης and ὁ θεός have been related in New Testament studies.[18]

This section will deal mainly with the identity, attributes, and purposes of the creator in Hebrews, since the main goal of this research is to judge the relationship between Hebrews and first-century cosmogonies. As shown in chapter 2, there is considerable information about the creator's identity, attributes, and purposes in first-century cosmogonies. Nevertheless, it is also necessary to deal with the creator since, as Delitzsch asserted, it seems that in Hebrews "God's will was to be, not a mere δημιουργός, but also a κτίστης."[19] However, it must be recognized that the will of God is not unambiguous in Hebrews' text, i.e., it must be demonstrated. Particularly since in Hebrews the word δημιουργός appears, but not κτίστης, even though δημιουργός—derived from δήμιος (public) and ἔργον (work)—is not preferred by the writers of both Old and New Testament documents, although κτίστης is.[20]

---

supernatural beings—for instance the Eleatic School in earlier times or the Discovery Institute today—and neither of them show important advances on cosmogonic presuppositions.

16. Alongside the nouns θεός, υἱός, κύριος, Χριστός and Ἰησοῦς, in Hebrews the following nouns can be identified, which due to their features in some specific contexts, could be defined as supernatural beings: ἄγγελος (cf. 1:4–7), ἀρχιερεύς (cf. 7:26), πνεῦμα (cf. 3:7; 9:8), λόγος (cf. 4:12), μελχισέδεκ (cf. 5:6).

17. Alford, *Alford's Greek Testament*, 4:5, 39, 45.

18. Also, the context of 1 Peter 4:19 implies that the noun κτίστης has as its referent the articulate ὁ θεός. Moreover, as Bigg asserts, the phrase πιστῷ κτίστῃ (to a faithful Creator), may be a reminiscence of the prayer of Jonathan in 2 Maccabees 1:24, which begins, κύριε, κύριε ὁ θεός, ὁ πάντων κτίστης. Bigg, *Critical and Exegetical Commentary*, 182. More recently, Schreiner also related the noun κτίστης to θεός. See Schreiner, *1, 2 Peter, Jude*, 229.

19. Delitzsch, *Commentary on the Epistle to the Hebrews*, 2:218.

20. Kistemaker, *Exposition of the Epistle to the Hebrews*, 367.

On the other hand, as McDonough states, Hebrews seems to show Jesus as the creator but in so doing, Hebrews rejects some kind of identification between God's Wisdom and Jesus, since for him—i.e., McDonough—in 11:3 the word ῥῆμα is really Jesus. So McDonough affirms "that when the author thinks about the creation of the world, he [sic] chooses to associate it with God's speaking rather than with God's Wisdom."[21]

Further, from early times until today there has been abundant debate among scholars about the nature of Jesus when performing his actions of creation. Suh, through the labels "elevation-line" and "restitution-line," placed two different Christological views in relation with the creation. According to Suh, the "elevation-line" is held by Duns Scotus, Karl Barth, Karl Rahner, and Hendrikus Berkhof, and in this view the earthly Jesus is central in the creative process. The "restitution-line" meanwhile, will assert that it is the eternal Son, the pre-incarnate Christ, who is central in the creative process. The latter view, according to Suh, is held by Irenaeus, Abraham Kuyper, Herman Bavinck, G. C. Berkouwer, and Arnold A. Van Ruler.[22] Nevertheless, the work of Suh does not solve the problem of the real identity of the creator.[23] Likewise, McDonough considers three theologians from the early centuries—Justin Martyr, Irenaeus, and Athanasius—and three, more current, German theologians—Wolfhart Pannenberg, Jürgen Moltmann, and Karl Barth—in order to determine the role of Christ in the creative act. McDonough observes that in the writings of these theologians "Christ becomes a depersonalized cosmic principle" or as he will generalize in his conclusions, "there has been a tendency among theologians to depersonalize the work of the Messiah in creation."[24] So there is evidently no consensus among theologians regarding the role of Christ in the origin of all things, what his condition was, and even whether he was present there.

Consequently, the identity of the creator, whether it was θεός, Χριστός or any other or all of them is still under debate. Nevertheless, the purpose of this research is not to determine who the creator in Genesis or in the entire New Testament is, but rather, who the creator is in Hebrews.

21. McDonough, *Christ as Creator*, 198.

22. Suh, "Creation-Mediatorship of Jesus Christ."

23. As Letham affirms, what is important in the work of Suh is that if "the union of God and man accomplished in the incarnation" is considered, then necessarily "a radical new element into God's relation with creation," especially in its first moment—creation—must be reoriented. Letham, "Review of, Chul Won Suh," 213.

24. McDonough, *Christ as Creator*, 251, 259.

With an awareness of the broad discussion regarding the identity of the creator in biblical studies, the next pages of this section will focus on the identity, features, and purposes of the creator in Hebrews.

Identity of Hebrews' Creator

Hebrews begins similarly to Genesis, since both have as the subject of their first sentence the noun "God,"[25] and it is not coincidence, since ὁ θεός is the most prominent subject in Hebrews as well as in the whole Bible. Also, as in Genesis, Hebrews portrays the nominative ὁ θεός in 1:2 as the one who speaks (cf. Gen 1:3, LXX), but also as the one who makes τοὺς αἰῶνας δι' υἱοῦ.[26] It is interesting to note that Hebrews deliberately avoids excessive use of the nominative articular ὁ θεός and substitutes it with pronouns or places it as a tacit element in important sentences.[27] On the other hand, of the twenty-two times where the articular nominative ὁ θεός is used in Hebrews, seven times are used in the literary component

---

25. The same can be affirmed about the use of God—ὁ θεός—in Hebrews that was stated by Kidner about Genesis and its use of the noun God: "it is no accident that *God* is the subject of the first sentence of the Bible [Hebrews]. . . . The passage, indeed the Book, is about him first of all; to read it with any other primary interest is to misread it." Kidner, *Genesis*, 47.

26. In 1:1–2 ὁ θεός is portrayed as the one who spoke long ago in different times and in various ways to the fathers by the prophets, as well as the one who ἐποίησεν τοὺς αἰῶνας (1:2). Meanwhile, Genesis 1:3 is the first moment when it is recorded that God spoke, and in the first verse of the Bible he is portrayed as the one that "ἐν ἀρχῇ ἐποίησεν τὸν οὐρανὸν καὶ τὴν γῆν" (Gen 1:1, LXX).

27. For instance, in the general introduction to Hebrews (1:1–4) ὁ θεός could be explicitly used at least three more times without interfering with its poetic arrangement. This fact—avoiding the use of ὁ θεός—happens in a very evident way in chapters 1–3, but also in its cosmogony in at least four key-sections. 1) In 1:10–12, he is the one who makes some assertions about the Son—even ὁ θεός is not present there. 2) In 2:10, he is the one for whom and by whom all things are, but also ὁ θεός is not present there. 3) In 8:1–2, he is the owner of the throne, but ὁ θεός is also not present in that text. 4) In 12:25–27 he is the one who speaks, from heaven, but also there the noun is not present. However, as Ellingworth recognizes, in this section (12:25–27) it is difficult to identify the subject of the actions, since the mention of Jesus in v. 24 can support the argument in favour of identifying Christ and not God, as "the one who speaks." But, as Ellingworth also asserts, the syntactic context of "λαλέω (1:1) as well as the semantic context of the verse, makes it more likely that ὁ θεός is the subject, or the one who speaks. See Ellingworth, *Epistle to the Hebrews*, 684. Attridge adds that "The one who speaks (τὸν λαλοῦντα) is certainly the God whose voice was heard at Sinai, and whose speech has been a major theme in Hebrews generally." Attridge, *Hebrews*, 379.

of Hebrews' cosmogony. In 3:3–4 he is the one that built everything,[28] in 4:3–5 he is the one that finished his works in the foundation of the world, the owner of the rest and who had rested in the seventh day from all his works; this imagery is repeated in 4:10. Meanwhile, in 9:24–26 he is the one in the presence of whom Christ appears on behalf of believers, while in 11:3, he is the one that brought the universe into existence by the power of the word, while in 11:9–10, he is the builder and maker of the city for which Abraham was waiting.

Nevertheless, the sentence ὁ θεός κτίστης ἐστίν (God is the creator) is not found in Hebrews; on the contrary, it says that κύριος is the one who "laid the foundation of the earth in the beginning" (1:10), and that δι' οὗ—υἱοῦ—ὁ θεὸς ἐποίησεν τοὺς αἰῶνας (cf. 1:1–2). Thus, the presence of three nouns: θεός, κύριος, and υἱός, gives rise to a problem regarding the identity of the creator in Hebrews. As already asserted, the noun κύριος in Hebrews' cosmogony pinpoints the Hebrew noun יהוה of the Old Testament, but it also functions in a sort of apposition to the nouns, υἱός, Χριστός, and Ἰησοῦς in the New Testament. Thus, it can be stated that all these names, including the Hebrew יהוה, pinpoint one person that was always interacting with human beings.[29] Besides, Hebrews 1 clearly indicates that υἱός and κύριος are only one being, and it is also indisputable that υἱός, Χριστός, and Ἰησοῦς are different nouns—perhaps titles—used to identify this same person.[30] Therefore, in 1:10, he who "laid the foundation of the earth in the beginning" must be Jesus in his preincarnate

---

28. Attridge, *Hebrews*, 110.

29. It is broadly accepted that there is a deep connection between the angel of the Lord—מלאך יהוה—and the preincarnate appearance of the Messiah; see Goldberg, "Angel of the Lord." Also, as Flink asserts, it is very probable that early Christianity argued for a pre-existence of Jesus of Nazareth identifying him with the יהוה of the Old Testament. See Flink, "Reconsidering the Text," 125. A good document asserting that Jesus was the יהוה of the Old Testament is the publication of Quarles, *Theology of Matthew*, 5–190.

30. As already shown, Hebrews uses the noun κύριος sixteen times: eleven times in text with an evident context of quotations (cf. 1:10; 7:21; 8:8, 9, 10, 11; 10:16, 30; 12:5, 6; 13:6), three times it is evident that it refers to Jesus (cf. 2:3; 7:14; 13:20), and only twice its use is not very clear (cf. 8:2; 12:14). But due to the historical context, its use in 12:14 must refer to Jesus also, since the predominant hope among the early Christians was to meet Jesus again, particularly because of the promise that he himself made (cf. Luke 12:40; John 14:3, 19). Therefore, it seems that Hebrews uses the noun κύριος to identify the actions and words of יהוה in the Old Testament, as well as to identify the actions and words of Jesus in the New Testament, and consequently in Hebrews יהוה, υἱός, Χριστός, and Ἰησοῦς are the same person.

condition. However, a big problem arises here, since as can be seen in Figure 5.3, the subject of the PC is ὁ θεός, therefore the one that addresses Him—κύριος—must be ὁ θεός,³¹ i.e., it seems that in Hebrews' cosmogony there are two persons in interaction. What is also interesting is that ὁ θεός addresses υἱός as κύριος, which means that ὁ θεός considers υἱός as a divine being, particularly if it is considered that υἱός is also identified as ὁ θεός in Hebrews (cf. 1:8–9). Therefore, Hebrews posits two divine beings in its cosmogony. On the other hand, it is important to remember that ὁ θεὸς ἐποίησεν could be considered as a hyperbaton³² of the Hebrew בָּרָא אֱלֹהִים (cf. Gen 1:1 LXX). Therefore, in Hebrews' cosmogony, ὁ θεός is used with the plural sense of the Hebrew noun אֱלֹהִים who is the creator in Genesis 1, and who performs his—their—creative action through one being that belongs to this plural being, which in Hebrews is identified with the noun υἱός.³³ Therefore, even though ὁ θεός, with the plural sense of אֱלֹהִים, is the creator—i.e., the two beings that interact in Hebrews' cosmogony—his actions in order to create were accomplished through one of the members of this plural being. So the specific creator in Hebrews is named—also in other texts of the New Testament—as the Son, Christos, Jesus, or Lord.³⁴

31. Hebrews 1:10 is a quotation from Psalm 102, and as Guthrie has asserted, this Psalm has generated a plethora of complex speculations on its exact genre, unity of form, setting, and appropriate interpretation, therefore its use and understanding in Hebrews is difficult. In the Hebrew Bible the conversation is between יהוה and אֶל in the LXX as Guthrie asserts it seems to be between κύριος and someone "addressed as "Lord," which according to Guthrie must be the divine Wisdom or the Messiah, a view shared also by Lane and Bruce, see Guthrie, "Hebrews," 940. Nevertheless, in Hebrews κύριος is who is addressed and therefore it seems that Hebrews changes the roles in the conversation, and consequently the addresser in Hebrews must be the addressed in Psalm 102, which in the LXX is identified by the dative of ἐγώ and in the Hebrew Bible by the noun אֶל. Therefore, the Hebrew יהוה who is the addresser in the Scriptures of Israel must be the κύριος in Hebrews who is also clearly identified with Jesus in Hebrews.

32. As Trotter affirms, "hyperbaton is a little-used device, but one that clearly identifies the author as rhetorically trained." It is the separation of words naturally belonging together, i.e., the Greek authors can change the word order to suit their purposes. He asserts that Hebrews' author "uses hyperbaton by quoting OT passages and then reusing them in ways that draw special attention to the interpretations he [sic] gives them." Trotter, *Interpreting the Epistle to the Hebrews*, 171.

33. Bruce asserts that the use of υἱός here must be understood as referring to someone superior to the angels, see Bruce, *Epistle to the Hebrews*, 53. And since in the cosmogonic context the only superior being is God himself as uncreated being, while all the other created things share the same quality, here the noun υἱός must be understood as referring to one of the members of the Godhead.

34. It is important to note here that even though the adjectives θεότης or θειότης are never used in Hebrews to depict the divinity of the person referred to by the nouns υἱός,

Thus Hebrews' cosmogony seems to assume the existence of at least two different beings with equal value and will, and therefore the creator is ὁ θεός υἱός even though ὁ θεός seems to be constituted not only by υἱός.

On the other hand, the noun υἱός, used in a sort of apposition to Jesus,[35] appears first in 1:2 where it is used to indicate the personal agent by whom the action of the verb ἐποίησεν was accomplished.[36] In addition, the prepositional phrase ἐν υἱῷ—see AJ1 in Figure 5.1—due to its context, must be understood as a hypostatic phrase; thus υἱός is not an instrument but the agent by which ὁ θεός in his plural sense, performs the actions of creation and recreation.[37] Nevertheless, it must be recognized that a different theological comprehension could give rise to a different conclusion. However, the previous assertion is also supported by the use of the prepositional phrase δι' οὗ in 1:2 since it expresses the ultimate cause and sole agency and not instrumentality.[38] Consequently, ὁ θεός with its plural sense is the creator, but υἱός, also called κύριος, Χριστός, and Ἰησοῦς in Hebrews, executes the creative actions.[39]

κύριος, Χριστός, and Ἰησοῦς it is indisputable that Hebrews asserts that Jesus is God.

35. As already asserted, the noun υἱός in 1:2—also in other Hebrews' texts (cf. 1:8; 3:6; 7:28)—is functioning as a proper name of Jesus but highlighting his hypostatic condition; also, Allen and Lane seem to understand this when they comment on this text, see, Allen, *Hebrews*, 131; Lane, *Hebrews 1–8*, 30.

36. Koester asserts for instance that "in 1:2 the Son was the agent 'through whom' God made the universe, whereas God himself is the agent in 2:10." See Koester, *Hebrews*, 227.

37. It is interesting to note that the noun υἱός is mainly used in the New Testament in referring to Jesus while he was accomplishing his redemptive work, and only in 1:2 is it used in a context that shows him as the creator of everything. However, its use here (1:2) alongside the adverb also—καὶ—could mean that other actions of ὁ θεός has also been made by the one who is called υἱός here. A good treatment on the noun υἱός and its use in Hebrews as a title is found in Cortez, "Jesus as 'Son' of God," 471–86.

38. That υἱός is not an instrument of God, but is God himself is also asserted by Allen when he affirms "Jesus is the effulgence of God's glory because he shares the same divine nature as the Father, yet he is distinct from the Father in his person. . . . The preincarnate Christ shared in the divine glory because he is "God of very God." . . . Furthermore, in this revelation, Jesus does not reveal something other than himself, nor does he reveal something other than God." Allen, *Hebrews*, 119.

39. About the identity of υἱός, Bruce asserts that "the Greek word χαρακτήρ, occurring only in [1:2] in the New Testament, expresses even more emphatically than εἰκών which is used elsewhere, that Christ is the "image" of God (2 Cor 4:4; Col 1:15)." Thus God is really in Christ, namely what God essentially is, is made manifest in Christ. Bruce also states that "To see Christ is to see what the Father is like," See Bruce, *Epistle to the Hebrews*, 48. But it is more likely that to see Christ is to see what the Godhead is like. On the other hand, to affirm that υἱός or Ἰησοῦς performs the creative action does

Features of Hebrews' Creator

In Hebrews' cosmogony, ὁ θεός and υἱός are the creators[40] and their attributes are portrayed in particular ways. In 4:3–5 the creator can be seen as a worker, i.e., he is not a passive being but an active being; he is not in the position of supervisor but of laborer. Therefore, in Hebrews the creator, in order to create, works directly and personally.[41] Further, another characteristic of Hebrews' creator is that he is willing to develop relationships with his creation, that is to say, he is a social being, not a solitary one.[42] Also, the accidence and syntactic context of the verb κατηρτίσθαι (was created) in 11:3 suggests that when the creator creates something, His creation is placed close to him, i.e., he is not a distant being, but a close being.[43] Moreover, even though according to 4:10, God is a being that is in motion, i.e., he is not a static being, the text does not imply that he leaves his creation alone, because his motion is inside his creation.[44] Thus, in the cosmogony of Hebrews, the Creator is surrounded by his creation.

---

not mean that he is the only one that can perform actions in the Godhead, but it seems that in Hebrews, especially in its cosmogony υἱός is who accomplishes at least the work of creation, redemption, and recreation.

40. As it was showed in the anterior section, ὁ θεός refers in the cosmogony of Hebrews to the Godhead as the creator, while υἱός refers to a specific being that is in charge to create. Thus, in Hebrews' cosmogony the attributes of both of them must be unify in order to know what are the characteristics of the creator, since both are the creator without existence of contradiction, as it was showed in the anterior section.

41. As affirmed in the previous chapter, due to the grammatical and syntactic context of 4:3–5, and particularly due to the use of the article, the work of God can be understood as a personal and direct work and not as a kind of supervisory or administrative function. Namely, the creative action is not performed through some agent or intermediary, it is something done by God himself or by the creator himself.

42. From the first verse of the Hebrews, which says that "God, who at various times and in various ways spoke in time past to the fathers by the prophets" (1:1) through to its end (cf. 13:20–21) God can be seen trying to keep a relationship with his creation. Furthermore, the use of the conjunction ὥσπερ in 4:10 alongside its grammatical and literary context, implies that the action of ceasing (κατέπαυσεν) or rest must be synchronised with the rest or ceasing of the actions of his creation—synchronization that could be temporary but also conditional—in order that it can accomplish its purpose.

43. From Genesis, where God went looking for Adam and Eve, through to Revelation where God comes down with his holy city, the Bible always shows God in a close relationship with his creation. I agree with Gregory when he affirms: "In a sense the creation is always closely related to the Creator, and has no separate, independent existence: 'thy heavens' (Ps 8:3), 'in him we live, and move, and have our being' (Ac 17:28)." See Gregory, "Union."

44. The εἰς is used seventy-four times—the most-used preposition in Hebrews—and

On the other hand, the accidence of the verb εἰσῆλθεν (cf. 9:11–12) implies a gnomic *aktionsart*—i.e., a temporal action not defined—which implies the creator's motion in temporal freedom. That is, the Creator is able to come and go,[45] to intervene in his creations, to produce new things both outside and inside his creations, and to leave for a moment what he is doing, in order to have communion with his creations—but even so, he always finishes his works. So the creator has a life full of activities which elapse in an undefined temporal framework. In addition, from 8:1–2 it can be understood that although the creator may not necessarily need a place to dwell, he prefers to have one. Also, just as he can enter in the greater and perfect place made by him, he can also enter into places prepared for him by his creation (cf. Exod 25:8; 1 Kgs 6:13; 8:10–13).[46]

Purposes of Hebrews' Creator

Although Hebrews is not explicit about the reason for which the creation was made or why the creation exists, everything that God does appears to be for the benefit of human beings.[47] Also, according to 8:1–2 κύριος has made a real σκηνή for him, and the context clarifies that it was made to minister on behalf of the believers. Likewise, according to 11:10, the

posits a motion, even when this preposition is in some cases used in a temporal sense: it is used eight times in combination with the verb εἰσέρχομαι and the noun κατάπαυσις (cf. 3:11, 18; 4:1, 3, 5, 10, 11), nine times with the noun αἰών (cf. 1:8; 5:6; 6:20; 7:17, 21, 24, 28; 13:8, 21), four times with the adjective διηνεκής (cf. 7:3; 10:1, 12, 14) and once with the adjective παντελής (cf. 7:25). This preposition has a special place in New Testament theology since it posits the motion between the creator and creation, in both directions. Rojas, "En Busca del κεντρον," 493–94.

45. 9:26 does not affirm that Χριστός cannot move from that moment on.

46. Although it is possible to misunderstand 7:18–19 as saying that the Jewish sanctuary was useless or without value, Hebrews never asserts as much. What Hebrews does assert is that the new era is characterised by better—κρείττων—things. Thus, the Jewish sanctuary fulfilled its purpose, even though, the people did not understand it, which was to point to the better things to come. Attridge, commenting on 6:9, asserts that "the author is 'convinced' (πεπείσμεθα) that better things are in store for his addressees." Attridge, *Hebrews*, 174.

47. For instance, from the context of 1:1 ὁ θεός spoke primarily for the benefit of ἡμῖν—us. Moreover, it is evident that in Hebrews everything that the Godhead does is for the benefit of his creation, with emphasis on the believers and human beings. So it can be affirmed with Neill that, "God is kindly, and has ordered His creation for the benefit of man." Neill, "Bible in English History," 101. LaRondelle also claims that "The Christian doctrine of creation confesses that creation is a benefit because it is the work of God in Jesus Christ." LaRondelle, *Our Creator Redeemer*, 14.

creator creates for his creation, i.e., because the creation needs created things to enjoy and to exist—to remain or to outlive—continually. Moreover, in 2:10 the purpose of the creation is described with the formula δι' ὅν—according to the EC3 in the SP1—which pinpoints that everything was done for the sake of God, not for the sake of some other intermediary agent,[48] but for his glory.[49] On this, it is important to understand that in Hebrews to glorify God means primarily to please, obey and serve him (cf. 2:1–4; 3:12; 5:11–14; 10:19–25), in a context of happiness, surety, and brotherly love to Christ (cf. 2:14–18; 3:1–3; 6:19–20; 9:13–14; 10:35–39). That is, the creation must feel the privilege and happiness of being his creation. Finally, according to Hebrews' cosmogony, the creator created everything with the purpose of having communion with it.[50]

Procedure in Hebrews' Cosmogony

Creating something usually implies some action(s) and some procedure(s) that also involves methods, sources and time. Hebrews portrays that the creator, in order to create, executed some actions, used some methods, employed some source(s), and that all this happened in a temporal reality.

---

48. Attridge also asserts that the phrase δι' ὅν ... δι' οὗ—for whom and through whom—which describes God here, "is closer to Stoic than to Platonic conceptions, since it does not refer to an intermediary agent of creation." Attridge, *Hebrews*, 82.

49. Although God, due to his nature, does not need anything in order to exist as a glorious being, from the cosmogonic context of Hebrews it emerges that God needs to be surrounded by his creation, not to be glorified by them, but because he loves his creation and a response of love from his creation glorifies him. Therefore, I agree with Lenski when he states that the two διά clauses declare that all the things that exist do so for his glory. See Lenski, *Interpretation of the Epistle to the Hebrews*, 80.

50. In Hebrews God is always in motion towards his creation and trying to move his creation towards him, specifically humanity, which implies relationship and communion. More specifically, from the grammar and syntactic structure of 4:3–5 since the *aktionsart* of the participle γενηθέντων (were finished) implies an action that is antecedent to its leading verb εἰσερχόμεθα (we enter), when God finalizes his action of creating, he opens the possibility of rest. So even though to enter into the rest could not be considered as a purpose from the syntactic perspective, it was the course of action of the creator according to Hebrews. Consequently, the creator works for the rest of his creation and also for his own rest, and in this regard again, the rest of God really implies a communion with his creation. This purpose is clearer in Genesis, where the humans are invited to participate in the rest of God although they did nothing.

Actions of the Creator

The actions of the Creator in the context of Hebrews' cosmogony are mainly expressed through verbs.[51] For purposes of this research, these verbs will be divided into two groups on the basis of the viewpoint that the author is trying to convey, i.e., verbs with imperfective and perfective aspect.[52] However, it must be noted that not all of the verbs will be dealt with here, since some of them are more deeply linked with other aspects of Hebrews' cosmogony and will consequently be treated in other sections.

Perfective Aspect

The perfective aspect is the external viewpoint of the actions, i.e., the text portrays the action as a whole and as being seen from a distant point, which in the cosmogonic context must be understood as a temporal reference. In 1:10 the aorist verb ἐθεμελίωσας (laid the foundation) portrays a summary or all-encompassing view of one real—due to its indicative mood—action. So the perfective aspect of this verb affirms that the entire creation from its very basis was set by the creator.[53] Thus in Hebrews'

---

51. The main verbs used in the cosmogony of Hebrews are the lemmas: λαλέω, εἶπον (to speak, cf. 1:1; 4:4), θεμελιόω (to lay the foundation, cf. 1:10), ποιέω (to make, cf. 1:2; 12:27), κατασκευάζω (to build, cf. 3:3-4), πήγνυμι (to erect, cf. 8:2), καταρτίζω (to prepare, to finish, cf. 11:3), καταπαύω (to rest, cf. 4:4, 10), φέρω (to uphold, cf. 1:3), γίνομαι (to became, cf. 11:3), ἑλίσσω (to fold, cf. 1:12), σαλεύω (to shake, cf. 12:26-27), σείω (to stir, cf. 12:26), τελειόω (to make perfect, cf. 2:10). However, in the cosmogony of Hebrews there are two words which could also be considered as words that portray actions of the creator, the adjective χειροποίητος—involving the root ποιεω—which basically portrays God using his hands in order to do something, and the noun καταβολή—involving the root βαλλω—which portrays God as establishing the foundations of everything.

52. Campbell defines the verbal aspect as the simplest viewpoint, both from the outside and from the inside, which the author or speaker portrays with respect to the action, event, or state. He asserts that "the view of an action, event, or state from the outside is called perfective aspect, while the view from the inside is called imperfective aspect." And he illustrates it by declaring that when the reporter reports "the street parade from a helicopter, [s/he] sees the whole parade from a distance," and it must be reported using the perfective aspect of the verb—the external viewpoint. But if s/he reports the parade from the level of the street, his/her view of the parade is quite different, s/he watches as it unfolds before him/her, and this viewpoint, from the street, represents what we call imperfective aspect—the internal viewpoint. Campbell, *Basics of Verbal Aspect*, 19-20.

53. Although Hebrews is not trying to demonstrate what this basis is, it can be asserted that God has laid the foundation of everything, namely the basis—perhaps

cosmogony, an important action of the Creator is to lay the foundation or basis, i.e., to create everything.

Likewise, the use of the aorist verb κατέπαυσεν (rested) in 4:3–5, which, besides its perfective aspect, implies an ingressive *aktionsart*, and posits that God does not pass from the state of activity to the state of inactivity or immobility, and its use in 4:10 also reinforces the idea of the ingressive *aktionsart*. Therefore, according to these texts the Creator stops one action—i.e., to create—only to begin a new action—i.e., to rest.[54] Thus, even though the Creator ceases his work of creation, he does not cease at all, he continues his activity in relation to his creation but in a different type of action—a friendly and protective relationship.[55] Everything mentioned above, together with the external viewpoint of the action—i.e., the perfective aspect—supports the position that the rest of the Creator is a change of activity and not the start of inactivity. That is, Hebrews affirms that the Creator is not creating all the time and has other activities to do. Due to the perfective aspect used here, although Hebrews is not showing in detail what these activities are, it is revealing perhaps the most important of them—according to the broader context of Hebrews' cosmogony—i.e., he is upholding all things by the word of his power (cf. 1:3). In short, the Creator is not always creating, he changes his activities and never goes to a state of inactivity; also, the detail of every action cannot be seen, but what can be seen is the final result, fully accomplished by the action of the Creator.

Other verbs that carry the same sense in Hebrews' cosmogony, i.e., verbs that portray actions that were, are and will be fully accomplished by the Creator—even though it is not possible to see the detail of these actions, nor experience them nor see them from a closer viewpoint—are

---

the primary elements or laws—of everything. Therefore, it can be considered a cosmogonic presupposition.

54. Also in 4:3–5 the prepositional phrase ἀπὸ πάντων τῶν ἔργων αὐτοῦ—from all of his works—indicates that one action of the Creator in the cosmogonic context is to leave his creative work, namely to separate himself from it and change his activities. However, since in 4:3–5 the context says that the Creator leaves all—πάντων—his works and not some of them, it is possible to reaffirm that his rest mainly consist in a moment of communion with his creation.

55. It does not mean that the Creator only takes some time to take care of his creation; on the contrary, it means that from the time when the creation is finished the main activity of the creator becomes to take care of his creation. On the other hand, the Creator's rest can be emulated by his creation and even though it could be realized every day, Hebrews will emphasise that it must be realized in one day, which Hebrews identifies as τῇ ἡμέρᾳ τῇ ἑβδόμῃ (the seventh day).

portrayed through verbs' lemmas such as: λαλέω, εἶπον (to speak, cf. 1:1; 4:4), ποιέω (to make, cf. 1:2; 12:27), πήγνυμι (to erect, cf. 8:2), and ἑλίσσω (to fold, cf. 1:12). Thus, Hebrews emphasizes that even though it is not possible for every human being to experience or to see the Creator speaking, making, creating, erecting or folding up something as a partner in these actions, they are a reality, since the results of all these actions of the creator are evident. Consequently, Hebrews' cosmogony affirms that in order to create, God accomplished some actions privately, i.e., the way in which these actions were performed are not revealed to the creation.

Imperfective Aspect

The imperfective aspect is the internal viewpoint of the actions, i.e., the text is portraying the action as being seen from an inner point, which in the cosmogonic context must be referring to some kind of supernatural involvement—perhaps vision, since the text is transmitting the facts as if its author was a personal witness of these actions. Thus for instance, the use of the perfect verb[56] κατηρτίσθαι (was created) in 11:3, which posits, as already stated, the creation of something new—not a recreation or the fashioning of something—something that did not exist before, implies not only a close and personal intervention of the creator, but also an inner viewpoint of the action by the author. Since it is logically impossible, the only possible explanation to this redaction in Hebrews is that the writer participated in this divine action through a supernatural experience, such as a vision or prophetic dream(s). But it is also possible that Hebrews is using the verb κατηρτίσθαι (was created) with this accidence due to the author of Hebrews having experienced this creative power. Thus, according to Hebrews, it is only possible to see the creative power of the creator in action if the creator decides to reveal it—to someone special—therefore, the power that brought everything into existence in the beginning could be witnessed. Namely, the creator is exercising his creative power in front of the eyes of the believers; so in Hebrews, the author and the believers are witnesses—although not of the beginning of everything—of the creative power of the Creator.[57]

---

56. Despite the difficulty on the aspect of the perfect tense of the verb, Campbell asserts, "Nevertheless, regarding the perfect as encoding imperfective aspect provides the best power of explanation and therefore is the position adopted here." Campbell, *Basics of Verbal Aspect*, 103.

57. It begs the question in what way could the creative power of the creator have

Other verbs that carry the same sense in Hebrews' cosmogony, i.e., verbs that portray actions that were, are, and will be ongoing actions, with the sense of repetition, which from the perspective of Hebrews are actions that could be seen in more detail, as well as could be experienced or observed by the audience of Hebrews, are portrayed through verbs' lemmas such as: κατασκευάσας (to build, cf. 3:4),[58] γίνομαι (to come to exist, to bring into existence, cf. 11:3), φέρω (to uphold, cf. 1:3), σαλεύω (to shake, cf. 12:26–27), σείω (to stir, cf. 12:26). Thus, Hebrews states that it is possible for every human being to experience or to see the Creator building, giving birth to new existences, upholding his creation, and shaking and stirring it.[59]

Methods Used to Create

As already asserted, Hebrews does not intend to be a treaty on cosmogony, and consequently there are no explicit declarations about methods used by the Creator to create; however, there are some important inferences that

---

been shown to the believers—including the author—at the time of Hebrews? From its very beginning Hebrews emphasizes the arrival of a new age (cf. 1:2) which is consistently related, in Hebrews, to the creation topic. So it is possible that Hebrews, in showing the creative power of the creator as being actioned in its time, could be referring to the origin of this new age, or perhaps Hebrews is referring to the incarnation of Jesus Christ (cf. 2:9). But it is also possible that Hebrews is referring here to the conversion—i.e., the creation of a new creature—that every Christian has experienced in his/her life (cf. 6:6; Eph 4:24; Col 3:10).

58. It is important to clarify that, as already asserted, the verb in the present tense, κατασκευάσας—build—in 3:4, posits that the creative actions of the Creator were a process and not an instantaneous act, and in this respect Hebrews agrees with Genesis, where the creation is shown as an action which was developed step-by-step through a process that took six days in order to be fully complete. However, the imperfective aspect of the verb, portrays that the actions of the Creator were attested by the author and the audience of Hebrews, but since this is logically impossible, the explanation for this redaction in Hebrews must be that the writer participated in this divine action through a supernatural experience, such as a vision or a prophetic-dream. But it is also possible that Hebrews is using the verb κατασκευάσας—build—because the author of Hebrews believed that every newborn and every new thing that appears on the earth is the creation of God.

59. Here it is important to note that the verbs σαλεύω (to shake, to agitate, cf. 12:26–27) and σείω (to shake to and fro, cf. 12:26) are used in Hebrews in a context that implies future actions. Therefore, even though these divine actions could easily be related to seismic movements, it is more likely that they are portraying future actions related to the end of the world of sin.

can be made on this issue. For instance, 1:1–4 reads: "He—ὁ θεός—made the universe through Him—υἱός." As already mentioned, this text does not set υἱός in an instrumental position, even though in English the use of the preposition "through" could give this idea. The preposition is showing the ultimate cause and sole agency and not the instrument issued by ὁ θεός in order to create. Therefore, this text shows that ὁ θεός—the Godhead, not the Father as if he were superior to the Son—is creating "through" υἱός, as a delegated responsibility and not as an instrumentality function. Consequently, ὁ θεός—the Godhead—in order to create, uses a method that could be called *delegation of functions*. Therefore, Hebrews asserts that the Godhead decided that the function of creating will rest on υἱός.

Now, this υἱός called in 1:10–12 κύριος is the one of whom ὁ θεός—the Godhead—declares "You, Lord, laid the foundation of the earth in the beginning and the heavens are the work of your hands." Here the verb ἐθεμελίωσας (laid the foundation) expresses an important notion about the method used by υἱός to create the universe.[60] As already shown, this verb is used in the LXX forty-one times and only five times in the New Testament, and from the four times where this verb is used in the New Testament, apart from 1:10, its meaning is related to something that was set previously in order to develop something bigger over it (cf. Matt 7:25; Eph 3:17; Col 1:23; 1 Pet 5:10). Further, its use in the LXX supports this assertion.[61] It can also be seen that the lemma θεμελιόω is used in a context that has a special connection with the notion of laws and regulations (cf. Ps 118:152; Prov 3:19; 8:23; Job 38:4, LXX),[62] and in conjunction with its

---

60. According to Allen, the expression in 1:10 "You laid the foundations—θεμελιόω," is an idiomatic expression for the act of creation" Allen, *Hebrews*, 183. And this assertion can be supported due to the use of θεμελιόω in the LXX, in Pss 101:26; 103:5; and Isa 48:13, since there the Creator—identified in the LXX with the nouns θεός and κύριος and in the Hebrew text with the nouns אֱלֹהִים and יהוה—says "my hand has founded—ἐθεμελίωσε—the earth, and my right hand firmed up the heaven." (Isa 48:13, cf. Ps 101:26, LXX). In addition, the LXX says, "He laid the foundation (ἐθεμελίωσεν) of the earth upon its stability; it will not be moved forever and ever" (Ps 103:5, LXX) in a literary context that is clearly identical to that of Hebrews 1:10 (cf. also Zech 12:1; Isa 51:13, 16).

61. Of the forty-one times the verb θεμελιόω is used in the LXX, in some instances it is used to identify something that is placed as a basis on which something bigger is ordered or developed (cf. 3 Kgdms 6:1c; 7:47; 2 Chron 8:16; 31:7; 1 Esd 5:55; 2 Esd 3:6, 10; Isa 44:28, LXX).

62. The use of the verb θεμελιόω in Job 38:4, LXX, is evidence that this word can refer to that which today is known as natural laws. It is important to understand this text in the context of Job 26:7, where it is clearly stated that "there are no physical

use in the New and Old Testament, also with a connotation of perpetuity. Therefore, υἱός in the beginning or initially (cf. Gen 1:1), created something that could be physical elements and laws,[63] or maybe only laws, that would be used and would rule his future creation. Therefore, the Creator, in order to create, used a method that could be called a logical process.

On the other hand, even though in 9:24 (cf. 9:11) Hebrews seems to convey the idea that the heaven or some heavenly places are not something made with hands (χεῖρες) i.e., created entities, this text does not contradict 1:10–12 which declares: "the heavens are the work of your hands—i.e., τῶν χειρῶν υἱοῦ."[64] First, it is essential to note here, as Allen asserts, that the noun χείρ (hand) is used in 1:10–12 as metonymy, referring to divine power,[65] but as already stated, the use of the word χείρ also implies closeness and direct action. Therefore, in order to create, the Creator—i.e., ὁ θεὸς δι' υἱοῦ (cf. 1:1–4)—used a method that could be called a powerful personal intervention. This assertion is supported by 2:10, where, according to Attridge, God is alluded to with the formula δι' ὅν . . . καὶ δι' οὗ (for whom and through whom) which "is closer to Stoic

---

foundations" to the globe, in fact, as Wiersbe affirms, "Job 26:7 clearly states that the world hangs on nothing, and this was written in a day when learned men taught that the world was held up by huge turtles or other creatures" or that it was supported by pillars sunk into the sea. Wiersbe, *Wiersbe's Expository Outlines*, Job 38:1—42:6. Alden also states, "Job's assertion that the earth hangs on nothing is amazingly accurate and certainly counters the charge that the Bible's writers held that the earth stood on something else." Alden, *Job*, 11:259. Therefore, the foundation referred to here cannot be the "lower part of a structure upon which the structure rests" as Reyburn rightly asserts; see Reyburn, *Handbook on the Book of Job*, 696. It is more likely that the foundation refers not only to the inauguration but to the whole process of creation, which, as Hooks asserts, this particular passage (Job 38) suggests was carefully planned; see Hooks, *Job*, 427. And according to the context of Job 38, the careful planning would have contemplated the formulation of the laws that rule the whole creation.

63. As Burton asserts, "Creation did not only result in the appearance of physical objects, but also involved the establishment of invisible phenomena. The principle of 'rulership' (*archē*) was first established on the fourth day of creation... [and] on the sixth day, God invested humans with rulership (*archē*) over all animal and plant life (Gen 1:26ff). [On the other hand] Paul, in Colossians 1:16, reasons that the 'invisible' creation also includes 'thrones, lords, and authorities.'" Burton, "Faith Factor," 40–41.

64. Given the aim of this section, which is to identify a methodology used by the Creator in order to create, the problem that arises with the use of οὐρανός—heaven—in Hebrews both in singular and in plural, will be addressed in what follows, with the intention of establishing whether the singular οὐρανός in 9:24 is a created entity or not.

65. Allen, *Hebrews*, 183.

than to Platonic conceptions, since it does not refer to an intermediary agent of creation."⁶⁶

However, perhaps the more important assertion on methods used by the Creator in Hebrews is found in 11:3, since the AJ1—ῥήματι θεοῦ, see Figure 5.11—asserts that "the universe was created by God via His word." As already argued, ῥήματι is functioning as a dative of means but also as a dative of agency,⁶⁷ and it is modifying θεοῦ, not as an instrument, but as an agent. So ῥῆμα is the power that belongs to every being of the Godhead as a person, but it is also the power to which all of them submit—i.e., they are submitted to the word of the Godhead.⁶⁸ So the will of the Godhead regarding the creation was executed through the power of the Son.⁶⁹ In Hebrews no other being has the power of ῥῆμα, since it is not only the capacity to talk—of course God can speak⁷⁰—but the

---

66. Attridge, *Hebrews*, 82. However, it is important to highlight that it does not imply that Hebrews has Stoic influence or even that it is a Stoic document, since the presence of some isolated ideas, words or similar phrases are not determinant to infer dependence or influence. As Ferguson claims, "two groups [that] use the same method does not necessarily mean that one is copying the other," and "Although Christianity had points of contact with Stoicism, the mysteries, the Qumran community, and so on, the total worldview was often quite different, or the context in which the items were placed was different." See Ferguson, *Backgrounds of Early Christianity*, 2–3.

67. See footnotes 167 and 168 from chapter 5.

68. Here it is important to note that ῥήματι is not a being, but it is apparently a law or every declaration that the Godhead asserts. Namely, every assertion of the Godhead not only subjugates the creation but also Themselves, therefore the Godhead is submitted to his own word.

69. Even though Allen, commenting on 11:3, posits that ῥήματι must be understood as dative of means (cf. Allen, *Hebrews*, 545.), he also asserts that ῥῆμα is used in Hebrews *exclusively* of God—the Father—speaking and the Son's speaking, referring to "his providential will and has the force of a command that the universe obeys." ῥῆμα is not focusing on the content of what is mentioned "but rather on the act of utterance," which according to him is the power that sustains the universe. Allen, *Hebrews*, 123. Therefore, ῥῆμα belongs to the Son, since it is he who expressed the creative words, but it can also be said that he—the Son—belongs to ῥῆμα since ῥῆμα is the expression of the will of God—the Father to Allen. Westcott also asserted that "the world was called into being by an utterance (ῥῆμα) of God" and also that it is sustained for the expression—ῥῆμα—of the divine will. Westcott, *Epistle to the Hebrews*, 14.

70. In 11:3, more specifically in the AJ1—see Figure 5.11—which notes that God created the universe via his word, some kind of connection—allusion—to Psalm 33:9 can be found which says "For He spoke, and it was done"—ὅτι αὐτὸς εἶπεν, καὶ ἐγενήθησαν (Ps 32:9, LXX). Therefore, even though there is no an explicit verb in 11:3 that says that God spoke and the universe was made, the genitive θεοῦ along with the dative ῥήματι implies the action of the verb εἶπεν in order to create. Thus, Hebrews asserts that God spoke in order to create. Kidner, commenting on Genesis 1, also affirms

capacity of creating or doing something that is the will of the Godhead, directed and performed only by someone that is part of the Godhead. And since ῥῆμα is analogous to πίστις[71] it must produce the thing in the moment when it is triggered, and only God can trigger it since it only belongs to the Godhead. So, υἱός, in order to create something, does not need anything more than to know the will of the Godhead, which actually is also his will. Namely, when he has the will, he has all he needs in order to create, for he has the ῥῆμα, i.e., he speaks and things come into existence. Consequently, the Creator uses a method to create that could be called an utterance of goodwill.[72]

Sources Used to Create

As already noted, according to 11:3 the Creator only needs the will of the Godhead and his ῥῆμα in order to create, therefore, the main source used by the Creator in order to create is his own will and his own ῥῆμα. Along with it, it must be noted that in 2:10 Hebrews affirms that ὁ θεός is the ultimate cause—not the proximate cause—and the sole cause and is therefore also the source of the creation. However, in conformity with the cosmogonic context of Hebrews, it is important to clarify that it does not mean that the creation is a kind of extension of God—i.e., pantheism—it only means that everything came from ὁ θεός—the Godhead, i.e., according to 2:10 the source of creation is God himself.

On the other hand, as can be seen in Figure 5.11, in 11:3 the genitive used—θεοῦ—is the AJ1 of the infinitive verb κατηρτίσθαι (to create) which in this context introduces the agent of the action. Namely, it is functioning as a prepositional phrase showing the agent who performs the verbal action, and therefore it must be in connection with the verb through some preposition. But since the preposition is not present here, a fact that has generated diverse interpretations, it is appropriate to add

---

that 11:3 implies that until God spoke, nothing existed. Kidner, *Genesis*, 48.

71. See comments under the subdivision 5.3.10.2.

72. Christianity has asserted from its very beginning that God is love and that his will is the best for his creation, therefore Guthrie is right when affirms that Hebrews shows a full picture of God's love, and also when he declares that the world was created by the word of God through his Son (1:2; 11:3), and that it—the creation—is sustained by the Son's powerful word. Guthrie, *Hebrews*, 48. It is important to note here that Guthrie ascribes ῥῆμα to υἱός in 1:2 and in 11:3, which in a cosmogonic context seems perfectly correct.

Cosmogonic Presuppositions in Hebrews

it for a better comprehension of the text.[73] However, in so doing, various possibilities arise, as can be seen in Figure 6.1.

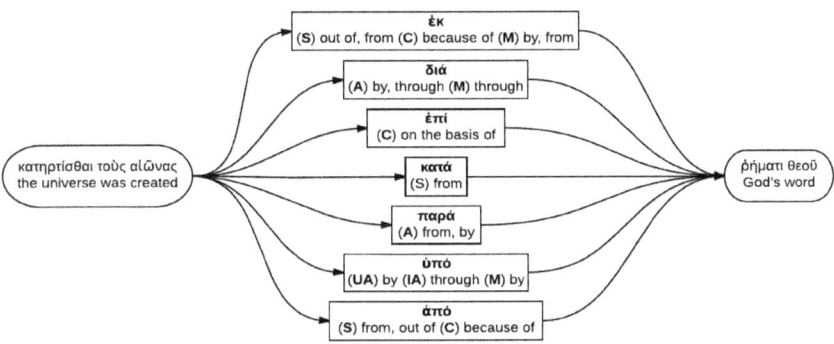

Figure 6.1 Prepositions that complete the idea of Hebrews 11:3.[74]

From Figure 6.1, there are at least seven common prepositions that could be used with the genitive θεοῦ,[75] the dative ῥήματι is the SP3 and

---

73. It is important to clarify here that the conclusion in this research about the absence of the preposition is that it was intentional, therefore this assertion does not intend to suggest that it is necessary to add a preposition in the biblical text or that the preposition was present in the *autographa*. Nevertheless, there are two issues that need to be clarified in this respect: first, it is convenient to add it in order to visualize the different possible interpretations, in order to make a more responsible evaluation of the different possibilities and thus to obtain a better interpretation of the text. Second, since the preposition must be added before the phrase ῥήματι θεοῦ some might think that the prepositional object should be ῥήματι, but the context impels one to consider θεοῦ as the prepositional object, since the dative ῥήματι can only receive as its preposition ἐν, παρά and σύν, and all of them do not fit in the context. For instance, it cannot be said that Hebrews is saying that the universe was created "in the word of God" or "along the word of God" or maybe even "in proximity to the word of God." Thus, even though θεοῦ does not appear alongside the preposition, it ought to be the prepositional object. This phenomenon also occurs in John 5:44—παρὰ τοῦ μόνου θεοῦ, from the only God—and in Rom 4:17—κατέναντι οὗ ἐπίστευσεν θεοῦ, in the presence of him whom he believed—where θεοῦ is the object of παρά and κατέναντι respectively. Here it must be mentioned again that the dative ῥήματι is functioning here as a dative of means but also as a dative of agency, even though a superficial reading of the text could posit it as an instrumental dative, which, in this case due to the general cosmogonic context of Hebrews is impossible.

74. The abbreviations in brackets correspond to their common uses with the genitive case, and they are as follows: (S) = Source; (C) = Cause; (A) = Agency; (M) = Means; (UA) = Ultimate Agency; (IA) = Intermediate Agency.

75. It is important to note that there are some prepositions that are not very

not the object in the prepositional phrase—see Figure 5.11—therefore it is not the focus of this section. At the starting point of this analysis, all the uses where the preposition implies a simple cause (C) must be discarded, so the preposition ἐπί can be discarded. It is also important to note that in the thirty-eight verses in the New Testament where the genitive anarthrous θεοῦ is used in connection with some preposition, it is never used with the preposition ἐπί and κατά. Besides, it can be seen that its main use is with the prepositions ἀπό—twenty-two times—ἐκ—six times—and παρά—five times. Moreover, it is notable that in Hebrews the genitive θεοῦ is only used in prepositional phrases led by the prepositions χωρίς (apart from, cf. 2:9), ὑπό (by, cf. 5:4, 10), and ἀπό (from, cf. 3:12; 6:7), however, the anarthrous θεοῦ is only used with ἀπό. On the other hand, it seems that the context of Hebrews' cosmogony requires the use of ἀπό in this place, since the object is ὁ θεός and not υἱός, because the use of the preposition ὑπό could be expected with υἱός, since ὑπό expresses an immediate and active causation. ἀπό, however, expresses a more remote and less active causation, and ὑπό posits the direct origination of an action while ἀπό posits an indirect one.[76] Therefore, it seems that ἀπό could be the preposition that would assist with the interpretation of the text; however, it also seems that the absence of ἀπό here is deliberate, so that the reader would infer that neither ὑπό nor ἀπό is wrong. Nevertheless, it seems that the preposition ἀπό fits better in the context of Hebrews' cosmogony, since even though the Godhead is the source of everything, it is from υἱός that came the ῥῆμα in order "that that which can be seen came into existence," and so 1:2 is not in contradiction with 11:3.

Furthermore, in 11:3 it reads: "so that that which can be seen came into existence from (ἐκ) what is not visible." Here the preposition ἐκ is used as a preposition of source, with a spatial sense, and not expressing the severance of some relationship, in the sense that the creation is something that has been detached from something and therefore it became something different or apart but with the same essence. Nothing is taken away from the invisible in order to develop the visible, the invisible is the

---

common in the New Testament that could also work with the genitive, κατέναντι—before, in the sight of—and ὡς—as, like. However, due to their inadequate semantic in their contexts, they are not considered as possible options.

76. Regarding the use of ὑπό and ἀπό Harris declares that ἀπό sometimes expresses agency with a passive verb, but it usually expresses source or separation, but with the sense of indirect origination. For more information about ὑπό and ἀπό see, Harris, *Prepositions and Theology*, 57–68, 219–24.

place or the area from where the visible came, as Hughes affirms regarding this text,

> [11:3] Excludes, on the one hand, dualism and, on the other, pantheism: dualism, because the self-existent God is the sole source and principle of all existence; and pantheism, because God, though infinite and omnipresent, is absolutely other than and above his creation, immanent indeed but also transcendent.[77]

Thus, the source of the creation is ὁ θεός himself—the Godhead—namely the only one Who is called invisible in the New Testament and Who dwells in the inaccessible light (cf. 1 Tim 6:11–16; Col 1:15).[78] It is important to note in this respect that the participle φαινομένων does not mean nonexistent; conversely, it implies the existence of something (cf. Matt 1:20; 2:7; John 5:35; Jas 4:4, 14; 2 Pet 1:19). So 11:3 is saying that everything came into existence from something that exists but that is impossible to see. Therefore, this sentence (11:3) is only reaffirming that everything came from the Godhead, that the real source of everything is ὁ θεός,[79] without there being any contradiction with the assertion that all came through the Son who is visible to the creation.

---

77. Hughes, *Commentary on the Epistle to the Hebrews*, 452. The affirmation supports the thesis of this research, even though Hughes asserts that the particle of negation μὴ is not working with the participle φαινομένων. Conversely, he asserts, it must be working with γεγονέναι, so he understands the phrase as "so that what is seen has not come into being from things which appear." However, he does this because he assumes that Hebrews certainly does not mean that "what is seen was made out of things which do not appear" in the sense that the visible world was made from invisible entities. However, he also admits that if God is the invisible source of the visible universe, this is true enough. Nevertheless, he has problems with this conclusion since the plural φαινομένων—things which do not appear—can hardly be intended as a designation of God. However, as it was shown, this plural fits perfectly with ὁ θεός, if 'Him' is understood as referring to the Godhead, an entity constituted by three divine beings. See Hughes, *Commentary on the Epistle to the Hebrews*, 452–53.

78. Even though the visibility or invisibility of God can be debated, it seems more accurate, according to the cosmogonic context of Hebrews, to conclude that the invisible God can only be seen through the face of Jesus, the incarnate God. See also the conclusion of Allen in Allen, "Visibility of the Invisible God," 266–70.

79. Even though Attridge could disagree with some assertions in this research, he also asserts that it is more likely that the negation—μή—ought to be construed with the participle φαινομένων, "in which case it would affirm that the world has an invisible source." Attridge, *Hebrews*, 315.

Time and Creation

In Hebrews there is not one sentence or phrase that asserts something like "God created the time" or "when the time did not exist" or something indicating that this world came from eternity or that it came from a specified number of years ago. Nevertheless, in 11:3 there is a temporal frame that surrounds the text; for instance, the infinite κατηρτίσθαι (was created) implies that the action of the main verb, which in this case is νοοῦμεν (we understand), happens after the infinitive. On the other hand, the negated participle φαινομένων—things that are not visible—assumes the existence of the invisible before the existence of the visible. So there is a historical development with a temporal framework in Hebrews' cosmogony, i.e., the existence of the believers is subsequent to the existence of the creation,[80] while the existence of the creation is subsequent to the existence of the invisible. So, a chronological order is noted here, and the existence of time is presupposed in Hebrews' cosmogony, even though it must be recognized that the instance of its starting point cannot be affirmed.[81]

Likewise, the accidence of the verb γεγονέναι (come into existence) in 11:3 implies an action that happens before the action described by the verb κατηρτίσθαι (was created). So, even though it seems to be contradictory, due to the morphological accidences, the universe came into existence before it was created. However, it is important to note that the

---

80. It does not mean that human beings are not created beings or that they are part of another creation, it simply means that the human being was not present when everything not according to the likeness and image of God was created. Ellingworth also asserts that εἰς τό—AJ2 see Figure 5.11—introduces, not a second event which is the result of the first, but a logical result or implication, and he also says that it is much more natural to take ἐκ as causal—AJ3 see Figure 5.11. Ellingworth, *Epistle to the Hebrews*, 568.

81. In 1983 the theologian-philosopher Fernando L. Canale called into question the timeless view of God in his doctoral dissertation, "A Criticism of Theological Reason." Canale questions that biblical ontology calls for an understanding of time as a primordial presupposition, that the God of revelation is not a timeless God but one who has entered time. See Canale, "Toward a Criticism of Theological Reason." More information can be found in the section "The Timeless View of God" in Gulley, *Systematic Theology*, 4–11. This view could also be supported in the cosmogony of Hebrews with its use of ἐλάλησεν—he has spoken—in 1:1 which expresses that something happened—summary *aktionsart*—without further specifications, i.e., when God spoke is not the main interest of the author of Hebrews. The interest of Hebrews seems to be to highlight that God spoke at various times, i.e., his action of speaking was realized in chronological time, therefore the idea of God moving in time exists in Hebrews.

prepositional phrase led by εἰς τό—"so that what" see the AJ2 in Figure 5.11—implies consequence or result, which means that must be understood as "with the result that," and not "in order that"; i.e., it can be an expression of result rather than purpose.[82] Therefore, the morphological accidence, which implies antecedence, seems to be in contradiction to the syntactic arrangement of the words, which implies progression or result. Nevertheless, this sort of apparent contradiction could be indicating—and therefore allows the assertion—that both actions happened in the same moment: so, created (κατηρτίσθαι) and coming into existence (γεγονέναι) happened in the same moment. Therefore, it seems that Hebrews affirms that there was not a time when the creation was without order, i.e., in Hebrews the creator created the things not needing to shape them at a future time. It could mean that in Hebrews' cosmogony every step followed by the Creator in order to create is consecutive and part of a very well-organized plan.

On the other hand, as already asserted, the accidence of the verb ἐποίησεν—He made—in 1:2 could imply a punctiliar *aktionsart* or a summary *aktionsart*. However, since the noun θεός in the New Testament is the subject of at least thirty-seven aorist verbs from which at least twenty-four are indicatives implying actions and not feelings, here in 1:2, ἐποίησεν ought to imply a punctiliar *aktionsart* (cf. Matt 15:4; Acts 2:24; 3:15; 4:10; 10:15; 13:30), which "expresses an action that is once-occurring and instantaneous."[83] However, in the few instances where the verb ἐποίησεν is functioning with the noun θεός as its subject it implies a summary *aktionsart*, (cf. Luke 8:39; Acts 2:36; 14:27; 15:12; 21:19) and it therefore seems to be more apt in this context (1:2) to understand it as such. So it is important to clarify that even though the Creator has the

---

82. The word "consequence" could give the idea that the preposition εἰς has a causal use here, but it does not. Matey asserted that the preposition εἰς is almost never translated as causal—i.e., ecbatic use. Nevertheless, Mantey in two articles argued for a causal translation. Mantey, "Causal Use of Eis in the New Testament," 45–48; Mantey, "On Causal Eis Again," 309–11. Nevertheless, as Porter, Wallace, and Harris affirm this kind of usage is very unlikely, however, it should not be discarded. Wallace, *Greek Grammar Beyond the Basics*, 369–71; Harris, *Prepositions and Theology*, 90–92. On the other hand, Porter would state that "this preposition, which can be used to refer to a directed action, can also describe the purpose or result of that action." Porter, *Idioms of the Greek New Testament*, 152. In this case it seems that in accordance with the cosmogonic context of Hebrews a resultative translation fits better.

83. Campbell, *Colossians and Philemon*, xxiv.

power to make things without needing a long period of time,[84] here Hebrews seems to show a presupposition founded in the account of Genesis 1, where God uses six days to create the world.

Likewise, in 1:10, the AJ1 κατ' ἀρχάς (in the beginning) is used to portray the temporal reference of the EC1 σὺ τὴν γῆν ἐθεμελίωσας (You laid the foundations of the earth) which depicts the beginning of the earth.[85] And as already shown, the AJ1 κατ' ἀρχάς in Hebrews' cosmogony in all likelihood refers to Genesis 1, and so it is an allusion to the Hebrew noun רֵאשִׁית (cf. Gen 1:1, LXX), which in the Bible is used to posit the very beginning of the history of this planet. In addition, the use of the verb ἐθεμελίωσας (laid the foundation) which implies a punctiliar *aktionsart*, posits the action of the verb happening once and in an instantaneous moment. Namely, while the creation of everything was carried out through a process which implies some time, the colocation of the foundations of the creation, as already asserted, did not take a long time, but was an instantaneous action.

However, it is important to note that there is no indication in Hebrews about the time between the ἐθεμελίωσας (laid the foundation) of the earth and the culmination of the whole process of the creation. Nevertheless, if this assertion is understood as the creation being in two steps, in which the first refers to a chaotic moment of disorder, then it could be seen as contradictory to a previous assertion that "Hebrews asserts that there was not a time when the creation was without order."

---

84. The Bible says that God can make or do what he wants without taking a long time in order to accomplish his goal (cf. Pss 33:6; 148:5–6). However, it is important to note that it does not imply that he will never use time or a process in order to do something—conversely, it reveals more evidence of God doing things through time and through a process (1:1; cf. Gen 1–2). The earthly ministry of Jesus could exemplify it very well: in order to fulfill his mission, he used at least three and a half years, but in order to heal the paralytic, he did not use any process. It was something that he did instantaneously (cf. John 5:8–9).

85. Here it is important to clarify that in Hebrews the phrase ἀπὸ καταβολῆς κόσμου—since the foundation of the world—used in 9:24–26 which evidently has a temporal sense, is also used to posit the beginning of the earth. However, it is interesting that here the death of Christ is possibly related to the foundation of the world, which can be understood in two ways: firstly, the appearance of sin in Genesis is considered as the foundation of the world; or secondly, as a more tropological declaration, sin and the beginning of the world belong to the same measurement of time. Therefore, since tropology is the use of figurative language which refers to the interpretation of the scripture as a source of moral guidance, it is more likely that Hebrews, even though it is not defining the time of creation, is relating the creation and the beginning of sin to the same measurement of time, or at least to two moments very close in time.

Nevertheless, the creation of the basic element or elements does not necessarily imply disorder: it could be a very orderly creation or it could be referring to the initial moment of the creative action of the Creator.[86] In this cosmogonic context Hebrews mentions the seventh day (ἐν τῇ ἡμέρᾳ τῇ ἑβδόμῃ) in 4:3–5, which certainly pinpoints that Hebrews—or at least its author—suggests that the creation was made in six days, as Genesis 1 shows in its account, which is in accordance with the cosmogonic context and literary dependence of Hebrews' cosmogony. Therefore, even though it could be debatable, Hebrews seems to show a presupposition or simply take over its tradition's position, that the time taken to create the realm of the human being is the same as related in Genesis, viz. six days.

The Creation in Hebrews' Cosmogony

The more important topic in cosmogony is the creation itself, and Hebrews has insights about the nature, content, features, purpose, and development of the creation; however, due to the purpose of this research, only the aspects of these matters which are linked to the cosmogonic topic will be addressed here.

The Nature of Creation

The first thing to be affirmed about the creation in Hebrews is that according to 1:10 the creation is today, as it was in the beginning, the handiwork of God, since the verb εἰσίν (are)—see SC1 in Figure 5.3—implies a state of being rather than a process. Therefore, its nature needs to be regarded as something given by God, and therefore something very good.[87] But even though the nature of something is generally closely re-

---

86. Here it is important to assert that the phrase κατ' ἀρχάς κύριε τὴν γῆν ἐθεμελίωσας (You, Lord, laid the foundation of the earth in the beginning) must be closely related, even though they are not synonymous, to the phrase ἀπὸ καταβολῆς κόσμου (since the foundation of the world) also used in the literary component of Hebrews' cosmogony (cf. 4:3; 9:26). As Mueller asserts, these phrases "identify the starting point for this world's history." See Mueller, "Creation in the New Testament," 53–54. On the other hand, Mortenson affirms that the phrase in 4:3 also refers to the first moment or first day of creation week. See Mortenson, "Jesus, Evangelical Scholars," 77–78.

87. According to 1:10 the creation is the ἔργα—the works—of God's hand, and since in the five times in which ἔργα is used in Hebrews in connection with God (cf. 1:10; 3:9; 4:3, 4, 10) it is used in a positive way, the creation ought to be something very

lated to its origin, from Hebrews it is not possible to affirm—as will be shown—that the creation and God share the same nature, although they could share some similarities. So for instance, from 2:10 and 11:3 it can be deduced that the nature of the creation shares the same features of the nature of the creator, since the main source of the creation is the creator. However, there are also significant differences: for instance, in 11:3 the creation is capable of being seen, while the creator is not allowed to be seen. Therefore, the nature of the creation is capable of being seen, i.e., it has a physical nature,[88] an assertion that could be supported by the use of the noun πόλις in 11:10 which, as already asserted, posits a physical entity.[89] Therefore, everything that can be seen must be a created thing according to Hebrews.

Furthermore, in 1:10–12 as Lane notes, the use of words such as ἀλλάσσειν (to change), ἑλίσσειν (to roll up), ὡς ἱμάτιον (like a garment), and ἀλλαγήσονται (they will be changed), provides a vivid image of change and stresses the frequency and casualness[90] of the nature of the created order. Therefore, the nature of creation could be illustrated by

---

good (cf. Gen 1:31). This assertion is reinforced by the use of τῶν χειρῶν—of (your) hands—as a genitive of quality, since this kind of genitive posits the superior quality of the creation, i.e., that which is created by God is always of a better quality. Only in 3:9 can a sort of potentially negative sense of ἔργα be seen, however, in its broader context this text must be understood as referring to the protective actions of God during the forty years when the Israelites lived in the desert.

88. For instance, Hebrews asserts that God has prepared a body for Christ, i.e., only through some created being is it possible to see God. Therefore, the body of Christ before his death and after his resurrection must be a physical body, i.e., the God who became human continued as God/human after his resurrection. For more information on the physical and bodily resurrection of Christ see Geisler, *Baker Encyclopedia of Christian Apologetics*, 665–70. Therefore, if God can be seen, it can only be possible through a created body of Jesus Christ.

89. As already asserted in 11:10 the phrase τὴν πόλιν (the city) which refers to a heavenly place for which Abraham was waiting, could be understood in Hebrews as a literal city—see section titled "Morpho-syntactic analysis of the key-sentence 11" in chapter 5. Besides, it can be inferred that the place referred to here by πόλις is a heavenly place, which must be a physical place, since the creation in Hebrews' cosmogony can only be inside another created reality, which in turn must be physical also. Maybe that is why only υἱός can go and return to the uncreated realm—The Godhead. Also, Ellingworth asserts that "in this passage the author does not pause to make an explicit contrast between heavenly and earthly cities" Ellingworth, *The Epistle to the Hebrews*, 585. Attridge, meanwhile, asserts that "This city is rather the heavenly Jerusalem" Attridge, *Hebrews*, 324. And both of them, although not in an explicit way, consider this place as some kind of physical heavenly place.

90. Lane, *Hebrews 1–8*, 31.

the nature of a garment due to its mutability,[91] i.e., due to its fragility and tendency to change, but also due to its ephemerality. Therefore, an important Hebrews' cosmogonic presupposition is that the nature of creation set it as an entity lacking eternity and capable of mutation, change and elimination.[92] This assertion is also support for the use of the adverb ὡς in 12:25–27—see SP6 in Figure 5.13—which accentuates that the nature of the creation is something capable of being changed or renewed, as well as destroyed or removed.[93] Which is opposite to the nature of the Creator.

On the other hand, according to 8:1–2 the things that God makes are the true ones, while the things that the creation—i.e., the human beings—makes are not true. Here it is important to understand that the word ἀληθινῆς does not mean "true" in a basic or external sense,[94] but in a

91. In this sense, the nature of the creation is very different to the nature of the creator. Lane also asserts that in 1:10–12 "the accent falls upon the mutability of the created order," which includes the angels, so the argument in 1:10–12 is parallel to that in 1:7–8 "where the mutability of the angels is contrasted with the eternal, unchangeable character of the Son." See Lane, *Hebrews 1–8*, 31.

92. Also in Hebrews 8:1–2 one can read about a creation of God that is called ἀληθινῆς (true) however, interestingly enough, the same text that says this "true" Sanctuary was erected by the Lord, affirms that this creation is not eternal, since it has a beginning, clearly expressed by the verb ἔπηξεν (erected). So even though this special creation could be called eternal for it will never be destroyed, it is not eternal in the sense that God is. This text can favour the idea that heavenly things, since they are also created things, are entities lacking in eternity and capable of mutation, change and elimination. And so, Hebrews affirms that the Creator is not part of the heavenly things, but that He is above the heavenly things.

93. It is important to note that Hebrews 12:25–27 could be understood as referring to a judgment that includes the heavenly realm (cf. 12:26) or "heavenly things" (cf. 9:23), see, Cortez, "Creation in Hebrews," 313–14. It cannot be denied that this text, although tricky to interpret, has important insights on cosmogony, which naturally will have implications in its final interpretation. Here, for purposes of this section it is enough to mention that this text holds a positive view of creation and not a negative one, an assertion that will be developed going forward.

94. The basic or external sense must be understood as the determination of the truthfulness of something on the basis of its comparison with something else, so, for example, a teddy bear could be labelled as false in comparison to the "true" bear. However, the teddy bear is also a true toy. As Powell asserts, the understanding of ἀλήθεια in the New Testament is deeply dependent on the Hebrew אֱמֶת, since the Hebrew word posits right, moral and relational actions and not only intellectual knowledge. Therefore, even though ἀλήθεια carries a more intellectual connotation under the Hellenistic influence, in Hebrews it must be understood in a sense heavily influenced by the Hebrew meaning. See Joanna Dewey and Mark Allan Powell, "Truth" in *The HarperCollins Bible dictionary*, ed. Mark Allan Powell (New York: HarperCollins, 2011), 1072.

more profound sense, i.e., true in its essence and purpose.[95] For instance in 10:22, ἀληθινῆς καρδίας (true heart) does not mean that some believers draw near God with unreal hearts. It is evident that no one can go to God without his real heart, but the emphasis here is that one does it in the right way while others do not, and therefore some achieve the purpose of drawing near to God while others do not. So in Hebrews the comparison between ἀληθινός and ἀντίτυπος—i.e., true and copy usually understood as true and false cf. 9:24—is not asserting that the things that belong to this creation are not real while the heavenly things are real. Moreover, Hebrews asserts that both are real and that both are created things in equality of conditions,[96] but it is important to notice here that the word ἀληθινῆς is used in order to assert that the human creation cannot fully achieve its

---

95. Bultmann noted that the word ἀληθινός has the sense of that which truly is, or of that which is eternal, particularly if it is in relation to some divine thing. See Kittel, Friedrich, and Bromiley, *Theological Dictionary of the New Testament*, 1:250–51. Besides, it is important to note that the use of the word ἀληθινός in the New Testament usually implies purpose and not essence, for instance in John 4:23 the word is used to make a distinction between two different kinds of worshipers, and it does not mean that the "true worshipers" are real humans while the others are not. It is evident that both are real humans and worshipers, but one kind does it correctly while the other does not. Also, the word ἀληθινός in John 1:9 is not saying that Jesus was a type of lantern, but it is showing his purpose, also in John 6:32, Jesus is not a real bread, but only he can satisfy the real physical and spiritual need of the people. Other similar uses can be found in Luke 16:11; John 4:23; 15:1. Therefore is better to understand ἀληθινός as an indicator of plenitude in the sense that it can fulfil the purpose of its creation.

96. However, in 9:11–12 the use of the adjectives μείζονος (greater), and τελειοτέρας (more perfect) could lead to misinterpretation of the text and lead to the conclusion that οὐ χειροποιήτου (not made with hands) implies that the earth and the entire environment of the human being is part of one inferior creation, since they usually are labeled as made with hands, even though Hebrews never asserts it in regard to the earth but only to the heavens (cf. 1:10–12). However, as already asserted, this text pinpoints that the creation of God is greater and more perfect in comparison to human's creations, i.e., the creation of God, as already asserted, can create—develop—some things, but these things are never of same value as God's Creation. Thus, in Hebrews there are two kinds of creation: 1) the creation of God and 2) the "creation," which really are inventions, constructions or modifications of God's creation. Only in this sense can it be asserted that the human being lives in a world of darkness, not because this world is a shadow but because the things that humanity produces cannot fully satisfy the necessity of the humanity, and in this sense they are not really useful—i.e., they are not ἀληθινός. This assertion can be emphasized for the use of the adjective τελειοτέρας (more perfect) since they are clearly comparing the things made by the human with the things made by God. Therefore, although it is not part of the cosmogonic topic, the nature of the things made by God are superior, and even though they are not eternal in and of themselves, they have a superior nature in relation to human "creations."

purposes, and that only God's creations can fully achieve it.[97] Therefore, it is part of the nature of God's creation to fully fulfil its purpose, i.e., what is created by God will always try to reach the purpose for its creation. Finally, even though the creation holds a special nature, from 9:11, 24 it can be asserted that everything that is created is not worthy of adoration.[98]

Characteristics of Creation

The characteristics of the creation could, although not necessarily, be considered as part of its nature, however for the purpose of this research it is better to consider it so, since in Hebrews' cosmogony, both nature and characteristics are provided by the Creator as inherent features of the creation. For instance, from 8:1–2, which affirms that the man is not the builder of the true sanctuary and tabernacle, the creation has the capacity

---

97. The use of the noun ἄνθρωπος—human being or person—in 8:1–2 posits that humanity cannot do things like God. Also, it is important to note that Hebrews does not use the verb ἔπηξεν (erected) as the verb of ἄνθρωπος, and it could indicate that they cannot do things as God does. On the other hand, it is interesting to note that the word ἄνθρωπος, as already shown, is used in the LXX to translate the noun אָדָם used in Genesis 1–2, therefore humanity in its original condition, as well as in its actual condition, cannot do things like God does them. It is important to note because it reveals that the methodology and process in which humanity does things is not analogous with the process through which God creates.

98. In order to assert that nothing that is created deserves adoration, it is necessary to understand Hebrews 9:11–12, 24–26. The text asserts that τὸν οὐρανόν (the heaven) is a place which is not made with hands and Hebrews 9:11–12 asserts that the heavenly tabernacle is not made with hands. The questions here are, what are these places? And, what means that they are not made with hands? In order to answer the first question, it is necessary to assert that since the use of the word ἀντίτυπα (a copy) which refers to the earthly sanctuary built by Moses, is used in a sort of contingence to the word τύπος used in Exodus 25:40, LXX, what Moses showed in the mountain was heaven itself, the place where God dwells, a place not made for humans but made by God himself, and therefore the heavenly tabernacle and τὸν οὐρανόν refers to the place where God dwells. In order to answer the second question, it is necessary to understand that the adjective χειροποιήτου (handmade) along with the use of the adjective ἀχειροποίητος (not made with hands) is almost always used to make reference to the Jewish tabernacle in the New Testament, where, as already shown, it is used only four times outside of Hebrews (cf. Mark 14:58; Acts 7:48; 17:24). On the other hand, the LXX uses this adjective fifty times as a kind of abbreviation or metonymy which refers to idols made by human hands (cf. Lev 26:1, 30; Isa 2:18; 10:11; 16:12; 19:1; 21:9; 31;7; 46:6; Dan 5:4, 23; 6:27; Wis 14:8; Jdth 8:18, LXX). Therefore, in this context, the adjective means that what is not made with hands is not made by humans but made by God, but also that it is not an idol since it is not worthy of adoration, because it is a creation of God, not God Himself.

to develop, namely to procreate and also to produce other things, but only on the basis of God's creation.[99] Likewise, 12:25–27 asserts that the creation will suffer a metanoia, which implies that the creation can transform itself, but Hebrews also asserts that it can only be eliminated by its Creator.[100] On the other hand, a reading of 9:24–26 outside of its wider literary context, which includes the Old Testament, can lead to the interpretation that God can never dwell in some place made by human beings, especially if it is read with Acts 7:48. However, the Old Testament shows that humans have the potential to make something where God can voluntarily decide to dwell in, i.e., in the creations of his creation (cf. Exod 25:8; 29:45).

On the other hand, the use of the noun ἱμάτιον (garments) in 1:11 alongside the noun περιβόλαιον (cloak) could lead to the misinterpretation of the text and lead to the conclusion that the creation is something that is not very good, particularly if it is understood without taking into account its syntactic context. However, according to the syntactic structure of 1:10–12 which could be considered as a kind of chiasmus[101]—as can be seen in Figure 6.2—the nouns ἱμάτιον and περιβόλαιον are not referring to the quality of the creation but to how it will operate in the eschatological view of Hebrews.

---

99. In Hebrews' cosmogony the creation is capable of being renewed, improved or eliminated for its Creator (cf. 1:10–12; 12:25–27), and therefore the creation has the capacity to procreate or create on the basis of God's creation (cf. 8:1–2; 11:11–12; 13:4). So it can be inferred that in Hebrews, due to its use of Genesis 1, the creation in its state of perfection can also be developed—this does not, however, mean imperfection, but growing in the sphere of perfection.

100. The use of the noun μετάθεσιν (removal) in 12:25–27 could be confusing, perhaps implying that the world in Hebrews is everlasting, but this phrase, in the context of the book, allows one to see that everything that is created is not inherently eternal, neither earth nor heaven. Perhaps they were made with the purpose of existing forever, but Hebrews clearly states that it can be eliminated by its creator (cf. 1:11–12). If in 12:25–27 the noun μετάθεσιν (removal) is not referring to the creation, then it could imply that the creation is eternal, an assertion that cannot fit in the general cosmogonic context of Hebrews. Conversely, this text could be considered as the most explicit reference to creation as an element that does not enjoy eternity, and that, due to its condition, the Creator will renew it once for all in the future. However, this topic, even though it is more deeply related to eschatology than cosmogony, will be developed further on, due to its importance for the cosmogonic assertions in this research.

101. It could be called "Indirect Chiasmus" or "Alternate correspondence," the difference between the Chiasmus proper and this other form of Chiasmus is found in the fact that the first is not congruent with the form of the letter Chi (X). More about it can be found in Bullinger, *Figures of Speech*, 363–93.

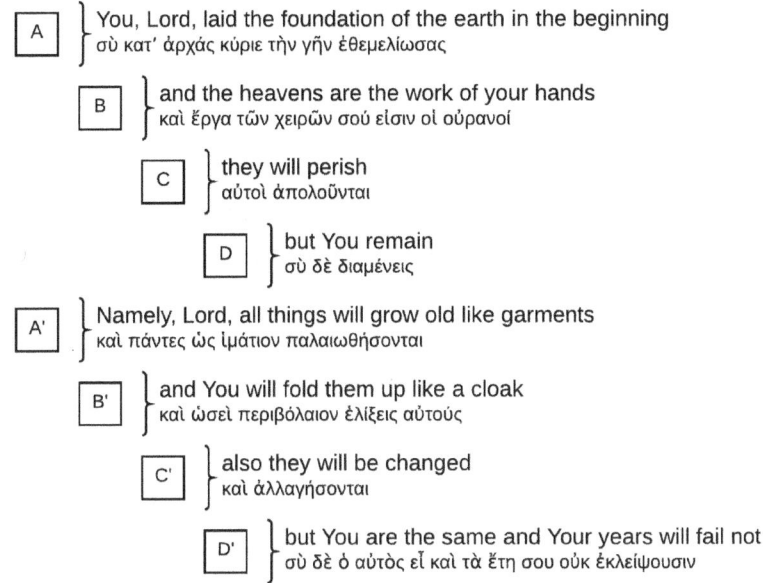

Figure 6.2 Chiastic structure of Hebrews 1:10–12.

The earth will not fold up like the heavens, while the heavens will not grow old like the earth. But both heaven and earth are not qualified in some negative respect; conversely they are both the creation of God and they are therefore both very good. Nevertheless, this text helps one to understand the sovereignty of the Creator, since he can do with his creations as the owner does with his clothes. Therefore, the Creator can act upon the different parts of his creation in different ways and he can allow that the different parts of his creation experience different situations.

On the other hand, in 9:11–12 the noun Χριστός, used as a sort of apposition word to Ἰησοῦς and υἱός (cf. 3:6; 13:8), is used mainly to identify one person of the Godhead in his incarnated condition. This Χριστός is the one who enters into a place which does not belong to this creation, so Hebrews appears to show that the humans can move to places which belong to other creations of God (cf. 11:10). This assertion, in 9:11–12, is supported by the phrase οὐ χειροποιήτου (not made with hands) in reference to the place where Christ enters, which refers to a place not made by humans. Therefore, it seems that in Hebrews there is a presupposition that the creation can experience a move from one creation to another creation, or at least the rational beings that belong to that creation.

The Content of Creation

What can be asserted from Hebrews about the things that God created? The content of creation is perhaps a more difficult topic to identify in Hebrews' cosmogony. It is asserted here that Hebrews uses at least six words to refer to the creation, αἰών, οἰκουμένη, κόσμος, οὐρανός, γῆν, and πᾶς. The first word to appear in Hebrews is αἰών in 1:2, and as already asserted, it is almost impossible to determine its meaning in Hebrews, from its morphology and syntactic configuration. But since αἰών is found in the section that functions as the basis to the main points that will be developed in the entire document, τοὺς αἰῶνας in 1:2 must imply something wide, all-covering or all-embracing. Proponents of the theories around the understanding of this noun can be divided into three groups: those who regard the semantic of the word as portraying a temporal meaning,[102] those who see a spatial meaning in it,[103] and those who understand it as both temporal and spatial.[104] However, as Bruce notes, its context requires that its meaning not be restricted to "ages"—temporal sense—neither in 1:2 nor in 11:3, and consequently he asserts that the whole created universe of space and time is meant by the τοὺς αἰῶνας.[105] It is also important to note what was remarked long ago by Lünemann, when he stresses that in both cases (1:2; 11:3) the emphasis is upon ἐποίησεν instead of τοὺς αἰῶνας,[106] i.e., Hebrews' focus is in God as creator, so there is nothing that can exist if God has not created it. However, it is interesting to note that Delitzsch, for instance, posits that 11:3 is closely connected

---

102. Hewitt, *Epistle to the Hebrews*; Miller, *Epistle to the Hebrews*; Westcott, *Epistle to the Hebrews*.

103. Hughes, *Commentary on the Epistle to the Hebrews*; Ellingworth, *Epistle to the Hebrews*; Lane, *Hebrews 1–8*; Delitzsch, *Commentary on the Epistle to the Hebrews*, 1:43.

104. Guthrie, *Letter to the Hebrews*; Lenski, *Interpretation of the Epistle to the Hebrews*; Bruce, *Epistle to the Hebrews*; Kistemaker, *Hebrews*.

105. Bruce asserts that there is ample evidence for this later use of αἰών, in singular and plural alike, to denote the world of space (cf. Exod 15:18, LXX, "The Lord reigns over the world [βασιλεύων τὸν αἰῶνα] for ever and ever"; Wis 13:9; 14:6; 18:4, LXX), Bruce, *Epistle to the Hebrews*, 47.

106. Lünemann, *Critical and Exegetical Handbook*, 67.

in meaning with 1 Timothy 1:17 which posits God as King eternal, immortal, invisible, the only wise being that deserves honor and glory.[107] It is also interesting that Westcott recognizes that τοὺς αἰῶνας "consists of parts which fulfil different functions and contribute in their measure to the effect of the whole."[108] Likewise, Ellingworth recognizes that

> τοὺς αἰῶνας, here [11:3] as in 1:2, may presuppose a plurality of worlds, but this is not the author's present concern. It is just possible to understand τοὺς αἰῶνας as plural in meaning, referring to visible and invisible worlds, that is, "the heaven and the earth" (Gn. 1:1) as having been both created by the word of God (Gn. 1:3, etc.).[109]

Therefore, it seems to be more correct that τοὺς αἰῶνας should be understood as portraying both a temporal and a spatial meaning, the position that it is assumed in this research, particularly if it is considered that the singular noun could be translated as referring to this creation or to this realm, in various texts of the New Testament (cf. Matt 13:22; Luke 16:8; 20:34; Rom 12:2; 1 Cor 1:20; 2:6, 8; 3:18; 2 Cor 4:4: Gal 1:4). Therefore, the plural τοὺς αἰῶνας could be referring to all creations and realms that came from God including the space and time in which they exist. Here it is important to make a distinction between the noun αἰῶνας and κόσμος in Hebrews. There are five times in which the noun κόσμος is used in Hebrews and in all these instances it clearly refers to this earth (cf. 4:3; 9:26; 10:5; 11:7, 38). Thus, in Hebrews the content of God's creation is constituted by this planet called Earth but also by everything that surrounds it, which is now known as the universe, including also the time in which it exists.[110]

On the other hand, the anarthrous adjective πᾶς, used forty-eight times in Hebrews, seems to highlight the belonging of an entity to a group that shares characteristics,[111] while the articular τὰ πάντα, used five

---

107. Delitzsch, *Commentary on the Epistle to the Hebrews*, 1:43.

108. Westcott, *Epistle to the Hebrews*, 312.

109. Ellingworth, *Epistle to the Hebrews*, 569.

110. The phrase "This planet called Earth but also for everything that surrounds it," does not mean that this research supports the astronomic model called geocentrism. It means that the Earth is the reason for the existence of other parts of this creation. Nevertheless, τοὺς αἰῶνας in 1:2 portrays not only this creation, but the universe as a whole, i.e., all creations of God included all things including time, planets, minor planets, moons, stars, galaxies, contents of intergalactic space, and all matter, and energy.

111. However, the adjective πᾶς is also used without an article in Hebrews'

times in Hebrews, all in a cosmogonic context (cf. 1:3; 2:8, 10), seems to work as a noun, which indicates the universe in its totality.[112] However, the anarthrous πᾶς is also found in the literary component of Hebrews' cosmogony (cf. 1:2, 11; 3:4; 4:4), and therefore it seems that Hebrews is asserting that not only the whole universe is the creation of God, but also everything that belongs to this entire universe.

Along with what has been said, it must be noted that the noun γῆ (earth) used in 1:10 posits, as already shown, the planet Earth and not only some part of it, such as the dry part. And although this text does not make an explicit declaration that it is God who created the Earth, the context of Hebrews' cosmogony impels its assertion, since that which exists must be created by God, because God created the basic elements and he also created the world as it is seen. Also following the same train of thought, 1:10 asserts that in addition to creating the earth, God also created the οἱ οὐρανοί (the heavens). In 1:10 the SC1 is linked to its head sentence—see EC1 in Figure 5.3 σὺ τὴν γῆν ἐθεμελίωσας (You laid the foundation of the earth)—with the conjunction καὶ, used here to add an additional element to the same train of thought, therefore the οἱ οὐρανοί are also the creation of God. Nevertheless, the use of the noun οὐρανός in number plural (cf. 1:10; 4:14; 7:26; 8:1; 9:23; 10:34 [Byz.]; 12:23, 25) and singular (cf. 9:24; 11:12; 12:26) could give rise to some problems. However, in these texts Hebrews uses the plural and singular indistinctly and may be influenced by the LXX and the Hebrew text of Genesis:[113] for

cosmogony, and even though Owen affirmed that it also refers to the totality of the creation, it is important to recognize that the adjective πᾶς has different nuances which depends on its accidence and syntaxes. Owen, *Hebrews by John Owen*, 15. A very thorough treatment of the word can be found in Kittel et al., *Theological Dictionary of the New Testament*, 5:888–89.

112. According to Allen, Hebrews use of the article with πᾶς indicates all things in their unity. Thus, he understands that "the author of Hebrews has a penchant for expressing the totality of the universe in this way since in 2:8 [s/he] altered the LXX by adding the article before πάντα, and then again twice in v. 10 [s/he] used the articular construction." Allen, *Hebrews*, 123. Also, as already shown, in 2:10 τὰ πάντα implies the universe as a whole, including the things that are not perceptible to the human being. Further, Salmond affirms that τὰ πάντα explains "the widest possible and most comprehensive universality, including the sum total of created objects, wherever found, whether men or things." Nicoll, *Expositor's Greek Testament: Commentary*, 3:262. More about it can be found in, Kittel et al., *Theological Dictionary of the New Testament*, 5:888–89.

113. Here it is important to note that "while both the Hebrew Bible and the LXX agree that there is only one earth, the Hebrew Bible suggests a plurality of heavens, in contrast to the singular heaven of the LXX." So, as Burton asserts, "later Jewish

instance, Hebrews locates Jesus seated at the right hand of the throne of God in the heavens (cf. 8:1). It also asserts that Jesus appears in the presence of God in the heaven (cf. 9:24); similarly, Hebrews says that the stars are in the heaven (cf. 11:12) and also affirms that the heavens (cf. 1:10)—which due to its context must include the stars—are the creation of God.

Nevertheless, as already shown, οὐρανός is used in Hebrews mainly to refer to the habitat of God (cf. 8:1; 9:23, 24), but also to posit the place where the heavenly bodies are located, which according to Hebrews is between the habitat of God and the habitat of human beings (cf. 4:14; 7:26; 11:12). Therefore, it seems that Hebrews' use of the noun οὐρανός is very similar to the contemporary use of the Spanish noun *cielo*, in common conversation or in a sermon. Namely, the plural and singular use of οὐρανός could be due to the sermonic nature of Hebrews, and so it could be referring to the different layers of the atmosphere and also to the creation where God dwells. However, no matter what the interpretation of the plural and singular οὐρανός could be, it is clear that Hebrews posits that the habitat of the Creator was also created for him.

Finally, it is important to recognize that according to 9:11–12, Χριστός enters in some place which Hebrews says is not ταύτης τῆς κτίσεως—i.e., it does not belong to this creation. Here the first thing that must be recognized is that the text is not saying that this other place, where Χριστός enters, is an uncreated place, the text is only asserting that this place does not belong to this creation. So the place where Χριστός enters could be understood in two ways: as not being part of this creation of God or as having not been developed by human beings. And since both readings are possible in the Hebrews' cosmogony context, Hebrews could be upholding that the whole creation is constituted by different creations.[114] Nevertheless, it is important to clarify that in Hebrews there is no difference

---

thinkers took the reference to plural heavens seriously and often spoke of seven heavens, and even Paul speaks about a man he knew who was caught up into the "third heaven" (cf. 2 Cor 12:2) and he also refers to the creation of all things in the "heavens" and the earth (cf. Col 1:16)." Burton, "Faith Factor," 40.

114. The existence of various creations could also be supported by the use of the noun κτίσεως—creation—with its article τῆς in 9:11–12, along with the pronoun demonstrative ταύτης—this, since, as Wallace affirms, one main function of the article is to stresss identity, distinguishing one entity from another or among others of the same value or conditions. Wallace, *Greek Grammar Beyond the Basics*, 210. Porter is clearer when he asserts that "When the article is used, the substantive may refer to a particular item." Porter, *Idioms of the Greek New Testament*, 104.

in quality or value among the creations of God, the only differences that could be asserted relate to the functions and commencements of his creations. Therefore, in Hebrews there are not different statuses among God's creation, only different functions, conditions, and beginnings.

Details of Creation

Hebrews does not show how the creation is configured, but it shows different areas that form part of God's creation. Although it is not possible to assert whether these different entities, which are God's creation, are part of the creation that set up the environment of human beings, they allow the assertion that the handiwork of God is constituted by different creations. Thus for instance, according to 2:5–9, as Lane notes, humanity does form part of God's creation,[115] but as Guthrie and Lane also assert, the angels could also be posited as created beings even though they belong to another creation,[116] and the use of Psalm 8 in 2:5–9 is strong evidence that Hebrews portrays the human being as the creation of God.[117] Therefore, Hebrews develops its arguments on the presupposition that the human being is the creation of God.

It is also important to note that the terms οὐρανός and γῆ in 1:10 are used in a sort of hendiadys in Genesis 1:1, LXX, in order to show one complementary entity, i.e., two things that belong together and form one creation.[118] So it seems that the creation of different elements or areas

---

115. Lane asserts that the description in Hebrews 2:5–9 corresponds to the divine intention expressed in Genesis 1:26–28. He also highlights that "humans were entrusted with the cultural mandate to subdue the earth and to put everything in subjection to themselves." This divine intention awakes "the expectation that all that had been placed under human dominion at the time of the creation would yet be subject to humanity in the world to come." Lane, *Hebrews 1–8*, 46.

116. For instance, Guthrie states that Hebrews asserts that one kind of creation can be the creation of spirits, namely the angels. Guthrie, *Hebrews*, 72. Also see, Lane, *Hebrews 1–8*, 17.

117. However, it is important to clarify that since the goal of this research is not the origin of the humanity—a topic which, more specifically, belongs to general cosmology or anthropology—this text will not be focused on. However, it is evident that Hebrews sees the human being as part of the creation of God.

118. In Genesis the best case that can illustrate this assertion is the creation of the human being, which according to Genesis 1:26 is a singular being, called אָדָם, a name that according to Genesis 5:1 is given to the male and female part of this creation. Namely, men and women are complementary beings, not two different beings, but one being constituted by two parts, which could also be demonstrated by the fact that the existence

forms one creation, i.e., God's creations are called creation only when all its elements are formed. On the other hand, since in 4:3–5 the word used for the creation is κόσμος, and as already shown, this word implies in Hebrews the spatial and physical habitat of the human being and not the totality of the cosmic system, in the sense of the universe,[119] some parts of the universe, to which the realm of the human being belongs, form part of one moment of creation, while the whole universe, which is also the creation of God, is constituted by different moments of God's creation. Thus, the whole creation of God is constituted by different projects of creation.

But regarding the creation of the whole environment of the human being, it must be noted that, according to 4:3–5, the creation was finished before the rest, i.e., the rest of God was prepared in order that the creation has at its disposal the rest of God. It seems that in Hebrews the rest of God is not part of the creation itself but is rather a special kind of creation that complements the creation. This rest, as already affirmed, in Hebrews is identified as the seventh day (ἐν τῇ ἡμέρᾳ τῇ ἑβδόμῃ) in harmony with Genesis 2:1–3. Thus, there were at least two big moments which cover the creation of the environment of humanity: the first could be called the creation of components and the second the creation of the rest, which as has already been asserted opens the possibility of communion with the creator.

On the other hand, in 8:1–2 in an undefined moment—gnomic *Aktionsart* of the verb ἔπηξεν—God erected a true sanctuary, which means that it could have been erected in human history or even before. Also, from the literary context of this text Hebrews asserts that the creation, which could be called the dwelling place of God, is a physical and real place and not a kind of spiritual or mythological place. This assertion is also supported by 11:10, since the accidence of the verb ἐξεδέχετο (he waited) implies a stative *aktionsart* expressing expectation and surety. This implies that in Hebrews the city for which Abraham waited was a real one, even though the context clearly states that this city is not an earthly one—not a creation that belongs to this creation—but a heavenly one, the city of God (cf. 12:22).

---

of the male and female is deeply dependent on the relation between each other.

119. A very good study on the word κόσμος can be found in Kittel et al., *Theological Dictionary of the New Testament*, 3:868–95.

The Development and Fate of Creation

Even though there is no explicit information in Hebrews about the condition of the creation in its very beginning—Genesis for instance portrays a condition "before sin" and "after sin"—Hebrews holds the presupposition that the creation is changing for the worse (cf. 1:10–12). Likewise, Hebrews affirms the existence of the condition without sin (cf. 4:15) and with sin (cf. 2:17; 7:26). Moreover, Hebrews asserts that the humanity needs to be saved from sin (cf. 9:28) and from the fear of death (cf. 2:15). So, Hebrews presupposes that the current condition of the creation, including human beings, is not an ideal condition and, due to its eschatological view, Hebrews portrays a perfect condition in the future (cf. 9:28; 12:28; 13:14). On the other hand, since the main concern of Hebrews is not cosmogony, even though it is relevant to its argument, there are no direct assertions about the purpose of the creation, but it is evident that it was made primarily to serve as the environment to humanity, as well as the place where they can meet with the Creator (cf. 12:18–24). Likewise, it seems that in Hebrews, due to the accidence of the verb παλαιωθήσονται (it will grow old) in 1:11, which implies a summary *aktionsart*, the creation is not something that can keep its qualities in the same condition forever—i.e., its potentialities can dwindle with the passing of time. In order to develop this important assertion to support the purpose of this research, it must be stated that 1:1–4 and 8:1–2 allows the assertion that the survival of the creation is always dependent upon the Creator.[120]

The End of Creation

There are more statements about the end of the creation in Hebrews—perhaps due to its eschatological perspective—than any other issue related to cosmogony. From its very beginning Hebrews shows a positive

---

120. In its very beginning, Hebrews asserts that the Son upholds "all things by the power of His word" (1:3), and from there Hebrews reveals a creation that is always dependent on its creator. So, for instance, the verb ἔχομεν (we have) in 8:1–2, which implies a stative *aktionsart*, posits that the creation has a permanent minister, i.e., Jesus is permanently ministering in favor of his creation, to both living and non-living beings (cf. Rev 11:18), even though his actions in respect of these two categories—i.e., the living and non-living beings—are not the same. But also, the term λειτουργός (minister) can imply that as the priest of the first century, the Son is acting in permanent relation to his people. Therefore, as Schenck states, the destiny of the whole creation depends on the Sonship of Jesus. Schenck, "Keeping His Appointments," 99–102.

view on creation, for instance υἱός upholds it by the power of his word (cf. 1:1-4), which evidences that the Creator values the creation. In this context it is important to note that Hebrews uses the noun οἰκουμένη (inhabited earth) in order to make reference to the world to come (cf. 2:6) and as the place where υἱός will be placed, i.e., in the world to come (cf. 1:6).[121] Likewise, the noun οἰκουμένη is equated by Lane with the age to come (cf. 6:5) and the city to come (cf. 13:14)[122] and interestingly enough, these texts have allusions to Psalms 92:1; 95:10, LXX, which show God as taking full governance of his creation—an allusion to these psalms are also found in 12:28. Therefore, in order to understand 12:25-27 it is necessary to understand all these other texts along with Haggai 2:6, the text that is quoted in this section of Hebrews.

The noun οἰκουμένη, in the thirteen times it is used outside of Hebrews, refers to the earth—i.e., the environment of the human being. Even Lane does not agree that the powers of the age to come (cf. 6:5) and the city to come (cf. 13:14) should be placed on this earth.[123] Therefore, "the kingdom that cannot be shaken" (12:28, ESV) which is delivered to those who hold fast to the confidence and firm to the end and who will rejoice in their salvation (3:6 cf. Matt 10:32, NKJV), must be a kingdom placed on the earth. In this context it is important to note that 1:10 asserts that οὐρανοί and γῆ—i.e., the heavens and the earth—that is to say the whole creation, will suffer the action of the verb ἀπόλλυμι, i.e., will perish, which

---

121. Here it is important to note that, even though Bruce connects this text with exaltation of Christ, he maintains that if "again" (πάλιν) is read along with "brings in" (εἰσαγάγῃ) the meaning must be, "And when he brings the firstborn into the world a second time." And even though this interpretation was disputed strongly by Westcott, Bruce asserts that Westcott's arguments are not as conclusive as he maintains. See Bruce, *Epistle to the Hebrews*, 56. Therefore, this text could be referring to the second coming of Jesus as holds Käsemann, *Wandering People of God*. And this assertion could also be supported by Hebrews 9:28.

122. Lane, *Hebrews 1–8*, 46. Guthrie states that since Psalms 92:1, and 95:10, LXX, are the source for οἰκουμένη in 1:6; 2:5, and both Psalm passages proclaim that this world, established with the reign of God, shall not be shaken, then "The explicit allusion to 'a kingdom that cannot be shaken' in 12:28 indicates that these passages were not far from the writer's mind when s/he penned it." Guthrie, "Hebrews," 920.

123. Allen is right when he maintains that Lane is wrong in his interpretation of οἰκουμένη as being an extraterrestrial place or reality, since, as Allen maintains, this "noun is commonly used to denote 'the inhabited earth' and not 'heaven' or some generic meaning like 'future world,' 'future life,' or 'heavenly world.'" Allen, *Hebrews*, 203. Then, the new earth as well as the city to come and the age to come must be placed on or must be this same earth.

carries the sense of being ruined as well as the loss of its primal condition[124] (cf. Matt 10:6, 39; Mark 1:24; Luke 9:25; 15:4, 9, 24, 32). In addition, the ingressive *aktionsart* of ἀπόλλυμι in 1:10 asserts that the creation has changed its original direction towards its destruction,[125] and due to the media voice of the verb, this change of direction in Hebrews' text is performed by the creation itself, not induced by God. So the movement of the creation up to a certain point in time was not towards its destruction, but when it changed, its fate also changed. However, as already asserted, the Creator in Hebrews greatly values his creation, and therefore the idea that the creation will be destroyed seems incongruent with the general cosmogonic context of Hebrews, but the idea that the creation will be restored to its ideal condition—i.e., without sin and under the government of God—is perfectly consistent. Thus, as Guthrie asserts,

> The quotation in 1:10–12 foreshadows the day of the Lord (9:28; 10:36–39) and the shaking of the earth, the eschatological judgment to be visited upon the earth at the end of the age . . . (12:25–29; cf. 1 Cor. 7:31; 1 John 2:8; Rev. 21:1). On that day only the kingdom of God will remain.[126]

And as already asserted, this kingdom of God must be placed on this physical earth but after having suffered a very extreme transformation, which can be seen in 1:12 since it asserts that when the creation is growing old the Son will fold up it (ἑλίξεις),[127] an action that, due to

---

124. It must be noted here that the pronouns, they—αὐτοὶ—in 1:11 includes both the "earth" and the "heavens" (1:10), and the verb ἀπολοῦνται has the sense of "destroy," but also "lose," "be lost," and, "be ruined." See Allen, *Hebrews*, 183; Newman, *Concise Greek-English Dictionary*, 22.

125. This assertion could also be supported since in 1:10 Hebrews, using the prepositional phrase ὡς ἱμάτιον (like a garment), answers the question, how or in what way—i.e., similar to what—will the creation grow old? The answer here is "like a garment or cloths," i.e., it will grow old with time and use.

126. However, it must be recognised that, according to Guthrie, this world is not the place of the kingdom of God that will remain. He asserts that when the material universe will pass away . . . the kingdoms of this world having been utterly destroyed, then, the Son will become "Lord." Guthrie, "Hebrews," in *Commentary on the New Testament Use of the Old Testament*, 939–41.

127. The morphology and syntax in which the verb ἑλίξεις (you will fold up) is placed in 1:12 is showing that when the creation grows old, the Lord will begin a new action, He will fold up all things. Here it is also necessary to assert again that this verb—ἑλίξεις—does not imply destruction, but to cause something "to take the shape of a roll, roll up." See Arndt et al., *Greek-English Lexicon*, 317.

the semantic of the verb ἑλίσσω (roll up), must be a very quick action.[128] In addition, it is necessary to assert that the verb ἀλλάσσω (change) in 1:12 clearly states that the creation will not be annulled, destroyed or replaced but changed, with the sense of its basic meaning, which is "to make otherwise."[129] Therefore, in this first part, Hebrews shows that the creation is going to its self-destruction, but also that in an abrupt future moment it will be renewed by the intervention of its Creator. And as already affirmed, this first part is deeply linked with 12:25–27, texts which affirm that the Creator will shake not only the earth but also the heavens, which indicates the μετάθεσιν (removal) of what can be stirred up, since they are created things, in order that what cannot be stirred up may remain (cf. 12:27).

As already asserted, 12:25–27 must be understood on the basis of its context—i.e., the whole Hebrews' text—along with Haggai 2:6, text that is quoted in this section. In light of Haggai 2:6, as is clearly stated by Cortez, it is possible to read this passage as being "parallel to 4:12–13 where the author warns the readers that the word of God will judge them," and in 12:27, affirms Cortez, "the author warns the readers that they need to pay attention to Him who warns from heaven, otherwise they will face the judgment, or shaking, of God."[130] Moreover, it is clear that this text is linked to the judgment of God, however, in light of what has been noted before, this judgment must be executed on this earth, and not in the heavens. It is important also to note that the phrase ἔτι ἅπαξ (still once again) constituted by two adverbs, must be understood as "the last one."[131] Therefore, it seems that the fate of the creation is to be shaken to and fro (σείω)—not to be stirred up (σαλεύω), an action which is clearly related with Exodus 19:18—once more and forever, so it will never happen again. The text finally asserts that when the Creator shakes the earth and the heavens to and fro (σείω), the μετάθεσιν (removal) of the created things is

128. Liddell et al., *Greek-English Lexicon*, 534. It is also important to note that this quick action of folding up will be done for the Son—κύριος—and not for the creation itself.

129. Kittel, Friedrich, and Bromiley, *Theological Dictionary of the New Testament*, 1:251.

130. Cortez, "Creation in Hebrews," 315.

131. Cortez seems to agree with this assertion when he states that "Here, the expression carries the sense of 'once for all' (cf. ἐφάπαξ) removal of 'what can be shaken' as in 7:27, 9:12 and 10:10. In other words, we could translate this expression as 'yet once more and forever.'" Cortez, "Creation in Hebrews," 312. See also section entitled "Morpho-syntactic Analysis of the Key-sentence 12" in chapter 5.

also carried out, both heavenly and earthly, in order that the heavenly and earthly things that will not be stirred up (σαλεύω) will remain.[132]

Here it is important to note first that the noun μετάθεσις (removal) really conveys a sense of change of some features of an entity rather than the change or removal of the entity altogether. In addition, its context in Philo,[133] as in Hebrews (cf. 7:12; 11:5) can imply a radical change, i.e., the final product of this transformation could be considered as a new entity, and only in that sense could the word "removal" be affirmed as the translation of μετάθεσιν here in 12:27. On the other hand, it is important to note that what is removed—perhaps it is better to say recreated (μετάθεσις)—is what is stirred up (σαλεύω), while what is shaken (σείω) will indirectly experience the μετάθεσιν. So what will be shaken (σείω) and indirectly removed and/or recreated (μετάθεσις), the text clearly states, will be the earth and the heavens, i.e., the whole creation.[134] However, what will be removed and/or recreated directly is something—not everything—that belongs to God's creation and that, according to the text, will be stirred up (σαλεύω); moreover the text defines these things through the plural participle πεποιημένων (things that have been created). This participle is used in the New Testament, as well as in Hebrews to refer firstly to the creative action of God (1:7 cf. Rev 14:7), and secondly to the creative actions—both physical and spiritual—of humans (cf. Matt 6:3; 7:21; 13:41; Luke 10:37), and here this participle, due to the cosmogonic context of Hebrews, must be understood as referring to both senses. It is also important to understand the noun μετάθεσις (removed and/or recreated) and the verb σαλεύω (to stir up), as already asserted, carries somewhat of an appositional sense. Therefore, since the plural participle σαλευομένων in

---

132. Here it is important to note that the participle σαλευομένων (to stir up) and the noun μετάθεσιν (the removal) refers to one moment and also to one action. On the other hand, the participle σαλευόμενα (to stir up) due to its accidence implies a contemporaneous action to the verb μείνῃ (may remain) therefore, to remove, to stir up, and to remain, happen at the same time, i.e., they are consequences of one divine action.

133. As already shown, the more important use of the noun μετάθεσιν by Philo appears in Aet. 113, where he uses the word in quoting to someone who believes that the world will never be destroyed, only transformed. As already asserted in footnote 195 from chapter 5, he further uses this noun along with three other words, which are: 1) πρόσθεσιν, 2) ἀφαίρεσιν, 3) μετάθεσιν, 4) ἀλλοίωσιν, which are usually translated as addition, subtraction, transposition, transmutation, and which literally mean: 1) addition of a part, 2) taking away, 3) change of position, transformation, 4) alteration, change.

134. As already asserted, the union of τὴν γῆν καὶ τὸν οὐρανόν (the earth and the heaven) could imply the whole creation of God, i.e., the τοὺς αἰῶνας of 1:2 and 11:3, so it could mean that another creation of God could also participate in this divine action.

the New Testament implies motion and not elimination (cf. Matt 11:7; Mark 13:25; Acts 2:25; 16:26; 2 Thess 2:2) some part of the whole creation, which needs to be removed, will be removed in order to recreate the whole creation, but what does not need to be removed, will remain. So, the end of the creation is to be renewed by a divine action that implies judgement, which will be executed on this very earth, with the consequence that some of the creations of both God and humans will be eliminated, while some of them will remain. Therefore, even though the creation is not inherently eternal, it will remain forever in its new condition according to 12:28.

Chapter Conclusion

This chapter started with the purpose of establishing the cosmogonic presuppositions in Hebrews. But this chapter first established that Hebrews' cosmogony does not need to be disregarded as old or not pertinent to the current time—on the contrary, it could contribute valuable insights to current cosmogonic theories which could also be called myths or presuppositions.

The presuppositions about the identity of the Creator in Hebrews are clearly portrayed through the nouns θεός and υἱός, with the latter also identified in Hebrews by the nouns κύριος, Χριστός, and Ἰησοῦς. Nevertheless, from Hebrews it is not possible to affirm the existence of various creators, since in Hebrews ὁ θεός, with its plural sense, is the creator, and υἱός is the one who executes the creative actions. Likewise, the attributes of the Creator in Hebrews are various. He is not a passive being, but an active being; his a social being, not a solitary one; he is a close being, not a distant one; he is not a static being, he is surrounded by his creation; and the Creator intervenes and interacts with his creation. Also, in Hebrews' text there is the assumption that the Creator made the creation with the purpose of having communion with it.

Presuppositions in Hebrews about the procedure followed by the Creator in order to create can be divided into two categories. Actions portrayed through verbs with perfective aspect, i.e., Hebrews presupposes that in order to create, the Creator has accomplished some actions privately, that is, the way in which these actions were performed are not revealed to the creation. Second, actions portrayed through verbs with imperfective aspect, i.e., Hebrews presupposes that the believer is a witness of the creative actions of the Creator, since they, but also every human being, can experience and see the Creator building, giving birth to new existences, upholding his creation, and shaking and stirring it.

Even though there is no explicit assertion in Hebrews about the method used by the Creator in order to create—i.e., it is showed as a presupposition—it was identified that Hebrews holds four main presuppositions about it. The four main presuppositions are placed in this research under the following labels:

1. Delegation of functions;
2. Development of a logical process;
3. Powerful personal intervention; and
4. Utterance of goodwill.

On the other hand, regarding the sources used by the Creator in order to create, Hebrews holds the presupposition that everything that exists came from an existent invisible source, i.e., ὁ θεός is the ultimate cause of everything. Nevertheless, Hebrews does not hold a pantheistic view of the creation, since Hebrews will assert that the ῥῆμα of the Creator was used in order to create everything. Regarding the time in Hebrews' cosmogony, it seems to show a presupposition built in Genesis 1—its own tradition—that everything was created in a temporal framework, which can be understood as six literal days.

Regarding the creation itself, Hebrews holds diverse presuppositions, with the more significant ones being:

1. The whole creation of God holds a nature that set it as an entity lacking eternity and capable of mutation, change, and elimination, as well as an entity that can be seen.
2. The creation of God is capable of fulfilling its purpose and in order to endure, it holds the capacity to procreate and can create other things on the basis of God's primary creation.
3. The whole creation of God is constituted by different creations, which include this planet called Earth and everything that surrounds it—i.e., the whole universe. It also includes the time in which the whole creation exists.
4. Hebrews presupposes that there are not different statuses among God's creation—i.e., angels, humans, Earth, or heavenly cities—only different functions, conditions, and beginnings.

5. Hebrews presupposes that the creation will endure forever, but not because it is inherently eternal and not in its actual condition, but after a powerful intervention by the Creator in which some of the creation will be eliminated while some of it will remain.

Up to this point, almost all the minor purposes of this research have been achieved—see subsection "Research Purpose" in chapter 1—and presented here and in the previous chapters. Nevertheless, the main purpose of this research is to judge the relationship between Hebrews' cosmogonic presuppositions and its first-century philosophical context. So after having exposed Hebrews' cosmogonic presuppositions in this chapter, the next chapter will compare these with the cosmogonic presuppositions present in first-century cosmogony, i.e., it will function as a comprehensive conclusion of this research.

7

Hebrews' Cosmogony and First-Century Cosmogonies

FROM THE TIME OF Emile Durkheim, possibly even much earlier, up until today it can be stated that all systems of ideas—i.e., presuppositions—which tend to explain things, and give a complete explanation for the existence of the world, are a type of religion, i.e., to some extent it can be affirmed that each cosmogony is a different religion.[1] Therefore, to explain the cosmogony of Hebrews is to explain its religion,[2] and to evaluate it in

---

1. The French sociologist Emile Durkheim claimed that "there is no religion that is not both a cosmology and a speculation about the divine" and that "to a greater and lesser degree, all known religions have been systems of ideas that tend to embrace the universality of things and to give us a representation of the world as a whole," see Durkheim, *The Elementary Forms*, 8, 141. Since cosmogony could be considered a key topic of cosmology, every religion is developed on cosmogonic presuppositions. See Robert A. Oden, Jr., "Cosmogony" in *ABD*, vol. 1, ed. David Noel Freedman (New York: Doubleday, 1992), 1162–71.

2. We are not talking about the theology of Hebrews but about its internal beliefs, i.e., its presuppositions, and even though Hebrews was an important document to some specific Christian group—perhaps groups—in the first century, it was shrouded in obscurity—i.e., as an incomprehensible and unimportant document—for a long time. See Allen, *Hebrews*, 23. So to explain Hebrews' cosmogony is to make Hebrews more understandable and pertinent, but also to allow it—the book or the author—to express its system of ideas on which its theology is developed. In this document beliefs, presuppositions and systems of ideas are the same, i.e., a thought tacitly assumed beforehand at the beginning of a line of argument. Nevertheless, it does not mean that the presupposition is assumed without reasons or without previous logical, methodical and systematic formulation. They are called presuppositions for they are not present in the text or argument but serve as support or basis for the theology of Hebrews in

its first-century philosophical context is to embark upon a comparison of religions, on the cosmogony topic, in the first-century world. However, it is important to highlight that the evaluation is always—particularly in cosmogony—between presuppositions or, as Durkheim stated, systems of ideas. Consequently, and being aware of the magnitude of the topic, the evaluation of cosmogonic presuppositions of Hebrews in its first-century philosophical context will be done only in regard to four aspects: (1) the literary component;[3] (2) the creator; (3) the procedure; and (4) the creation. Nevertheless, before making these more specific evaluations on Hebrews' cosmogony, it is important to highlight two things: First, the general presuppositions that lead the argument of Hebrews and on which all other presuppositions rest is that the Old Testament is constituted by the words of God, that it presents a unified revelation of truth, and that the Old Testament bears witness to past, present, and future actions of Christ.[4] Second, a plethora of thoughts[5] characterized the first century CE. Tenney appropriately illustrates that time when he states,

> Like the rivers which ran into the Mediterranean Sea from all sides, pouring into it their sediment and feeding its waters, so the many peoples comprised within the constantly expanding domain of Rome brought into it all their cultural contributions. Africans, Teutons, Greeks, Jews, Parthians, and Phrygians mingled in the provinces and cities and shared their national heritages.[6]

---

this case. On the other hand, theology is constituted by the explicit arguments present in the text, i.e., the religious beliefs and theory which are systematically presented in Hebrews' text.

3. As already asserted, in this document the literary component pinpoints the most pertinent vocabulary used in first-century literature, including Hebrews, in order to reveal the different cosmogonies of that time.

4. Guthrie for instance also asserts that the author of Hebrews developed his whole argument on the basis of his belief that "the Old Testament consists of the words of God," since his Old Testament quotations are almost always framed as coming directly from the mouth of God. The author accepts the Old Testament as the words of God and feels no compulsion to explain the texts—moreover, s/he simply states them as offering facts, which for him/her are absolute truth. Further, Guthrie asserts that the author of Hebrews has "the presupposition that God speaks consistently and systematically" through the entire Old Testament, and also that it bears witness to Christ. Guthrie, *Hebrews*, 73–74.

5. Klauck for instance asserts that "in the early imperial period, the classical philosophical schools continued to exist, with some modification, and indeed even experienced in part a new momentum." Klauck, *Religious Context of Early Christianity*, 332.

6. Tenney, *New Testament Times*, 67.

Therefore, it can be asserted that Hebrews was written in a complex and pluralistic society, and that the cultural and intellectual milieu in which its ideas and themes were developed are not only the Hellenistic or Hebrew thoughts present in first-century CE.

The Literary Component

Strictly speaking, the literary component is not part of the cosmogonic presuppositions in Hebrews, rather, it is part of the available evidence, i.e., it can be corroborated and demonstrated, not on the basis of arguments, but in concrete form. So the literary component is constituted by the most prominent texts, which in turn are constituted by words, which form the core points around which a cosmogonic discourse of Hebrews is presented, as well as the discourse of first-century cosmogony. So chapter 4, on the basis of the text of the NA^{28}, shows that Hebrews is constituted by 303 verses which in turn are constituted by 4953 words,[7] which in turn make up 178 sentences,[8] and among them there are twelve sentences which are constituted by 174 words that can be considered as the literary component of Hebrews' cosmogony. These 174 words are divided into twenty-four nouns, twenty-five verbs, nine adjectives, eight conjunctions, seven prepositions, six adverbs, five pronouns, plus the article and the particle οὐδέ (and not) among which the nouns, verbs, and adjectives are more significant for the purpose of this section. On the other hand, the same evaluation—i.e., the methodology which has been used in Hebrews—in order to obtain the main cosmogonic vocabulary, is for a project like this one almost impossible to do with all the literature of the first century.

Nevertheless, chapter 3 of this research, following a different methodology, displays it.[9] So, it is very likely that the main vocabulary of first-

---

7. Here it is important to note that in other versions or manuscripts the number of words could be different, so for instance in the Byz. text Hebrews has 4,799 words, while in the TR it has 5,013 words, while in the Codex Sinaiticus Hebrews has 4,694 words.

8. This number, 178 sentences, is the number provided by Lukaszewski et al., however, as already shown in chapter 4. Porter et al. argued for the presence of 366 sentences, while Leedy, meanwhile, maintains that there are 181 sentences in Hebrews and Andi and Tan believed that Hebrews is composed of 247 sentences. For more information, see chapter 4, "Exclusion in Macrostructures."

9. The evaluation to obtain the main cosmogonic vocabulary of the first century has been done through a review of previous research on cosmogony or cosmology thought of the first century, as well as in a review of primary source(s). So the main

century cosmogony was constituted by seventy-one words in total, which in turn are constituted by thirty nouns, twenty-one verbs, and twenty adjectives as can be seen in Table 3.6. These will be compared with the main vocabulary found in Hebrews' cosmogony, in order to determine the relationship between Hebrews' cosmogony and first-century philosophy. The comparison of this main vocabulary will be done in Hebrews' usage of nouns, verbs, and adjectives, in relation to selected literature of the first century, which will be organized in three categories: (1) Jewish literature; (2) Greek and Roman literature; and (3) Christian literature. Two of these categories will be further subdivided into two groups, the Jewish literature into the Septuagint and other documents, and the Christian literature into the New Testament and other documents.[10]

---

vocabulary on cosmogony during first-century philosophy comes from: 1) forerunning thoughts to the first century, for instance ideas expressed by personalities such as: Heraclitus, Parmenides, Socrates, Plato, and Aristotle, as well as from the testimony of Cicero (106–43 BCE) and Nicolaus of Damascus (65–64 BCE); 2) writings of the first century, such as the documents produced by Philo, Josephus, and Plutarch of Chaeronea, and; 3) the testimony of some personalities that lived between the second and fifth century CE, such as Tertullian (ca. 155–240 CE), Hippolytus (170–235 CE), Diogenes Laertius (180–240 CE), Lactantius (ca. 240–320 CE), Eusebius (ca. 260–340 CE), and Augustine (354–430 CE). It is evident that not all the documents produced during these centuries have some insights on cosmogonic presuppositions of the first century. However, as far as could be established, from them Philo has twenty-four documents that have important insights on his cosmogony, Aristotle eight, Plato three, and all the others together have sixteen documents. Along with this, some insight on the cosmogony of the first century can be found in the apocrypha and pseudepigrapha. Also, the Septuagint, as it is natural, shows special insights on first-century cosmogony, particularly in 2 Baruch, 2 Enoch, and Wisdom of Solomon. Likewise, even though it could be argued otherwise, the Nag Hammadi Library also provides some insights about first-century philosophy. Therefore, as is evident, it is impossible to summarize all these documents to obtain the main vocabulary of first-century cosmogony. However, it is important to highlight that all this documentation can provide important insights about the main vocabulary used in first-century cosmogony. So for instance, the Sepher Yetzirah, a document that has been harshly challenged on its time of origin as well as on its originality, can provide important information about the cosmogony of the first century in spite of these problems, either as a witness of it or as a forerunner thought to it.

10. Logos 7 software was used to do the counting. The specific documents used for the Jewish literature were: 1) *Septuaginta: With Morphology*; 2) Philo, *Philo*; 3) Josephus and Niese, *Flavii Iosephi*; and 4) Penner and Heiser, *Old Testament Greek Pseudepigrapha*, which includes morphologically tagged and lemmatized Greek texts for eighty-one books, letters, and fragments of Greek pseudepigraphal texts. The specific documents used for the Greek and Roman literature are the documents under the library Greek Classics of Logos 7 and the Perseus Classics Collection which include works of personalities such as Aristophanes, Aristotle, Cicero, Homer, Hippocrates,

Cosmogonic Verbs in First-Century CE Literature

As can be seen in Table 7.1, there are thirty-one verbs that could be considered part of the cosmogonic vocabulary of first-century literature: six are not found in the vocabulary of Hebrews' cosmogony, ten are exclusive of Hebrews' cosmogony, and fifteen are used as common cosmogonic verbs in first-century literature.

	Greek Verb	Meaning	Literature				
			Jewish		Greek & Roman	Christian	
			LXX	PJP		ApAF	NT
Present in the cosmogony of first century philosophy	γεννάω	beget, engender, produce	253	454	941	56	97
	ἐποχέομαι	be carried upon, ride upon, rest	0	21	32	0	0
	κτίζω	create, to found	67	115	540	26	15
	μεταβάλλω	change, to turn about	32	217	959	1	1
	προγίγνομαι	come forward, pre-exist	3	9	200	0	0
	προνοέω	provide for, care for, take thought for	9	122	162	3	3
Present in the cosmogony of Hebrews and first century philosophy	ἀλλάσσω	change, exchange, alter	42	51	237	11	6
	ἀπόλλυμι	destroy, perish, lose, be ruined	93	443	2847	53	90
	βλέπω	see, observe, perceive, watch	133	231	956	93	131
	γίνομαι*	to become, be born, be produce	2222	4174	36509	373	668
	δεῖ	it is necessary, inevitable, one must	1	401	33312	76	101
	δηλόω	reveal, make clear	37	662	1659	49	7
	εἰμί	be, exist, happen, become	6829	15076	307739	1556	2462
	καταπαύω	rest, stop, cease, hinder	67	38	174	9	4
	κατασκευάζω	build, prepare, make ready	28	422	2072	1	11
	μένω	remain, stay, persist	89	396	2860	35	118
	νοέω	understand, perceive, think	31	153	1003	45	14
	πάσχω	suffer, endure	18	553	4909	56	7
	πήγνυμι	pitch a tent, build, set up, fix	41	110	799	4	1
	ποιέω	make, do, manufacture, prepare	3386	2779	27452	353	568
	φαίνω	shine, become visisble, appear	66	347	7046	43	31
Present in Hebrews cosmogony	εἰσέρχομαι	enter, go in, enter, invaded	709	276	995	77	194
	ἐκδέχομαι	wait for, expect, receive from	15	94	208	3	6
	ἑλίσσω	roll up, turning, be entangled	2	5	269	0	2
	ἔχω	have, hold, possess	501	3565	39867	427	708
	θεμελιόω	lay a foundation, found firmly	41	7	54	6	5
	καταρτίζω	create, produce, prepare, restore	17	1	40	19	13
	παλαιόω	wear out, become old, decay	28	2	792	3	4
	πρέπω**	be fitting, be proper, be suitable	10	86	1021	15	7
	προσφέρω	bring, offer, present	165	249	1034	34	13
	σαλεύω	to stir, to waver, afflict, to shake	78	44	68	1	15

Table 7.1 Comparison of cosmogonic verbs in first-century literature.[11]

Plato, Seneca, Plutarch, Sophocles, Cornelius Tacitus, Tertullian, Xenophon, and many more. The specific documents used for the Christian literature were: 1) Nestle and Nestle, *Nestle-Aland*; 2) Brannan, *Greek Apocryphal Gospels*; and 3) Lightfoot and Harmer, *Apostolic Fathers*.

11. The abbreviations LXX, PJP, ApAF, and NT correspond with the explanation given in footnote 10 from current chapter, namely: LXX = Septuagint; PJP = Philo, Josephus and the Pseudepigrapha; ApAF = Apocryphal and Apostolic Fathers.

* Regarding γίνομαι it must be asserted that in Greek literature the verb is usually

Table 7.1 shows that there are both differences and similarities between Hebrews and the philosophical cosmogony of the first century. It is evident that most of the verbs used in first-century cosmogony were also used in Hebrews' cosmogony. Nevertheless, it can be seen that verbs such as: μεταβάλλω (change or to turn about), ἐποχέομαι (be carried upon or ride upon), προγίγνομαι (come forward or preexist), προνοέω (provide or care for), γεννάω (beget or engender), κτίζω (create or to found), were never used in Hebrews' cosmogony. The avoidance of the use of these verbs seems to be intentional, since for instance, Hebrews chose to use φέρω (carry, sustain, care, guide, cf. 1:3) which evidently has a major semantic range, in place of προνοέω (provide or care for) which has a minor semantic range.[12] The same could be asserted of Hebrews' use of ἀλλάσσω (change or alter) in place of μεταβάλλω (change or to turn about). It is also interesting to note that Hebrews avoids the use of κτίζω (create) which is consistently used in the New Testament in a cosmogonic context (cf. Matt 19:4; Mark 13:19; Rom 1:25; 1 Cor 11:9; Eph 2:10, 15; 3:9; 4:24; Col 1:16; 3:10; 1 Tim 4:3; Rev 4:11; 10:6) in order to assert that God created everything. Hebrews uses the verb καταρτίζω (create or prepare) in its place which embraces semantically the verb κτίζω (create) and adds ideas, such as, to make adequate and produce (cf. 11:3).[13]

On the other hand, it is interesting to note that verbs such as ἑλίσσω (roll up or be entangled), παλαιόω (wear out or decay), σαλεύω (to stir or to waver) and θεμελιόω (lay a foundation) are used exclusively in Hebrews' cosmogony. So, in its verb usage, Hebrews shows a slight difference in the way in which the actions—verbs—are portrayed in its cosmogony, which will be more evident in the following sections of this chapter.

---

found in the form of γίγνομαι. See Thayer, *Greek-English Lexicon*, 115.

** Regarding πρέπω it must be recognized that Philo uses this verb once in a cosmogonic context when he affirms that the character of God impels him "to change disorder into order, and not order into disorder," so he affirms that the undertaking of creating the world was a fitting employment for him (cf. Philo, *Aet.* 40).

12. The Greek lexicon using the concept of semantic domains, Louw and Nida, clearly shows the difference between φέρω and προνοέω in semantic range. See Louw and Nida, *Greek-English Lexicon of the New Testament*, 2:208, 56.

13. Louw and Nida for instance place the word κτίζω—create—only under the semantic domains of Make and Create, while the verb καταρτίζω—create or prepare—is placed under the semantic domains of Adequate, Qualified, Happen, Be, Become, Exist, Make and Create. See Louw and Nida, *Greek-English Lexicon of the New Testament*, 1:162, 513, 679.

Cosmogonic Nouns in First-Century CE Literature

As can be seen in Table 7.2, there are forty-two nouns that could be considered part of the cosmogonic vocabulary of first-century literature. Of the forty-two, eighteen are not found in the vocabulary of Hebrews' cosmogony, eleven are exclusive to Hebrews' cosmogony, and thirteen are used as common cosmogonic nouns in first-century literature. So, Table 7.2 could show either that there are differences between Hebrews and philosophical cosmogony in the first century, or that there are similarities.

It is possible to make some conclusions from Table 7.2. First the forty-two nouns can be classified into two groups: (1) general vocabulary—words that can be found in a different context, even though sometimes they could have a special meaning in a specific context—and, (2) specialized vocabulary for cosmogony. Of the two, the latter is more pertinent in order to determine the similarities or differences between the main vocabulary that constitutes Hebrews' cosmogony and first-century cosmogonies. So the following words can be considered as specialized vocabulary: ἐκπύρωσις (conflagration), ἰδέα (idea), κόσμοι (worlds), νοῦς or νόος (mind or god), ὁμοιομερεία or ὁμοιομερής (*homoeomeries* or homogeneous molecules),[14] στοιχεῖον (fundamental principle), χάος (chaos), δημιουργός (builder), αἰών (universe),[15] and μετάθεσις (transformation).[16] What is interesting is that of these ten nouns, only one—δημιουργός—is shared by Hebrews and the general cosmogony found among first-century philosophy.

---

14. This word is used by Laertius—cf. Laertius *Vit. Phil.* 2.8—and could mean having like parts, similarity of composition, having parts like each other and the whole but also of the parts themselves, like each other or the whole. See Liddell et al., *Greek-English Lexicon*, 1224.

15. From the explanation given below—see ** in footnote 17 from current chapter—the noun αἰών could only be considered as specialized vocabulary in Hebrews' cosmogony. Moreover, its use in Aristotle also seems to have the same sense of lifetime or the whole time (cf. Aristotle, *Met.* 1072b.25–29, 1075a.5–9).

16. It is possible that some could argue, saying that μετάθεσις is used by Aristotle in a cosmogonic context, when he states "These are the things whose nature remains the same after transposition, but whose form does not, e.g., wax or a coat," Aristotle, *Met.* 1024a.1–4. However, in that text he is talking about the nature of the "whole" and not about the nature of the creation, cf. Aristotle, *Met.* 1023b.25–24a.4.

Hebrews' Cosmogony and First-Century Cosmogonies 241

	Greek Noun	Meaning	Literature				
			Jewish		Greek & Roman	Christian	
			LXX	PJP		ApAF	NT
Present in the cosmogony of first century philosophy	ἀήρ	air, sky, space	10	301	1184	5	7
	δύναμις	power, strength, force, capability	591	1343	7523	86	119
	εἰκών	image, likeness, mental representation	55	165	2418	7	23
	ἐκπύρωσις	conflagration	0	20	19	0	0
	ἰδέα	idea, kind, form, outward appearance	8	236	616	9	0
	κόσμοι	worlds, cosmoses, universes	2	10	169	1	0
	κτίστης	creator, founder	7	34	46	3	1
	λόγος	word, message, the Logos	1239	2241	17521	129	330
	νοῦς*	mind, intellect, understanding, god	30	747	2185	13	24
	ὁμοιομερεία*	homoeomeries or homogeneous molecules	0	0	21	0	0
	ὄνομα	name, title	1049	1026	5164	149	229
	πατήρ	father, forefather, ancestor, progenitor	1447	1715	6058	152	413
	ποιητής	doer, maker, inventor, lawgiver	1	127	1887	0	6
	πῦρ	fire	528	614	2391	39	71
	στοιχεῖον	elements, fundamental principle, heavenly body	3	115	505	4	7
	ὕδωρ	water	675	599	3437	57	76
	ὕλη	existing essence, wood, forest	8	254	1249	4	1
	χάος	chaos, infinite space, unformed matter	2	7	42	0	0
Present in the cosmogony of Hebrews and first century philosophy	ἄνθρωπος	humanity, man	1426	2313	11128	213	550
	ἀρχή	beginning, ruler, power	236	1130	9195	31	55
	γῆ	earth, land, ground, people	3174	1751	6261	111	250
	δημιουργός	builder, maker, craftsworker	2	125	373	7	1
	ἔργον	work, deed, action, product	591	1005	6364	114	169
	ἡμέρα	day, time	2573	1561	5912	151	389
	θεός	God, deity, goddess	4009	5847	13305	833	1317
	κόσμος	world, order, cosmos, universe	72	944	1613	83	186
	κτίσις	creation, creature, institution	16	52	88	21	19
	οὐρανός	heaven, sky	682	829	1146	84	273
	πόλις	city, town	1579	2518	22109	47	163
	τεχνίτης	designer, artisan, craftsperson, artificer	12	99	282	4	4
	χείρ	hand	1945	846	4992	90	177
Present in Hebrews cosmogony	αἰών**	universe, age, eternity	749	333	277	114	122
	ἱμάτιον	cloak, garment, clothing	223	59	614	14	60
	καταβολή	foundation, sowing, building	1	21	30	2	11
	κύριος	Lord, master, sir	8608	1438	2089	810	715
	λειτουργός	servant, minister, assistant	14	17	17	3	5
	μετάθεσις	change, transformation, removal	1	14	39	0	3
	περιβόλαιον	cloak, a wrapper, mantle	11	5	7	0	2
	πίστις	faith, belief, trust	59	394	1112	115	243
	ῥῆμα	a spoken word, an utterance	546	125	520	62	68
	σκηνή	tabernacle, tend, hut	436	193	600	6	20
	Χριστός	Christos, anointed	52	61	1	247	529

Table 7.2 Comparison of cosmogonic nouns in first-century literature.[17]

17. For the abbreviations—LXX, PJP, ApAF, and NT—see footnotes 10 and 11 from current chapter.

* It is necessary to clarify that in Roman and Hellenistic literature νοῦς is usually used instead of νόος, and that the words ὁμοιομερεία and ὁμοιομερής seem to have been used indistinctively.

** Regarding the use of αἰών in a cosmogonic context it could be argued that it is also used outside of Hebrews in the literature of first-century cosmogony, since the word is used for instance by Plato six times—four as the noun αἰών and two as the

Even though Hebrews does share some general vocabulary with the common vocabulary of first-century cosmogony, it does not share the specialized vocabulary in cosmogony. Thus, first of all, Hebrews is not a document about cosmogony; and second, the cosmogony of Hebrews could be different to other current cosmogonies in the first century.

Moreover, there is some kind of correlation in vocabulary use between Jewish and Greek and Roman literature, but not so with Christian literature. For instance, it can be seen in Table 7.2 that some of the specialized words such as ἐκπύρωσις (conflagration), ἰδέα (idea), κόσμοι (worlds), and χάος (chaos), are used in Jewish and Greek and Roman literature but never in Christian literature. Other terms, meanwhile, are scarcely used in Christian literature in comparison to their use in Jewish and Greek and Roman literature, for instance, νοῦς or νόος (mind or god), στοιχεῖον (fundamental principle), and ὕλη (all existing essence).

Cosmogonic Adjectives in First-Century CE Literature

There are 24 adjectives that could be considered part of the cosmogonic vocabulary of first-century literature. Of the 24, 15 are not found in the vocabulary of Hebrews' cosmogony, four are exclusive to Hebrews' cosmogony and five are used as common cosmogonic adjectives in first-century literature. Thus, Table 7.3 shows that there are differences between Hebrews and philosophical cosmogonies in the first century.

---

adjective αἰώνιος—(cf. Plato, *Ti.* 37d–38c). Nevertheless, it is important to highlight that there is a very big difference between the sense that carries this word in Hebrews and in the general literature of the first century, which includes other documents which constitute the New Testament. Here it is important to highlight what Bitter asserts in his review on the research of Keizer about just one word, αἰών, since in spite of this very insightful research constituted by more than three hundred pages, he asserts "but we remain in the dark as to the question what *aiōn* in substance really means in the different writings. There is unquestionably more to say about *aiōn* than that it means, next to time and life, 'entirety' instead of 'eternity', or that it is ' . . . time made into a meaningful whole." Bitter, "Review of 'Helleen M. Keizer," 237–40. cf. Keizer, "Life-Time-Entirety." So what was asserted in chapter 5 can be reaffirmed, that even though the word is used in other documents, the sense in which it is used in Hebrews' cosmogony—i.e., portraying the whole temporal and spatial realm included also the heavenly places—is exclusive to Hebrews.

Hebrews' Cosmogony and First-Century Cosmogonies 243

Greek Adjective		Meaning	Literature				
			Jewish		Greek & Roman	Christian	
			LXX	PJP		ApAF	NT
Present in the cosmogony of first century philosophy	ἀγένητος	uncreated, unoriginated	0	103	41	0	0
	ἀΐδιος*	eternal	0	81	398	1	0
	αἴτιος	cause, source	7	473	4967	0	5
	ἀνώλεθρος	indestructible	0	3	26	0	0
	ἀόρατος	invisible, unseen	3	133	71	13	5
	ἀσώματον	bodiless, incorporeal	0	117	82	2	0
	ἄτομος	indivisible, atom, instant	0	8	128	0	1
	ἄφθαρτος	imperishable, uncorrupted	2	130	95	8	8
	γενητός*	originated, generated	0	98	1056	0	0
	κενός	void, empty, vain	78	169	1688	29	18
	ὁρατός	visible, to be seen	4	78	504	6	1
	πρῶτος	first, before, earliest	245	1978	12629	91	155
	σπερματικός	seminal, the power of generating	0	11	7	0	0
	τεχνικός	artistic, skilful, technical excellence	0	22	141	0	0
	φθαρτός	perishable, corruptible	4	91	95	10	6
Present in the cosmogony of Hebrews and first century philosophy	ἕβδομος	seventh, seventh day, sabbath	134	263	313	5	9
	ἴδιος	one's own, particular, private	79	858	4153	58	114
	μέγας	large, great, big	913	2454	18264	163	243
	πᾶς	every, all, each, everything	6821	8142	36895	813	1243
	τέλειος	perfect, mature, complete	19	475	1171	25	19
Present in Hebrews cosmogony	ἅγιος	holy, sacred, dedicated	831	435	100	148	233
	ἀληθινός	true, sincere, authentic	50	51	372	16	28
	ἀντίτυπος	antitype, copy, representation	0	6	103	2	2
	χειροποίητος	made by hands, manual work	15	29	43	0	6

Table 7.3 Comparison of cosmogonic adjectives in first-century literature.[18]

From Table 7.3, some conclusions on the use of adjectives can be made—similar to the section on nouns. Firstly, the twenty-four adjectives can also be classified into two groups: 1) general vocabulary; and 2) specialized vocabulary. The following words can be considered as specialized vocabulary: ἀγένητος (uncreated); ἀΐδιος (eternal); ἀνώλεθρος (indestructible); ἀσώματον (incorporeal); ἄτομος (indivisible); γενητός (originated); σπερματικός (seminal); and ἀντίτυπος (antitype). And of these eight adjectives only one is used in Hebrews—ἀντίτυπος—and it is never used as a specialized word in cosmogonies outside of Hebrews. So Hebrews does not use any of the other seven words that could be considered part of the specialized vocabulary of current first-century cosmogonies.

18. For the abbreviations—LXX, PJP, ApAF, and NT—see footnotes 10 and 11 from current chapter.
   * It is necessary to clarify that in Roman and Hellenistic literature ἀϊδής and ἀίδιος are usually used instead of ἀΐδιος, and that the words γεννητός and γενητός were used indistinctively or perhaps they belonged to different times, but they carry the same sense.

Secondly, there is more correlation between the use of adjectives in Jewish literature and Greek and Roman literature than in Christian literature in relation to both other groups. So for instance, αἴτιος (cause, source) used abundantly in the literature of the first century and also in a cosmogonic context, is only used five times in the New Testament, and it is never used in a cosmogonic context in Hebrews (cf. 5:9) or in its other uses (cf. Luke 23:4, 14, 22; Acts 19:40). The same can be stated about words such as ἀόρατος (invisible), ἄφθαρτος (imperishable), κενός (void), ὁρατός (visible), and φθαρτός (perishable).

Consequently, on the basis of adjective-, noun- and verb-usage in Hebrews and in first-century literature about cosmogony, it can be affirmed that Hebrews proposes, to a great degree, a different cosmogony to those present in first-century CE.

The Creator

Regarding the Creator, the first cosmogonic presupposition found in Hebrews is that he is ὁ θεός (cf. 1:1–4) but that υἱός, who could be identified as κύριος and יהוה in the Old Testament Greek and Hebrew respectively, performs the creative action,[19] not as an instrument but as the ultimate cause and sole agency.[20] Nevertheless, it is important to highlight that in first-century philosophy, anti-creationism—a kind of evolutionism—was present from the time of the Ionian School (ca. 624–428 BCE)—although it could have been present prior to 624 BCE. People like Anaxagoras (ca. 510–428 BCE) posited the existence of some kind of natural law, which he calls νοῦς—i.e., the eternal mind—as responsible for the organization of the tiny particles from which the realm of the human being is constituted. On the other hand, the Eleatic School (ca.

---

19. As already asserted, in Hebrews' cosmogony the articulate noun ὁ θεός holds a plural sense. On the other hand, in Hebrews' cosmogony the words, wills, and actions of ὁ θεός are expressed, accomplished, and realized through the υἱός. However, it is also important to say that Hebrews never directly or indirectly asserts that the Godhead does not do anything in order to create the world. On the contrary, Hebrews posits clearly the indirect participation of various beings—i.e., the Godhead—in the process of creation (cf. 1:1–4; 2:10; 9:14).

20. See the analysis of the prepositional phrase δι' οὗ in 1:2 in chapter 4 of this research. However, that υἱός is not an instrument of God, but is God himself as also asserted by Allen when he states that Jesus is "God of very God, so Jesus does not reveal something other than Himself, nor does He reveal something other than God." Allen, *Hebrews*, 119.

580–430 BCE) affirmed the existence of an unchanging, unlimited, infinite, immobile, eternal, and immutable being, whom they called *God*.[21] However, it is important to highlight that for them this being is not a creator, strictly speaking, since for them, apart from this "being," nothing exists,[22] because this being is everything,[23] which is a pantheistic view of creation. The Stoics (ca. 335–51 BCE), meanwhile, followed the same reasoning, since they understood the λόγος—reason or mind—not only as the soul of the world, god,[24] the ruler of the creation,[25] but also as the seminal reason, who is able to adapt matter to itself in order to develop the creation.[26] Therefore, Turner is right when he labels Stoicism as pantheism,[27] although, Stoic cosmogony can also be seen as a combination of Ionianism and Eleaticism. Socrates, meanwhile, adopted the intelligent cause—νοῦς—proposed by Anaxagoras, and from it he formulated the principle that "whatever exists for a useful purpose must be the work of an intelligence,"[28] and therefore he posited the existence of some entity that is above the creation.[29] However, it is important to mention here that Plato maintains that Socrates believed in the eternity of the world,[30] so it can be stated that for Socrates this "intelligence" is more like a fashioner or the "intelligent cause" of order, apart from the eternal substance from which everything is constituted. In addition, Plato (ca. 427–347 BCE) posits the existence of some Living Being,[31] in whom is the non-physical idea which is chosen by the δημιουργός, who is not a divine or personal

---

21. Aristotle, [*Xen.*] 977.1.10–14.
22. Henry, *God, Revelation, and Authority*, 5:44.
23. Plato, *Soph.* 242d.
24. Diogenes, *Vit. Phil.* 7.135.
25. Perkins, "Stoicism," 993.
26. Diogenes, *Vit. Phil.* 7.136, 138.

27. Turner, *History of Philosophy*, 161. Also, Torres claims that the Stoics defended a kind of pantheism in which the λόγος extends over all things. See Mas Torres, *Historia de la Filosofía Antigua*, 220.

28. Turner, *History of Philosophy*, 79, 82. Xenophon is the source for this conclusion, because this argument, as far as can be established, was never used by Socrates, nevertheless it can be implied from his anthropological and moral arguments. cf. Xenophon, *Mem.* 1.4.2–19; 4.3.14–17.

29. Forbes was right when he asserts that Socrates regarded the world as the "handiwork of some wise artifice." Forbes, *Socrates*, 213–17.

30. Plato, *Phdr.* 245d.
31. Vlastos, *Plato's Universe*, 27.

ruler but a manual laborer,[32] in order to fashion everything. On the other hand, Aristotle (ca. 384–322 BCE) considers himself a Platonist,[33] but at the same time he also understood the creation as an eternal entity as did Socrates, and consequently his cosmogonic view and particularly his comprehension about the creator is not well-defined.[34] Therefore it can be said that Aristotle neither adds anything new nor clarifies anything about the creator. Likewise, middle Platonism also affirms the existence of a creator,[35] but does not add anything new since it simply tries to explain Plato's assertions about the creator who, however, is not, strictly speaking, a creator.

On the other hand, in Pythagorean cosmogony—Pythagorean School (ca. 570 BCE)—God is not present, i.e., the origin of all things is proposed as having no theistic supernatural connection.[36] Likewise, the Atomistic School (ca. 500 BCE) held that everything came to its existence due to physical laws that rule the ἄτομος—atoms,[37] and not by any corporeal or incorporeal agency or by chance.[38] In addition, it is very likely that Skeptics (ca. 365 BCE), Eclectics (ca. 266 BCE), and the Scientific Movement (ca. 400 BCE) held a view on the creator similar to the Pythagorean or Atomistic School. Or at least it is very likely that they supported the idea of non-existence of some creator; however, it is very difficult to make an assertion with certainty in this regard, due to the scarce documentation on their cosmogony.

Epicureanism (ca. 341 BCE), meanwhile, developed its cosmogony on the old Atomistic School and added chance to it, because in Epicurus' cosmogony the world came into existence by chance,[39] without purpose, and without the intervention of some god or gods.[40] On the

---

32. Vlastos, *Plato's Universe*, 26–27.

33. See Aristotle, *Met.* 992a.10–14.

34. Turner for instance affirms that Aristotle, like his master Plato, did not have a clear or even coherent concept about God or the supernatural being, i.e., the creator. Turner, *History of Philosophy*, 143.

35. See Plutarch, *De Defect.* 22; *Plat.* 8.4.

36. Stenudd, *Cosmos of the Ancients*, 61–63.

37. Aristotle, *De an.* 403.2.30–404.1.29; *Ph.* 203.1.20–24; Lactantius, *Inst.* 7.3,7.

38. Adams, *Constructing the World*, 46.

39. Mas Torres, *Historia de la Filosofía Antigua*, 200.

40. It is important to mention that Epicurus believed in the existence of gods; however, to him, they are only a different race or perhaps a superior or more evolved race of living beings. cf. Lactantius, *De Ira D.* 4.

other hand, among the Jews of the first century, even though they were widely divided,[41] the existence of a supernatural being—God—as the creator is evident, and although most of them were deeply influenced by Hellenism, it did not change the Jewish understanding of God as the creator—in most cases—but rather the understanding of the creation.[42] So for instance, Philo shows the constructor—δημιουργός—and the creator—θεός—as the same person,[43] while in an apparent contradiction he also uses the intervention of intermedium realities in his cosmogony. Finally, the existence of the creator is also present in Gnosticism, and even though it is unlikely that Gnosticism existed in the first century, the gnostic creator, which to them is a δημιουργός, is a lesser, inferior, false and bad god,[44] and was in total opposition to Hebrews' Creator.

Therefore, first of all it can be asserted that Hebrews does not share anything—on the creator—with Ionians, Pythagoreans, Atomists, Skeptics, Eclectics, Scientific Movement, or Epicureans, while it shares the assertion about the existence of some creator with Eleatics, Stoics, Socrates, Plato, Aristotle, Middle Platonism and Jewish sects. However,

---

41. Although it is very likely almost impossible to determine with absolute certainty the wide range into which Judaism was divided in the first century, groups, sects and minor groups that have their origin in Intertestamental Judaism were present. Judaism of the first century was constituted by a mix of ideas present in the thought of groups such as: Essenes, Maccabees, Pharisees, Sadducees, Zealots, Sicarii, Samaritans, Hellenists, Galileans, Herodians, Scribes, Therapeutae, Magical Judaism, Disciples of John the Baptist, the Fourth Philosophy, whose can be the Zealots of the New Testament, Hemerobaptists, Masbotheans, Meristae, and Genistae, among others. See Scott, *Jewish Backgrounds of the New Testament*, 30, 195–218, 29–30; Hengel, *Judaism and Hellenism*, 60; Grabbe, "Hellenistic City of Jerusalem," 6.

42. It is possible to assert a change in the understanding of the creation in Judaism, due to the presence of different cosmogonies therein evidenced by some of its literature, and the apocrypha and pseudepigrapha of the Old Testament, the Apocalypse of Baruch, the Sepher Yetzirah, and Philo could serve as clear evidence of it. cf. 2 Bar 21:4; 2 En. 24:2; Wis 11:17; Philo, *Opif.* 19–23.

43. Philo, *Opif.* 170–71.

44. Among gnostic schools the false and bad god was sometimes identified as Ahriman, El, Saklas, Samael, Satan, Yaldabaoth, or Yahweh. According to Rosscup, Gnosticism posited that each of these beings gave rise to the next in order and each, in turn, became more remote from the Pleroma until, at last, the thirteenth aeon was so far distant that he could enter into contact with matter. This aeon created the world of matter recorded in the Old Testament, and was the Jehovah of the Old Testament, an inferior being whom gnostics styled the demiurge. For them he was only an emanation out of the pure, Supreme being. Since God could not defile himself in contacting matter, or flesh, the incarnation of God was unthinkable in Gnosticism. See Rosscup, *Exposition on Prayer*, 5:2658.

there seem to be great differences in the comprehension of the identity, nature, attributes, and purpose of the creator between Hebrews and these other schools of thought present in some way in first-century philosophy. For instance, the Eleatics and the Stoics see the creator as a being that fragments himself in order to create—which posits a pantheistic view of the creation—while Hebrews evidently presupposes that the Creator and the creation are different things (cf. 1:10–12). However, it is important to note that in Hebrews there is no antagonistic sense in this difference,[45] as in Socrates, Plato, and particularly in the gnostic view on the creator. Philo's presupposition about the nature of the creator is also in opposition to that of Hebrews.[46]

Moreover, Hebrews' general presupposition is that the creator is a good and perfect being who does not belong to a group of gods organized in different levels, which is evidently an important idea in first-century cosmogony.[47] In addition, Hebrews holds some presuppositions that are not evident in the first-century philosophical context about the creator. These ideas include, for instance, the presupposition that the Creator became human and that he holds a physical nature[48] after his incarnation (cf. 2:6, 14; 5:1–4; 9:11–14, 24), and moreover, that he is always in motion inside of his creation (cf. 1:10; 4:3–5, 10; 9:11–12, 26;

---

45. For the explanation of the sentences σὺ δὲ διαμένεις (but You remain, cf. 1:11) and σὺ δὲ ὁ αὐτὸς εἶ καὶ τὰ ἔτη σου οὐκ ἐκλείψουσιν (You are the same and Your years will fail not, cf. 1:12), where the conjunction δέ has an adversative function, see its analysis in chapter 4.

46. Guthrie, "Hebrews," 952. Philo also states that the nature of the creator is superior to the nature of the creation. cf. Philo, *Migr.* 193.

47. Hebrews' view of the creator is in opposition to gnostic presuppositions about the creator, as well as very different to the view of Socrates, Plato, Aristotle, and Middle Platonism, since the Creator of Hebrews is not the god or gods placed in the highest level of divinity, because Hebrews does not have an assumption of different levels of divinities. However, it is important to recognize that it is very difficult to "establish beyond any doubt what he [Socrates] did believe." See Janko, "Socrates the Freethinker,"

48. Further information, although not necessarily correct at all, can be found in the work of Apuleius *De Deo Socratis*—On the God of Socrates. See Apuleius et al., *Works of Apuleius*, 351. For Neoplatonism and the creator, see Moore, "Middle Platonism."

48. Even though some assumed that the nature of Jesus after his resurrection was not corporeal, as Geisler asserts, the Bible is very clear about the nature of the resurrection. It is the same physical, material body of flesh and bones that died. See Geisler, *Baker Encyclopedia of Christian Apologetics*, 665–70. Therefore, the physical condition of Jesus after his resurrection must also be held in his exalted condition as υἱός "at the right hand of the Majesty on high" (cf. 1:3).

11:3), since in Hebrews the Creator is not a distant nor a static being.[49] In addition, another presupposition is that the Creator made everything with the purpose of having communion with his creation, which should live in obedience and service to him (cf. 2:1–4; 3:12; 5:11–14; 10:19–25) in a context of happiness, confidence and a brotherly love relationship to its incarnate creator, Christ (cf. 2:14–18; 3:1–3; 6:19–20; 9:13–14; 10:35–39).[50] These presuppositions, along with the identification of the Creator with the Godhead and more specifically with the person of υἱός are exclusive to Hebrews (cf. 1:1–4, 8; 4:14–16; 9:14). So, concerning the Creator, Hebrews holds a different presupposition of what was present in first-century philosophy, and the Jewish view of the Creator comes closest to Hebrews' view.

The Procedure

The procedure by which the creation came into existence was viewed differently in particularly two main ways in the first century: a first group that accepted the existence of some supernatural being or beings in its cosmogony, and another group that did not hold this view. The second group is constituted by Ionians, Pythagoreans, Atomists, Skeptics, Eclectics, and people that belong to the Scientific Movement, and to Epicureanism. All of them, with some variations, hold the view that everything came into existence due to the combination of physical, natural, and mathematical laws—Ionians, Atomists, and Pythagoreans—and chance—Epicureanism—or due to some of them.[51]

49. From the first verse of Hebrews, which says that "Long ago, at many times and in many ways, God spoke to our fathers by the prophets" (1:1, ESV) through to its end (cf. 13:20–21), it is evident that God is trying to keep a relationship with his creation. Moreover, the grammatical and syntactic context of 4:3–5, 10 shows, as already expounded in chapter 4, that ὁ θεός is a personal and direct worker and not a kind of supervisory or administrative worker, who through some agent or intermediary accomplished his will, i.e., somehow all the individual members of the Godhead must be active in the creation.

50. The creation in Hebrews was for the sake and glory of God—the Creator—which in Hebrews' context means primarily to please, obey and serve him, in a direct relationship with him. However, it is also important to clarify that the Creator in Hebrews loves his creation and he is the one that tries to keep this relationship. Cf. Attridge, *Hebrews*, 82; Lenski, *Interpretation of the Epistle to the Hebrews*, 80.

51. For instance, the Ionians believed that when the multitude of ὁμοιομέρειαι— tiny particles like seeds—mix together they bring about the origin of every creature. The Atomists, meanwhile, posited that the ἄτομος were brought together by their equal

On the other hand, those who accepted the existence of some supernatural being as the one who performs the procedure by which everything came into existence can be subdivided into other branches. For instance, the Eleatics believed in the fragmentation of the creator, since for them everything is part of the creator.[52] Socrates seems to assert that everything is the product of divine design,[53] even though it seems that he believed in the eternity of the world.[54] Plato states that the creator—the demiurge—used physical elements, such as fire, earth, air and water,[55] in order to make everything; and likewise, Aristotle believed that the κόσμος is ἀγένητος—uncreated.[56] Consequently, the procedure for the existence of the creation is different from one view to another; nevertheless, it seems that at least Aristotle, who probably tried to mix all previous assertions, posited a kind of evolution—which could be shared by the others—as the procedure for the existence of reality.[57] The Stoics asserted that in order to develop the creation the λόγος—reason or mind—adapted matter to itself, while middle Platonism asserted that the creator transformed matter into the receptacle of evil in order to create.

Another subgroup of those who accepted the existence of a supernatural being in their cosmogony is Judaism, which in the first century was non-monolithic, a fact that is evidenced by the existence of different positions on the procedure by which reality came into existence. For instance, the Sepher Yetzirah states that the creator made everything from the ten Sephiroth, meanwhile the Wisdom of Solomon says that the creator uses his powerful hand, and the Apocalypse of Baruch says that he uses his word and spirit. Philo, meanwhile, shows a more complex

---

weight. Cf. Aristotle, *Met.* 1010a.10–14; *De an.* 405.25–29; 403.2.30–404.1.29; *Ph.* 185.2.15–24; 203.1.20–24; *Cael.* 298.2.30–34; Lactantius, *Inst.* 7.3, 7. Regarding the Ionian School, particularly Heraclitus' theory, the best explanation has been given by Plato who asserts that in the opinion of Heraclitus all things flow and nothing stays. cf. Plato, *Crat.* 401–2.

52. Plato, *Soph.* 242d.
53. McPherran, *Religion of Socrates*, 282.
54. See Plato, *Phdr.* 245d.
55. And for this reason, "the demiurge makes it as much like his model as he can, limited, of course, to the limitations imposed by the fact that it consists of matter." Vlastos, *Plato's Universe*, 27.
56. Philo, *Aet.* 10.
57. Aristotle asserted that the actual corn, as well as the human being, are the development of some prior seed and are also the seeds from which a future entity will be developed. cf. Aristotle, *Met.* 1049b.15–24.

procedure in which the creator brought everything about in three steps inside a timeless reality:[58] 1) the creation of the model before time; 2) the creation of incorporeal things from the model; and 3) the creation of corporeal things.[59] But he also asserts that the world is constituted by γῆ (earth), ὕδωρ (water), ἀήρ (air), and πῦρ (fire), the four elements characteristic of the speculative presuppositions on cosmogony. He also asserts that γῆ (earth) through some process became water, which in turn became air and which in turn became fire, and that they will disappear following a reverse process until they become γῆ (earth) again.[60]

Hebrews, meanwhile, regarding the procedure by which the creation came into existence, holds the presupposition that the creator made it in a systematic and organized way. So for instance, Hebrews asserts that the Creator, in order to create, laid the foundation (ἐθεμελίωσας) of his creation, i.e., the basis of everything (cf. 1:10–12), which according to the general context of Hebrews' cosmogony must be the laws and not the physical elements that hold the creation. On the other hand, it is important to note that from Hebrews' use of the perfective aspect in important verbs of its cosmogony—such as the lemmas: λαλέω, εἶπον (to speak, cf. 1:1; 4:4); ποιέω (to make, cf. 1:2; 12:27); πήγνυμι (to erect, cf. 8:2); and ἑλίσσω (to fold, cf. 1:12)—another important presupposition in Hebrews' cosmogony emerges, i.e., the detail about the procedure by which the creation came into existence is something concealed.[61] Namely, the way in which these actions were performed is not revealed to the creation, but on the contrary, it is the final result or the complete actions portrayed by these verbs which evidence that everything came by the will and work of an intelligent Creator.

However, this does not mean that Hebrews does not have anything to say about the procedure by which everything came into existence. Indeed, there are important general insights—presuppositions—about it in Hebrews. So for instance, it was asserted in the preceding chapter that in

---

58. Winston, *Philo of Alexandria*, 11. Cf. Philo, *Opif.* 26, 67; *Leg.* 1.2; *Sacr.* 65.

59. See Philo, *Opif.* 19, 25, 29.

60. Philo, *Aet.* 107, 110.

61. The conclusion that these actions are private arise from the fact that the perfective aspect implies a complete action, i.e., "it presents events in summary, from a distance and does not view the details of how the action took place." See Campbell, *Basics of Verbal Aspect*, 34. Action that, according to Porter, does not show some reference to time or duration, i.e., it could be instantaneous actions or some action that was occurring over a long period of time. See Porter, *Idioms of the Greek New Testament*, 21.

order to create, the Creator used a method that could be called a logical process,[62] or a delegation of functions, which asserts that the Godhead decided that the function of creating would rest on υἱός (cf. 1:1–4) as a delegated responsibility and not as an instrumentality function. Likewise, it was asserted that the Creator used a method referred to here as a powerful personal intervention (cf. 1:1–4, 10–12; 2:10; 9:11, 24),[63] a presupposition that according to Attridge is nearer to the Stoic one, since they do not refer to an intermediary agent of creation.[64] In addition, it was also asserted that the Creator used a method of creating that could be called an utterance of goodwill (11:3), which follows a careful plan, scheme, or project.

On the other hand, Hebrews' use of the imperfective aspect portrays actions that were, are, and will be ongoing actions—with the sense of repetition—which the Creator performs before the believers.[65] Verbs

62. For the support of this assertion see chapter 5 of this research and the analysis of the verb θεμελιόω (to lay the foundation) in chapter 4; see also chapter 6, section "Methods Used to Create." What is important to mention here is that the creation must be a carefully planned activity, which, according to the context in which the verb θεμελιόω is used in the LXX (cf. Ps 118:152; Prov 3:19; 8:23; Job 38:4; 3 Kgdms 6:1; 7:47; 2 Chr 8:16; 31:7; 1 Esd 5:55; 2 Esd 3:6, 10; Isa 44:28, LXX) and in the New Testament (cf. Matt 7:25; Eph 3:17; Col 1:23; 1 Pet 5:10), ought to have contemplated the formulation of the laws that rule the whole creation. Burton also asserts "creation did not only result in the appearance of physical objects, but also involved the establishment of invisible phenomena," i.e., the principles of governance had to be established first. See Burton, "Faith Factor," 40–41.

63. For the support of this assertion see chapter 5 of this research and the analysis of the noun χείρ (hands) in chapter 4, see chapter 6, section "Methods Used to Create."

64. Attridge, *Hebrews*, 82. As already asserted in footnote 66 from chapter 6, it is important to highlight that it does not imply that Hebrews has Stoic influence, or worse, that it is a Stoic document, since the presence of some isolated ideas, words, or similar phrases are not determinative of dependence or influence. Moreover, as Ferguson states, "two groups using the same method does not necessarily mean that one is copying the other," and he also asserts that "Although Christianity had points of contact with Stoicism, the Mysteries, the Qumran community, and so on, the total worldview was often quite different, or the context in which the items were placed was different." And that is also applicable to Hebrews in its perceived relationship to other movements in the first century CE. See Ferguson, *Backgrounds of Early Christianity*, 2–3. Moreover, it is important to highlight that Attridge seems not to take into account that Stoicism mainly held a kind of pantheistic view of creation, which is in total opposition to Hebrews.

65. The imperfective aspect of the verb is the opposite of the perfective aspect, i.e., it shows a closer view of verbal actions. It shows the details as being seen by those who are in relation to the written text, namely the verbal actions are perceived by the language users as being in progress, in other words, its internal structure is seen as

used with this verbal aspect in Hebrews' cosmogony are: κατασκευάσας (to build, cf. 3:4); γίνομαι (to come to exist, to bring into existence, cf. 11:3); φέρω (to uphold, cf. 1:3); σαλεύω (to shake, cf. 12:26–27); and σείω (to stir, cf. 12:26). As already mentioned, Hebrews' presupposition is that it is possible for every human being to see the Creator in action, building, giving birth to new existences, upholding his creation, and shaking and stirring it. In addition, the assumption—presupposition—that the Creator never rests, that he is in a permanent state of activity (cf. 4:3–5) since he is always interacting with his creation in order to develop relationships and protect it (cf. 1:3), could also be considered as exclusive presuppositions of Hebrews. From this procedure, it can be asserted that Hebrews' cosmogony has more similarities with some Jewish cosmogonies than with other cosmogonies present in the first century.

The Sources

Regarding the source used by the Creator in order to create everything, Hebrews asserts that it was only his ῥῆμα—a spoken word or an utterance—and therefore, Hebrews presupposes that the only source used by the Creator in order to create was his own ῥῆμα (cf. 2:10; 11:3). This assertion is in opposition to what was asserted by the Eleatic School and by the Stoics. In Stoicism and Eleaticism the creator is also the source of everything, but as already shown, they have a kind of pantheistic view.[66] The most similar view in the first century regarding the source of creation can be found among the Jewish people, since some among them—i.e., apocalyptic Judaism—believed that God created everything from nothing.[67]

On the other hand, most presuppositions in the first century assumed that the creation came from some physical element, since the

---

unfolding. Porter, *Idioms of the Greek New Testament*, 21.

66. About the Eleatic School, cf. Aristotle, [*Xen.*] 977.1.10–14. Plato, *Soph.* 242d. Henry, *God, Revelation, and Authority*, 5:44. About the Stoics see Diogenes, *Vit. Phil.* 7.136, 138; Turner, *History of Philosophy*, 161; Mas Torres, *Historia de la Filosofía Antigua*, 220.

67. See 2 Bar. 21:4; cf. 2 En. 24:2. Also, Philo shows some insight about the creation from nothing (cf. Philo, *Somn.* 1.76). However, Philo's idea that everything came from some preexistent matter is more abundant in his writings (cf. Philo, *Opif.* 22; *Aet.* 5; *Spec.* 1.226). More about apocalyptic Judaism can be found in Collins, *Apocalyptic Imagination*; Flusser, *Judaism of the Second Temple Period*; Attridge et al., *Semeia*; Aune et al., *Semeia*.

Greeks believed the gods had not created the world out of nothing.[68] For instance, the Ionian School, and among them Anaxagoras in particular, posited that everything came from a multitude of tiny particles (ὁμοιομέρειαι) like seeds,[69] as well as water, fire, air, and land. On the other hand, the Pythagoreans believed that everything was built on numbers, from an eternal fiery seed.[70] The Atomistic School posited that everything came from atoms, while Socrates maintained that the source is something unknown, eternal, and indestructible. Plato, meanwhile, held that the source is the pattern, which is a real, perfect, and eternal world, but also that the demiurge used fire and earth—i.e., solid elements—and air and water—i.e., liquid elements—in order to fashion the cosmos out of this chaotic elemental matter. Aristotle followed the assertion of Plato, and it is very likely that the Skeptics and the Scientific Movement also held a very similar presupposition about the source from which everything came into existence. Stoicism, Epicureanism, Middle Platonism, and even most of the Jewish cosmogonies also followed this same idea.[71] Therefore, there are no similarities between Hebrews and most first-century cosmogonies regarding the sources from which all things came into existence.

The Time

As already asserted numerous times, Hebrews does not claim to be a cosmogonic document, and therefore, a careful and deep reading between the lines must be undertaken to identify its cosmogonic presuppositions. Consequently, there are only slight suggestions regarding time in Hebrews' cosmogony. Nevertheless, as already shown in chapter 5, the existence of time is presupposed in Hebrews' cosmogony, although it must be recognized that its starting point cannot be affirmed (cf. 11:3),[72] and

---

68. Kittel et al., *Theological Dictionary of the New Testament*, 3:69.

69. Aristotle, *Ph.* 203.1.20–24. Freeman asserts that Anaxagoras stated that this world exists because the ὁμοιομέρειαι were mixed together. Freeman, "Anaxagoras," 65.

70. See Aristotle, *Met.* 987b.10–14; 1090a.20–24, 30–39; *Frag.* 28, 61. More information can be found in Macdonald Cornford, *Plato's Cosmology*, 57.

71. For the bibliographical support of these assertions see chapter 3, particularly subtitles "Forerunner Thoughts for First-century Cosmogonies" and the conclusion of the chapter.

72. For the argument on which this assertion is developed see chapter 6, section "Time and Creation," in this research.

consequently, Hebrews also asserts that there was not a time when time did not exist. Likewise, Hebrews presupposes that the Creator used some time in order to create, and, due to its general context, it is very likely that this time could be similar to that portrayed in Genesis 1–2.[73] In addition, even though Hebrews presupposes that the creation of everything was carried out through a process, which implies the passing of some time, the laying of its foundation is not connected to a specific time period.[74]

On the other hand, it must be recognized that in first-century cosmogonies, there were more explicit assertions regarding time. For instance, one of the more important presuppositions about time was that it had always existed, i.e., from eternity. It was the Eleatic School that posited it first, but since Ionians, Pythagoreans, Atomists, Sceptics, the Scientific Movement, and Gnosticism share the presupposition that everything came from some eternal source, it is very likely that they also believed time had always been present. Socrates may also have held this idea about time, but Plato introduced a new idea about time: he asserted that time had been created. Plato held the presupposition that there is a timeless reality without motion, and that everything, and especially time, was the moving image of the unmoving eternity.[75] Philo, Stoics, Epicureans, and Middle Platonism followed this Platonic presupposition, which ensured that time was restricted to human beings—i.e., the physical creation—and that outside of this reality there is a timeless reality. What

---

73. Since Hebrews, in almost all its cosmogonic presuppositions, is contrary to Philo, and since Philo has no literal reading of Genesis 1–2, it is possible that Hebrews interprets these chapters literally. Moreover, it is recognized that Hebrews' usage of Old Testament is typological and not allegorical, i.e., Hebrews understands the Old Testament as real history with typological implications as to its time and the future. "Jewish exegesis of the first century can be classified under four headings: literalist, midrashic, pesher, and allegorical," and all of these can be found in Hebrews. On the other hand, it must be recognized with Punt that Hebrews was clearly a "child of many worlds," since its thought—here its hermeneutic could be included—was held in common with various traditions. More information about it can be found in Punt, "Hebrews, Thought-Patterns and Context," 152; Dyer, "Epistle to the Hebrews in Recent Research," 112–22; Longenecker, *Biblical Exegesis in the Apostolic Period*, 14; Docherty, *Use of the Old Testament in Hebrews*.

74. As argued in chapters 4 and 5 of this document, the analysis of the phrase σὺ τὴν γῆν ἐθεμελίωσας (You laid the foundations of the earth) where the verb ἐθεμελίωσας (laid the foundations) implies a punctiliar *aktionsart*. The use of temporal references from the Old Testament also supports this assertion (cf. 1:10; 3:17; 5:7; 10:1; 11:30), as does its use of antediluvian histories (cf. 11:4–7).

75. Plato, *Ti.* 37–38. More information about it can be found in Von Leyden, "Time, Number, and Eternity," 35–52.

stands out is that in Hebrews there is no clear and direct assertion about the nature of time, particularly in its cosmogonic context,[76] and therefore it seems that Hebrews is not interested in what its surrounding learned society has to say about time.

The Creation

Regarding the creation itself, as already shown in chapter 6, the first assertion of Hebrews that could be considered a cosmogonic presupposition about creation itself is that it is the handiwork of the Creator—God, the supreme being—i.e., it is the result of a personal intervention of the Creator (cf. 1:2, 10). Conversely, most first-century presuppositions on cosmogony asserted that the whole realm surrounding humanity, and humanity itself, did not come into being by the action of some creator, whether personal or impersonal—i.e., the Ionians, Pythagoreans, Eleatics, Atomistics, Sceptics, the Scientific Movement, and Epicureans. Further, some first-century presuppositions on cosmogony asserted that creation is not the result of a personal intervention of some supreme being—i.e., Socrates, Plato, Aristotle, Stoics, Middle Platonism, and Philo.[77] The only

---

76. There are more than fifty temporal references in Hebrews, nevertheless, not one of them has an assertion about the nature of time. With the exception of 13:8, all the others could be labeled as some temporal reference that posits some historical event, in the past, present, or future. Even the use of the noun αἰών, as clearly asserted by Buchanan, refers to a long period of time that displays some historical event such as, "some king's rule, the rule of some nation over another, a period of war, peace, or something like that." Buchanan, *Book of Hebrews*, 58.

77. It is possible to divide all cosmogonies in the first century into two larger groups. These two groups as far as can be established were never labeled in the first century as creationism, evolutionism, theism, deism or any other category, since these are very new words. Even though the term "creationism" goes back to 1880, Darwin used the term "creationists" in his second letter written to J. D. Hooker on 5 July 1856, to describe a proponent of creationism. "Darwin Correspondence Project" https://www.darwinproject.ac.uk/letter/DCP-LETT-1919.xml. Evolutionism, meanwhile, in its basic form—i.e., evolution—has its first known use in 1616, although its use in describing a cosmogonic theory was only applied from the second half of the nineteenth century onwards. Due to the similarities in the essential presuppositions and since it could be irresponsible and unnecessary to label these different cosmogonies with new terminology, this research will categorize first-century cosmogonies using two contemporaneous words, creationism and evolutionism. So Socrates, Plato, Aristotle, Stoics, Middle Platonism, Philo, Judaism, and Christianity could be said to fall into the category of creationism. On the other hand, Ionians, Pythagoreans, Eleatics, Atomists, Skeptics, the Scientific Movement, and Epicureans posited some kind of primitive

similar assertion to Hebrews is found in Wisdom of Solomon 11:17.[78] In addition, Hebrews shows a positive view of creation, i.e., in Hebrews the creation is something valuable and worthy of care of its creator (cf. 1:1–4, 6; 2:6).[79] Socrates, meanwhile, perceived the creation as being something useful—i.e., a positive view—while Plato, Aristotle and Neo Platonism labelled it as something imperfect.[80] Apparently, following on from these assumptions, Epicureanism considered it as an entity without purpose, and Gnosticism as something negative and even deserving of destruction.[81]

On the other hand, however, Hebrews portrays the creation as an entity lacking eternity and capable of mutation, change, and elimination.[82] Interestingly, most cosmogonies present in the first century portrayed the reality—i.e., creation—as constituted by eternal matter, capable of mutation and change, but incapable of total elimination—i.e., the Ionians, Pythagoreans, Eleatics, Atomists, Socrates, Aristotle, Sceptics, the Scientific Movement, Middle Platonism, and Gnosticism. Plato, meanwhile, asserted that the creation will end in some future moment, an assumption apparently followed by Epicureanism and Philo, who, for his part,

---

evolutionism. More information about the origin of the words can be found at http://www.etymonline.com/.

78. Here it is important to remember however, that the second part of Wisdom of Solomon 11:17 is in total opposition to Hebrews' presupposition about the source of everything, since it says "For your hand, which is all powerful, and created the world out of formless matter."

79. In asserting that creation is good, Hebrews is in ful harmony with the theology of creation in the New Testament, since even though the presence of evil powers such as Satan exists in the New Testament who introduce evil into the world, the New Testament will affirm that creation is something very good (cf. Gen 1:31; Matt 10:26–33; Mark 10:1–12; Acts 7:44–50; 17:22–34; Rom 1:20; Col 1:15–16).

80. Nevertheless, it is important to recognise that Plato also supported the idea of the beauty of creation. cf. Plato, Ti. 29–30.

81. The Gnostic idea about creation is very negative which can be seen clearly in its concept of salvation, since it defines salvation as an escape from both the world and the restrictive bodily tomb. More about Gnosticism can be found in Wright, *Creation, Power and Truth: The Gospel in a World of Cultural Confusion*, 26–29.

82. The analysis of words present in 1:10–12; 8:1–2; 12:25–27 such as ἀληθινῆς (truly), ἔπηξεν (erected), ἀλλάσσειν (to change), ἑλίσσειν (to roll up), ἱμάτιον (garment), ἀλλαγήσονται (they will be changed), παλαιωθήσονται (will grow old), μετάθεσιν (removal), as was shown in chapter 5 of this research, provides a vivid image of change and stresses the frequency and contingency of creation. See Lane, *Hebrews 1–8*, 31. However, it is important to take into account what Schenck asserts in this respect that "in the Sonship of Jesus depends the destiny of the whole creation." Schenck, "Keeping His Appointment," 99–102.

asserts that even though the creation can be eliminated, it will not be, since the nature of the creator does not allow him to do so. In this respect, Philo and Hebrews seem to share a similar presupposition; nevertheless, it is more likely that Philo, Epicurus, and Plato presupposed the eternal existence of matter or something similar from which everything came into existence. Moreover, Hebrews presupposes that both heavenly and earthly things are real, created equal, with the capacity to fully achieve their purpose, but are, however, unworthy of adoration,[83] for only the Creator is worthy of it. In this presupposition Hebrews is totally distinct from Philo, Plato, and most first-century cosmogonies, since some of them held a pantheistic view on creation, while others held that there is nothing which could be considered as a superior or heavenly reality, and still others that these two realities are different in quality, nature, power, and value.[84] However, Hebrews will assert that there is no difference in value among the creations of God, that is, heavenly and earthly things have the same value in the sight of the Creator.

Another cosmogonic presupposition in Hebrews is that the whole creation of God is constituted by different creations.[85] So the realm of the human being forms part of one creation, while the whole universe is constituted by different creations of God, and this could be considered as resembling a common thought in first-century cosmogony, namely, the existence of an unlimited number of cosmoses.[86] Nonetheless, Hebrews'

83. As shown in chapter 5 of this research, the analysis of words such as ἀληθινός and ἀντίτυπος—true and copy wrongly understood as true and false (cf. 9:24), μείζονος (greater), τελειοτέρας (more perfect), οὐρανός (heaven), ἄνθρωπος (human), ἔπηξεν (erected), χειροποιήτου (handmade), ἀχειροποίητος (not made with hands), supports this assertion (cf. 8:1–2; 9:11–12, 24–26).

84. Philo for instance holds a view about creation that could be considered a sort of incipient gnostic idea, i.e., that creation has different levels of perfection; for instance, he asserted that a human being was created with a more perfect sand and not with a common one. Besides, he stated that the first human was perfect because of the creator—God—but the actual human being is not fully perfect because the human is the creation of other humans. cf. Philo, *Opif.* 137–40.

85. However, it is important to mention here that among God's creation, there are different functions, conditions, and beginnings. So for instance, humanity is part of one of God's creations, while the angels are part of another creation of God. cf. Lane, *Hebrews 1–8*, 17, 46; Guthrie, *Hebrews*, 72.

86. Nevertheless, the more common way in which the unlimited number of cosmoses was designated in first-century cosmogony was by the use of the noun κόσμος (world) in its plural form κόσμοι (worlds) which is never used in Hebrews. Therefore, it seems that the unlimited number of cosmoses is not similar to the diverse creations in Hebrews. More about the usage of the noun κόσμος can be found in Kittel et al.,

presupposition that one creation can move to other creations, i.e., that there is interaction between the different creations (cf. 13:2), and also between the creator and his creations, is very distinct from the common presuppositions in first-century cosmogonies. Only Philo, using different intermediary realities, mentioned some relationship between creations and between the Creator and his creation, but the intermediary realities are not part of Hebrews' cosmogonic presuppositions.[87] Likewise, Hebrews' cosmogonic presupposition that the purpose of creation is to serve as the habitat for humanity, as well as the place where they can meet with the Creator (cf. 1:6; 9:28; 12:28), is only partly found in first-century cosmogonies. Most first-century cosmogonies held that this world or creation serves as habitat for humanity, but none of them held that this habitat is the place where the creator and humanity meet. Likewise, Hebrews' assumption that the creation is heading to its self-destruction, and also that in the future it will abruptly be renewed by the intervention of its Creator (cf. 1:10–12; 12:25–27),[88] is partly found in first-century cosmogonies. The significant presupposition in Hebrews' cosmogony that the creation will be renewed, i.e., that God will recreate everything because sin damaged it, is, however, not found in first-century cosmogonies. Consequently, even though in Hebrews the creation is not inherently eternal, it will remain forever, not in its actual condition, but in its recreated condition (cf. 12:28), a presupposition that also is not found in first-century cosmogonies.

Finally, Hebrews' presupposition that everything that could be seen, whether spirits, cities, or humans, must be a created thing (cf. 1:7; 2:2; 11:10;

Theological Dictionary of the New Testament, 3:868–95.

87. In Philo the intermediary world or the intermediary realities are inhabited by various entities or various intermediary realities called *logos*, *sophia*, angel, humans, son, and others, and among them, as was asserted in chapter 3, the λόγος is the outstanding entity. However, even though it could be disputed, it is evident that Hebrews' cosmogony never uses some words used by Philo in reference to the intermediary realities in a similar sense. More explanations of both positons, i.e., use or non-use of intermediary realities in Hebrews, can be found in Buchanan, *To the Hebrews*; Dey, *Intermediary World*.

88. This particular Hebrews' cosmogonic presupposition—the creation will be renewed in the future—is also in harmony with the New Testament about the future reality, since it is widely known and accepted that one of the more important issues in the New Testament is the παρουσία—coming—of Jesus Christ (Matt 24:3, 27, 37, 39; 1 Cor 15:23; 1 Thess 2:19; 3:13; 4:15; 5:23; 2 Thess 2:1, 8; Jas 5:7–8; 2 Pet 3:4, 12) in a second and final moment (cf. 9:28).

12:22; 13:2), is not found in first-century cosmogonies. Consequently, on the basis of all that was stated before, the following becomes clear:

1. Hebrews' presuppositions on creation itself share more ideas with Jewish literature than other cosmogonic literature of the first century.

2. First-century cosmogonic presuppositions can be considered a plethoric mixture of thoughts, where incipient Gnosticism was present and syncretic presuppositions were in apogee, and where speculative, contemplative, and exclusive presuppositions were combined.[89]

3. Hebrews holds a new cosmogonic perspective in its time, built on coherent presuppositions mostly developed in its reading of Jewish literature, among which the Old Testament and particularly Genesis 1–3 takes a predominant place.

---

89. The first refers to presuppositions that were shaped mainly by the thoughts of pre-Socratic philosophy, in which five schools were predominant: 1) the Ionian School; 2) the Pythagoreans; 3) the Eleatics; 4) the Atomists; and 5) the Sophists. The second refers to presuppositions that were fashioned mainly on the thoughts of three personalities; they are Socrates (ca. 469–399 BCE), Plato (ca. 427–347 BCE), and Aristotle (ca. 384–322 BCE). The third refers to presuppositions that were fashioned mainly on the thoughts of six schools of thought: 1) the Stoics; 2) the Epicureans; 3) the Sceptics; 4) the Eclectics; 5) the Scientific Movement; and 6) the Philosophy of the Romans. But as already asserted, there is a kind of marked syncretism on cosmogony among the people of the first century.

8

General Conclusion

THIS LAST CHAPTER SERVES only as a summary of the full research, but will also showcase the main findings as well as some questions that arose during the process of study and that could serve as preliminary questions for future researchers.

Brief Research Summary

This research project began with the question: What are the relationships between Hebrews' cosmogonic presuppositions and its first-century philosophical context? This question was posed in chapter 1 as the main problem to be tackled in this research. Consequently, and since the focus of this research is Πρὸς Ἑβραίους—[the discourse] to the Hebrews—chapter 2 presents the introductory issues of Hebrews such as authorship, audience, and background, amongst others, focusing on their cosmogonic implications.

Since the second variable of this research is the cosmogony of the first century, chapter 3 deals with the different cosmogonies that could have been present during the time of Hebrews' composition. What was found in this chapter is that the first century was a kind of sedimentary lake of thought, where different hybrid cosmogonies were present. Presuppositions from times of cosmogonic speculation, contemplation, and exclusion, plus cosmogonic thoughts from Stoicism, Epicureanism, middle Platonism, Judaism, and even Gnosticism, were all found in the first century—however, neither in a systematic nor disjointed way, but rather in a syncretic form. The clearest and most evident instance of this is Philo. In addition, it was interesting to note that some first-century cosmogonic presuppositions show interesting similarities with cosmogonic presuppositions which are present today—of course, some differences and, in some cases, new theories altogether are in play today. For instance, chaos, eternal matter, intermediary agents, pantheism, evolutionism, theistic and deistic evolutionism, parallel universes, and even incipient presuppositions about relative and quantum theories as proposed by Hawking for the origin of the universe arguably were prefigured in first-century cosmogonies.

Chapter 4 begins the reading of Hebrews' text with the goal of determining the literary component of Hebrews' cosmogony, which was found to be constituted by twelve clauses, which in turn are constituted by 174 words, which represent eighty-six lemmas and nine morphological categories. In addition, this chapter locates these twelve clauses in Hebrews' literary structure, and also deals with their genre and figures of speech included in the clauses, as well as with their probable textual dependence. This chapter also tackles textual issues within the twelve clauses that are claimed to constitute the cosmogonic core in Hebrews. Nevertheless, the structural analysis leaves a sense of dissatisfaction, since its value for the outlining of Hebrews' cosmogony was not as expected, mainly due to the marked differences among proposals about it. Nonetheless, the genre and figures of speech analysis, as well as the analysis of the textual dependence of Hebrews' cosmogony, also shows that Hebrews' cosmogony is constituted by assertions about the Old Testament and on Genesis 1–2 mainly. Finally, the linguistic analysis of Hebrews' cosmogony shows that small changes in the Greek text on which the interpretation is based will inevitably bring the greatest influences in the interpretation of the text. Fortunately, in the twelve identified key-sections—see chapter 4 section "Exclusion in Microstructures"—there was only one textual issue—see chapter 4, "Textual Issues of Hebrews Cosmogony"—i.e., only one instance in which the Greek Hebrews' text was changed with respect to the text present in the NA^{28}.

Chapter 5, meanwhile, analyzes the clauses present in Hebrews' cosmogony with special emphasis on its literary component. It could be considered the main chapter in this research, since it provides the foundational analysis of the Greek text upon which interpretation has been established, so it provides syntactic, semantic, and contextual insights on clauses and independent words of Hebrews' cosmogony. The achievements of this chapter are diverse, and do not need to be summarized; nevertheless, the influence of its conclusions can be seen not only in chapter 6 and 7 but also in preceding chapters, particularly in chapter 4.

From chapter 6 onwards, this research begins to present conclusions that answer the primary question of this research. Chapter 6 attempted to illuminate Hebrews' cosmogony and, in order to make it more comprehensible, it divides the topic into three main sections. The first section concerns the identity of the Creator as well as his attributes and purposes. The second section focuses on the procedure used to create, i.e., it displays the actions, methods, and sources which, according to Hebrews, were used by the Creator, as well as the role of time in this process. The third section deals with the creation itself and shows its nature in Hebrews, as well as its content, development and destiny. The most important achievement of this chapter is that even though Hebrews appears not to have much to say about cosmogony, its arguments have profound cosmogonic presuppositions. So for instance, it seems that if Hebrews does not first declare υἱός as the Creator, its Christology could lose its main basis.

Chapter 7, then, gathers together Hebrews' cosmogonic presuppositions and the first-century's cosmogonies in order to judge the relationship between them—i.e., to fulfill the main purpose of this research. Consequently, this chapter presents four sections in which different elements and thoughts are compared—i.e., between the cosmogony of Hebrews and the cosmogony of first-century philosophy. The first section compares the literary component of Hebrews' cosmogony, namely the verbs, nouns, and adjectives that are mostly used in the cosmogonic content in Hebrews and in the first century. The second section deals with the presupposition present in Hebrews and in first-century philosophy about the creator. The third section deals with the procedure used by the creator in order to create, and the last section deals with the presupposition about the creation itself. What was found in this chapter is that Hebrews presents a different cosmogony: even though some ideas can be found in both Hebrews and in some first-century literature, the final product—i.e., Hebrews' cosmogony—is different to the other cosmogonies present in the first century.

Main Research Findings

The first finding of this research was that there is a gap in the spectrum of knowledge produced on the epistle to the Hebrews. Hebrews has been studied for different reasons and different scholars tackled diverse issues; however, its cosmogony was mostly ignored. Although its cosmology, Christology, hermeneutics, structure, genre, dependence, background of thought, and other topics, were in some cases studied in depth—and in others scarcely touched—its cosmogony was regarded as less important in its content. This was the first main finding of this research and it was addressed in chapter 1. Consequently, this research tries to fill part of this gap and therefore tries to answer the primary question, which was divided into six secondary questions: (1) Does the comprehension of introductory questions about Hebrews influence the understanding of its cosmogony? (2) What are the cosmogonic presuppositions and literary content present in first-century philosophy? (3) What is the cosmogonic literary component of Hebrews? (4) What are the grammatical features that can assist in extracting the cosmogonic presuppositions in Hebrews? (5) What are the cosmogonic presuppositions in Hebrews? (6) What are the similarities and differences between the cosmogonic presuppositions in Hebrews and first-century philosophy? The main findings of this research answer these secondary questions, which collectively address the primary question.

The main finding in chapter 2 is that there is not consensus among scholars regarding Hebrews' introductory issues such as authorship, audience, background of thought, genre, and even date—not today nor in the past. But the main assertion to be deduced from this chapter is that the theories regarding the introductory issues of Hebrews will greatly affect the understanding of its cosmogony—and perhaps other topics too. Consequently, in order to achieve a better comprehension of Hebrews' cosmogony, this research chooses to concentrate its study on the text of Hebrews rather than on other issues that could influence its interpretation—i.e., a textually-focused study allows for dedicated attention to Hebrews' text and not to its relationship to a particular tradition or stream of thought about its author. Nevertheless, the text's historical context cannot be avoided altogether, and therefore this research was influenced by the assumption that Hebrews was written before the fall of Jerusalem (70 CE) but after the beginning of the second half of the first century. From chapter 3, meanwhile, it can be asserted that the first century was characterized by different cosmogonies, since the syncretic thought of different schools, such as Platonic or Ionians for instance, gave rise to a combination of assertions and therefore positing new cosmogonies was the custom of the time. Nevertheless, the terminology and more central cosmogonic thoughts in the first century were widely known since deliberation on this topic was rampant at the time.

Likewise, the most important finding of chapter 4 was the identification of the literary component of Hebrews' cosmogony—i.e., the cosmogonic content of Hebrews. It identified twelve key-sections with twelve key-clauses, which are mainly quotations, allusions, or some kind of echoes of some text of the Old Testament. This chapter displays another important methodological issue, i.e., the development of a methodology that allows the discovery of a document's position on topics other than its main topic. In the subsequent chapter—i.e., chapter 5—the grammatical analysis of the literary component of Hebrews' cosmogony allows one to make some important assertions.

1. Words such as ἀληθινός, ἀντίτυπος, ῥῆμα, καταρτίζω, amongst other verbs, nouns, and adjectives, seem to hold a special connotation in Hebrews' cosmogony.

2. Most of the words seem to portray a meaning that is some kind of reflection of the Hebrew and Greek text of the Scriptures of Israel.

3. It seems that in Hebrews' text there is an intentional avoidance of usage of words with heavy cosmogonic semantics in the first century.

4. The syntax of some key clauses in Hebrews' cosmogony is carefully elaborated in order to portray a special meaning.

5. The meaning of the noun αἰών in Hebrews' cosmogony is impossible to determine by a grammatical analysis. It is important to remember in this respect that the grammatical analysis is constituted by at least four different analyses: the analysis of the functions of the words, and of the morphology, lexicology, and syntax of the words.

Chapter 6, meanwhile, shows the cosmogonic presuppositions present in Hebrews, and since it is redundant to repeat was has already been asserted, here it will suffice to confirm that it is shown in the conclusion of chapter 6. And finally, chapter 7 of this research shows that Hebrews' cosmogony is a new cosmogonic perspective in its time; however, it must be highlighted that it cannot be considered just one more cosmogony among the other syncretic cosmogonies of its time, since the main feature among the others is that they share vocabulary and thought. Hebrews' cosmogonic presuppositions, however, show novelty in vocabulary and thought, which seem to be built on its reading and interpretation of the Old Testament, particularly Genesis 1–2, and possibly of reality.

Finally, since the primary question of this research reads as follows: "What are the relationships between Hebrews' cosmogonic presuppositions and its first-century philosophical context?" this research allows one to answer it by asserting that there is no relationship of dependence in presuppositions but only in the usage of some general vocabulary. However, this relationship is not antagonistic or confrontational, since Hebrews seems not to try to correct these other cosmogonies but only presents its particular and coherent point of view.

Future Research Questions

All research answers one or more questions, and in some cases it raises more questions, as is the case with this research. From chapter 1 to this last chapter there are diverse issues that can be addressed in other research which intends to examine Hebrews' text. So for instance, it could be interesting to consider the relationship between Hebrews and its assertion about the temple made without hands (cf. 9:11) and with the declaration which says "We heard Him say, 'I will destroy this temple made with hands, and within three days I will build another made without hands'" (Mark 14:58 NKJV). So a lot of deep intertextual research between Hebrews and other New Testament writings can be performed—a field which seems a bit neglected—as well as with Old Testament writings, and other documents present in the first century.

However, it could be more interesting to study the importance of Hebrews' cosmogony in relation to other more prominent topics of its content, for example, the relationship of Hebrews' cosmogony with its eschatology or its Christology. Likewise, the soteriology of Hebrews, which basically asserts "the removal of sin" (cf. 9:26, LEB) could be compared to its cosmogony to see if Hebrews holds the view of a sinless creation at the beginning, a topic that due to time and space was neglected in this research. Linguistic studies could also be very promising, since, for instance, the use of tenses and prepositions seems to follow an interesting pattern in Hebrews. Finally, it could be interesting to do some kind of study in which an evaluation of how the view on some introductory issue, such as authorship for instance, can influence its interpretation. This kind of study would need to compare two different possibilities of authorship in relation to the interpretation of one determined topic.

One thing is undeniable about Hebrews: it is a spring of seminal thoughts which, in its process of expanding, became a renewed spring of novel seminal thoughts; that is to say, it is a fount that never stops giving.

Bibliography

Adams, Edward. *Constructing the World: A Study in Paul's Cosmological Language.* Edinburgh: T. & T. Clark, 2000.
Adamson, Peter. "98—For a Limited Time Only: John Philoponus." *History of Philosophy without Any Gaps* (podcast), October 14, 2012. https://historyofphilosophy.net/philoponus.
Adamson, Robert. *The Development of Greek Philosophy.* Edited by R. P. Hardie and W. R. Sorley. Edinburgh: Blackwood, 1908.
Adan-Bayewitz, David, et al. "Preferential Distribution of Lamps from the Jerusalem Area in the Late Second Temple Period (Late First Century B.C.E.–70 C.E.)." *BASOR* 350 (2008) 37–86.
Aland, Barbara, et al., eds. *Greek Bible Text From: Novum Testamentum Graece.* Stuttgart: Deutsche Bibelstiftung, 2012.
Aland, Barbara, et al., eds. *The Greek New Testament: Apparatus.* Stuttgart: Deutsche Bibelgesellschaft; American Bible Society; United Bible Societies, 2014.
Alden, Robert L. *Job.* Vol. 11. 42 vols. The New American Commentary. Edited by E. Ray Clendenen. Nashville, TN: Broadman & Holman, 1993.
Alford, Henry. *Alford's Greek Testament: An Exegetical and Critical Commentary.* Vol. 4. 4 vols in 6. 7th ed. Grand Rapids, MI: Guardian, 1976.
Allen, David Lewis. *Hebrews.* New American Commentary 35. Nashville, TN: B & H Group, 2010.
Allen, R. Michael. "The Visibility of the Invisible God." *JRThe* 9.3 (2015) 249–69.
Alon, Ilai. "Socrates in Arabic Philosophy." In *A Companion to Socrates,* edited by Sara Ahbel-Rappe and Rachana Kamtekar, 317–26. Malden, MA: Blackwell, 2006.
Anderson, John E. "Creation." In *The Lexham Bible Dictionary,* edited by John D. Barry et al., np. Bellingham, WA: Lexham, 2016. Logos edition.
Apuleius, et al. *The Works of Apuleius: A New Translation Comprising the Metamorphoses, or Golden Ass, the God of Socrates, the Florida, and His Defence, or a Discourse of Magic.* Translated by Thomas Taylor. London: Bell, 1914.
Archer, Gleason L. *Encyclopedia of Bible Difficulties.* Grand Rapids, MI: Zondervan, 1982.
Arndt, William, et al., eds. *A Greek-English Lexicon of the New Testament and Other Early Christian Literature.* Chicago, IL: University of Chicago Press, 2000.
Attridge, Harold W. *The Epistle to the Hebrews: A Commentary on the Epistle to the Hebrews.* Hermeneia: New Testament 21. Edited by Helmut Koester. Philadelphia: Augsburg Fortress, 1989.

———. "Paraenesis in a Homily (Λόγος Παρακλήσεως): The Possible Location of, and Socialization in, the 'Epistle to the Hebrews.'" *Semeia* 50 (1990) 210–26.
Attridge, Harold W., et al. *Semeia*. Vol. 14, *Apocalypse: The Morphology of a Genre*. Edited by John Joseph Collins. Missoula, MT: SBL, 1979.
Aune, David E., et al. *Semeia*. Vol. 36, *Early Christian Apocalypticism: Genre Social Setting*. Edited by Adela Yarbro Collins. Decatur, GA: SBL, 1986.
Bacon, B. W. "Heb 1, 10–12 and the Septuagint Rendering of Ps 102, 23." *ZNW* 3 (1902) 280–85.
Balz, Horst Robert, and Gerhard Schneider, eds. *Exegetical Dictionary of the New Testament*. 3 vols. Grand Rapids, MI: Eerdmans, 1990.
Barclay, William. *The Letter to the Hebrews: Revised Edition*. Louisville, KY: Westminster John Knox, 1976.
Barrett, Frank J., and Suresh Srivastval. "History as a Mode of Inquiry in Organizational Life: A Role for Human Cosmogony." *Hum. Rel.* 44.3 (1991) 231–54.
Bartley, James, et al., eds. *Nuevo Comentario Bíblico: Siglo Veintiuno*. El Paso, TX: Casa Bautista de Publicaciones, 1999.
Bateman, Herbert W. *Charts on the Book of Hebrews*. Grand Rapids, MI: Kregel, 2012.
Benton, Christopher P. "An Introduction to the Sefer Yetzirah," The Maqon Journal for Studies in Rabbinic Literature, Past Maqom Journal Articles, no 27., 1. http://www.maqom.com/journal.html
Berkhof, L. *Principles of Biblical Interpretation*. Grand Rapids, MI: Baker, 1950.
Bigg, Charles. *A Critical and Exegetical Commentary on the Epistles of St. Peter and St. Jude*. International Critical Commentary on the Holy Scriptures of the Old and New Testaments. Edinburgh: T. & T. Clark International, 1901.
Bitter, R. A. "Review of 'Helleen M. Keizer, Life-Time-Entirety. A Study of Αιων in Greek Literature and Philosophy, the Septuagint and Philo. Diss. Univ. V. Amsterdam 1999." *Mnemosyne* 55.2 (2002) 237–40.
Blundell, Sue. *The Origins of Civilization in Greek & Roman Thought*. London: Croom Helm, 1986.
Bohnsack, Ralf, et al., eds. *Qualitative Analysis and Documentary Method: In International Educational Research*. Germany: Barbara Budrich-Esser, 2010.
Bolen, Todd. "Where Did the Possessed-Pigs Drown?" In *Lexham Geographic Commentary on the Gospels*, edited by Barry J. Beitzel and Kristopher A. Lyle, 194–218. Bellingham, WA: Lexham, 2016. Logos edition.
Bolle, Kees W. "Cosmology: And Overview." In *Encyclopedia of Religion*, edited by Lindsay Jones, 3:1991–98. Farmington Hills, MI: Thomson Gale, 2005.
Bornhäuser, D. *Empfänger Und Verfasser Des Briefes an Die Hebräer*. Gütersloh: Bertelsmann, 1932.
Brakke, David. *The Gnostics: Myth, Ritual, and Diversity in Early Christianity*. Cambridge, MA: Harvard University Press, 2010.
Brannan, Rick. *Greek Apocryphal Gospels, Fragments and Agrapha: Texts and Transcriptions*. Bellingham, WA: Lexham, 2013.
———, ed. *The Lexham Analytical Lexicon to the Greek New Testament*. Bellingham, WA: Lexham, 2012.
Brannan, Rick, et al., eds. *The Lexham English Septuagint*. Bellingham, WA: Lexham, 2012.
Brickhouse, Thomas, and Nicholas D. Smith. *Plato (427—347 Bce)*. Internet Encyclopedia of Philosophy. Edited by James Fieser and Bradley Dowden. Martin, TN: The University of Tennessee at Martin, 1995.

Brown, J. Vallance. "The Authorship and Circumstances of 'Hebrews'—Again!" *BSac* 80.320 (1923) 505–38.
Brown, Raymond E., and John P. Meier. *Antioch and Rome: New Testament Cradles of Catholic Christianity*. New York: Paulist, 1983.
Bruce, F. F. *The Epistle to the Hebrews*. Rev. ed. New International Commentary on the New Testament. Grand Rapids, MI: Eerdmans, 1990.
———. *New Testament History*. New York: Doubleday Religious Group, 1983.
Buchanan, George Wesley. *The Book of Hebrews: Its Challenge from Zion*. Intertextal Bible Commentary. Eugene, OR: Wipf & Stock, 2006.
———. *To the Hebrews*. The Anchor Bible 36. Garden City, NY: Doubleday, 1972.
Bullinger, Ethelbert William. *Figures of Speech Used in the Bible*. London: Eyre & Spottiswoode, 1898.
Bultmann, Alexander. *A Grammar of the New Testament Greek*. Andover, MA: Draper, 1891.
Bultmann, Rudolf K. "Is Exegesis without Presuppositions Possible? [1957]." In *Existence and Faith: Shorter Writings of Rudolf Bultmann*, edited and translated by Schubert M. Ogden, 289–96. Cleveland, OH: The World Company, 1960.
Burrell, David B., et al., eds. *Creation and the God of Abraham*. Leiden: Cambridge University Press, 2010.
Burton, Keith Augustus. "The Faith Factor: New Testament Cosmology in Its Historical Context." *JATS* 15.1 (2004) 34–46.
Campbell, Constantine R. *Basics of Verbal Aspect in Biblical Greek*. Grand Rapids, MI: Zondervan, 2008.
———. *Colossians and Philemon: A Handbook on Greek Text*. Baylor Handbook on the Greek New Testament. Waco, TX: Baylor University Press, 2013.
Canale, Fernando L. "Toward a Criticism of Theological Reason: Time and Timelessness as Primordial Presuppositions." PhD diss., Andrews University, 1983.
Carr, Edwin Stutely. "Greek Elements in Modern Religious Thought." *BSac* 53.209 (1896) 117–32.
Casiday, Augustine. "Platonism." In *Cambridge Dictionary of Christian Theology*, edited by Karen Kilby et al., 391–92. Cambridge: Cambridge University Press, 2011.
Chapman, Benjamin. *New Testament Greek Notebook*. Grand Rapids, MI: Baker, 1978.
Chapman, Benjamin, and Gary Steven Shogren. *Greek New Testament Insert*. 2nd revised ed. Quakertown, PA: Stylus, 1994.
Charles, Robert Henry, ed. *Pseudepigrapha of the Old Testament*. 2 vols. Oxford: Clarendon, 1913.
Childs, Brevard S. *The New Testament as Canon : An Introduction*. 1st Fortress Press ed. Philadelphia: Fortress, 1985.
Clarkson, M. E. "The Antecedents of the High Priest Theme in Hebrews." *AThR* 29 (1947) 89–95.
Cockerill, Gareth Lee. *The Epistle to the Hebrews*. The New International Commentary on the New Testament. Grand Rapids, MI: Eerdmans, 2012.
Cohen, S. Marc. "Plato's Cosmology: The Timaeus." https://faculty.washington.edu/smcohen/320/timaeus.htm.
Collins, John J. *The Apocalyptic Imagination: An Introduction to Jewish Apocalyptic Literature*. 2nd ed. The Biblical Resource Series. Grand Rapids, MI: Eerdmans, 1998.
Comfort, Philip. *Encountering the Manuscripts: An Introduction to New Testament Paleography & Textual Criticism*. Nashville, TN: Broadman & Holman, 2005.

Copan, Paul, and William Lane Craig. *Creation Out of Nothing: A Biblical, Philosophical, and Scientific Exploration*. Grand Rapids, MI: Baker, 2004.

Correa, S. Teófilo. "Intertextualidad y Exégesis Intra-Bíblica: ¿Dos Caras de la Misma Moneda? Breve Análisis de las Presuposiciones Metodológicas." *DavarLogos* 5.1 (2006) 1–13.

Cortez, Felix H. "Creation in Hebrews." *AUSS* 53.2 (2015) 279–320.

———. "Jesus as 'Son' of God: The Perspective of Hebrews." In *The End from the Beginning: Festschrift Honoring Merling Alomía*, edited by Benjamin Rojas et al., 471–86. Lima: Fondo Editorial Universidad Peruana Unión, 2015.

Costache, Adrian. *Gadamer and the Question of Understanding: Between Heidegger and Derrida*. Lanham, MD: Lexington, 2016.

Cotterell, Peter. "Review of Linguistics for Students of New Testament Greek by David Alan Black." *Them* 16.3 (1991) 28.

Cross, F. L., and Elizabeth A. Livingstone, eds. *The Oxford Dictionary of the Christian Church*. Oxford: Oxford University Press, 2005.

Davis, Paul K. *100 Decisive Battles: From Ancient Times to the Present*. New York: Oxford University Press, 1999.

Delitzsch, Franz. *Commentary on the Epistle to the Hebrews*. Translated by Thomas L. Kingsbury. 2 vols. Clark's Foreign Theological Library. Edinburgh: T. & T. Clark, 1874.

Dellutri, Salvador, and Ezequiel Dellutri. *La Aventura del Pensamiento: una Introducción al Fascinante Mundo de la Filosofía Occidental*. Miami: Editorial Unilit, 2002.

deSilva, David A. "Hebrews." In *The Bible Knowledge Background Commentary: John's Gospel, Hebrews–Revelation*, edited by Craig A. Evans and Craig A. Bubeck, 199–256. Colorado Springs, CO: Cook, 2005.

———. *An Introduction to the New Testament: Contexts, Methods and Ministry Formation*. Downers Grove, IL: InterVarsity, 2004.

———. *Perseverance in Gratitude: A Socio-Rhetorical Commentary on the Epistle "to the Hebrews."* Grand Rapids, MI: Eerdmans, 2000.

Dewey, Joanna, and Mark Allan Powell, "Truth." In *The HarperCollins Bible Dictionary*, edited by Mark Allan Powell, 1072–73. New York: HarperCollins, 2011.

Dey, Lala Kalyan Kumar. *The Intermediary World and Patterns of Perfection in Philo and Hebrews*. Dissertation Series No 25. Missoula, MT: SBL, 1975.

Docherty, Susan E. *The Use of the Old Testament in Hebrews: A Case Study in Early Jewish Bible Interpretation*. Wissenschaftliche Untersuchungen Zum Neuen Testament 2. Reihe 260. Tübingen: Mohr Siebeck, 2009.

Durkheim, Emile. *The Elementary Forms of the Religious Life*. Translated by Karen E. Fields. New York: The Free, 1995.

Dyer, Bryan R. "The Epistle to the Hebrews in Recent Research: Studies on the Author's Identity, His Use of the Old Testament, and Theology." *JGRChJ* 9 (2013) 104–31.

Ellingworth, Paul. *The Epistle to the Hebrews: A Commentary on the Greek Text*. New International Greek Testament Commentary. Edited by I. Howard Marshall and Donald A. Hagner. Grand Rapids, MI: Eerdmans, 1993.

Ellingworth, Paul, and Eugene Albert Nida. *A Handbook on the Letter to the Hebrews*. UBS Handbook Series. New York: United Bible Societies, 1994.

Ellis, E. Earle. "How the New Testament Uses the Old." In *New Testament Interpretation: Essays on Principles and Methods*, edited by I. Howard Marshall, 198–214. Milton Keynes, UK: Paternoster, 1979.

Erler, Michael. "Epicurus." In *The Oxford Encyclopedia of Ancient Greece and Rome*, edited by M. Gagarin and E. Fantham, 1:84–91. New York: Oxford University Press, 2010.
Evans, Craig A. *NT307 Archaeology and the New Testament*. Logos Mobile Education. Bellingham, WA: Lexham, 2014.
Ferguson, Everett. *Backgrounds of Early Christianity*. 3rd ed. Grand Rapids, MI: Eerdmans, 2003.
Filtvedt, Ole Jakob. "Creation and Salvation in Hebrews." *ZNW* 106.2 (2015) 280–303.
Fitzgerald, John T. "Cosmologies of the Ancient Mediterranean World." *IDS* 47.2 (2013) 1–7.
Flink, Timo. "Reconsidering the Text of Jude 5, 13, 15 and 18." *EFN* 20.39–40 (2007) 95–125.
Flusser, David. *Judaism of the Second Temple Period*. Translated by Azzan Yadin-Israel. Grand Rapids, MI: Eerdmans, 2007.
Forbes, J. T. *Socrates*. Edinburgh: T. & T. Clark, 1905.
Frazer, James George. *Creation and Evolution in Primitive Cosmogonies, and Other Pieces*. London: Dawsons, 1968.
Freeman, Kathleen. "Anaxagoras." *GR* 4.11 (1935) 65–75.
Friedman, Daniel. *The Genesis One Code*. New York: Park East, 2011.
Furley, David. "Cosmology." In *The Cambridge History of Hellenistic Philosophy*, edited by Keimpe Algra et al., 412–51. Cambridge: Cambridge University Press, 1999.
Gadamer, Hans-Georg. *Truth and Method*. Translated by Joel Weinsheimer and Donald G. Marshall. 2nd rev. ed. Bloomsbury Revelations. London: Bloomsbury, 2013.
Gaster, Moses. *The Samaritans: Their History, Doctrines and Literature*. Scheweich Lectures. London: Oxford Univeristy Press, 1925.
Gauli, Bardo M. "Cosmology and Natural Philosophy." In *Brill's Companion to Seneca: Philosopher and Dramatist*, edited by Andreas Heil and Gregor Damschen, 363–78. The Netherlands: Koninklijke Brill NV, 2013.
Geisler, Norman L. *Baker Encyclopedia of Christian Apologetics*. Baker Reference Library. Grand Rapids, MI: Baker, 1999.
Gilbert, George Holley. "The Greek Element in the Epistle to the Hebrews." *AmJT* 14.4 (1910) 521–32.
Gilbert, R. T. Foreword to *The Book of Formation, or Sepher Yetzirah Attributed to Rabbi Akiba Ben Joseph*, by Knut Stenring. v–xv. Berwick, ME: Nicolas-Hays, 2004.
Goddard, Angela. *The Language of Advertising: Written Texts*. Intertext Series. New York: Routledge, 2002.
Goldberg, Louis. "Angel of the Lord." In *Evangelical Dictionary of Biblical Theology*, edited by Walter A. Elwell, 23–24. Grand Rapids, MI: Baker, 1996.
Gowler, David B. "Socio-Rhetorical Interpretation: Textures of a Text and Its Reception." *JSNT* 33.2 (2010) 191–206.
Grabbe, Lester L. "The Hellenistic City of Jerusalem." In *Jews in the Hellenistic and Roman Cities*, edited by John R. Bartlett, 6–21. London: Routledge, Taylor & Francis Group, 2002.
———. "Jewish History: Roman Period." In *Dictionary of New Testament Background: A Compendium of Contemporary Biblical Scholarship*, edited by Craig A. Evans and Stanley E. Porter, 576–80. Downers Grove, IL: InterVarsity, 2000.
———. *Wisdom of Solomon*. London: T. & T. Clark, 1997.

Greenlee, J. Harold. *An Exegetical Summary of Hebrews*. 2nd ed. Dallas: SIL International, 2008.

Greenwood, Kyle. *Scripture and Cosmology: Reading the Bible between the Ancient World and Modern Science*. Downers Grove, IL: InterVarsity, 2015.

Gregory, Andrew. *Ancient Greek Cosmogony*. London: Duckworth, 2008.

Gregory, T. "Union." In *A Dictionary of Christ and the Gospels*, edited by James Hastings, 779–80. Edinburgh: T. & T. Clark, 1942.

Grelot, Pierre. *Une Lecture de L'épître aux Hébreux*. Lire La Bible 132. Paris: Éditions du Cerf, 2003.

Greshko, Michael, and National Geographic Staff. "Origins of the Universe." http://www.nationalgeographic.com/science/space/universe/origins-of-the-universe.

Gromacki, Gary R. "Genesis, Geology and the Grand Canyon." *JMT* 12.2 (2008) 26–68.

Gugliotto, Lee J. *Handbook for Bible Study: A Guide to Understanding, Teaching, and Preaching the Word of God*. Hagerstown, MD: Review and Herald Association, 2000.

Gulley, Norman R. "Basic Issues between Science and Scripture: Theological Implications of Alternative Models and the Necessary Basis for the Sabbath in Genesis 1–2." *JATS* 14.1 (2003) 195–229.

———. *Systematic Theology: Prolegomena*. Berrien Springs, MI: Andrews University Press, 2003.

Guthrie, Donald. *The Letter to the Hebrews : An Introduction and Commentary*. Tyndale New Testament Commentaries 15. Downers Grove, IL: InterVarsity, 1983.

———. *New Testament Introduction*. 4th ed. Downers Grove, IL: InterVarsity, 1996.

Guthrie, George H. "Hebrews." In *Commentary on the New Testament Use of the Old Testament*, edited by G. K. Beale and D. A. Carson, 919–93. Grand Rapids, MI: Baker, 2007.

———. *Hebrews*. The NIV Application Commentary. Grand Rapids, MI: Zondervan, 1998.

———. "Hebrews in Its First-Century Context: Recent Research." In *The Face of New Testament Studies: A Survey of Recent Research*, edited by Scot McKnight and Grant R. Osborne, 414–43. Grand Rapids, MI: Baker, 2004.

———. "Hebrews' Use of the Old Testament: Recent Trends in Research." *CurBR* 1.2 (2003) 271–94.

———. *The Structure of Hebrews: A Text-Linguistic Analysis*. Supplements to Novum Testamentum 73. Leiden: Brill, 1994.

Guthrie, George H., and J. Scott Duvall. *Biblical Greek Exegesis: A Graded Approach to Learning Intermediate and Advanced Greek*. Grand Rapids, MI: Zondervan, 1998.

Häberl, Charles G. "Iranian Scripts for Aramaic Languages: The Origin of the Mandaic Script." *BASOR* 341 (2006) 53–62.

Hacking, Philip H. *Opening up Hebrews*. Leominster: Day One, 2006.

Hagner, Donald Alfred. *Hebrews*. Understanding the Bible Commentary Series. Grand Rapids, MI: Baker, 2011.

———. *New Testament Exegesis and Research: A Guide for Seminarians*. Pasadena, CA: Fuller Seminary Press, 1999.

Hahm, David E. *The Origins of Stoic Cosmology*. Columbus: Ohio State University Press, 1977.

Harris, Murray J. *Prepositions and Theology in the Greek New Testament: An Essential Reference Resource for Exegesis*. Grand Rapids, MI: Zondervan, 2012.

Harrison, R. K., et al. *Biblical Criticism: Historical, Literary and Textual*. Grand Rapids, MI: Zondervan, 1978.

Hartnett, John G. "A Biblical Creationist Cosmogony." *ARJ* 8 (2015) 13–20.

Heidegger, Martin. *Being and Time: A Translation of Sein Und Zeit*. Translated by Joan Stambaugh. Albany, NY: State University of New York Press, 1996.

Heiser, Michael S., and Vincent M. Setterholm. *Glossary of Morpho-Syntactic Database Terminology*. Bellingham, WA: Lexham, 2013.

Helmbold, Andrew K. *The Nag Hammadi Gnostic Texts and the Bible*. Grand Rapids, MI: Baker, 1967.

Hengel, Martin. *Judaism and Hellenism: Studies in Their Encounter in Palestine During the Early Hellenistic Period*. 2 vols. London: SCM, 2003.

Henry, Carl F. H. *God, Revelation, and Authority: God Who Speaks and Shows*. 6 vols. Wheaton, IL: Crossway, 1999.

Herrera, Yoshiko M., and Bear F. Braumoeller. "Symposium: Discourse and Content Analysis." *QMMR* 2.1 (2004) 15–39.

Hetherington, Norriss S., ed. *Encyclopedia of Cosmology: Historical, Philosophical, and Scientific Foundations of Modern Cosmology*. Routledge Revivals. New York: Garland, 1993.

Hewitt, Thomas. *The Epistle to the Hebrews, an Introduction and Commentary*. 1st ed. The Tyndale New Testament Commentaries. Grand Rapids, MI: Eerdmans, 1960.

Holmes, Michael W., ed. *The Greek New Testament: SBL Edition*. Atlanta, GA; Bellingham, WA: SBL, 2011–13.

Hoogendyk, Isaiah, ed. *The Lexham Analytical Lexicon to the Septuagint*. Bellingham, WA: Lexham, 2014.

Hooks, Stephen M. *Job*. The College Press NIV Commentary. Joplin, MO: College Press, 2006.

Horwitz, Jonathan. *A Defence of the Cosmogony of Moses*. Baltimore, MD: Matchett, 1838.

Hsieh, Hsiu-Fang, and Sarah E. Shannon. "Three Approaches to Qualitative Content Analysis." *QHR* 15.9 (2005) 1277–88.

Hubler, James Noel. "Creatio Ex Nihilo: Matter, Creation, and the Body in Classical and Christian Philosophy through Aquinas." PhD diss., University of Pennsylvania, 1995.

Huffman, Carl. "Pythagoras." In *The Stanford Encyclopedia of Philosophy*, edited by Edward N. Zalta, n.p. https://plato.stanford.edu/entries/pythagoras/.

Hughes, David W. "Cosmogony (the Origin of Planetary Systems) and the Case for Teaching It at University." *Eur. J. Phys.* 24 (2003) 221–29.

Hughes, Philip Edgcumbe. *A Commentary on the Epistle to the Hebrews*. Grand Rapids, MI: Eerdmans, 1977.

Hurst, L. David. *The Epistle to the Hebrews: Its Background of Thought*. Vol. 65. Society for New Testament Studies: Monograph Series. Edited by Graham N. Stanton. Cambridge: Cambridge University Press, 1990.

Ingalese, Richard, and Isabella Ingalese. *Cosmogony and Evolution*. 1907. Reprint, Kila, MT: Kessinger, 1996.

Jackson, Jeffrey G., and Rick Brannan, eds. *New Testament Use of the Old Testament*. Bellingham, WA: Faithlife, 2015.

Janko, Richard. "Socrates the Freethinker " In *A Companion to Socrates*, edited by Sara Ahbel-Rappe and Rachana Kamtekar, 48–62. Blackwell Companions to Philosophy 34. Malden, MA: Blackwell, 2006.

Jensen, Richard A. *Envisioning the Word: The Use of Visual Images in Preaching*. Minneapolis, MN: Fortress, 2005.
Johnson, Luke Timothy. *Hebrews: A Commentary*. Louisville, KY: Westminster John Knox, 2006.
Johnson, Luke Timothy, and Todd C. Penner. *The Writings of the New Testament: An Interpretation*. Rev ed. Minneapolis, MN: SCM, 1999.
Josephus, Flavius, and Benedikt Niese. *Flavii Iosephi Opera Recognovit Benedictvs Niese*. Berolini: Apvd Weidmannos, 1888.
Jupp, Victor, ed. *The Sage Dictionary of Social Research Methods*. California: SAGE, 2006.
Kantenwein, Lee L. *Diagrammatical Analysis*. Bellingham, WA: Logos Research Systems, 2003.
Kaplan, Aryeh. *Sefer Yetzirah: The Book of Creation in Theory and Practice*. Rev. ed. York Beach, ME: Red Wheel Weiser, 1997.
Karleen, Paul S. *The Handbook to Bible Study: With a Guide to the Scofield Study System*. New York: Oxford University Press, 1987.
Käsemann, Ernst. *The Wandering People of God: An Investigation of the Letter to the Hebrews*. Minneapolis, MN: Augsburg, 1984.
Keizer, Heleen M. "Life-Time-Entirety: A Study of Aion in Greek Literature and Philosophy, the Septuagint and Philo." PhD diss., University of Amsterdam, 1999.
Ken, Penner, and Michael S. Heiser, eds. *Old Testament Greek Pseudepigrapha with Morphology: Alternate Texts*. Bellingham, WA: Logos Bible Software, 2008.
Ketter, Peter. *Hebräerbrief, Jakobusbrief, Petrusbrief, Judasbrief*. Freiburg im Breisgau: Herder, 1950.
Kidner, Derek. *Genesis: An Introduction and Commentary*. Tyndale Old Testament Commentaries 1. Edited by Donald J. Wiseman. Downers Grove, IL: InterVarsity, 1967.
Kim, Youngmin. "Cosmogony as Political Philosophy." *PEW* 58.1 (2008) 108–25.
Kistemaker, Simon J. *Exposición de la Epístola a los Hebreos*. Translated by Norberto E. Wolf. Comentario al Nuevo Testamento. Grand Rapids, MI: Libros Desafío, 1991.
———. *Exposition of the Epistle to the Hebrews*. Moffatt New Testament Commentary. Welwyn: Evangelical, 1984.
Kittel, Gerhard, et al., eds. *Theological Dictionary of the New Testament*. 10 vols. Grand Rapids, MI: Eerdmans, 1964.
Klauck, Hans-Josef. *The Religious Context of Early Christianity: A Guide to Graeco-Roman Religions*. Translated by Brian McNeil. Studies of the New Testament and Its World. Edited by John Barclay et al. Edinburgh: T. & T. Clark, 2003.
Koester, Craig R. *Hebrews: A New Translation with Introduction and Commentary*. The Anchor Bible 36. New Haven, CT: Yale University Press, 2001.
Kohler, Kaufmann, and Louis Ginzberg. "Yeẓirah, Sefer." In *The Jewish Encyclopedia*, edited by Isidore Singer, 12:602–9. 12 vols. London: Funk & Wagnalls, 1906.
Krebs, Robert E., and Carolyn A. Krebs. *Groundbreaking Scientific Experiments, Inventions, and Discoveries of the Ancient World*. Groundbreaking Scientific Experiments, Inventions, and Discoveries through the Ages. London: Greenwood, 2003.
Küçükoğlu, Hülya. "Improving Reading Skills through Effective Reading Strategies." *PSBS* 70 (2013) 709–14.
Ladd, George E. *The Pattern of New Testament Truth*. Grand Rapids, MI: Eerdmans, 1968.

Laertius, Diogenes. *Pythagoras*. Lives of Eminent Philosophers. Edited by R. D. Hicks. Cambridge: Harvard University Press, 1972.

Lane, William L. *Hebrews 1–8*. Word Biblical Commentary 47A. Dallas: Word, 1991.

———. *Hebrews 9–13*. Word Biblical Commentary 47B. Dallas: Word, 1991.

LaRondelle, Hans K. *Our Creator Redeemer: An Introduction to Biblical Covenant Theology*. Berrien Springs, MI: Andrews University Press, 2005.

Lea, Thomas D. *Hebrews, James*. Holman New Testament Commentary 10. Nashville, TN: Broadman & Holman, 1999.

Leedy, Randy. *New Testament Diagrams*. BibleWorks 10, 2016.

Leeming, David A. *Creation Myths of the World*. 2nd ed. Oxford: ABC-CLIO, 2010.

LeMon, Joel M., and Kent H. Richards, eds. *Method Matters: Essays on the Interpretation of the Hebrew Bible in Honor of David L. Petersen*. Atlanta, GA: SBL, 2009.

Lenski, R. C. H. *The Interpretation of the Epistle to the Hebrews and of the Epistle of James*. Columbus, OH: Lutheran Book Concern, 1938.

Letham, Robert. "Review of, Chul Won Suh. *The Creation-Mediator Ship of Jesus Christ: A Study in the Relation of the Incarnation and the Creation*. Amsterdam: Rodopi, 1982." *WTJ* 46.1 (1984) 213–16.

Liddell, Henry George, et al. *A Greek-English Lexicon*. Oxford: Clarendon, 1996.

Lieberman, Saul. *Hellenism in Jewish Palestine*. 2nd ed. Text and Studies of the Jewish Theological Seminary of America 18. New York: Jewish Theological Seminary of America, 1962.

Lightfoot, Joseph Barber, and J. R. Harmer. *The Apostolic Fathers*. London: Macmillan, 1891.

Lindars, Barnabas. *The Theology of the Letter to the Hebrews*. New Testament Theology. Edited by J. D. G. Dunn. 1991. Reprint, Cambridge: Cambridge University Press, 2003.

Linde, Andrei, and Arthur Mezhlumian. "Stationary Universe." *PLB* 307.1–2 (1993) 25–33.

Long, Anthony A. *La Filosofía Helenística: Estoicos, Epicúreos, Escépticos*. Translated by P. Jordán de Urríes. Madrid: Alianza Editorial, 1984.

———. "The Scope of Early Greek Philosophy." In *Early Greek Philosophy*, edited by A. A. Long, 1–21. Cambridge Companions. New York: Cambridge University Press, 1999.

Long, Charles H. *Alpha: The Myths of Creation*. New York: G. Braziller, 1963.

———. "Cosmogony." In *Encyclopedia of Religion*, edited by Lindsay Jones, 3:1986–88. Farmington Hills, MI: Thomson Gale, 2005.

Long, Fredrick J. *Kairos: A Beginning Greek Grammar*. Mishawaka, IN: Long, 2005.

Longenecker, Richard N. *Biblical Exegesis in the Apostolic Period*. 2nd ed. Grand Rapids, MI: Eerdmans, 1999.

Lookadoo, Jonathon. "Celestial Bodies." In *Lexham Theological Wordbook*, edited by Douglas Mangum et al., np. Lexham Bible Reference Series. Bellingham, WA: Lexham, 2014. Logos edition.

Losin, Peter. "Plato and Platonism." In *The History of Science and Religion in the Western Tradition: An Encyclopedia*, edited by Gary B. Ferngren et al., 123–29. New York: Garland, 2000.

Louw, Johannes P., and Eugene Albert Nida. *Greek-English Lexicon of the New Testament: Based on Semantic Domains*. 2 vols. New York: United Bible Societies, 1996.

Lovell, Bernard. *Emerging Cosmology*. Convergence. Edited by Ruth Nanda Anshen. Lincoln, NE: Columbia University Press, 1981.

Lucas, E. C. "Cosmogony." In *Dictionary of the Old Testament: Pentateuch*, edited by T. Desmond Alexander and David W. Baker, 1:130–39. Downers Grove, IL: InterVarsity, 2003.

Lukaszewski, Albert L. *The Lexham Syntactic Greek New Testament Glossary*. Bellingham, WA: Lexham, 2007.

Lukaszewski, Albert L., et al. *The Lexham Syntactic Greek New Testament, SBL Edition: Expansions and Anotations*. Bellingham, WA: Lexham, 2011.

Lünemann, Gottlieb. *Critical and Exegetical Handbook to the Epistle to the Hebrews*. Translated by Maurice J. Evans. Critical and Exegetical Commentary on the New Testament. Edinburgh: T. & T. Clark, 1882.

Lust, Johan, et al., eds. *A Greek-English Lexicon of the Septuagint*. Stuttgart: Deutsche Bibelgesellschaft, 2003.

Macdonald Cornford, Francis. *Plato's Cosmology: The Timaeus of Plato*. 1935. Reprint, Indianapolis: Hackett, 1997.

Mackie, Scott D. "Ancient Jewish Mystical Motifs in Hebrews' Theology of Access and Entry Exhortations." *NTS* 58.1 (2012) 88–104.

Mantey, J. R. "The Causal Use of Eis in the New Testament." *JBL* 70.1 (1951) 45–48.

———. "On Causal Eis Again." *JBL* 70.4 (1951) 309–11.

Mare, W. Harold. "Cosmogony, Cosmology." In *The Zondervan Encyclopedia of the Bible: A–C*, edited by Merrill C. Tenney and Moisés Silva, 1:1035–44. Grand Rapids, MI: Zondervan, 2009.

Mastora, Anna, et al. "Failed Queries: A Morpho-Syntactic Analysis Based on Transaction Log Files." First Workshop on Digital Information Management, Corfu, Greece, March 30–31, 2011. http://eprints.rclis.org/15845/.

Mas Torres, Salvador. *Historia de la filosofía antigua: Grecia y el Helenismo*. Madrid: Universidad Nacional de Educación a Distancia, 2003.

McCullough, J. C. "Some Recent Developments in Research on the Epistle to the Hebrews (Part I)." *IBS* 2.3 (1980) 141–65.

———. "Some Recent Developments in Research on the Epistle to the Hebrews (Part II)." *IBS* 3.1 (1981) 28–45.

McCune, Lorne A. "Intertestamental Period." In *The Lexham Bible Dictionary*, edited by John D. Barry et al., np. Bellingham, WA: Lexham, 2016. Logos edition.

McDonald, L. M. "Antioch (Syria)." In *Dictionary of New Testament Background: A Compendium of Contemporary Biblical Scholarship*, edited by Craig A. Evans and Stanley E. Porter, 34–37. Downers Grove, IL: InterVarsity, 2000.

McDonough, Sean M. *Christ as Creator: Origins of a New Testament Doctrine*. Oxford: Oxford University Press, 2009.

McGowan, Andrew B., and Kent H. Richards, eds. *Method and Meaning: Essays on New Testament Interpretation in Honor of Harold W. Attridge*. Atlanta, GA: SBL, 2011.

Mcguire-Moushon, J. A. "Divine Beings." In *Lexham Theological Wordbook: Lexham Bible Reference Series*, edited by Douglas Mangum et al., np. Bellingham, WA: Lexham, 2014. Logos edition.

McPherran, Mark L. *The Religion of Socrates*. Pennsylvania: The Pennsylvania State University Press, 1996.

Melvin, David P. *History of Israel, Post-Monarchic Period*. The Lexham Bible Dictionary. Edited by John D. Barry and Lazarus Wentz. Bellingham, WA: Lexham, 2012.

Mendels, Doron. *Identity, Religion and Historiography: Studies in Hellenistic History.* Journal for Study of the Pseudepigrapha Supplement Series 24. Edited by James H. Charlesworth and Lester L. Grabbe. Sheffield, UK: Sheffield Academic, 1998.

Michaels, Ramsey J. "Commentary on Hebrews." In *Cornerstone Biblical Commentary: 1 Timothy, 2 Timothy, Titus, and Hebrews,* 17:303–476. Carol Stream, IL: Tyndale, 2009.

Miller, Neva F. *The Epistle to the Hebrews: An Analytical and Exegetical Handbook.* Dallas: Summer Institute of Linguistics, 1988.

Moffatt, James. *A Critical and Exegetical Commentary on the Epistle to the Hebrews.* International Critical Commentary on the Holy Scriptures of the Old and New Testaments. Edinburgh: T. & T. Clark International, 1924.

Montgomery, James Alan. *The Samaritans: The Earliest Jewish Sect.* Philadelphia: Winston, 1907.

Moore, Edward. "Middle Platonism." *Internet Encyclopedia of Philosophy: A Peer-Reviewed Academic Resource.* http://www.iep.utm.edu/midplato/.

Mortenson, Terry. "Jesus, Evangelical Scholars, and the Age of the Earth." *MSJ* 18.1 (2007) 69–99.

Mosser, Carl. "No Lasting City: Rome, Jerusalem and the Place of Hebrews in the History of Earliest 'Christianity.'" PhD diss., University of St Andrews, 2004.

Mounce, William D. *Basics of Biblical Greek: Grammar.* Edited by Verlyn D. Verbrugge. 3rd ed. Grand Rapids, MI: Zondervan, 2009.

Mueller, Ekkehardt. "Creation in the New Testament." *JATS* 15.1 (2004) 47–62.

Mueller-Vollmer, Kurt, ed. *The Hermeneutics Reader: Texts of the German Tradition from the Enlightenment to the Present.* New York: Continuum, 1985.

Mukhanov, V. *Physical Foundations of Cosmology.* Cambridge: Cambridge University Press, 2005.

Myers, Allen C. *The Eerdmans Bible Dictionary.* Grand Rapids, MI: Eerdmans, 1987.

Neeley, Linda L. "A Discourse Analysis of Hebrews." *Occasional Papers in Translation and Textlinguistics* 3–4 (1987) 1–146.

Negev, Avraham. *The Archaeological Encyclopedia of the Holy Land.* New York: Prentice Hall, 1990.

Neill, Stephen. "The Bible in English History." *Chm* 75.2 (1961) 96–106.

Nestle, Eberhard, and Erwin Nestle. *Nestle-Aland: Novum Testamentum Graece.* Edited by Barbara Aland et al. 28th rev. ed. Stuttgart: Deutsche Bibelgesellschaft, 2012.

Neuendorf, Kimberly A. *The Content Analysis Guidebook.* Los Angeles: SAGE, 2002.

Newman, Barclay M., Jr. *A Concise Greek-English Dictionary of the New Testament.* Stuttgart: Deutsche Bibelgesellschaft, 1993.

Nichol, Francis D., ed. *The Seventh-Day Adventist Bible Commentary.* Vol. 7, *Ellen G. White.* 8 vols. Hagerstown, MD: Review and Herald Association, 1980.

Nicoll, W. Robertson, ed. *The Expositor's Greek Testament: Commentary.* 5 vols. Grand Rapids, MI: Eerdmans, 1956.

O'Brien, Peter Thomas. *The Letter to the Hebrews.* The Pillar New Testament Commentary. Grand Rapids, MI: Eerdmans, 2010.

Oden, Robert A., Jr. "Cosmogony." In *The Anchor Yale Bible Dictionary,* edited by David Noel Freedman, 1:1162–71. New York: Doubleday, 1992.

Omanson, Roger L. *A Textual Guide to the Greek New Testament: An Adaptation of Bruce M. Metzger's Textual Commentary for the Needs of Translators.* Stuttgart: Deutsche Bibelgesellschaft, 2006.

O'Neill, J. C. "How Early Is the Doctrine of Creatio Ex Nihilo?" *JTS* 53.2 (2002) 449–65.
Osborne, Grant R. *The Hermeneutical Spiral: A Comprehensive Introduction to Biblical Interpretation*. Rev. and expanded, 2nd ed. Downers Grove, IL: InterVarsity, 2006.
Owen, John. *Hebrews by John Owen*. Crossway Classic Commentaries. Edited by Alister McGrath and J. I. Packer. Wheaton, IL: Crossway, 1998.
Parker, David. *Learning New Testament Greek Now and Then*. Sydney: Sydney College of Divinity Press, 2008.
Patton, Michael Quinn. *Qualitative Research & Evaluation Methods*. Los Angeles: SAGE, 2001.
Pearson, Birger A. *Ancient Gnosticism: Traditions and Literature*. Minneapolis, MN: Fortress, 2007.
———. *Gnosticism, Judaism, and Egyptian Christianity*. Studies in Antiquity and Christianity 5. Minneapolis: Fortress, 1990.
Pellegrin, Pierre. "The Aristotelian Way." In *A Companion to Ancient Philosophy*, edited by Mary Louise Gill and Pierre Pellegrin, 235–44. Blackwell Companions to Philosophy 31. Malden, MA: Blackwell, 2006.
Pennington, Jonathan T., and Sean M. McDonough. *Cosmology and New Testament Theology*. Library of New Testament Studies 355. London: T. & T. Clark, 2008.
Perkins, Pheme. "Stoicism." In *The Harpercollins Bible Dictionary: Revised Edition*, edited by Mark A. Powell and Paul J. Achtemeier, 993–94. New York: HarperCollins, 2011.
Philo. *Philo: Greek Text*. 10 vols. Edited by F. H. Colson and G. H. Whitaker. The Loeb Classical Library. London: Heinemann, 1929–53.
Pixner, B. "The Jerusalem Essenes, Barnabas and the Letter to the Hebrews." In *Intertestamental Essays in Honour of Józef Tadeusz Milik*, edited by Z. J. Kapera, 167–78. Qumranica Mogilanensia 6. Kraków: Enigma, 1992.
Polkinghorne, John. "A Scientist Looks at the Epistle to the Hebrews." In *The Epistle to the Hebrews and Christian Theology*, edited by Richard Bauckham et al., 113–21. Grand Rapids, MI: Eerdmans, 2009.
Porter, Stanley E. *How We Got the New Testament: Text, Transmission, Translation*. Acadia Studies in Bible and Theology. Edited by Lee Martin McDonald and Craig A. Evans. Grand Rapids, MI: Baker, 2013.
———. *Idioms of the Greek New Testament*. 2nd ed. Sheffield, UK: Sheffield Academic, 1999.
Porter, Stanley E., et al. *The Opentext.Org Syntactically Analyzed Greek New Testament: Clause Analysis*. Bellingham, WA: Logos Bible Software, 2006.
———. *The Opentext.Org Syntactically Analyzed Greek New Testament: Glossary*. Bellingham, WA: Logos Bible Software, 2006.
Punt, Jeremy. "Hebrews, Thought-Patterns and Context: Aspects of the Background of Hebrews." *Neot* 31.1 (1997) 119–58.
Quarles, Charles L. *A Theology of Matthew: Jesus Revealed as Deliverer, King, and Incarnate Creator*. 1st ed. Explorations in Biblical Theology. Phillipsburg, NJ: P&R, 2013.
Ramm, Bernard L. "The New Hermeneutic." In *Baker's Dictionary of Practical Theology*, edited by Ralph G. Turnbull, 139–43. Grand Rapids, MI: Baker, 1967.
Ratzinger, Joseph. "La Interpretación Bíblica en Conflicto: Problemas del Fundamento y Orientación de la Exégesis Contemporánea." In *Escritura E Interpretación: los Fundamentos de la Interpretación Bíblica*, edited by Luis Sánchez Navarro and Carlos Granados, 19–54. Madrid: Ediciones Palabra, S.A., 2003.

Renan, Ernest. *Vida de Jesús*. Translated by Agustin G. Tirado. Madrid: Editorial Edaf, 1981.
Reyburn, William David. *A Handbook on the Book of Job*. UBS Handbook Series. New York: United Bible Societies, 1992.
Rissi, Mathias. *Die Theologie des Hebräerbriefs: ihre Verankerung in der Situation des Verfassers und seiner Leser*. Wissenschaftliche Untersuchungen Zum Neuen Testament 41. Tübingen: Mohr, 1987.
Ritzema, Elliot. "Platonism." In *The Lexham Bible Dictionary*, edited by John D. Barry et al., np. Bellingham, WA: Lexham, 2016. Logos edition.
Robbins, Vernon K. *Exploring the Texture of Texts: A Guide to Socio-Rhetorical Interpretations*. Valley Forge, PA: Trinity Press International, 1996.
———. "Socio-Rhetorical Interpretation." In *The Blackwell Companion to the New Testament*, edited by David E. Aune, 192–219. Oxford: Wiley-Blackwell, 2010.
Robertson, A. T. *A Grammar of the Greek New Testament in the Light of Historical Research*. 4th ed. New York: Hodder & Stoughton, 1923.
Rojas, Benjamin. "En Busca del κεντρον de la Epístola a los Hebreos." In *The End from the Beginning: Festschrift Honoring Merling Alomía*, edited by Benjamin Rojas et al., 471–86. Lima: Fondo Editorial Universidad Peruana Unión, 2015.
Roncace, Mark, et al. "Dictionary of Socio-Rhetorical Terms." http://www.religion.emory.edu/faculty/robbins/SRI/defns/.
Roothaan, John. *The Method of Meditation*. 1858. Reprint, New York: Kessinger, 2010.
Rosscup, James E. *An Exposition on Prayer: Igniting the Fuel to Flame Our Communication with God*. 5 vols. Chattanooga: AMG, 2011.
Rothschild, Clare K. *Hebrews as Pseudepigraphon: The History and Significance of the Pauline Attribution of Hebrews*. Wissenschaftliche Untersuchungen Zum Neuen Testament 235. Tübingen: Mohr Siebeck, 2009.
Safrai, S., and S. Stern, eds. *The Jewish People in the First Century*. Vol. 1, *Historical Geography, Political History, Social, Cultural and Religious Life and Institutions*. 2 vols. Netherlands: Van Gorcum, 1974.
Salmond, S.D.F. "The Epistle of Paul to the Ephesians." In *The Expositor's Greek Testament: Commentary*. Vol. 3. New York: George H. Doran Company, n.d.
Samuelson, Norbert M. *Judaism and the Doctrine of Creation*. Cambridge: Cambridge University Press, 1994.
Sandegren, C. "The Addressees of the Epistle to the Hebrews." *EvQ* 27.4 (1955) 221–24.
Schaff, Philip, and David S. Schaff. *History of the Christian Church*. 8 vols. 3rd ed. New York: Scribner's, 1910.
Schenck, Kenneth L. *Cosmology and Eschatology in Hebrews: The Settings of the Sacrifice*. Society for New Testament Studies Monograph Series 143. Edited by John M. Court. New York: Cambridge University Press, 2007.
———. "Keeping His Appointment: Creation and Enthronement in Hebrews." *JSNT* 19.66 (1997) 91–117.
Schmidt, W. H. "לֹא." In *Theological Lexicon of the Old Testament*, edited by Ernst Jenni and Claus Westermann, 107–12. Peabody, MA: Hendrickson, 1997.
Schnabel, E. J. "Scripture." In *New Dictionary of Biblical Theology*, edited by T. Desmond Alexander and Brian S. Rosner, 34–43. Downers Grove, IL: InterVarsity, 2000.
Schreiner, Thomas R. *1, 2 Peter, Jude*. The New American Commentary 37. Edited by E. Ray Clendenen. Nashville, TN: Broadman & Holman, 2003.
———. *Interpreting the Pauline Epistles*. 2nd ed. Grand Rapids, MI: Baker, 2011.

Scott, Ernest Findlay. *The Epistle to the Hebrews: Its Doctrine and Significance.* Edinburgh: T. & T. Clark, 1922.
Scott, Julius J., Jr. *Jewish Backgrounds of the New Testament.* Grand Rapids, MI: Backer, 1995.
Septuaginta: With Morphology. Stuttgart: Deutsche Bibelgesellschaft, 1996.
Smith, Jerome H., ed. *The New Treasury of Scripture Knowledge.* Nashville, TN: Nelson, 1992.
Smith, W. Andrew. "Clothing." In *Lexham Theological Wordbook*, edited by Douglas Mangum et al., np. Lexham Bible Reference Series. Bellingham, WA: Lexham, 2014. Logos edition.
Solmsen, Friedrich. "Aristotle and Presocratic Cosmogony." *HSCP* 63 (1958) 265–82.
Spicq, Ceslas. *L'épître aux Hébreux: I. Introduction.* Deuxième ed. Paris: J. Gabalda, 1952.
———. *Theological Lexicon of the New Testament.* Translated by James D. Ernest. 3 vols. Peabody, MA: Hendrickson, 1994.
Stanton, Graham N. "Presuppositions in New Testament Criticism." In *New Testament Interpretation: Essays on Principles and Methods*, edited by I. Howard Marshall, 60–71. Eugene, OR: Wipf & Stock, 2006.
Stausberg, Michael, and Steven Engler, eds. *The Routledge Handbook of Research Methods in the Study of Religion.* London: Routledge, 2011.
Stenring, K. *Sepher Yetzirah: The Book of Formation.* New York: Ktav, 1923.
Stenudd, Stefan. *Cosmos of the Ancients: The Greek Philosophers on Myth and Cosmology.* North Charleston, SC: CreateSpace, 2007.
Stewart, Roy A. "Creation and Matter in the Epistle to the Hebrews." *NTS* 12.3 (1966) 284–93.
Story, Dan. *Christianity on the Offense: Responding to the Beliefs and Assumptions of Spiritual Seekers.* Grand Rapids, MI: Kregel, 1998.
Stuart, Moses. *A Commentary on the Epistle to the Hebrews.* 3rd ed. Andover, MA: Draper, 1854.
Suh, Chul Won. "The Creation-Mediatorship of Jesus Christ: A Study in the Relation of the Incarnation and the Creation." PhD diss., Vrije Universiteit te Amsterdam, 1982.
Svendsen, Stefan Nordgaard. *Allegory Transformed: The Appropriation of Philonic Hermeneutics in the Letter to the Hebrews.* Tübingen: Mohr Siebeck, 2009.
Sweeney, James P. "Hebrews, Letter to The." In *The Lexham Bible Dictionary*, edited by John D. Barry, np. Bellingham, WA: Lexham, 2016. Logos edition.
Tan, Randall K., et al. *The Lexham Greek-English Interlinear Septuagint.* Bellingham, WA: Lexham, 2012.
Tenney, Merrill C. *New Testament Times.* Grand Rapids, MI: Eerdmans, 1975.
Thayer, Joseph Henry. *A Greek-English Lexicon of the New Testament: Being Grimm's Wilke's Clavis Novi Testamenti.* New York: Harper, 1889.
Thiselton, Anthony C. *A Concise Encyclopedia of the Philosophy of Religion.* Oxford: Oneworld, 2005.
Thomas, Robert L. *New American Standard Hebrew-Aramaic and Greek Dictionaries: Updated Edition.* Anaheim, CA: Foundation, 1998.
Thompson, James W. *Hebrews.* Paideia: Commentaries on the New Testament. Edited by Mikeal C. Parsons and Charles H. Talbert. Grand Rapids, MI: Baker, 2008.
———. "Outside the Camp: A Study of Heb 13:9–14." *CBQ* 40.1 (1978) 53–63.

———. "What Has Middle Platonism to Do with Hebrews?" In *Reading the Epistle to the Hebrews*, edited by Eric F. Mason and Kevin B. McCruden, 66:31–52. Resources for Biblical Study. Edited by Tom Thatcher. Atlanta, GA: SBL, 2011.
Tischendorf, Constantin von. *Novum Testamentum Graece Apparatum Criticum*. Lipsiae: Giesecke & Devrient, 1869–94.
Trotter, Andrew H. *Interpreting the Epistle to the Hebrews*. Guides to New Testament Exegesis 6. Grand Rapids, MI: Baker, 1997.
Turner, William. *History of Philosophy*. Boston: Athenæum, 1903.
Utley, Bob. *The Superiority of the New Covenant: Hebrews*. Study Guide Commentary Series: New Testament 10. Marshall, TX: Bible Lessons International, 1999.
Vanhoye, Albert. *Structure and Message of the Epistle to the Hebrews*. Subsidia Biblica 12. Roma: Editrice Pontificio Istituto Biblico, 1989.
Vine, W. E., et al. *Vine's Complete Expository Dictionary of Old and New Testament Words*. 2 vols. Nashville, TN: Nelson, 1996.
Vlastos, Gregory. *Plato's Universe*. Edited and with a new introduction by Luc Brisson. Las Vegas, NV: Parmenides, 2005.
Von Leyden, W. "Time, Number, and Eternity in Plato and Aristotle." *Phil. Q.* 14.54 (1964) 35–52.
Voorwinde, Stephen. "Hebrews' Use of the Old Testament." *VR* 73 (2007) 60–82.
Voulgaris, Christos. "Hebrews: Paul's Fifth Epistle from Prison." *GOTR* 44.1–4 (1999) 199–206.
Wallace, Daniel B. *Greek Grammar Beyond the Basics: An Exegetical Syntax of the New Testament*. Grand Rapids, MI: Zondervan, 1996.
Waltke, Bruce K. "The Creation Account in Genesis 1:1–3 Part I: Introduction to Biblical Cosmogony." *BSac* 132.1 (1975) 25–37.
Weber, Alfred. *History of Philosophy*. Translated by Frank Thilly. New York: Scribner's, 1896.
Wegner, Paul D. *A Student's Guide to Textual Criticism of the Bible: Its History, Methods & Results*. Downers Grove, IL: InterVarsity, 2006.
Westcott, Brooke Foss. *The Epistle to the Hebrews: The Greek Texts with Notes and Essays*. 3rd ed. Classic Commentaries on the Greek New Testament. London: Macmillan, 1903.
Westfall, Cynthia Long. *A Discourse Analysis of the Letter to the Hebrews: The Relationship between Form and Meaning*. Journal for the Study of the New Testament Supplement Series 297. London: T. & T. Clark, 2005.
Widder, Wendy. *Textual Criticism*. Lexham Methods Series. Edited by Douglas Mangum. Bellingham, WA: Lexham, 2013.
Wiersbe, Warren W. *Wiersbe's Expository Outlines on the Old Testament*. Wheaton, IL: Victor, 1993.
Williamson, Ronald. *Philo and the Epistle to the Hebrews*. Leiden: Brill, 1970.
Winer, Georg Benedikt. *A Treatise on the Grammar of the New Testament Greek: Regarded as a Sure Basis for New Testament Exegesis*. Edinburgh: T. & T. Clark, 1882.
Winston, David. *Philo of Alexandria: The Contemplative Life, Giants and Selections*. The Classics of Wertern Spirituality. Edited by Richard J. Payne. London: SPCK, 1981.
Wright, N. T. *Creation, Power and Truth: The Gospel in a World of Cultural Confusion*. London: SPCK, 2013.
Wu, Andi, and Randall Tan. *Cascadia Syntax Graphs of the New Testament: SBL Edition*. Bellingham, WA: Lexham, 2010.

Yadin, Yigael. "The Dead Sea Scrolls and the Epistle to the Hebrews." In *Aspects of the Dead Sea Scrolls*, edited by Yadin Rabin and Chaim Rabin, 36–55. Scripta Hierosolymitana 4. Jerusalem: Magnes, 1965.

Yoo, Yohan, and James W. Watts. *Cosmologies of Pure Realms and the Rhetoric of Pollution*. Routledge Studies in Religion. London: Routledge, 2021.

Zerwick, Max. *Biblical Greek Illustrated by Examples*. Edited by Joseph Smith. Rome: Editricce Pontificio Istituto Biblico, 1963.

Zesati Estrada, Carlos. *Hebreos 5:7–8: Estudio Histórico-Exegético*. Rome: Editrice Pontificio Istituto Biblico, 1990.

Zetterholm, Magnus. *The Formation of Christianity in Antioch: A Social-Scientific Approach to the Separation between Judaism and Christianity*. London: Routledge, 2003.

Zhang, Yan, and Barbara M. Wildemuth. "Qualitative Analysis of Content." In *Applications of Social Research Methods to Questions in Information and Library Science*, edited by Barbara M. Wildemuth, 308–19. Westport, CT: Libraries Unlimited, 2009.

Zinke, Edward E. "Faith-Science Issues: An Epistomological Perspective." *JATS* 15.1 (2004) 63–90.

Zuck, Roy B. *Basic Bible Interpretation: A Practical Guide to Discovering Biblical Truth*. Edited by Craig Bubeck. Colorado Springs, CO: Cook, 1991.

Ancient Document Index

OLD TESTAMENT

Genesis	105, 131, 184n5, 192, 192n25, 196n43, 198n50, 213, 223, 224n118
1	129, 131, 184, 194, 205n670, 212, 213
1:1	107, 129, 130n46, 204, 221
1:1 LXX	132, 192n26, 194, 212, 224
1:1–2	11n32
1–2	132, 212n84, 217n97, 255, 255n73, 262, 266
1–3	6, 105, 113, 129n42
1:3	192n26, 221
1–3	260
1:3 LXX	192
1:5 CSB	147n106
1:6–7	132
1:8 LXX	132
1:26	61, 224n118
1:26–28	224n115
1:28	105
1:31	213n87, 257n79
2	184
2:1–3	225
2:2	107, 147
2:2–3	131, 134, 134n62
2:16	105
3:3–4	192
3:9	105
3:19	107
4:3–5	192
4:10	192
5:1	147, 224n118
6:3	125n35
9:24–26	192
12–17	107
18:32 LXX	178

Exodus	
12:18	147n106
15:18	126n36
15:18 LXX	220n105
19:18	107, 230
20:10–11	147
22:26	135
24	107
25:8	197, 218
25:8–9	107
25:9	30
25:9 (25:8 LXX)	154
25–30	30
25:40	30, 162n145
25:40 LXX	162, 163, 217n98
26:30	30
26:33, 34	152
27:8	30
29:45	218
31:3 LXX	175

Leviticus

10:4	152
16	107
19:30	152
23:32	147n106
26:1 LXX	217n98
26:2	152
26:30 LXX	217n98

Numbers

12:7	107
24:6	107

Deuteronomy

22:12	135

Judges

5:5	107
6:39 LXX	178
8:26	135

1 Kings

6:13	197
8:1–2	197
8:10–13	197
11:10	197
12:26	123

2 Chronicles

8:16	203n61
8:16 LXX	252n62
10:16 LXX	123
31:7	203n61
31:7 LXX	252n62

Ezra

1:2–4	36n3
6:3–5	36n3

Nehemiah

5:5	170

Job

26:6	135
26:7	203n62, 204n62
38	204n62
38:1—42:6	204n62
38:4 LXX	203, 203n62, 252n62

Psalms

	105, 169
2:5–9	224
2:8	107
8	224
8:3	196n43
23	106n60
32:9 LXX	205n670
33:6	212n84
33:6, 9	107
33:9	107, 205n670
68:8	107
83:4 LXX	125n34
92:1 LXX	227, 227n122
95:10 LXX	227, 227n122
95:11	107
101:26 LXX	129, 203n60
101:27	135
101:27 LXX [102:26]	111, 112
102	193n31, 194n31
102:25 (101:26 LXX)	129
102:25–27	107
103:5 LXX	203n60
103:6	135
110:1	107
118:152	203
118:152 LXX	129, 252n62
119:152 (118:152 LXX)	129
148:5–6	212n84

Proverbs

3:19	203
3:19 LXX	252n62
8:23	203
8:23 LCC	252n62
16:4	107

Isaiah

2:18 LXX	217n98

10:11 LXX	217n98	**Haggai**	178
16:12 LXX	217n98	2:6	227, 229
19:1 LXX	217n98	2:6, 21	107
21:9 LXX	217n98	2:6 LXX	178
30:17	119n11	2:11	26n42
31:7 LXX	217n98	2:21	107
43:13	107		
44:28	36n3	**Zechariah**	
44:28 LXX	203n61	7:8	26n42
46:6 LXX	217n98	12:1	203n60
48:13	107		
48:13 LXX	203n60	**Malachi**	
50:3	135	2:7	26n42
51:13, 16	203n60		
51:16	203n60		
57:15	126n36		
59:17	135		

DEUTEROCANONICAL BOOKS

Jeremiah

15:12	135

1 Esdras

5:55	203n61
5:55 LXX	252n62
2 Enoch	237n9
24:2	57
2 Esdras	169
3:6, 10	203n61
3:6, 10 LXX	252n62
3:10	203n61
3:10 LXX	252n62
4:12 LXX	169n164
4:13 LXX	169n164
4:16 LXX	169n164
5:3 LXX	169n164
6:14 LXX	169n164

Ezekiel

16:13 LXX	135
27:7 LXX	135
34	106n60
42:20 LXX	153
43:21 LXX	153
44:1 LXX	153
44:15 LXX	153
45:7 LXX	153
47:12 LXX	153
48:10 LXX	153
48:18 LXX	153

Daniel

5:4	126n36
5:4 LXX	217n98
5:23 LXX	217n98
6:27 LXX	217n98
9:24	107
12:7	126n36

2 Maccabees

2:29	145n95
3:37 LXX	178
4:1	176
4:25 LXX	119n11
7:28	62n154, 63n159
7:39 LXX	119n11
10:2	176
11:1 LXX	119n11
11:24 LXX	180
12:21	134n62

Habakkuk

3:13 LXX	157

3 Kingdoms

6:1 LXX	252n62
6:10	203n61
7:47	203n61
7:47 LXX	252n62
12:26	123

3 Maccabees

2:2, 7	160
2:7	160
6:2	160

4 Maccabees

2:6	143n90
5:18	143n90
7:8	176
7:13	143n90
8:1 LXX [4 Macc 7:24]	144
8:16	143n90
18:24 LXX	125n34

Baruch

3:3	126n36

Book of Wisdom (Wisdom of Solomon) — 56, 57n114, 237n9, 250

2:6	160
5:7	160
11:17	57, 247n42, 257n78
13:9	126n36
13:9 LXX	220n105
14:6	126n36
14:6 LXX	220n105
14:8 LXX	217n98
15:13	176
16:24	160
18:4 LXX	220n105
18:16	119n11
19:6	160

Enoch

9:6 LES	126n36
22:14 LES	126n36

Judith

4:13	152
8:18 LXX	217n98
9:12	160
16:14	160
16:20	153

Odes Sol

1:18	126n36
13:14, 27 LXX	157n129

Pss. Sol.

9:18	126n36

Sirach

16:17	160
43:25	160
46:7, 16 LXX	170
49:16	160

Tobit

3:2	126n36
6:17	126n36
8:5, 15	160
14:7	126n36
14:15 LXX	125n34

PSEUDEPIGRAPHA (OLD TESTAMENT)

2 Baruch — 237n9

21:4	57, 247n42, 253n67

2 Enoch

24:2	247n42, 253n67

Apocalypse of Baruch — 57, 247n42, 250

Psalms of Solomon

8:7	160

DEAD SEA SCROLLS

Authoritative Teaching (The Nag Hammadi Library)

VI

22:34	65n165
32:16–33	65n165
223:17–20	65n165

ANCIENT JEWISH WRITERS

Josephus	54, 54n103, 55, 55n105, 154, 237n9

Jewish Antiquities

12.64	145n96
18.163, 164, 274	145n96

Jewish War

2.260, 409, 417	145n96
7.43–45	33n79

Philo of Alexandria	5, 5n18, 5n19, 27, 28, 28n53, 53, 55n105, 58–63, 62n154, 63n158, 65, 71, 104, 145, 230, 237n9, 247, 248, 250, 255, 255n73, 256, 256n77, 257, 258, 258n84, 259, 259n87, 262

De Abrahamo

18, 81	180n193

De aeternitate mundi

1–15	59n126
4	62n151
5	63n156, 253n67
5, 30, 140	62n152
7, 10, 75	58n120
8	41n28
8, 19	60n143
10	45n55, 250n56
40	239
97	59n129
106	60n144
107	59n133
107, 110	251n60
110	59n134
113	180n194, 180n195, 230
130, 145	60n136

De confusione linguarum

102	162n143

De fuga et invention

93	153n119

De gigantibus

19	125n35
22, 23	175n183
66	180n193

De Josepho

136	180n193
225	129n40

De migratione Abrahami

193	123n26, 248n46

De mutatione nominum

60, 130	180n193

De opificio mundi

7	58n120, 58n121
8–9	59n128
12	58n120
16	59n127
19, 25, 29	60n140, 251n59
19–23	58n123, 247n42
19–26	61n149

De opificio mundi (cont.)

20	58n122, 61n148
22	61n145, 62n153, 253n67
24–26	60n135
26, 67	60n142, 251
26–27	60n135
28	60n137
29	60n139, 60n141
64	60n138
72, 75	58n123
78	59n130
125	58n119
132	145n97
135	60n143
137–40	61n146, 258n84
156	58n124
170–71	58n125, 247n43
171	59n131

De plantatione

133	162n143

De posteritate Caini

64	134n62

De praemiis et poenis

17	180n193
63, 68	129n40
68	129n41

De providentia

2:19	125n35

De sacrificiis

65	60n142, 251n58

De sobrietate

45	145n97

De somniis

1.76	62n155, 253n67
1.92, 101, 107	135n69

De specialibus legibus

1.226	63n157, 253n67
3.36	145n97

De vita contemplative

63	129n40

De vita Mosis

1.279	145n97
2.51	160n137
2.74	30n63

In Flaccum

11, 138	129n40

Legatio ad Gaium

54, 125	145n97

Legum allegoriae

1.16, 18	134n62
1.2	60n142, 251
1.31	61n149
1.7	62n152
3.92	129n40

Philo

3	237n10

Quaestiones et Solutiones in Exodum

2, 68	61n147

Quis rerum divinarum heres sit

115	145n97
181	162n143
191	59n132

Quod deterius potiori insidari soleat

118	129n40

RABBINIC WORKS

Amoraim	55n105
Baraita	55n105
Haggadah	55n105
Halakah	55n105
Midrashim	55n105
Mishnah	55n105, 57n116
Rabbi Akiva	57

Sepher Yetzirah (The Book of Formation)

	56, 56n111, 56n112, 237n9, 247n42, 250
1:2, 10–12	56

Talmud	55n105, 57n116
Tannaim	55n105
Tosefta	55n105

NEW TESTAMENT

Matthew 104n54

1:20	209
2:2	117n6
2:7	209
6:3	230
7:21	230
7:25	203, 252n62
10:6, 39	228
10:26–33	257n79
10:32 NKJV	228
10:39	228
11:7	231
11:25	64
12:32	125n33
13:22	221
13:22, 39–40, 49	125n33
13:39–40	125n33
13:41	230
13:49	125n33
15:4	211
19:4	239
19:4–6	64
21:19	125n32
24:3	125n33
24:3, 27, 37, 39	259n88
24:27	259n88
24:37	259n88
24:39	259n88
25:24	64
26:61	157n131
28:20	125n33

Mark

1:24	228
3:29	125n32
4:19	125n33
6:34	106n60
10:1–12	257n79
10:30	125n33
11:14	125n32
13:19	239
13:25	231
14:27	106n60
14:58	217n98
14:58 NKJV	266

Luke 30, 104n54

1:33	125n32
1:55	125n32
1:70	125n33
6:49	117n6
8:39	211
9:25	228
10:21	64
10:37	230
11:50	64
12:11	128
12:40	193n30
12:53	122
15:4	228
15:9	228
15:24	228
15:32	228
16:8	125n33, 221
16:11	216n95
18:30	125n33
20:34	221
20:34–35	125n33
20:35	125
21:6	36n4
23:4	244
23:14	244
23:22	244

John

1:3	64, 106
1:9	216n95
1:24	64
4:5	122
4:14	125n32
4:23	216n95
5:8–9	212n84
5:17	64
5:35	209
5:44	207n73
6:32	216n95
6:45	117n6
6:51	125n32
6:58	125n32
8:35	125n32
8:51	125n32
8:52	125n32
9:32	125n33
10:2	106n60
10:11	106n60
10:28	125n32
11:26	125n32
12:29	117n6
12:34	125n32
13:8	125n32
14:3	193n30
14:16	125n32
14:19	193n30
15:1	216n95
19:39	119n11

Acts

	30, 31n67, 104n54
2:10	26n42
2:24	211
2:25	231
2:36	211
3:15	211
3:21	125n33
4:10	211
6:7	25, 33n79
6:8	26n42
7	6n21, 106n59
7:44–50	257n79
7:48	217n98, 218
10:15	211
13:30	211

14:17	64
14:27	211
15:12	211
15:18	125n33
16:9	157n131
16:26	231
17:16	174n180
17:22–34	257n79
17:24	64, 217n98
17:24–26	64
17:28	196n43
18:24	20n12
18:26	20n12
19:24, 38	175
19:38	175
19:40	244
20:17	26n42
20:18	26n42
20:28	26n42
21:19	211
21:38	54n103

Romans

	104n54
1:20	64, 257n79
1:25	125n32, 239
4:17	207n73
9:5	125n32
11:36	64, 125n32, 139n79
12:2	125, 125n33, 221
15:3	106n60
16:27	125n32

1 Corinthians

1:9	139n79
1:20	125n33, 221
2:6, 8	221
2:6–8	125n33
2:7	125n32
2:8	221
3:2	106n60
3:18	125n33, 221
7:31	228
8:6	23, 64, 106
8:13	125n32

10:11	125n32, 125n33	1:23	203
11:9	239	1:26	125n32, 125n33
11:33	174n180	1.23	252n62
15:23	259n88	2:15	128
16:11	174n180	3:10	202n57, 239

2 Corinthians

1 Thessalonians

4:4	125n33, 195n39, 221	2:19	259n88
		3:13	259n88
9:9	125n32	4:15	259n88
11:31	125n32	5:23	259n88
11:33	157n131		
12:2	65, 223n113		

2 Thessalonians

2:1	259n88

Galatians

		2:2	231
1:4	125n33, 221	2:8	259n88
1:5	125n32	3:14	157n131
4:7	139n79		

1 Timothy

Ephesians

		1:17	23, 125n32, 125n33, 221
1:4	64		
1:21	125n33	2:13	64
2:2	125n32, 125n33	4:3	239
2:7	125n33	6:11–16	209
2:10	239	6:17	125n33
2:15	239		
3:9	23, 106, 125n32, 125n33, 239	## 2 Timothy	
		4:10	125n32, 125n33
3:11	125n32, 125n33	4:18	125n32
3:17	203, 252n62		
3:21	125n32, 125n33	## Titus	
4:6	64		
4:24	202n57, 239	2:12	125n33
6:12	128		

Hebrews

Philippians

		1	193
4:20	125n32	1:1	25, 109n63, 192n27, 196n42, 197n47, 199n51, 201, 210n81, 212n84, 251

Colossians

204n63

1:15	195n39, 209		
1:15–16	257n79	1:1 ESV	249n49
1:15–18	64	1:1 ISV	105
1:15–19	23	1:1–2	92, 192n26, 193
1:16	106, 223n113, 239	1:1—2:4	99, 100n39
1:17	106	1:1–3	83, 84

Ancient Document Index

Hebrews (*cont.*)

1:1–4	76n7, 83, 84, 86, 90, 97, 100, 113, 118–26, 192n27, 203, 204, 226, 227, 244, 244n19, 249, 252, 257
1:1—4:16	99, 100n39
1:1–5	76n8
1:1–14	102
1:2	23n26, 64, 80, 81, 98, 99, 102, 106, 106n60, 107, 109n63, 112, 113, 124, 125, 125n32, 125n33, 126, 126n36, 192n26, 195, 195n35, 195n36, 195n37, 195n39, 199n51, 201, 202n57, 206n72, 208, 211, 220, 221, 221n110, 222, 230n134, 251, 256
1:2 NIV	22
1:3	106, 112, 170, 199n51, 200, 202, 222, 226n120, 239, 248n48, 253
1–3	192n27
1:4	106n60, 112, 119n9
1:4–7	190n16
1:5—2:8	76n7
1:5—4:14	97
1:5–14	100
1:6	227, 227n122, 257, 259
1:7	76n8, 230, 259
1:7–8	215n91
1:8	112, 124, 125n32, 125n33, 195n35, 196n44, 249
1:8–9	194
1:8–12	98
1:10	76n8, 80, 83, 84, 109n63, 128, 129, 130, 131, 193, 193n30, 193n31, 199, 199n51, 203n60, 212, 213, 213n87, 222, 223, 224, 228, 228n124, 228n125, 248, 255n74, 256
1:10–12	81, 83, 84, 86, 86n24, 92, 98, 100, 102, 107, 111, 112, 113, 126–36, 182, 192n27, 203, 204, 214, 215n91, 216n96, 218, 218n99, 219, 226, 228, 248, 251, 252, 257n82, 259
1:10a	83, 84
1:10b	83, 84
1:11	109n63, 218, 222, 226, 248n45
1:11–12	134n65, 218n100
1:11a	83, 84
1:11a–b	83, 84
1:11b	83, 84
1:11c	83, 84
1:11c–12a–b	83, 84
1:12	109n63, 201, 228, 229, 229n127, 248n45, 251
1:12a	83, 84
1:12b	83, 84
1:12c	83, 84
1:12c–d	83, 84
1:12d	83, 84
2:1–4	103n50, 198, 249
2:2	259
2:2–4	76n8
2:3	21, 26n42, 193n30
2:4	26n42
2:5	227n122
2:5–9	224, 224n115
2:5–18	100, 100n39, 102

2:6	76n8, 112, 155, 227, 248, 257	3:12	198, 208, 249
		3:13–14	76n8
2:8	112, 222, 222n112	3:14	24
2:9	202n57, 208	3:17	255n74
2:9–18	76n7	3:18	112, 196n44
2:10	81, 83, 84, 86–87, 92, 98, 100, 102, 107, 109n63, 113, 123, 136–39, 139n79, 192n27, 195n36, 198, 199n51, 204, 206, 214, 222, 222n112, 244n19, 252, 253	4:1	196n44
		4:1–10	76n7, 101
		4:1–13	100
		4:2–4	76n8
		4:2–10	101
		4:3	64, 83, 84, 109n63, 131, 142, 145, 146, 196n44, 213n86, 213n87, 221
		4:3–4	80, 81
2:10–13	100	4:3–5	83, 84, 87, 92, 98, 100, 102, 107, 113, 142–49, 196, 196n41, 200, 200n54, 213, 225, 248, 249n49, 253
2:12	76n8		
2:14	248		
2:14–18	198, 249		
2:15	226		
2:17	226		
3:1	100, 100n39	4:3–11	98
3:1 Byz	130	4:4	64, 83, 84, 109n63, 131, 142, 147, 199n51, 201, 213n87, 222, 251
3:1–3	198, 249		
3:1—4:1	100		
3:1—4:13	100		
3:1—4:16	102	4:4–5	83, 84
3:1–6	98, 100	4:4a	83, 84
3:1–19	76n7	4:4b	83, 84
3:2–4	76n8	4:5	142, 196n44
3:3	83, 84	4:6	112
3:3–4	83, 84, 87, 113, 139–42, 199n51	4:6–11	98
		4:7–8	76n8
3:4	80, 83, 84, 92, 98, 100, 102, 107, 109n63, 113, 202, 202n58, 222, 253	4:10	76n8, 80, 81, 83, 84, 87, 92, 98, 101, 102, 107, 109n63, 113, 131, 149–51, 196, 196n44, 199n51, 200, 213n87, 248
3:4a	83, 84		
3:4b	83, 84		
3:5	134n63		
3:6	24, 112, 134n63, 157, 162, 195n35, 219, 228	4:11	112, 196n44
		4:11—5:10	76n7
		4:11—10:25	100n39, 101
3:7	21, 190n16	4:12	190n16
3:8–10	76n8	4:12–13	229
3:9	21, 131, 213n87, 214n87	4:12–14	76n8
		4:14	24, 132, 222, 223
3:11	196n44	4:14—10:25	99

Hebrews (*cont.*)

4:14–16	249
4:15	226
4:16—10:18	97
5:1	76n8, 112
5:1–4	248
5:1—7:28	99
5:4	208
5:5	76n8
5:6	112, 124, 125n32, 190n16, 196n44
5:7	76n8, 255n74
5:7–8	5
5:9	76n8, 244
5:10	208
5:11	76n7, 112
5:11—6:12	76n7
5:11—6:20	103n50
5:11–14	76n8, 198, 249
5:12	26n42, 106n60, 112
5:12 CSB	33
6:1, 10	131
6:1–3	76n8
6:5	76n8, 124, 125n33, 170, 227
6:6	26n42, 202n57
6:7	76n8, 208
6:9	197n46
6:9–10	21
6:10	76n8, 131
6:12 NLT	33
6:13	76n8
6:13–20	76n7
6:16	76n8
6:19	134n63
6:19–20	198, 249
6:20	124, 125n32, 197n44
7:1–10	76n7
7:1—10:18	26n42, 102
7:2–3	76n8
7:3	197n44
7:4—10:25	101
7:8	76n8
7:10	76n8
7:11—8:6	76n7
7:12	180, 230
7:14	130, 193n30
7:15	26n42
7:16	76n8, 170n170
7:17	124, 125n32, 197n44
7:18–19	197n46
7:21	124, 125n32, 130, 193n30, 197n44
7:24	124, 125n32, 197n44
7:25	197n44
7:26	132, 190n16, 222, 223, 226
7:26–28	76n8
7:27	229n131
7:28	124, 125n32, 195n35, 197n44
8:1	132, 222, 223
8:1–2	76n8, 83, 84, 88, 92, 99, 101, 102, 107, 109n63, 113, 151–55, 157, 192n27, 197, 215, 215n92, 217, 217n97, 218n99, 225, 226, 226n120, 257n82, 258n83
8:1–6	101
8:1—10:18	101
8:1–13	101
8:2	80, 81, 83, 84, 130, 154, 155, 193n30, 199n51, 201, 251
8:3—10:18	99
8:5	30, 76n8
8:5 NIV	30
8:7—9:10	76n7
8:7–13	76n8
8:8	130, 193n30
8:9	130, 193n30
8:10	193n30
8:11	193n30
9:1–2	76n8
9:1—10:18	99
9:1–14	101
9:6	76n8, 156n126

9:6–10	84, 156n126	9:25–26a	83, 84
9:6–12	88, 155–60	9:25–28	99
9:7	156n126	9:26	80, 81, 109n63,
9:7–10	156n126		124, 125n32,
9:7b–12	83, 84		125n33, 145, 146,
9:8	156, 190n16		197n45, 213n86,
9:8–9	76n8		221, 248
9:10	156	9:26 LEB	266
9:11	80, 81, 83, 84, 92,	9:26–27	76n8
	154, 155, 156,	9:26b	83, 84
	156n126, 204,	9:28	106n60, 226, 228,
	217, 252, 266		259, 259n88
9:11—10:4	76n7	9:28 NKJV	29
9:11–12	76n8, 83, 84, 99,	10:1	76n8, 197n44,
	101, 102, 107,		255n74
	109n63, 113,	10:5	76n8, 146, 221
	197, 216n96,	10:5–23	76n7
	217n98, 219, 223,	10:7	76n8
	223n114, 248,	10:9	76n8
	258n83	10:10	229n131
9:11–14	248	10:11	76n8
9:12	155, 156,	10:12	197n44
	156n126, 229n131	10:13	174n180
9:13–14	198, 249	10:14	197n44
9:13–22	99	10:16	76n8, 193n30
9:14	131, 190, 244n19,	10:18	26n42
	249	10:19	97
9:14–15	76n8	10:19—12:2	101
9:15–18	101	10:19—13:25	100n39, 101
9:15–28	101	10:19–25	198, 249
9:18	76n8	10:21–22	77n8
9:19–22	101	10:22	216
9:23	132, 215n93, 222,	10:23	24
	223	10:24	131
9:23–24	76n8, 99	10:24–25	77n8
9:23–28	101	10:24–31	76n7
9:24	80, 81, 83, 84,	10:26–39	103n50
	109n63, 132, 204,	10:27	77n8
	204n64, 216, 217,	10:29	26n42
	222, 223, 248, 252	10:30	130, 193n30
9:24–26	83, 84, 88, 92, 99,	10:31	190
	101, 102, 107, 113,	10:31–32	77n8
	160–66, 212n85,	10:32–39	76n7
	217n98, 218,	10:34	21, 26n42
	258n83	10:34 [Byz.]	222
9:24a	83, 84	10:35–36	77n8
9:24b–26a	83, 84	10:35–39	198, 249
9:25	109n63	10:36–39	228

Hebrews (*cont.*)

11	168
11:1–3	99
11:1—12:27	103
11:1–40	76n7, 99, 101
11:3	64, 81, 83, 84, 88–89, 93, 99, 101, 103, 107, 109n63, 113, 124, 125, 125n32, 125n33, 126, 126n36, 166–72, 182, 193, 196, 199n51, 201, 202, 205, 205n69, 205n670, 206, 206n70, 206n72, 208, 209, 210, 214, 221, 230n134, 239, 249, 252, 253, 254
11:3 NKJV	6, 124
11:3–31	101
11:4–7	255n74
11:4–12	99
11:5	180, 230
11:6 ESV	184
11:7	77n8, 146, 221
11:9	84, 154
11:9–10	83, 84, 89, 113, 172–76, 193
11:10	80, 81, 83, 84, 93, 99, 101, 103, 107, 109n63, 113, 175, 214, 214n89, 219, 225, 259
11:10–13	77n8
11:11	145, 145n94
11:11–12	218n99
11:12	130, 132, 222, 223
11:13	168
11:16	77n8, 175
11:23–24	77n8
11:26	106n60
11:26–30	77n8
11:29	130
11:30	168n158, 255n74
11:34	77n8
11:38	77n8, 146, 221
11:39–40	168
12:1–11	76n7
12:1–29	101
12:5, 6	193n30
12:6	193n30
12:7	77n8
12:9–10	77n8
12:12 NKJV	33
12:12–13	77n8
12:12–17	76n7
12:14	193n30
12:16	134n63
12:18–19	77n8
12:18–24	102, 226
12:18–29	76n7
12:19	170, 170n169
12:22	175, 190, 226, 259
12:22–23	77n8
12:23, 25	222
12:24	106n60, 192n27
12:25	102, 222
12:25–27	77n8, 84, 89, 93, 101, 103, 103n50, 107, 113, 176–81, 192n27, 215, 215n93, 218, 218n99, 218n100, 227, 229, 257n82, 259
12:25–29	99, 228
12:26	180n192, 199n51, 202, 202n59, 215n93, 222, 253
12:26–27	199n51, 202, 202n59, 253
12:27	81, 83, 84, 109n63, 179n191, 180, 180n196, 199n51, 201, 229, 230, 251
12:28	226, 227, 227n122, 259
12:28 ESV	227
12:29	77n8
13:1	76n7
13:1–8	76n7
13:2	259
13:4	218n99
13:6	155, 193n30

Ancient Document Index   299

13:6–7	77n8
13:7	25
13:8	124, 125n32, 157, 162, 197n44, 219, 256n76
13:9	76n7
13:9–19	76n7
13:12	77n8
13:13	106n60
13:13 LEB	27
13:13–14 NKJV	33
13:14	175, 226, 227
13:14–15	77n8
13:15	106n60
13:17	25, 77n8
13:17–25	97
13:19–22	77n8
13:20	106n60, 193n30
13:20–21	97, 196n42, 249n49
13:20–25	76n7, 97
13:21	124, 125n32, 197n44
13:22	19, 33
13:22 CSB	32
13:22 NASB	19n11
13:22–25	97
13:24	25, 26n42, 34
13:24 CSB	32n73
13:24 NIV	33
13:24b	25

James

4:4, 14	209
5:7	174n180
5:7–8	259n88

1 Peter

	6n21
1:2	106n60
1:4	106n60
1:20	64
1:25	125n32
2:5	106n60
2:24	106n60
2:25	106n60
3:3	146n101
3:9	106n60
3:18	106n60
4:11	125n32
4:19	190, 190n18
5:10	252n62
5:11	125n32

2 Peter

1:19	209
3:4	259n88
3:5	65, 157n131
3:7	65
3:10–12	65
3:12	259n88
3:18	125n33

1 John

2:8	228
2:17	125n32

2 John

2	125n32

Jude

13	125n32
13, 25	125n33
25	125n32, 125n33

Revelation

	104n54
1:6, 18	125n32
3:14	106
4:9, 10	125n32
4:11	64, 106, 239
5:13	125n32
7:12	125n32
10:6	125n32, 239
11:15	125n32
11:18	226n120
14:7	230
14:11	125n32, 125n33
15:7	125n32
18:22	175
19:3	125n32
20:10	125n32
21:1	228
22:5	125n32

APOCRYPHA (NEW TESTAMENT)

Apocryphon of John   21n16

Gospel of Barnabas
5.5   146n100

EARLY CHRISTIAN WRITINGS

Aquinas   46

Summa Theologica
I.Q.44.a.1–a.4   46n58

Athanasius   191
Augustine   46, 237n9

Confessions
11.10   46n58
12.9, 12, 15, 29   46n58

De civitate Dei
2.4   46n58
12.16   46n58

Clement of Alexandria   24
Vitae Philosophorum   49n74
Clement of Rome   20n12
Diogenes Laertius   237n9
Duns Scotus   191
Eusebius   237n9

Historia ecclesiastica
3.38.2   20n12
6.13.1–2   20n12
6.14.1–4   24n30
6.25.13   22n21
14.1–4   20n12
66.25.13–14   22n20

Gospel of Philip   21n16
Gospel of Truth   21n16

Hegesippus   54, 54n103
Hippolytus of Rome   237n9

The Refutation of All Heresies
10.3   41n26

Ignatius of Antioch
Ignatius to the Magnesians
13.1   123n27

Irenaeus   191
Justin Martyr   54, 54n103, 191
Lactantius   237n9
Origen   20n12, 22
Tertullian   237n9, 238n10

De pudicitia
20.2   20n12

GRECO-ROMAN LITERATURE

Anaxagoras   38n8, 39, 39n16, 41, 42, 68, 245, 254, 254n69
Anaximander   38n8, 38n9
Anaximenes   38n8, 38n9, 42
Antiochus of Ascalon   53, 70

Apuleius
De Deo Socratis   248n47

Arcesilas   43n43
Archimedes   47, 67
Aristarchus   47, 67
Aristophanes   237n10
Aristotle   42, 44n43, 45–46, 45n49, 48n67, 66, 69, 237n9, 237n10, 246, 246n34, 247, 248n47, 250, 254, 256, 256n77, 257, 260n89

De anima

403.2.30–404.1.29	41n30, 246n37
405.25–29	38n11, 39n13, 250n51

De caelo

296.2.5–14	45n51
298.2.30–34	38n11, 250n51

De plantis

817a.1.25–29	39n17

De Xenophane

977.1.10–14	40n23, 245n21, 253n66

Fragmenta varia

28	39n19
28, 61	254n70
61	40n19

Metaphysica

102.4a1–4	240n16
983b.3.30–24	38n10
987b.10–14	39n19, 254n70
992a.10–14	246n33
1010a.10–14	38n10, 38n11, 250n51
1023b.25–24a.4	240n16
1048b.15–24	250n57
1049b.15–24	46n59
1072b.25–29	240n15
1075a.5–9	240n15
1090a.20–24	39n19, 254n70

Meteorologica

355.1.5–9	39n13

Physica

185.2.15–24	38n11, 250n51
203.1.20–24	39n15, 41n31, 246n37, 250n51, 254n69
205.1.1–4	39n12, 39n13

251.1.20–34	46n56
251.2.10–20	45n53
252.1.1–4	45n54
Chrysippus	50, 70
Cicero	237n9, 237n10

Academicae quaestiones

39	47n63

Cleanthes	50
Cornelius	238n10
Crantor	45n48
Crates	43n43
Democritus of Abdera	41, 68

Diogenes Laertius

Pythagoras 40n22

Vitae Philosophorum

2.8	240n14
7.134	49n75
7.135	49n71, 245n24
7.136, 138	49n73, 245n26, 253n66
7.137	50n78
7.138	50n79
7.140, 141	50n77
8.46	40n22
9.51	37n7
9.61	47n61
10.73	52n90
10.74	51n87
10.89	52n88
10.91	52n92

Empedocles	38n8
Epicurus	51, 51n86, 52, 52n95, 70, 246n40, 258
Euclid	47, 67
Eudorus of Alexandria	53, 70
Heraclitus of Ephesus	38–39, 38n8, 39n12, 39n13, 39n14, 43n42, 68, 237n9, 250n51

Hicetas	47, 67	*Phaedrus*	
Hippocrates	237n10	245d	245n30, 250n54
Homer	40n22, 237n10		

Lactantius

Sophista

		218c	37n7
De Ira Dei		242d	40n25, 245n23, 250n52, 253n66
4	52n94, 246n40		

Divine institutions

Theaetetus

2.9	52n95	152a 2–4	37n7
3.17	52n95	152a 6–8	37n7
7.3, 7	250n51		
7.3, 7	41n31, 246n37	*Timaeus*	43, 50, 53
		29–30	257n80
Epitome Divinarum Institutionum		37–38	255n75
70	52n95	37d–38c	242n17

Leucippus	41, 68	Pliny the Elder	55n105
Lucretius	52	Plotinus	53, 53n96, 65, 70
Nicolaus of Damascus	39, 55n105, 237n9	Plutarch of Chaeronea	50, 53, 70, 237n9, 238n10

De plantis

De Defectu oraculorum

1.2	39n17	22	53n98, 246n35

Numenius of Apamea	53, 70	*De Stoicorum repugnantiis*
Parmenides	40, 63, 63n159, 68, 237n9	39	50n81
Philo of Larissa	43n43, 44n43		
Plato	36, 42, 43, 43n39, 43n42, 43n43, 44n43, 44n46, 45, 45n48, 53, 66, 69, 237n9, 238n10, 241n17, 245, 246n34, 247, 248, 248n47, 250, 254, 255, 256, 256n77, 257, 258, 260n89	*Placita Philosophorum*	
		1.3.4	38n10
		Platonicae quaestiones	
		8.4	53n99, 246n35
		Polemon	43n43
		Posidonius	70
		Proclus	45n48
		Protagoras	43n42
		Ptolemy	47, 55n105, 67
		Pyrrho	47, 67
Cratylus		Pythagoras	39, 39n18, 40n22, 68
386	37n7		
401–2	38n11, 250n51	Seneca	238n10

Socrates	42, 66, 69, 237n9, 245, 245n28, 246, 247, 248, 248n47, 250, 254, 255, 256, 256n77, 257, 260n89	Xenocrates	43n43, 45n48
		Xenophon	40, 42, 68, 238n10
		Memorabilia	
		1.4.2–19	42n34, 245n28
		4.3.14–17	42n34, 245n28
Sophocles	238n10		
Speusippus	43n43, 45n48		
Strabo	55n105	Zeno of Citium	49, 50, 70
Tacitus	55n105, 238n10	Zeno of Elea	40, 68
Thales	38n8, 38n9		

www.ingramcontent.com/pod-product-compliance
Lightning Source LLC
Chambersburg PA
CBHW071231230426
43668CB00011B/1380